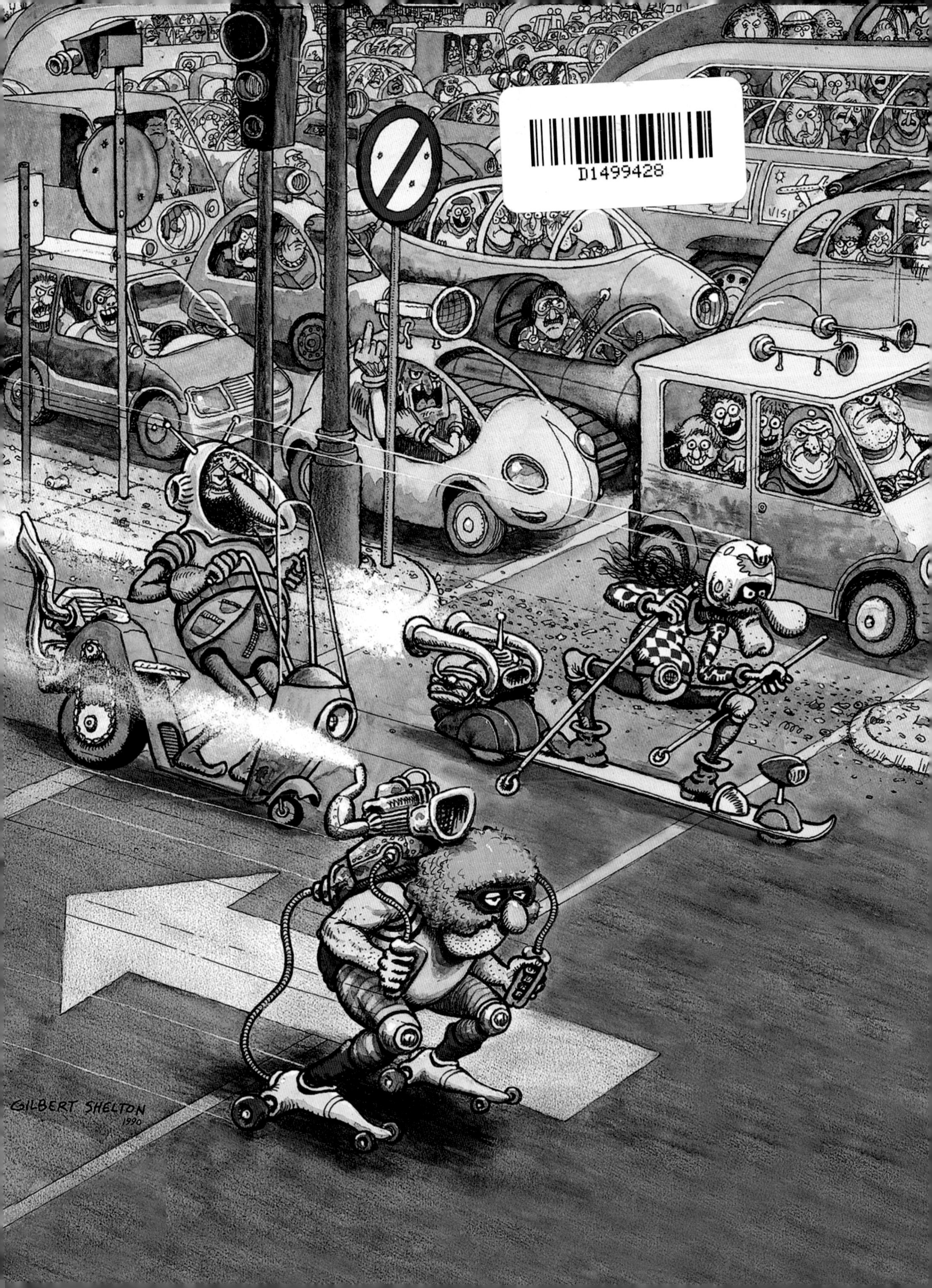
GILBERT SHELTON
1990

FREEWHEELIN'
FRANKLIN
FAT
FREDDY
PHINEAS
& FAT FREDDY'S CAT

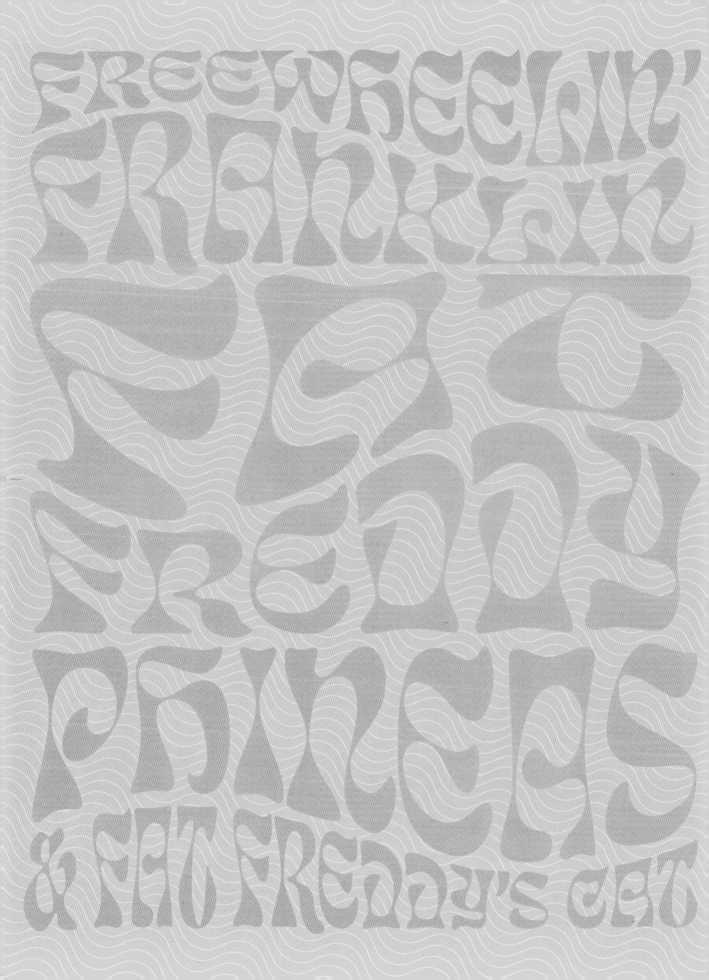

THE FABULOUS FURRY FREAK BROTHERS

in the 21st Century and Other Follies

by Gilbert Shelton
with Paul Mavrides and Dave Sheridan

Publisher: GARY GROTH
Senior Editor: J. MICHAEL CATRON
Assistant Editor: KIT BRASH
Designer: JUSTIN ALLAN-SPENCER
Production: PAUL BARESH
Associate Publisher: ERIC REYNOLDS

Fantagraphics Books, Inc.
7563 Lake City Way NE
Seattle, WA 98115
(800) 657-1100
Fantagraphics.com · Twitter: @fantagraphics · facebook.com/fantagraphics

Special thanks to Paul Mavrides, Fred Todd, Gary Panter, David Miller, Bill Griffith, and Heritage Auctions.

First Fantagraphics Books edition: January 2023
ISBN: 978-1-68396-558-9 | Library of Congress Control Number: 2021951598
Printed in China

NOW AVAILABLE

The Fabulous Furry Freak Brothers: The Freak Brothers in the 21st Century and Other Follies (Volume 5)
The Fabulous Furry Freak Brothers: The Idiots Abroad and Other Follies (Volume 6)

COMING SOON

The Fabulous Furry Freak Brothers: Grass Roots and Other Follies (Volume 4)

THE FABULOUS FURRY FREAK BROTHERS

in the 21st Century and Other Follies

by Gilbert Shelton
with Paul Mavrides and Dave Sheridan

Fantagraphics • Seattle

CONTENTS

THE FABULOUS FURRY FREAK BROTHERS
created by Gilbert Shelton

Gilbert Shelton (art and lettering) • **Dave Sheridan** (art) • **Paul Mavrides** (art)

☘ ☘ ☘

☘ ☘ ☘

The Fabulous Furry Freak Brothers

☘ ☘ ☘

The Fabulous Furry Freak Brothers Shorts

☘ ☘ ☘

Fat Freddy

☘ ☘ ☘

Fat Freddy's Cat

Fat Freddy's Cat Shorts

Fat Freddy's Comics & Stories #1

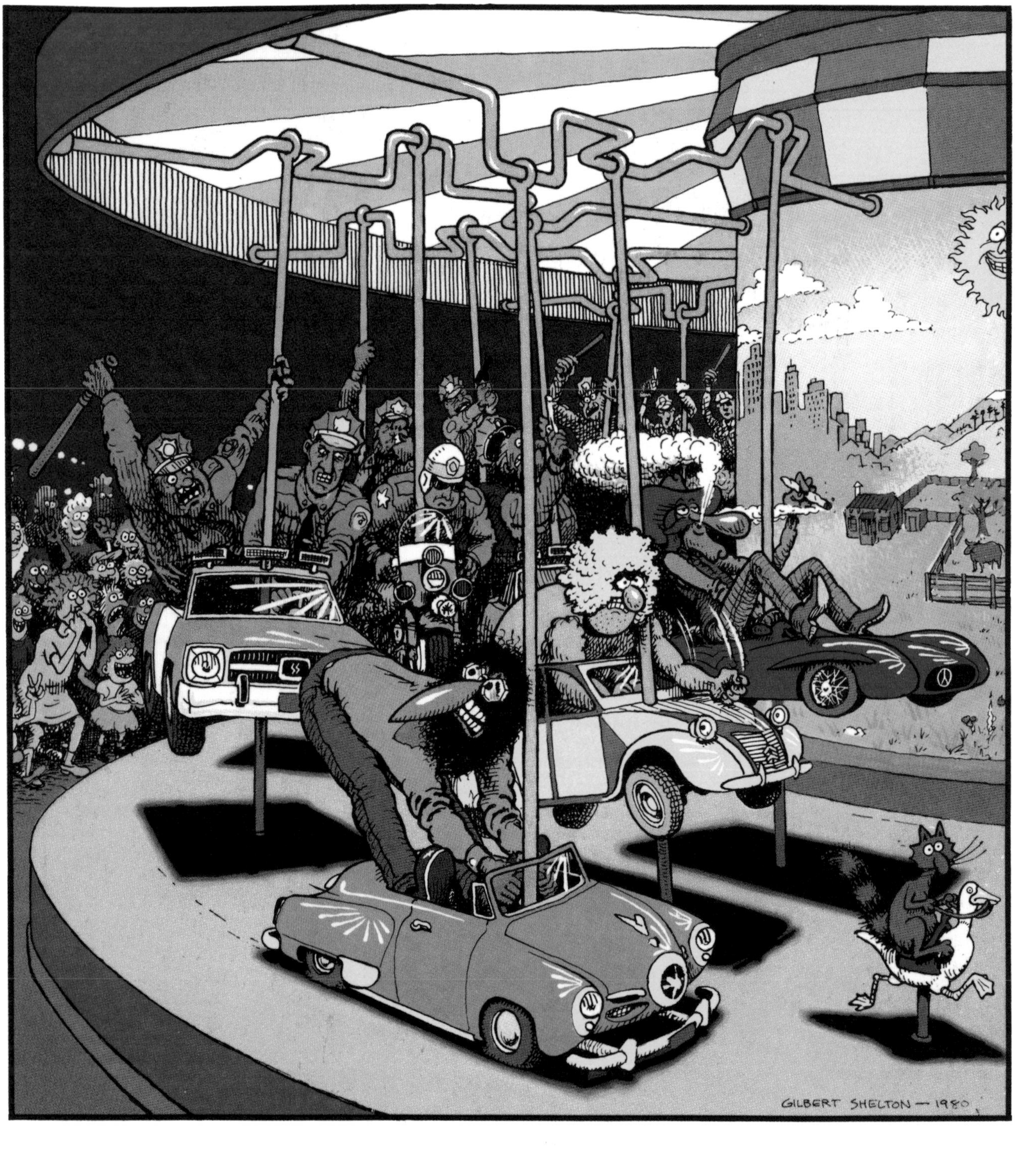
GILBERT SHELTON — 1980

INTRODUCTION

by Kit Brash

By 1979, Gilbert Shelton had been living in San Francisco and telling stories of The Fabulous Furry Freak Brothers for a decade. A two-year sabbatical in Europe led to a permanent relocation to France and to a change in Shelton's creative outlook. He and his collaborators had worked hundreds of gags and setups from the premise of three stoned doofuses (of varying levels of doofitude) looking for the easiest way to stay high and keep vibing in the world locus of hippiedom.

Now looking at a new Reaganized America from the perspective of an expatriate, Shelton began using the picaresque naiveté of the Freak Brothers for sharper satire. Many of the stories in this volume throw them into events, situations, and elements of culture that clearly mark the early 1980s as a harsher, more antagonistic time. The Brothers innate optimism (and cannabistic discombobulation) keeps their Candide-like spirits up, and the stories are no less hilarious and rollicking, but the settings and situations bite harder. Paul Mavrides's increasing involvement as a co-author and co-artist helps tighten the satire.

Even so, there's still plenty of domestic humor, cheap verbal gags, and kitty-related comedy.

This volume also features an exact reproduction of *Fat Freddy's Comics & Stories* #1. Shelton assembled an all-star squad of his fellow underground comix pioneers to pastiche, parody, and mock the popular genres of commercial comics. (The title itself is a riff on *Walt Disney's Comics & Stories*.) There are horror and sci-fi shorts based on 1950s EC Comics (see *The Fantagraphics EC Artists' Library* series if you're not familiar with EC), takes on the perennials of romance and superheroes (the latter a field also tilled by Shelton in his Wonder Wart-Hog series), and two of Marvel Comics' 1970s attempts at black-and-white magazines for "adult" audiences: Robert E. Howard's Conan, and that company's sad attempt at continuing Howard the Duck without his creator and writer, Steve Gerber.

The Freak Brothers' globetrotting epic *The Idiots Abroad* was created contemporaneously with the strips, shorts, and comics in this volume and is available in Volume 6 of this series. ✹

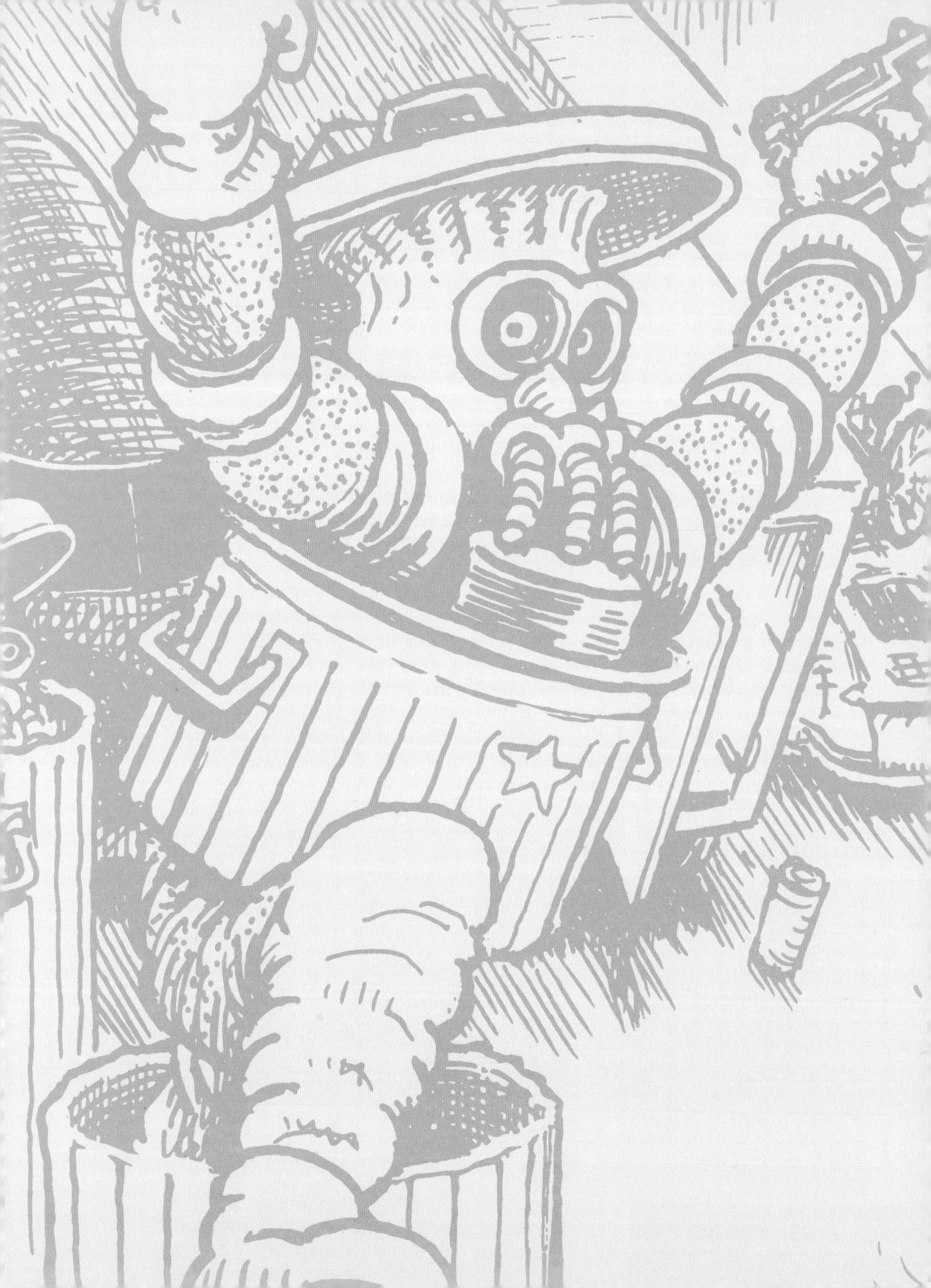

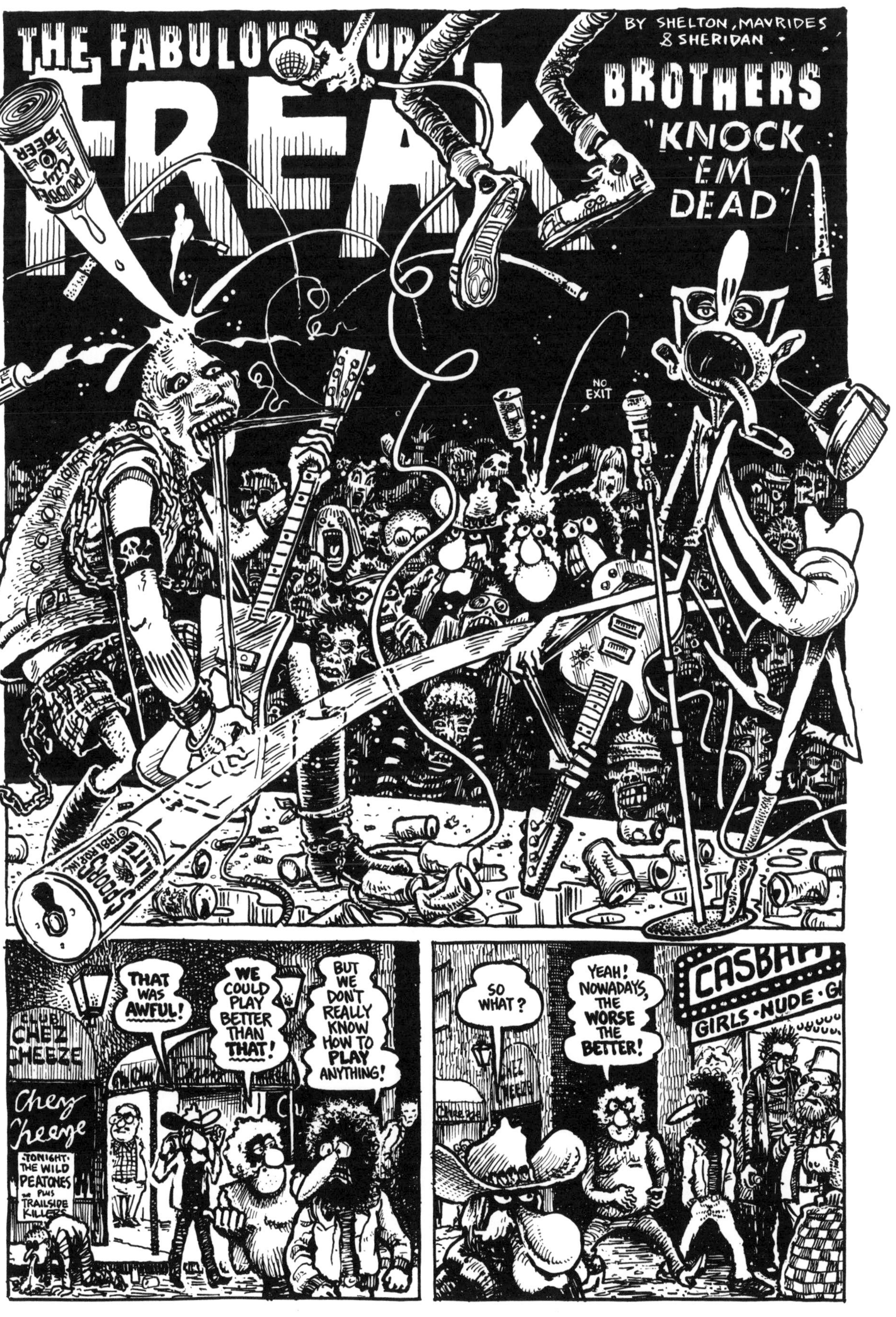
THE FABULOUS FURRY FREAK BROTHERS
BY SHELTON, MAVRIDES & SHERIDAN
"KNOCK 'EM DEAD"
NO EXIT
RUBBER CITY BEER
CLUB CHEZ CHEEZE
Chez Cheeze
TONIGHT THE WILD PEATONES PLUS TRAILSIDE KILLERS
THAT WAS AWFUL!
WE COULD PLAY BETTER THAN THAT!
BUT WE DON'T REALLY KNOW HOW TO PLAY ANYTHING!
SO WHAT?
YEAH! NOWADAYS, THE WORSE THE BETTER!
CASBAH
GIRLS · NUDE

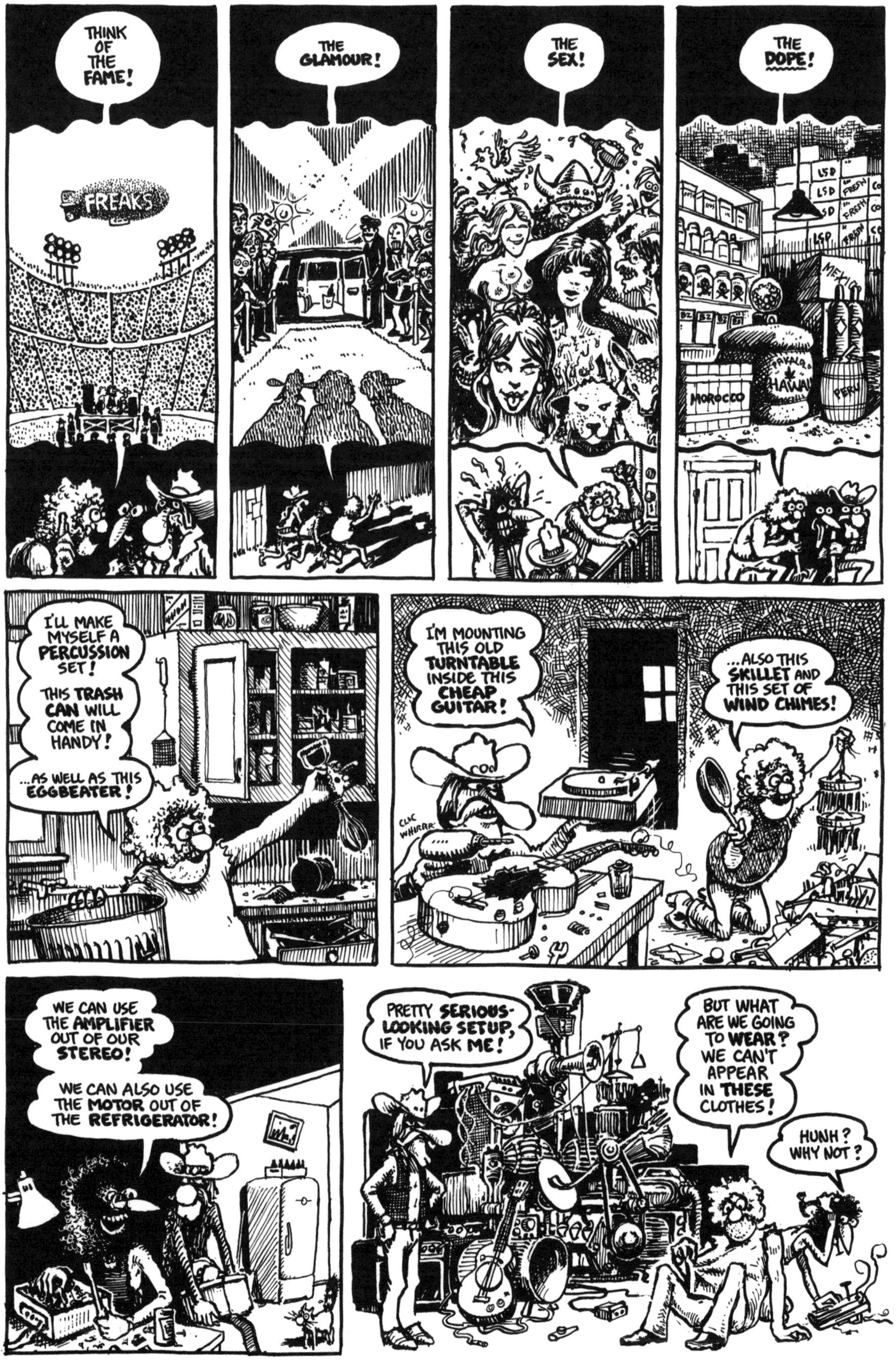
THINK OF THE FAME!
FREAKS
THE GLAMOUR!
THE SEX!
THE DOPE!
LSD
MOROCCO
HAWAII
PERU
I'LL MAKE MYSELF A PERCUSSION SET!
THIS TRASH CAN WILL COME IN HANDY!
...AS WELL AS THIS EGGBEATER!
I'M MOUNTING THIS OLD TURNTABLE INSIDE THIS CHEAP GUITAR!
CLIC WHIRRR
...ALSO THIS SKILLET AND THIS SET OF WIND CHIMES!
WE CAN USE THE AMPLIFIER OUT OF OUR STEREO!
WE CAN ALSO USE THE MOTOR OUT OF THE REFRIGERATOR!
PRETTY SERIOUS-LOOKING SETUP, IF YOU ASK ME!
BUT WHAT ARE WE GOING TO WEAR? WE CAN'T APPEAR IN THESE CLOTHES!
HUNH? WHY NOT?

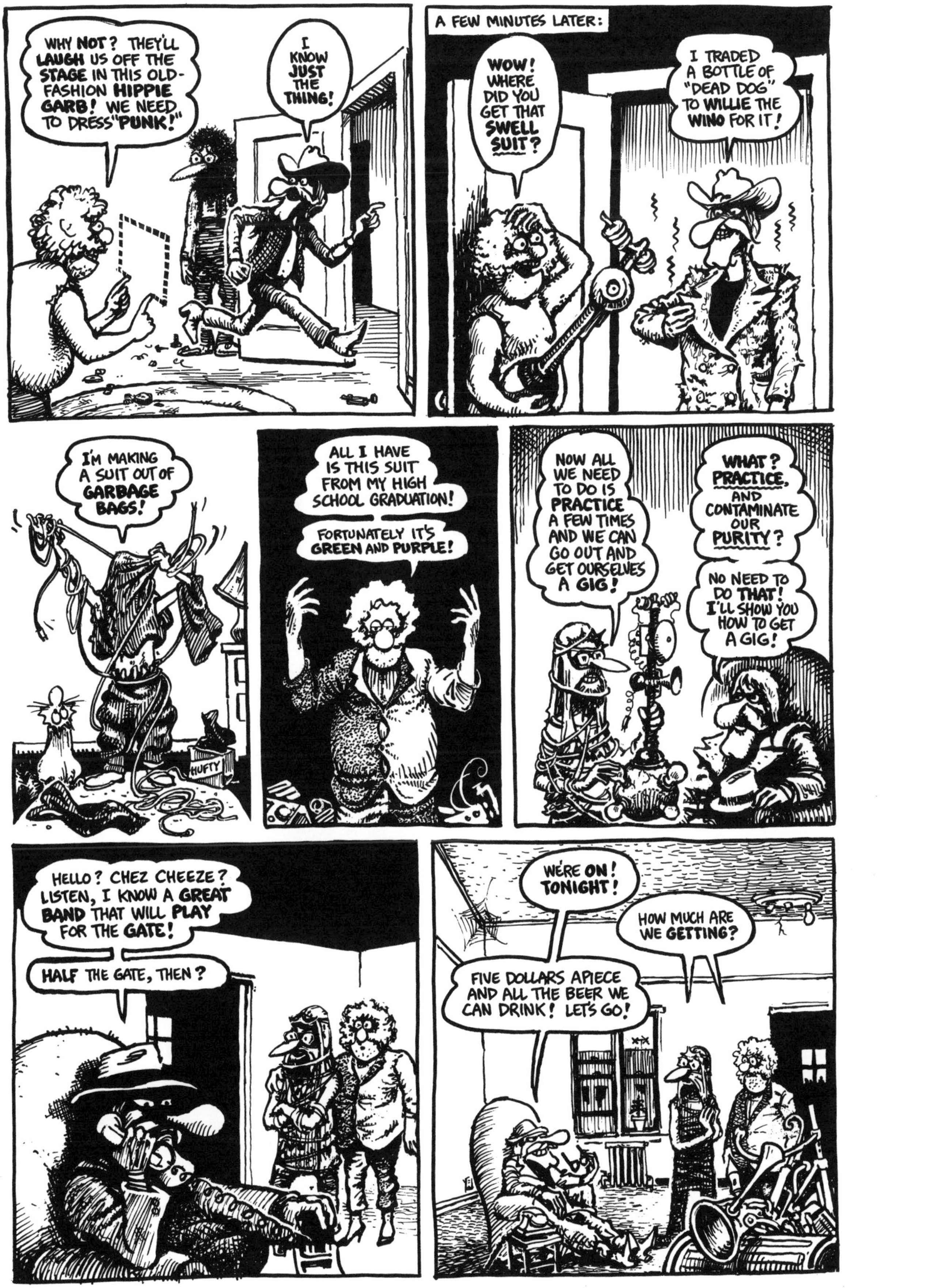
WHY NOT? THEY'LL LAUGH US OFF THE STAGE IN THIS OLD-FASHION HIPPIE GARB! WE NEED TO DRESS "PUNK!"
I KNOW JUST THE THING!
A FEW MINUTES LATER:
WOW! WHERE DID YOU GET THAT SWELL SUIT?
I TRADED A BOTTLE OF "DEAD DOG" TO WILLIE THE WINO FOR IT!
I'M MAKING A SUIT OUT OF GARBAGE BAGS!
HUFTY
ALL I HAVE IS THIS SUIT FROM MY HIGH SCHOOL GRADUATION!
FORTUNATELY IT'S GREEN AND PURPLE!
NOW ALL WE NEED TO DO IS PRACTICE A FEW TIMES AND WE CAN GO OUT AND GET OURSELVES A GIG!
WHAT? PRACTICE, AND CONTAMINATE OUR PURITY?
NO NEED TO DO THAT! I'LL SHOW YOU HOW TO GET A GIG!
HELLO? CHEZ CHEEZE? LISTEN, I KNOW A GREAT BAND THAT WILL PLAY FOR THE GATE!
HALF THE GATE, THEN?
WE'RE ON! TONIGHT!
HOW MUCH ARE WE GETTING?
FIVE DOLLARS APIECE AND ALL THE BEER WE CAN DRINK! LET'S GO!

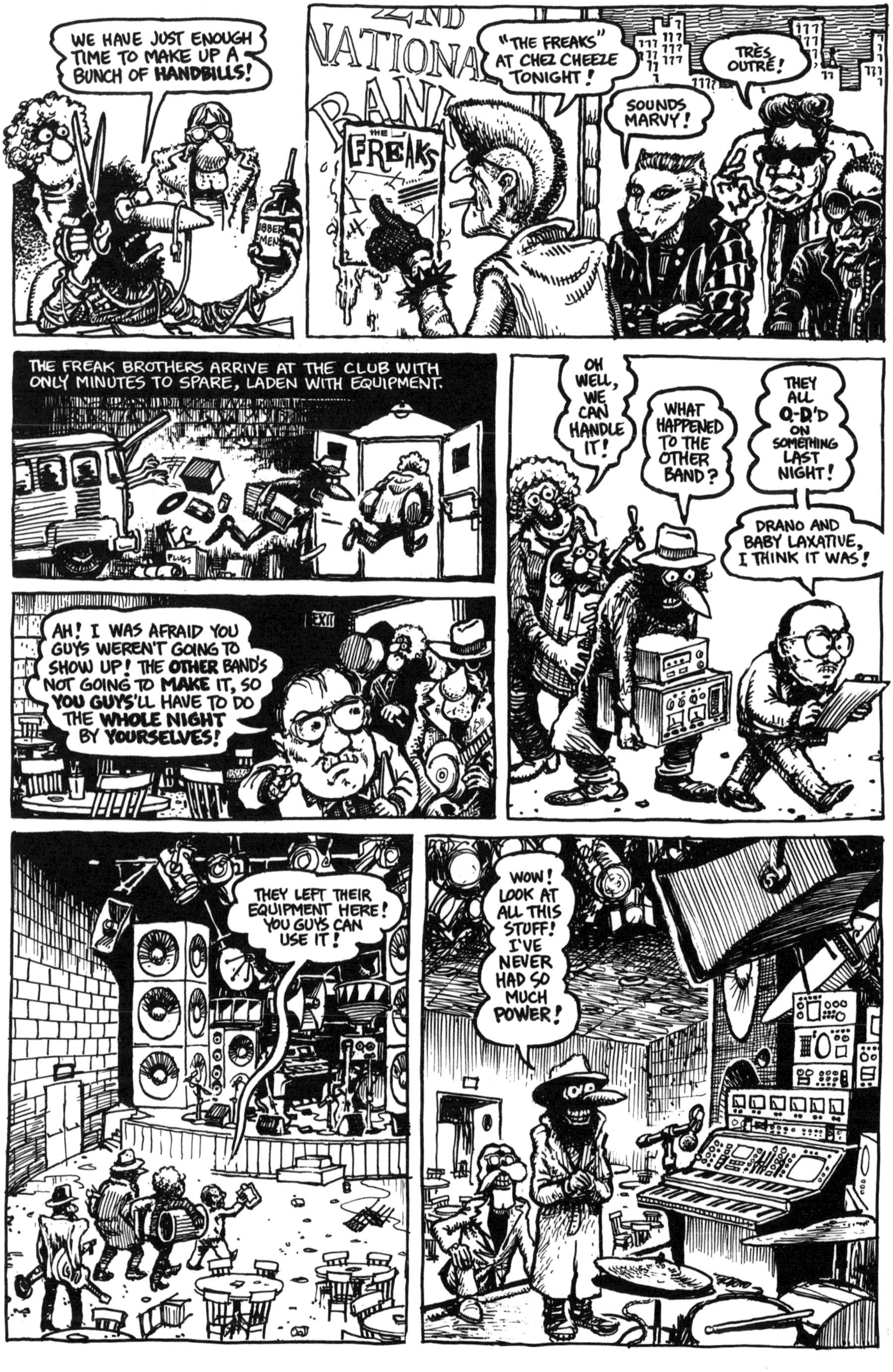
WE HAVE JUST ENOUGH TIME TO MAKE UP A BUNCH OF HANDBILLS!
"THE FREAKS" AT CHEZ CHEEZE TONIGHT!
SOUNDS MARVY!
TRÈS OUTRÉ!
THE FREAKS
2ND NATIONAL BANK
THE FREAK BROTHERS ARRIVE AT THE CLUB WITH ONLY MINUTES TO SPARE, LADEN WITH EQUIPMENT.
AH! I WAS AFRAID YOU GUYS WEREN'T GOING TO SHOW UP! THE OTHER BAND'S NOT GOING TO MAKE IT, SO YOU GUYS'LL HAVE TO DO THE WHOLE NIGHT BY YOURSELVES!
EXIT
OH WELL, WE CAN HANDLE IT!
WHAT HAPPENED TO THE OTHER BAND?
THEY ALL O-D'D ON SOMETHING LAST NIGHT!
DRANO AND BABY LAXATIVE, I THINK IT WAS!
THEY LEFT THEIR EQUIPMENT HERE! YOU GUYS CAN USE IT!
WOW! LOOK AT ALL THIS STUFF! I'VE NEVER HAD SO MUCH POWER!

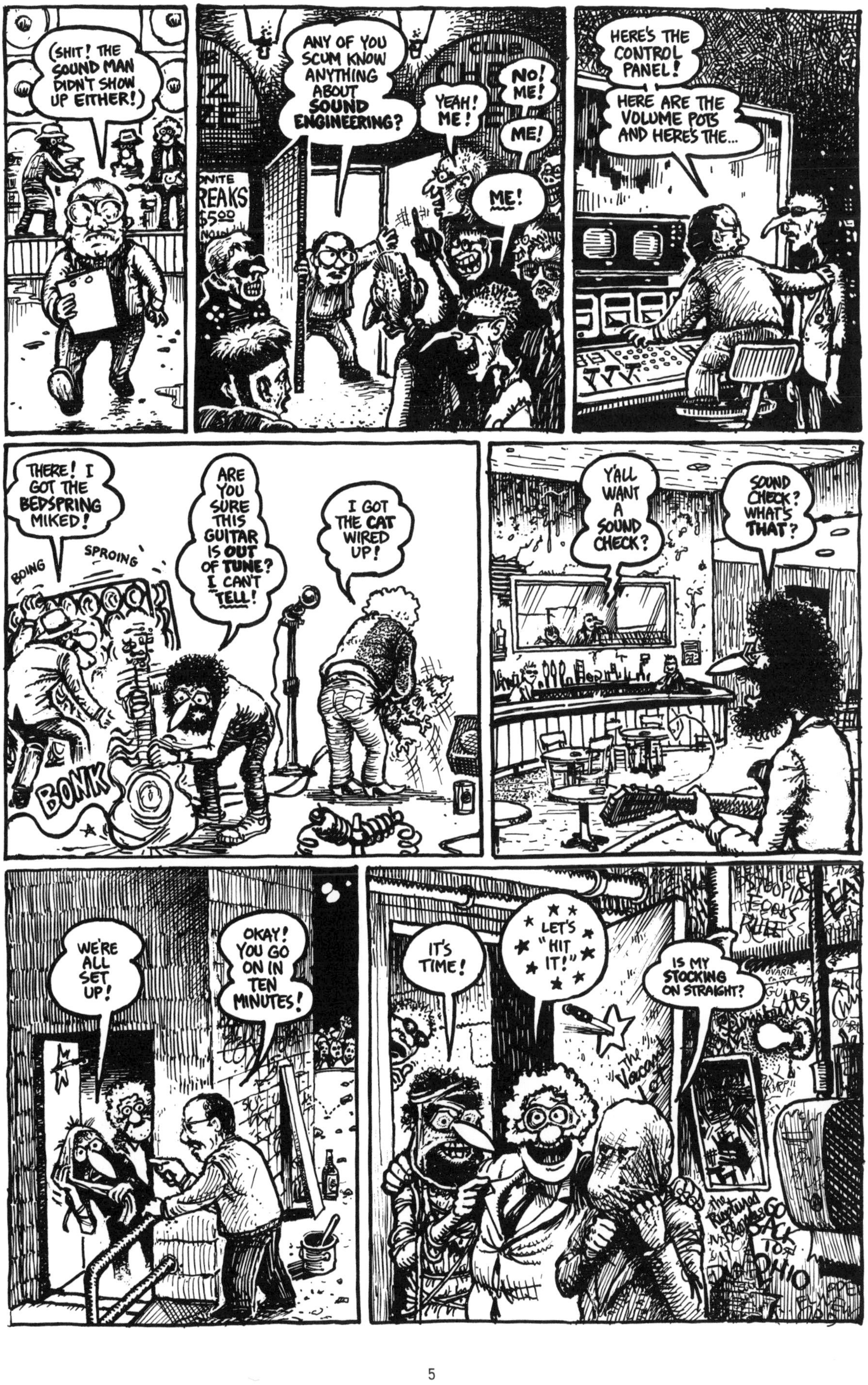
(SHIT! THE SOUND MAN DIDN'T SHOW UP EITHER!)
ANY OF YOU SCUM KNOW ANYTHING ABOUT **SOUND ENGINEERING**?
YEAH! ME!
NO! ME!
ME!
ME!
HERE'S THE CONTROL PANEL!
HERE ARE THE VOLUME POTS AND HERE'S THE...
THERE! I GOT THE BEDSPRING MIKED!
BOING
SPROING
ARE YOU SURE THIS GUITAR IS **OUT** OF **TUNE**? **I** CAN'T **TELL**!
BONK
I GOT THE **CAT** WIRED UP!
Y'ALL WANT A SOUND CHECK?
SOUND CHECK? WHAT'S **THAT**?
WE'RE ALL SET UP!
OKAY! YOU GO ON IN TEN MINUTES!
IT'S TIME!
LET'S "HIT IT!"
IS MY **STOCKING** ON STRAIGHT?

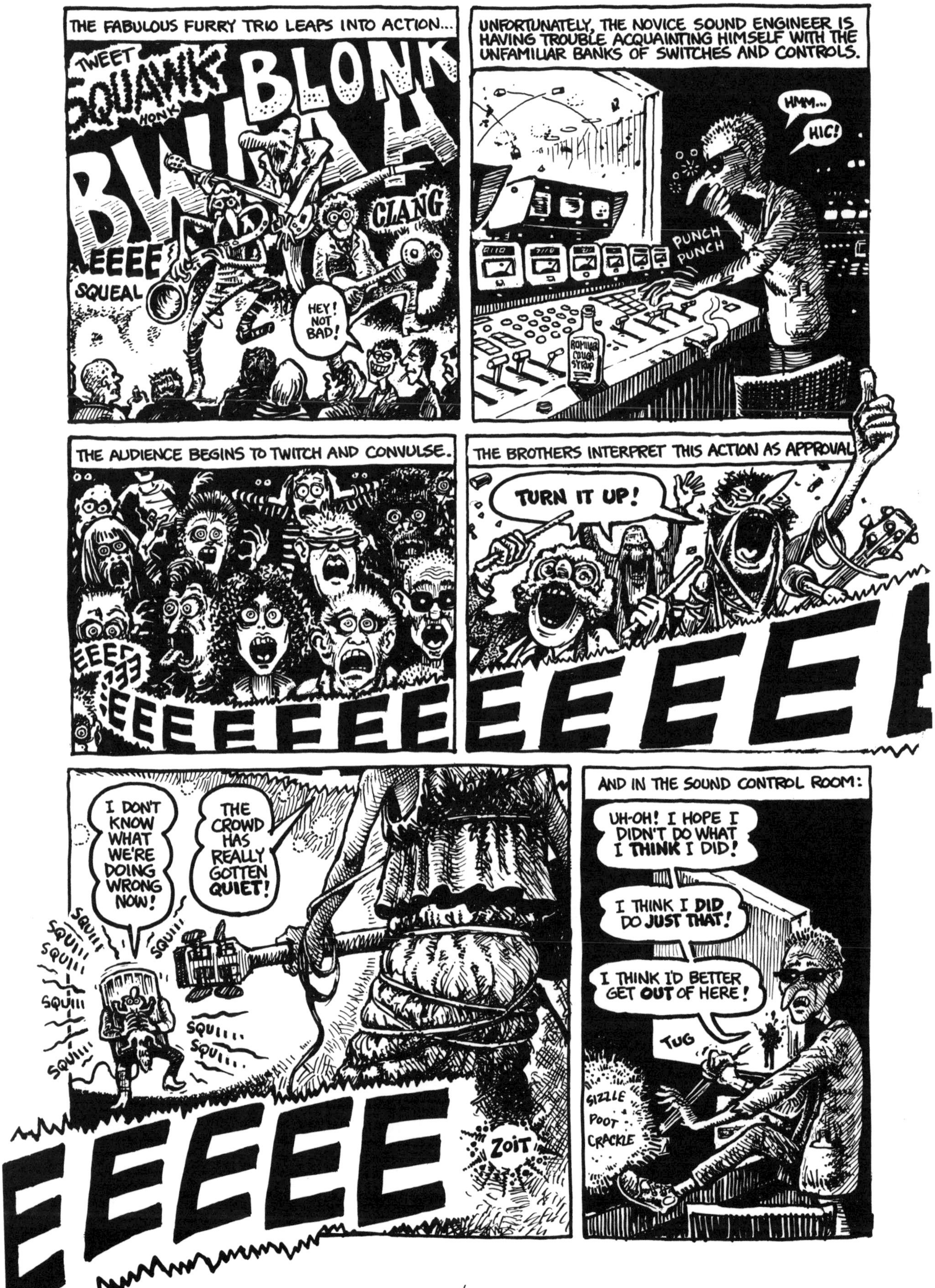
THE FABULOUS FURRY TRIO LEAPS INTO ACTION...
TWEET
SQUAWK
HONK
BLONK
BWAA
CLANG
EEEE
SQUEAL
HEY! NOT BAD!
UNFORTUNATELY, THE NOVICE SOUND ENGINEER IS HAVING TROUBLE ACQUAINTING HIMSELF WITH THE UNFAMILIAR BANKS OF SWITCHES AND CONTROLS.
HMM...
HIC!
PUNCH
PUNCH
ROMILAR COUGH SYRUP
THE AUDIENCE BEGINS TO TWITCH AND CONVULSE.
THE BROTHERS INTERPRET THIS ACTION AS APPROVAL
TURN IT UP!
EEEEEEEEEEEEE
I DON'T KNOW WHAT WE'RE DOING WRONG NOW!
THE CROWD HAS REALLY GOTTEN QUIET!
SQUI
SQUI
SQUI
SQUI
SQUI
SQUI
SQUI
SQUI
EEEEE
ZOIT
AND IN THE SOUND CONTROL ROOM:
UH-OH! I HOPE I DIDN'T DO WHAT I THINK I DID!
I THINK I DID DO JUST THAT!
I THINK I'D BETTER GET OUT OF HERE!
TUG
SIZZLE
POOT
CRACKLE

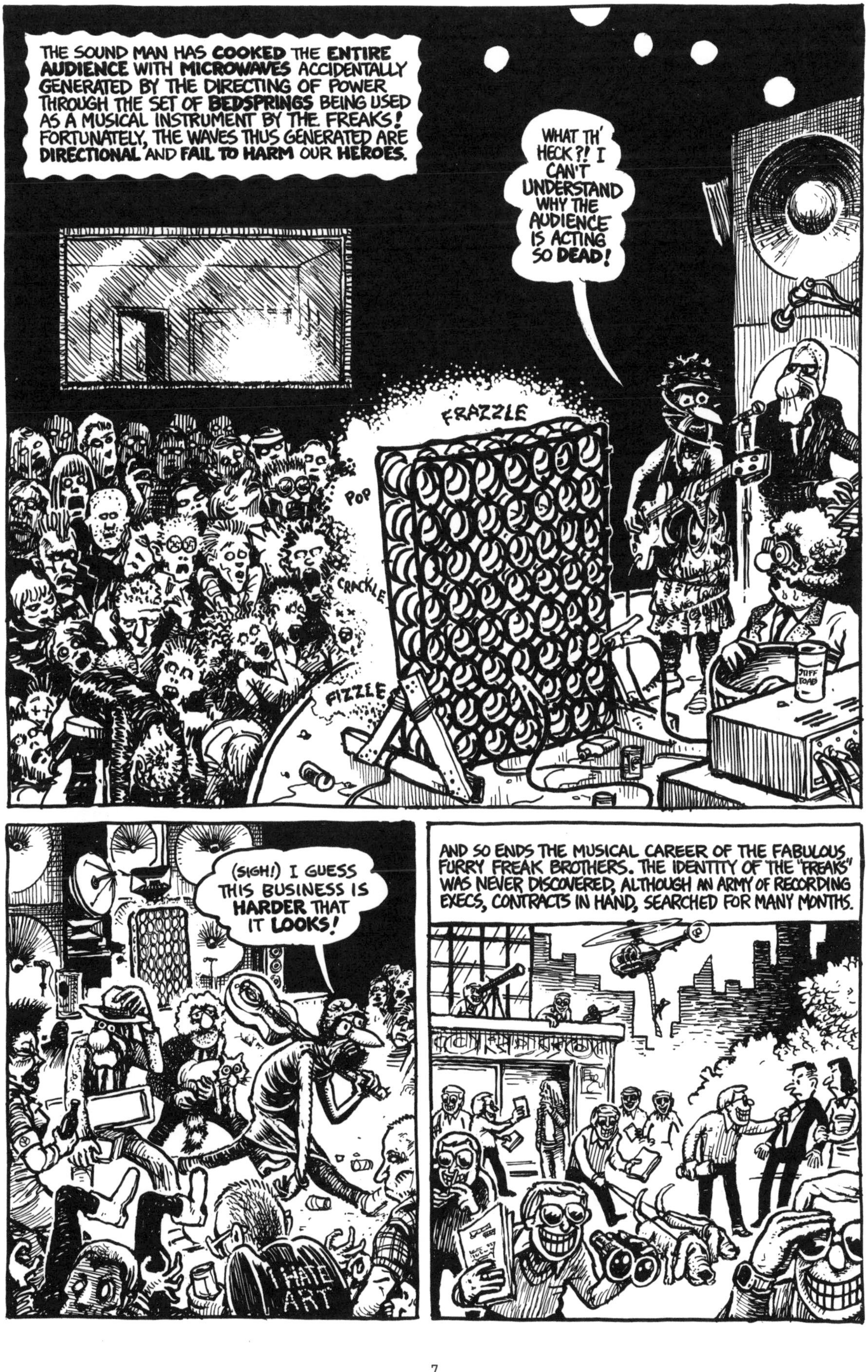
THE SOUND MAN HAS COOKED THE ENTIRE AUDIENCE WITH MICROWAVES ACCIDENTALLY GENERATED BY THE DIRECTING OF POWER THROUGH THE SET OF BEDSPRINGS BEING USED AS A MUSICAL INSTRUMENT BY THE FREAKS! FORTUNATELY, THE WAVES THUS GENERATED ARE DIRECTIONAL AND FAIL TO HARM OUR HEROES.
WHAT TH' HECK?! I CAN'T UNDERSTAND WHY THE AUDIENCE IS ACTING SO DEAD!
FRAZZLE
POP
CRACKLE
FIZZLE
(SIGH!) I GUESS THIS BUSINESS IS HARDER THAT IT LOOKS!
I HATE ART
AND SO ENDS THE MUSICAL CAREER OF THE FABULOUS FURRY FREAK BROTHERS. THE IDENTITY OF THE "FREAKS" WAS NEVER DISCOVERED, ALTHOUGH AN ARMY OF RECORDING EXECS, CONTRACTS IN HAND, SEARCHED FOR MANY MONTHS.

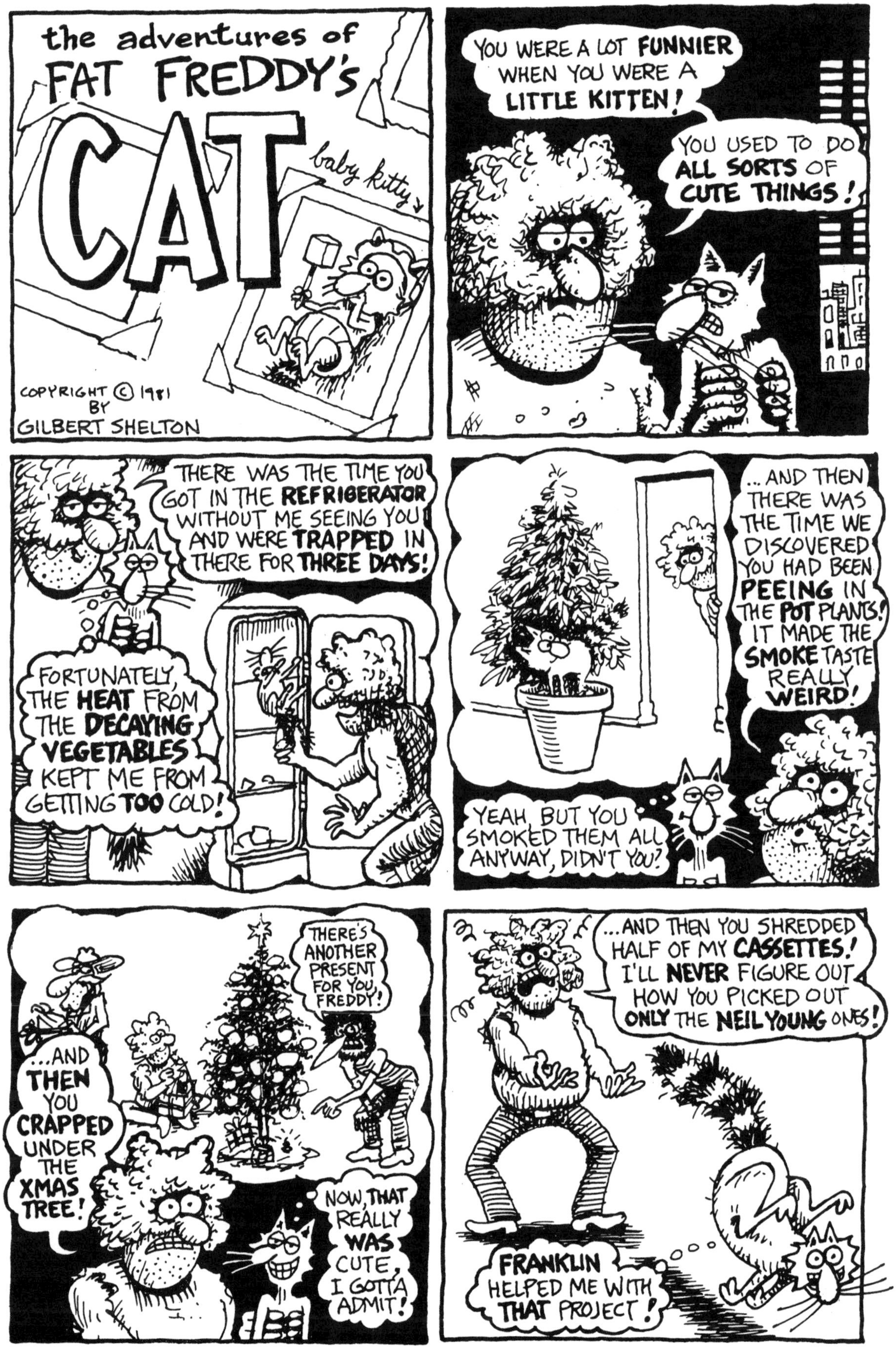
the adventures of
FAT FREDDY'S
CAT
baby kitty
COPYRIGHT © 1981 BY GILBERT SHELTON
YOU WERE A LOT FUNNIER WHEN YOU WERE A LITTLE KITTEN!
YOU USED TO DO ALL SORTS OF CUTE THINGS!
THERE WAS THE TIME YOU GOT IN THE REFRIGERATOR WITHOUT ME SEEING YOU AND WERE TRAPPED IN THERE FOR THREE DAYS!
FORTUNATELY, THE HEAT FROM THE DECAYING VEGETABLES KEPT ME FROM GETTING TOO COLD!
...AND THEN THERE WAS THE TIME WE DISCOVERED YOU HAD BEEN PEEING IN THE POT PLANTS! IT MADE THE SMOKE TASTE REALLY WEIRD!
YEAH, BUT YOU SMOKED THEM ALL ANYWAY, DIDN'T YOU?
...AND THEN YOU CRAPPED UNDER THE XMAS TREE!
THERE'S ANOTHER PRESENT FOR YOU, FREDDY!
NOW, THAT REALLY WAS CUTE, I GOTTA ADMIT!
...AND THEN YOU SHREDDED HALF OF MY CASSETTES! I'LL NEVER FIGURE OUT HOW YOU PICKED OUT ONLY THE NEIL YOUNG ONES!
FRANKLIN HELPED ME WITH THAT PROJECT!

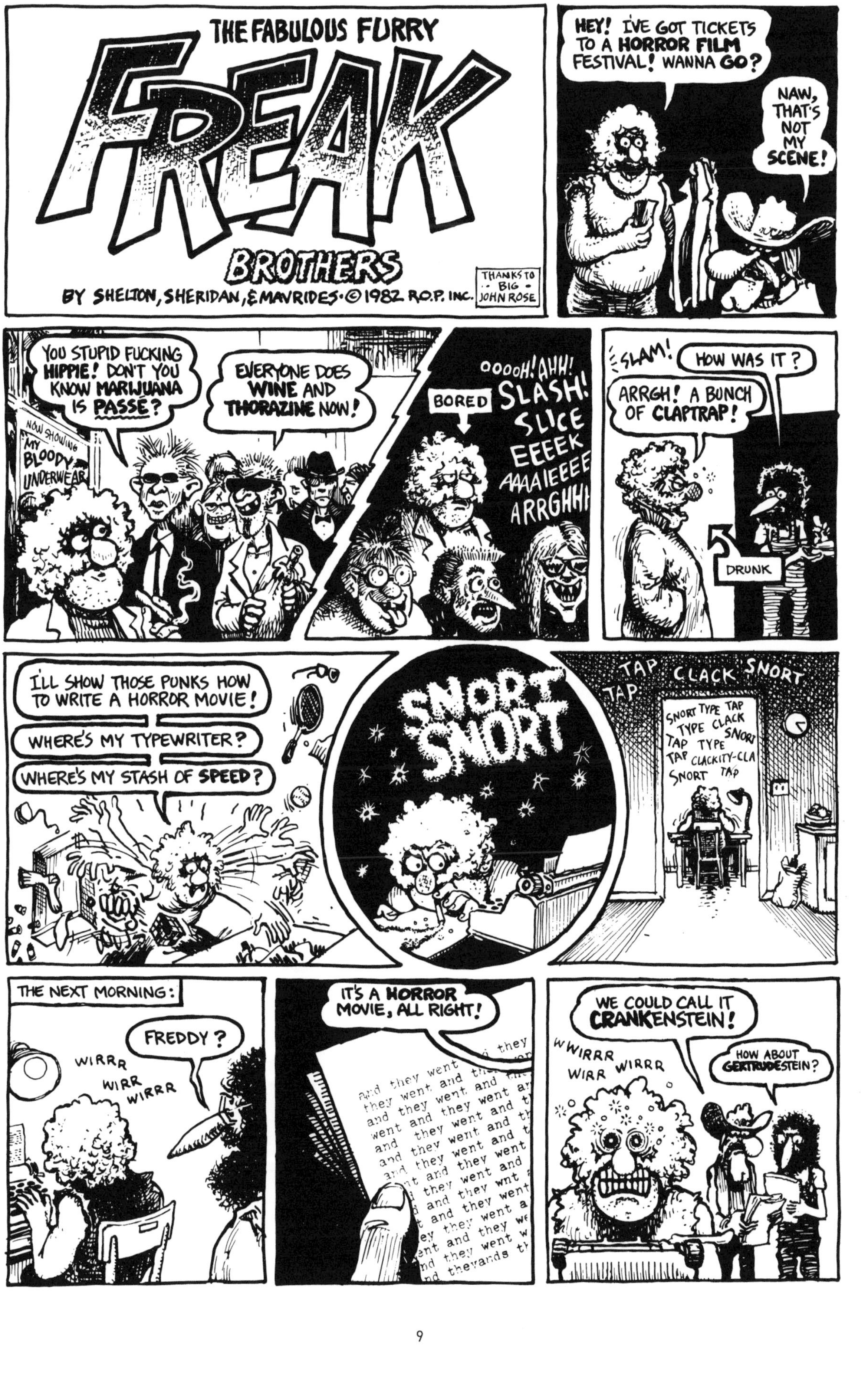
THE FABULOUS FURRY
FREAK
BROTHERS
BY SHELTON, SHERIDAN, & MAVRIDES · © 1982 R.O.P. INC.
THANKS TO · BIG · JOHN ROSE
HEY! I'VE GOT TICKETS TO A HORROR FILM FESTIVAL! WANNA GO?
NAW, THAT'S NOT MY SCENE!
NOW SHOWING MY BLOODY UNDERWEAR
YOU STUPID FUCKING HIPPIE! DON'T YOU KNOW MARIJUANA IS PASSÉ?
EVERYONE DOES WINE AND THORAZINE NOW!
BORED
OOOOH! AHH! SLASH! SLICE EEEEK AAAAIEEEE ARRGHHH
SLAM!
HOW WAS IT?
ARRGH! A BUNCH OF CLAPTRAP!
DRUNK
I'LL SHOW THOSE PUNKS HOW TO WRITE A HORROR MOVIE!
WHERE'S MY TYPEWRITER?
WHERE'S MY STASH OF SPEED?
SNORT SNORT
TAP TAP CLACK SNORT
SNORT TYPE TAP TYPE CLACK SNORT TAP TYPE TAP CLACKITY-CLA SNORT TAP
THE NEXT MORNING:
FREDDY?
WIRRR WIRR WIRRR
IT'S A HORROR MOVIE, ALL RIGHT!
WE COULD CALL IT CRANKENSTEIN!
WWIRRR WIRR WIRRR
HOW ABOUT GERTRUDESTEIN?

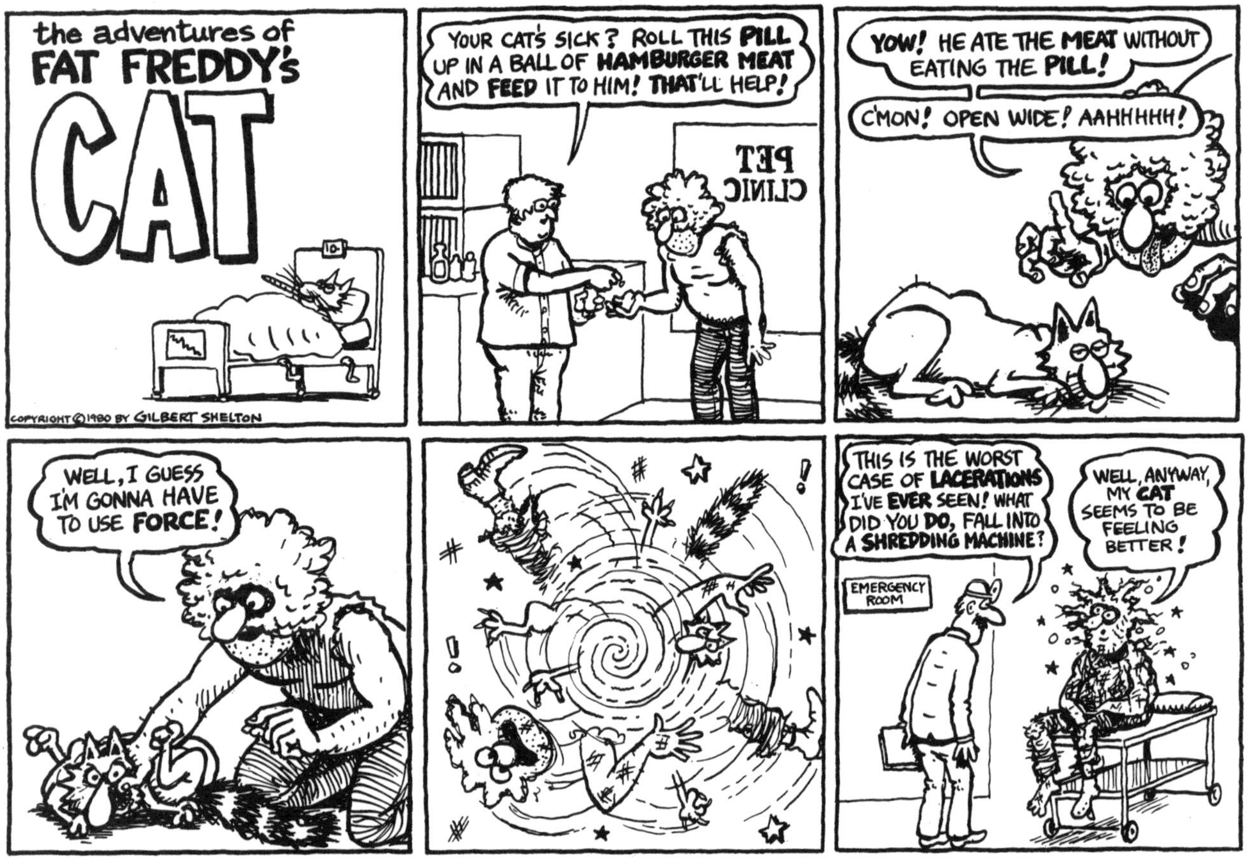
the adventures of
FAT FREDDY's
CAT
COPYRIGHT © 1980 BY GILBERT SHELTON
YOUR CAT'S SICK? ROLL THIS PILL UP IN A BALL OF HAMBURGER MEAT AND FEED IT TO HIM! THAT'LL HELP!
PET CLINIC
YOW! HE ATE THE MEAT WITHOUT EATING THE PILL!
C'MON! OPEN WIDE! AAHHHHH!
WELL, I GUESS I'M GONNA HAVE TO USE FORCE!
THIS IS THE WORST CASE OF LACERATIONS I'VE EVER SEEN! WHAT DID YOU DO, FALL INTO A SHREDDING MACHINE?
WELL, ANYWAY, MY CAT SEEMS TO BE FEELING BETTER!
EMERGENCY ROOM

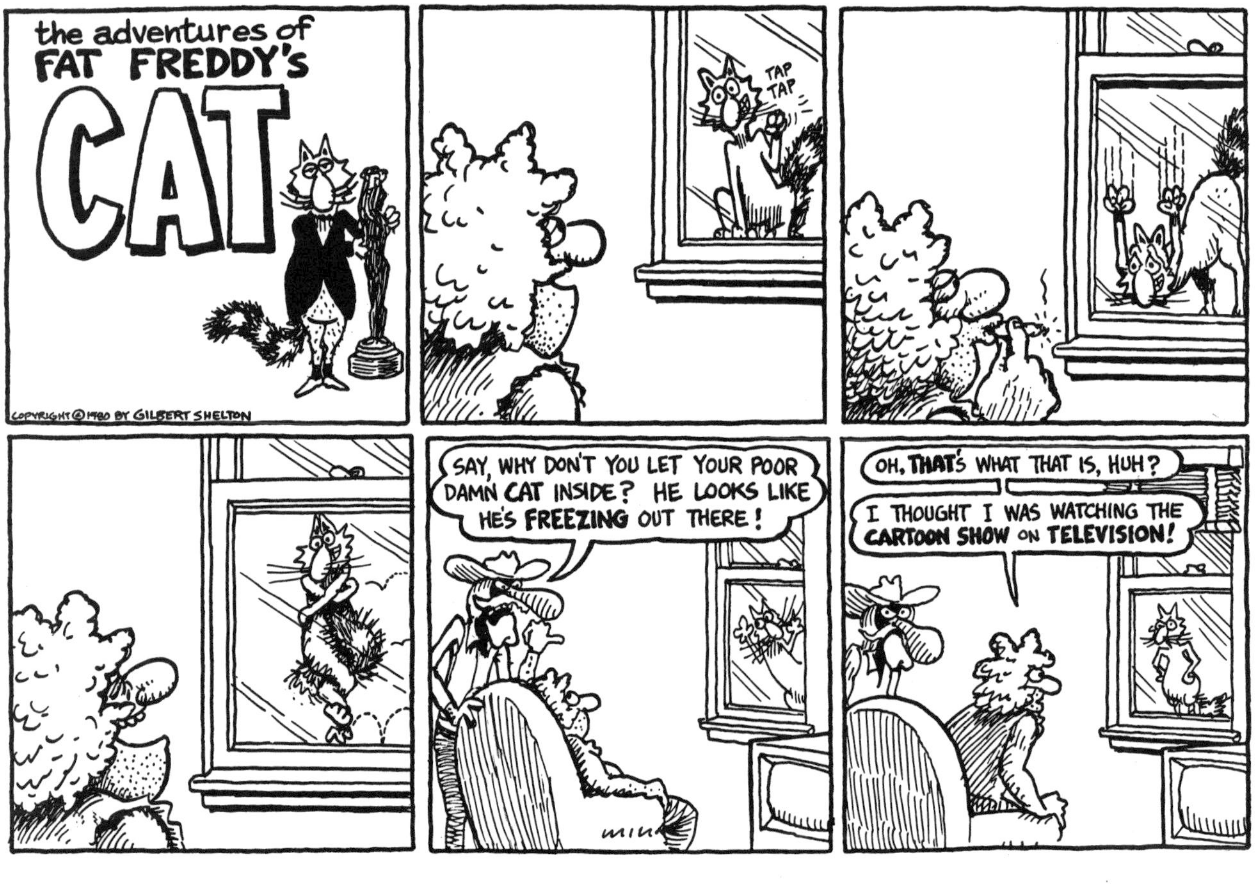
the adventures of
FAT FREDDY's
CAT
COPYRIGHT © 1980 BY GILBERT SHELTON
TAP TAP
SAY, WHY DON'T YOU LET YOUR POOR DAMN CAT INSIDE? HE LOOKS LIKE HE'S FREEZING OUT THERE!
OH, THAT'S WHAT THAT IS, HUH?
I THOUGHT I WAS WATCHING THE CARTOON SHOW ON TELEVISION!

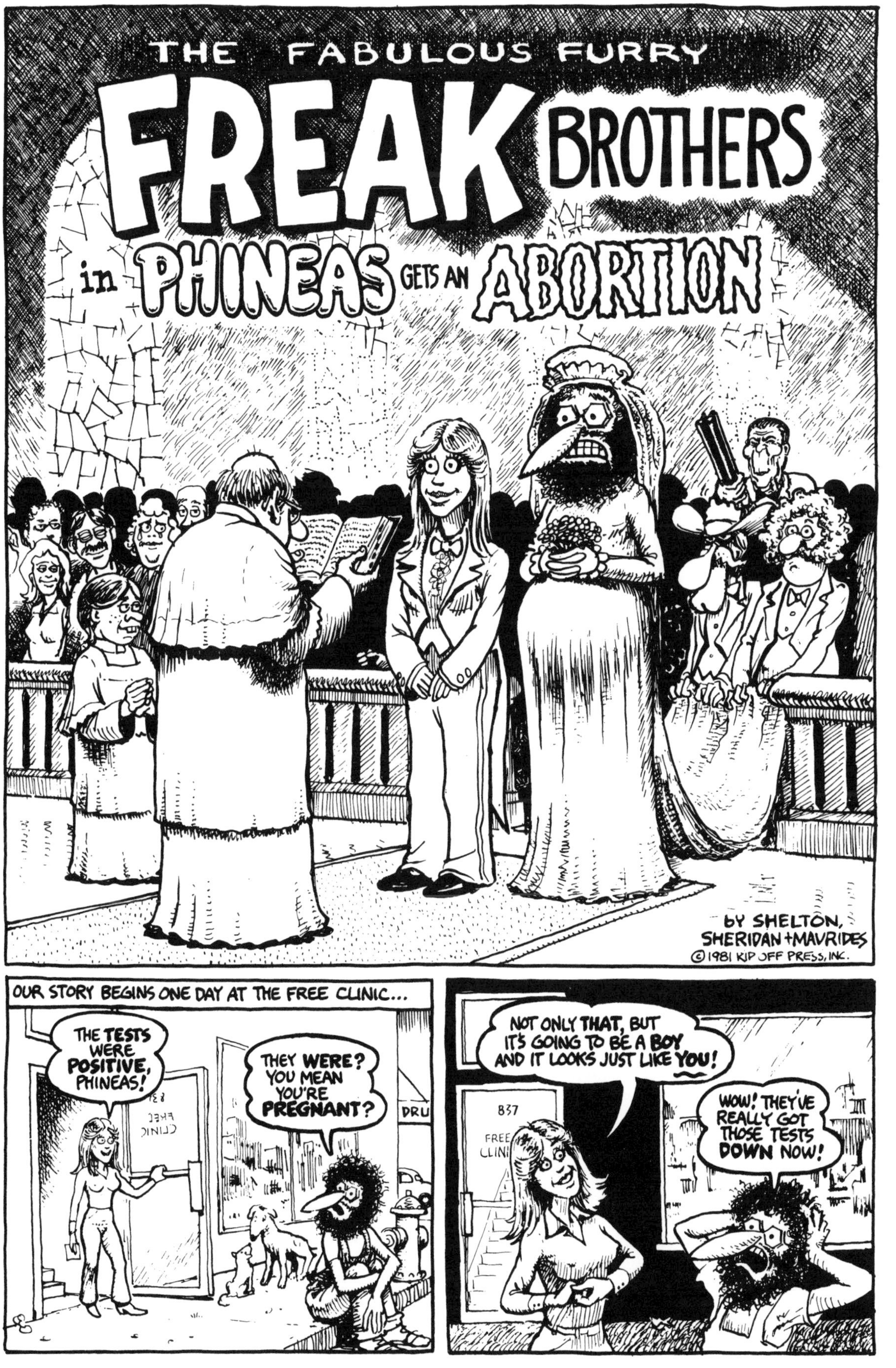
THE FABULOUS FURRY
FREAK BROTHERS
in PHINEAS GETS AN ABORTION
by SHELTON, SHERIDAN + MAVRIDES
© 1981 RIP OFF PRESS, INC.
OUR STORY BEGINS ONE DAY AT THE FREE CLINIC...
THE TESTS WERE POSITIVE, PHINEAS!
THEY WERE? YOU MEAN YOU'RE PREGNANT?
837 FREE CLINIC
DRU
NOT ONLY THAT, BUT IT'S GOING TO BE A BOY AND IT LOOKS JUST LIKE YOU!
WOW! THEY'VE REALLY GOT THOSE TESTS DOWN NOW!

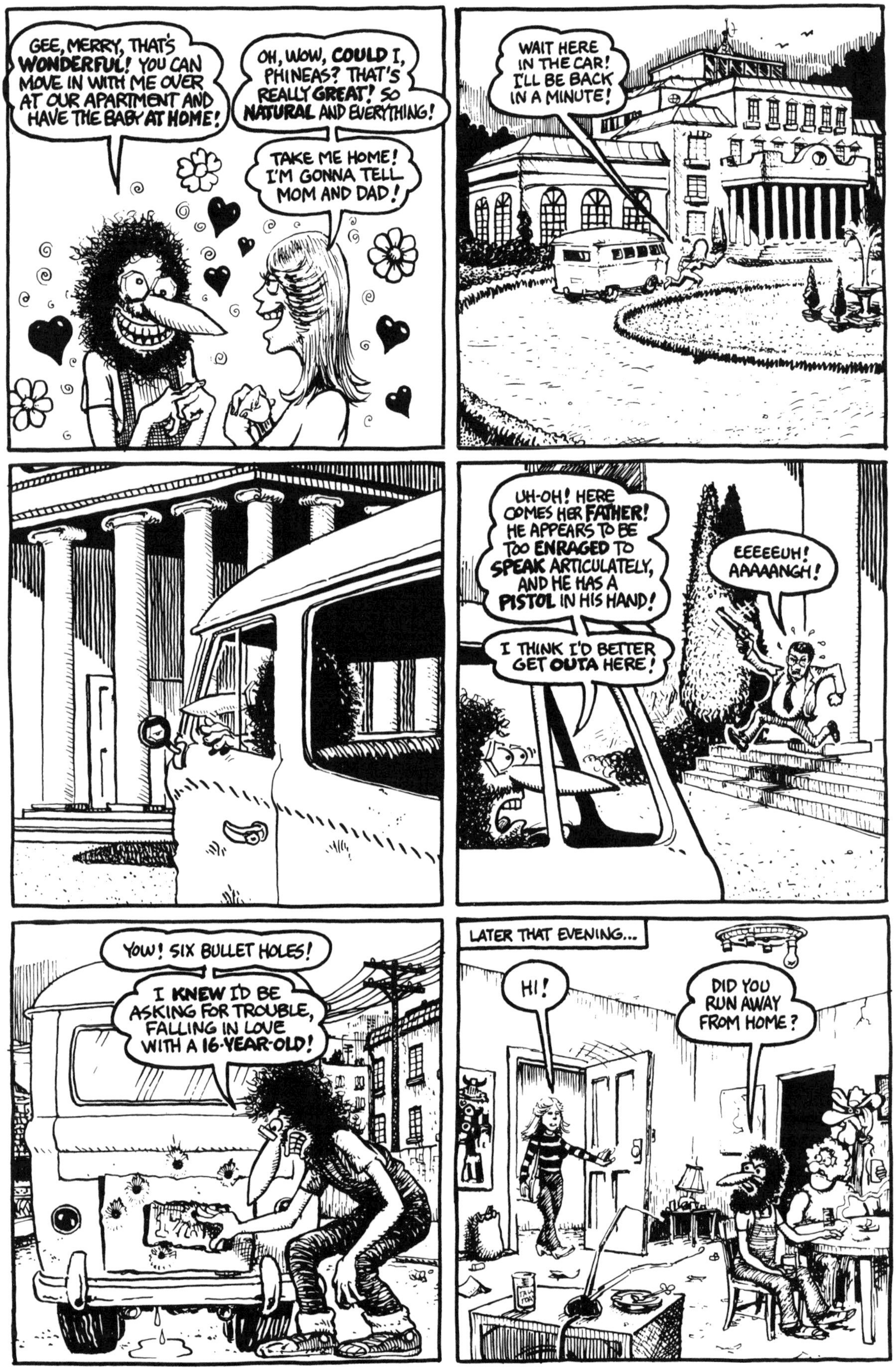
GEE, MERRY, THAT'S WONDERFUL! YOU CAN MOVE IN WITH ME OVER AT OUR APARTMENT AND HAVE THE BABY AT HOME!
OH, WOW, COULD I, PHINEAS? THAT'S REALLY GREAT! SO NATURAL AND EVERYTHING!
TAKE ME HOME! I'M GONNA TELL MOM AND DAD!
WAIT HERE IN THE CAR! I'LL BE BACK IN A MINUTE!
UH-OH! HERE COMES HER FATHER! HE APPEARS TO BE TOO ENRAGED TO SPEAK ARTICULATELY, AND HE HAS A PISTOL IN HIS HAND!
I THINK I'D BETTER GET OUTA HERE!
EEEEEUH! AAAAANGH!
YOW! SIX BULLET HOLES!
I KNEW I'D BE ASKING FOR TROUBLE, FALLING IN LOVE WITH A 16-YEAR-OLD!
LATER THAT EVENING...
HI!
DID YOU RUN AWAY FROM HOME?

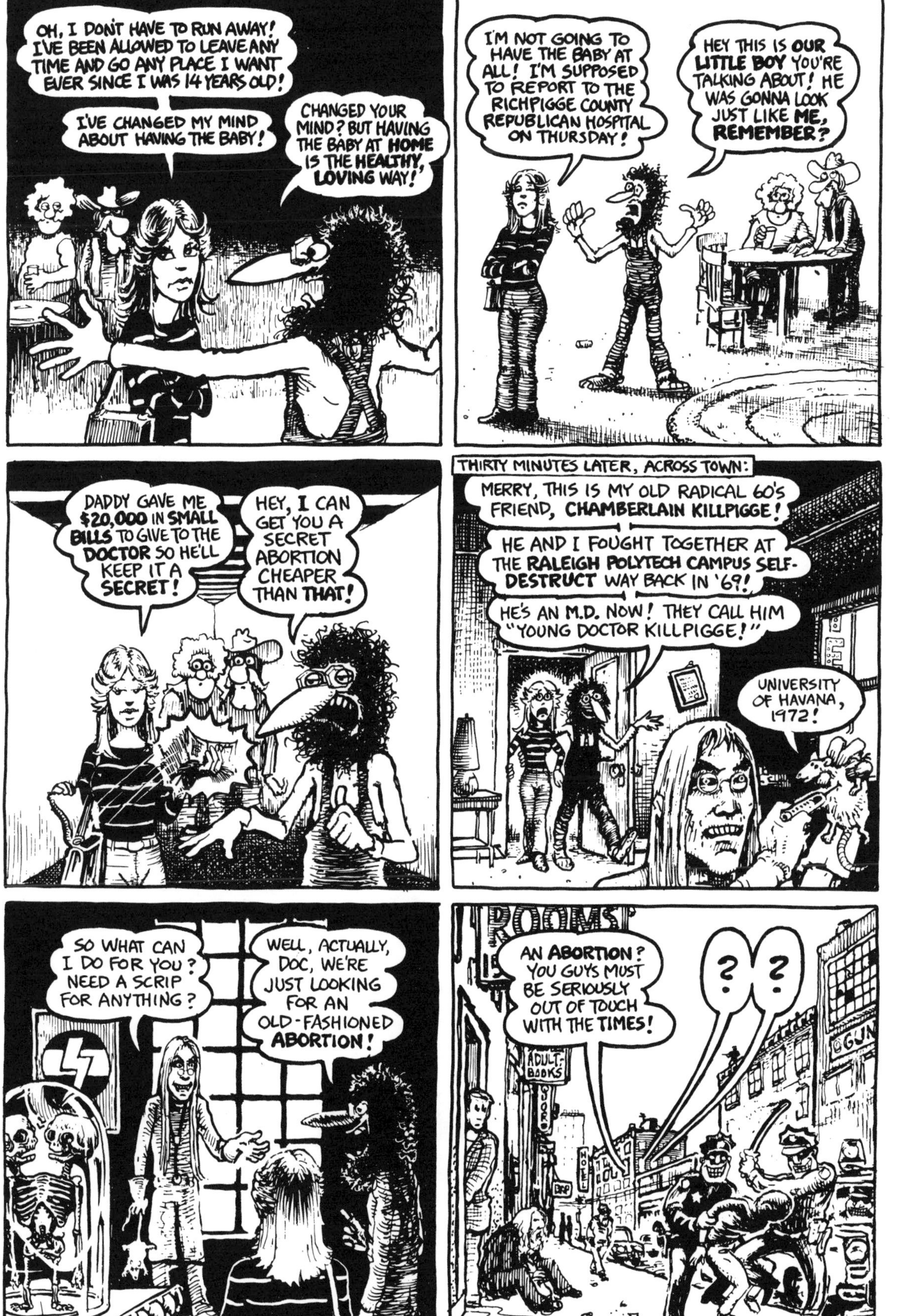
OH, I DON'T HAVE TO RUN AWAY! I'VE BEEN ALLOWED TO LEAVE ANY TIME AND GO ANY PLACE I WANT EVER SINCE I WAS 14 YEARS OLD!
I'VE CHANGED MY MIND ABOUT HAVING THE BABY!
CHANGED YOUR MIND? BUT HAVING THE BABY AT HOME IS THE HEALTHY, LOVING WAY!
I'M NOT GOING TO HAVE THE BABY AT ALL! I'M SUPPOSED TO REPORT TO THE RICHPIGGE COUNTY REPUBLICAN HOSPITAL ON THURSDAY!
HEY THIS IS OUR LITTLE BOY YOU'RE TALKING ABOUT! HE WAS GONNA LOOK JUST LIKE ME, REMEMBER?
DADDY GAVE ME $20,000 IN SMALL BILLS TO GIVE TO THE DOCTOR SO HE'LL KEEP IT A SECRET!
HEY, I CAN GET YOU A SECRET ABORTION CHEAPER THAN THAT!
THIRTY MINUTES LATER, ACROSS TOWN:
MERRY, THIS IS MY OLD RADICAL 60'S FRIEND, CHAMBERLAIN KILLPIGGE!
HE AND I FOUGHT TOGETHER AT THE RALEIGH POLYTECH CAMPUS SELF-DESTRUCT WAY BACK IN '69!
HE'S AN M.D. NOW! THEY CALL HIM "YOUNG DOCTOR KILLPIGGE!"
UNIVERSITY OF HAVANA, 1972!
SO WHAT CAN I DO FOR YOU? NEED A SCRIP FOR ANYTHING?
WELL, ACTUALLY, DOC, WE'RE JUST LOOKING FOR AN OLD-FASHIONED ABORTION!
ROOMS
ADULT BOOKS
STORE
HOTEL
AN ABORTION? YOU GUYS MUST BE SERIOUSLY OUT OF TOUCH WITH THE TIMES!
?
?

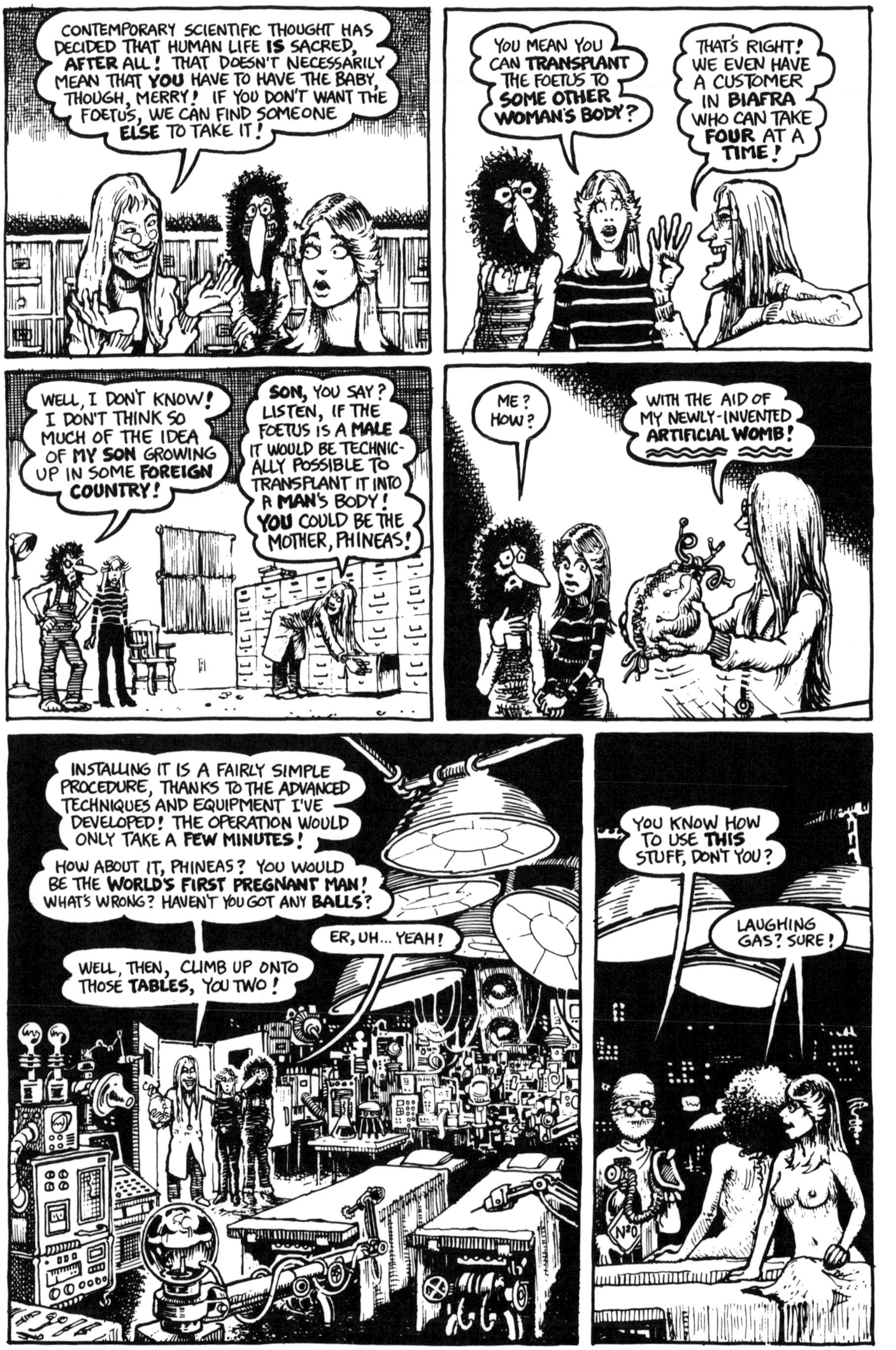
CONTEMPORARY SCIENTIFIC THOUGHT HAS DECIDED THAT HUMAN LIFE IS SACRED, AFTER ALL! THAT DOESN'T NECESSARILY MEAN THAT YOU HAVE TO HAVE THE BABY, THOUGH, MERRY! IF YOU DON'T WANT THE FOETUS, WE CAN FIND SOMEONE ELSE TO TAKE IT!
YOU MEAN YOU CAN TRANSPLANT THE FOETUS TO SOME OTHER WOMAN'S BODY?
THAT'S RIGHT! WE EVEN HAVE A CUSTOMER IN BIAFRA WHO CAN TAKE FOUR AT A TIME!
WELL, I DON'T KNOW! I DON'T THINK SO MUCH OF THE IDEA OF MY SON GROWING UP IN SOME FOREIGN COUNTRY!
SON, YOU SAY? LISTEN, IF THE FOETUS IS A MALE IT WOULD BE TECHNICALLY POSSIBLE TO TRANSPLANT IT INTO A MAN'S BODY! YOU COULD BE THE MOTHER, PHINEAS!
ME? HOW?
WITH THE AID OF MY NEWLY-INVENTED ARTIFICIAL WOMB!
INSTALLING IT IS A FAIRLY SIMPLE PROCEDURE, THANKS TO THE ADVANCED TECHNIQUES AND EQUIPMENT I'VE DEVELOPED! THE OPERATION WOULD ONLY TAKE A FEW MINUTES!
HOW ABOUT IT, PHINEAS? YOU WOULD BE THE WORLD'S FIRST PREGNANT MAN! WHAT'S WRONG? HAVEN'T YOU GOT ANY BALLS?
ER, UH... YEAH!
WELL, THEN, CLIMB UP ONTO THOSE TABLES, YOU TWO!
YOU KNOW HOW TO USE THIS STUFF, DON'T YOU?
LAUGHING GAS? SURE!
N2O

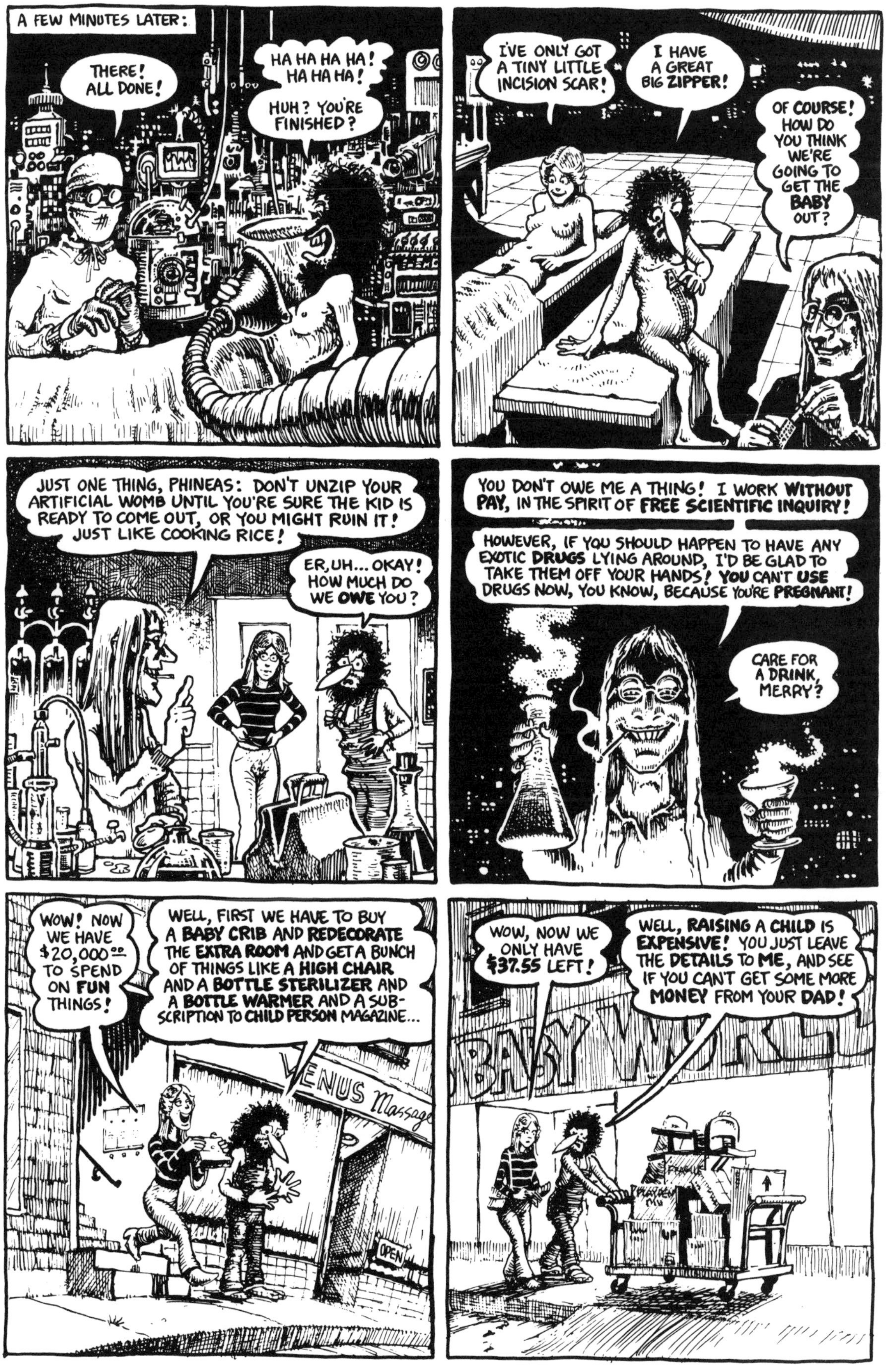
A FEW MINUTES LATER:
THERE! ALL DONE!
HA HA HA HA! HA HA HA!
HUH? YOU'RE FINISHED?
I'VE ONLY GOT A TINY LITTLE INCISION SCAR!
I HAVE A GREAT BIG ZIPPER!
OF COURSE! HOW DO YOU THINK WE'RE GOING TO GET THE BABY OUT?
JUST ONE THING, PHINEAS: DON'T UNZIP YOUR ARTIFICIAL WOMB UNTIL YOU'RE SURE THE KID IS READY TO COME OUT, OR YOU MIGHT RUIN IT! JUST LIKE COOKING RICE!
ER, UH... OKAY! HOW MUCH DO WE OWE YOU?
YOU DON'T OWE ME A THING! I WORK WITHOUT PAY, IN THE SPIRIT OF FREE SCIENTIFIC INQUIRY!
HOWEVER, IF YOU SHOULD HAPPEN TO HAVE ANY EXOTIC DRUGS LYING AROUND, I'D BE GLAD TO TAKE THEM OFF YOUR HANDS! YOU CAN'T USE DRUGS NOW, YOU KNOW, BECAUSE YOU'RE PREGNANT!
CARE FOR A DRINK, MERRY?
WOW! NOW WE HAVE $20,000.00 TO SPEND ON FUN THINGS!
WELL, FIRST WE HAVE TO BUY A BABY CRIB AND REDECORATE THE EXTRA ROOM AND GET A BUNCH OF THINGS LIKE A HIGH CHAIR AND A BOTTLE STERILIZER AND A BOTTLE WARMER AND A SUBSCRIPTION TO CHILD PERSON MAGAZINE...
VENUS Massage
OPEN
WOW, NOW WE ONLY HAVE $37.55 LEFT!
WELL, RAISING A CHILD IS EXPENSIVE! YOU JUST LEAVE THE DETAILS TO ME, AND SEE IF YOU CAN'T GET SOME MORE MONEY FROM YOUR DAD!
BABY

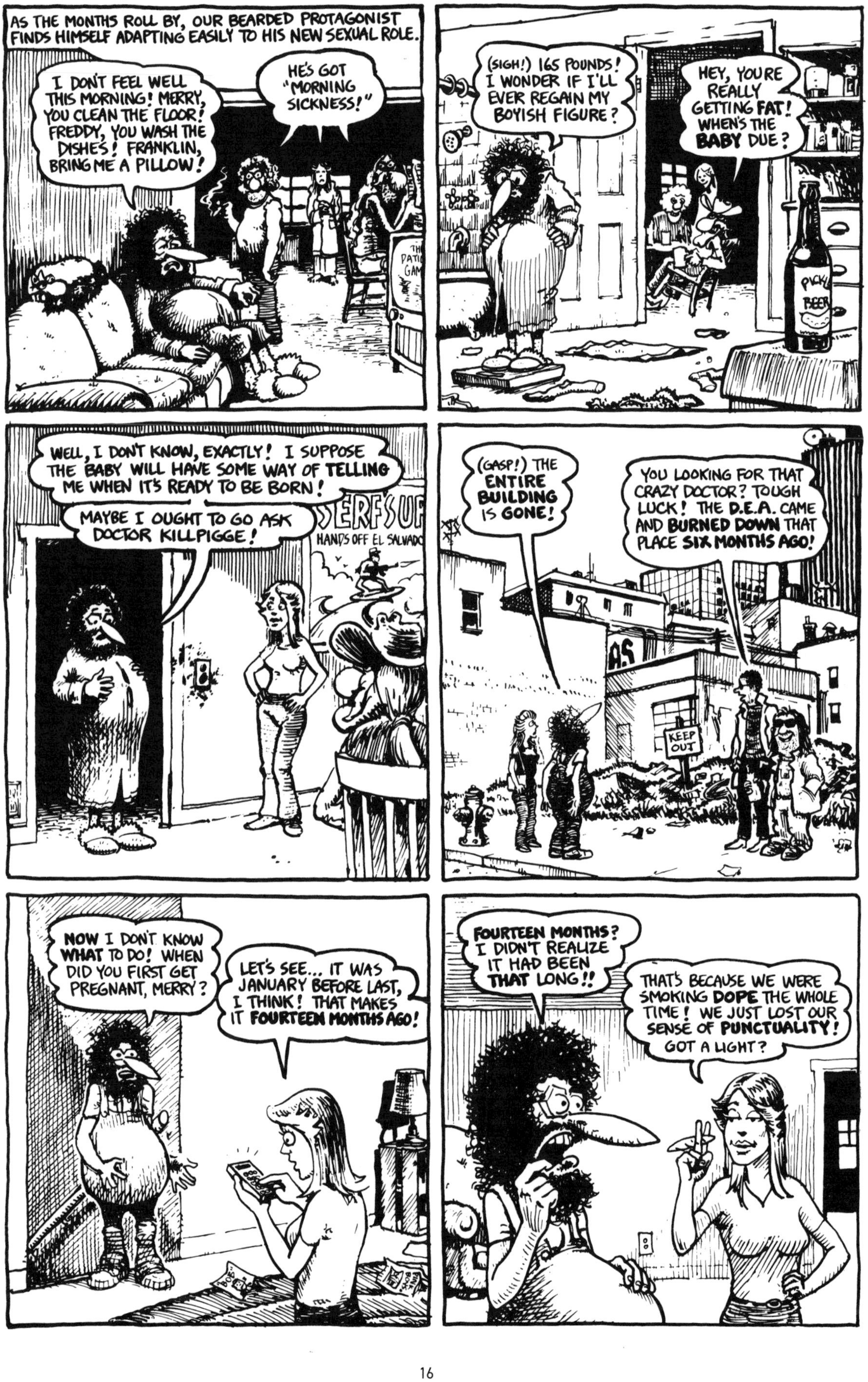
AS THE MONTHS ROLL BY, OUR BEARDED PROTAGONIST FINDS HIMSELF ADAPTING EASILY TO HIS NEW SEXUAL ROLE.
I DON'T FEEL WELL THIS MORNING! MERRY, YOU CLEAN THE FLOOR! FREDDY, YOU WASH THE DISHES! FRANKLIN, BRING ME A PILLOW!
HE'S GOT "MORNING SICKNESS!"
(SIGH!) 165 POUNDS! I WONDER IF I'LL EVER REGAIN MY BOYISH FIGURE?
HEY, YOU'RE REALLY GETTING FAT! WHEN'S THE BABY DUE?
WELL, I DON'T KNOW, EXACTLY! I SUPPOSE THE BABY WILL HAVE SOME WAY OF TELLING ME WHEN IT'S READY TO BE BORN!
MAYBE I OUGHT TO GO ASK DOCTOR KILLPIGGE!
HANDS OFF EL SALVADOR
(GASP!) THE ENTIRE BUILDING IS GONE!
YOU LOOKING FOR THAT CRAZY DOCTOR? TOUGH LUCK! THE D.E.A. CAME AND BURNED DOWN THAT PLACE SIX MONTHS AGO!
KEEP OUT
NOW I DON'T KNOW WHAT TO DO! WHEN DID YOU FIRST GET PREGNANT, MERRY?
LET'S SEE... IT WAS JANUARY BEFORE LAST, I THINK! THAT MAKES IT FOURTEEN MONTHS AGO!
FOURTEEN MONTHS? I DIDN'T REALIZE IT HAD BEEN THAT LONG!!
THAT'S BECAUSE WE WERE SMOKING DOPE THE WHOLE TIME! WE JUST LOST OUR SENSE OF PUNCTUALITY! GOT A LIGHT?

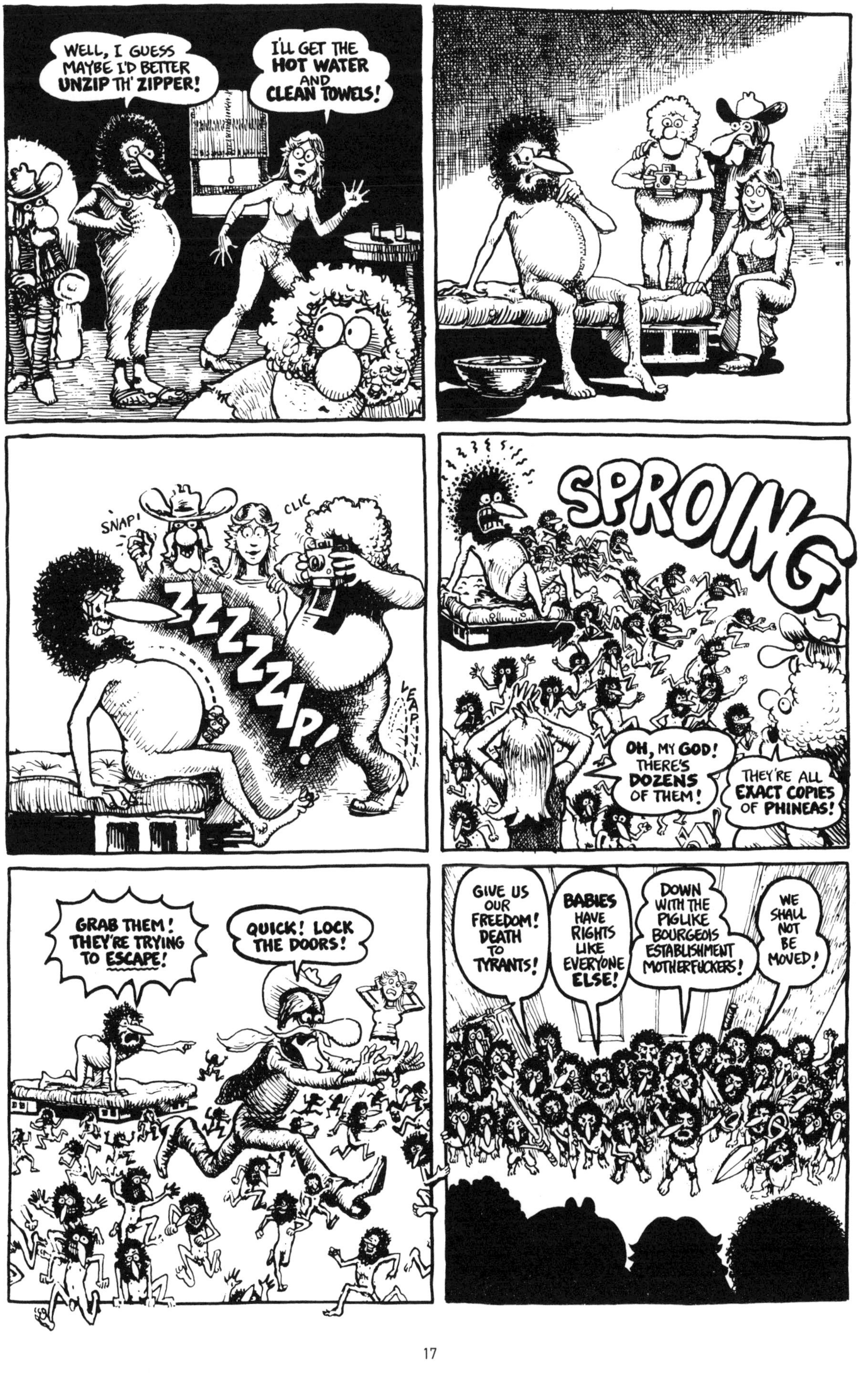
WELL, I GUESS MAYBE I'D BETTER UNZIP TH' ZIPPER!
I'LL GET THE HOT WATER AND CLEAN TOWELS!
SNAP!
CLIC
ZZZZZIP!
LEAP!
SPROING
OH, MY GOD! THERE'S DOZENS OF THEM!
THEY'RE ALL EXACT COPIES OF PHINEAS!
GRAB THEM! THEY'RE TRYING TO ESCAPE!
QUICK! LOCK THE DOORS!
GIVE US OUR FREEDOM! DEATH TO TYRANTS!
BABIES HAVE RIGHTS LIKE EVERYONE ELSE!
DOWN WITH THE PIGLIKE BOURGEOIS ESTABLISHMENT MOTHERFUCKERS!
WE SHALL NOT BE MOVED!

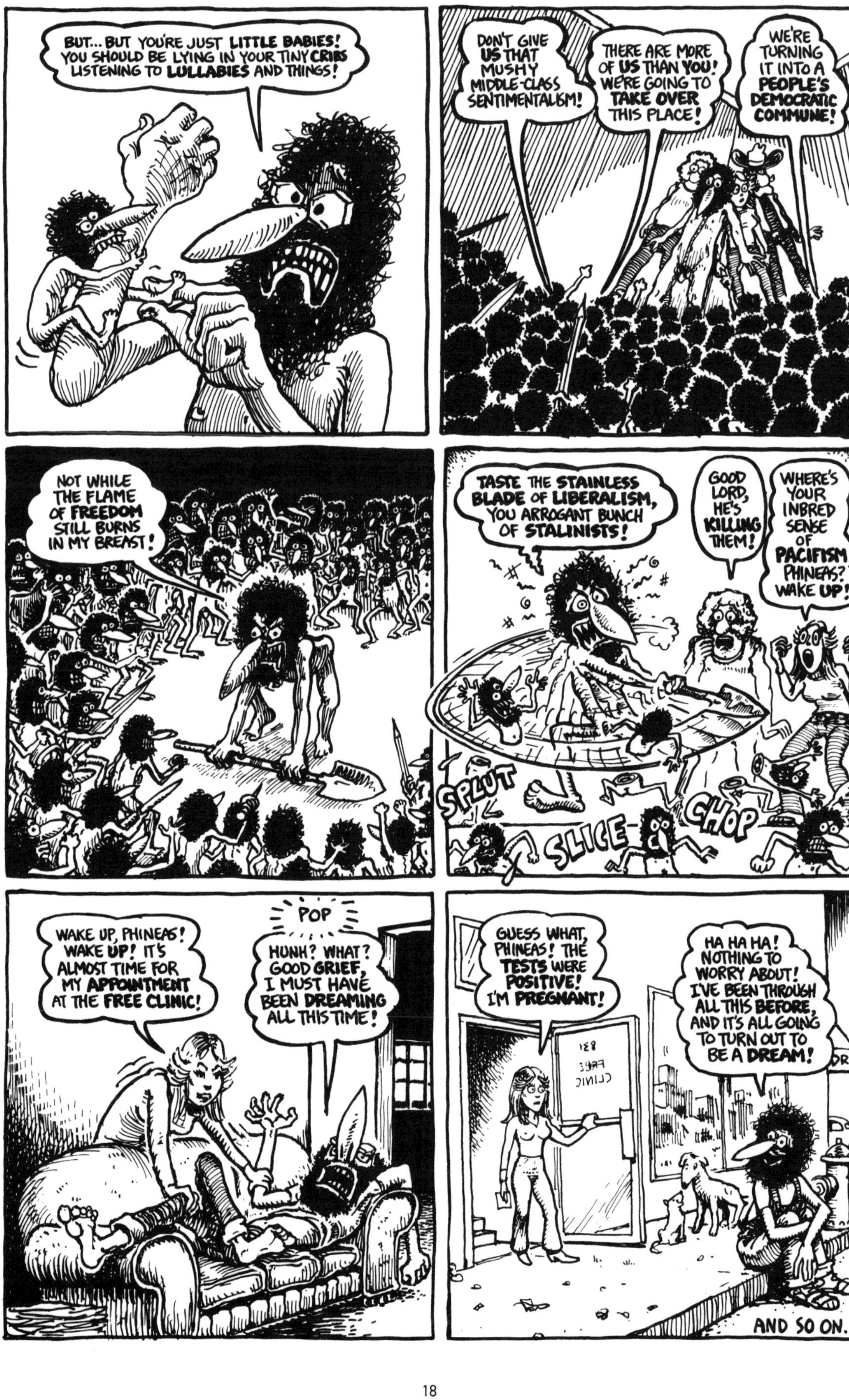
BUT... BUT YOU'RE JUST LITTLE BABIES! YOU SHOULD BE LYING IN YOUR TINY CRIBS LISTENING TO LULLABIES AND THINGS!
DON'T GIVE US THAT MUSHY MIDDLE-CLASS SENTIMENTALISM!
THERE ARE MORE OF US THAN YOU! WE'RE GOING TO TAKE OVER THIS PLACE!
WE'RE TURNING IT INTO A PEOPLE'S DEMOCRATIC COMMUNE!
NOT WHILE THE FLAME OF FREEDOM STILL BURNS IN MY BREAST!
TASTE THE STAINLESS BLADE OF LIBERALISM, YOU ARROGANT BUNCH OF STALINISTS!
GOOD LORD, HE'S KILLING THEM!
WHERE'S YOUR INBRED SENSE OF PACIFISM, PHINEAS? WAKE UP!
SPLUT
SLICE
CHOP
WAKE UP, PHINEAS! WAKE UP! IT'S ALMOST TIME FOR MY APPOINTMENT AT THE FREE CLINIC!
POP
HUNH? WHAT? GOOD GRIEF, I MUST HAVE BEEN DREAMING ALL THIS TIME!
GUESS WHAT, PHINEAS! THE TESTS WERE POSITIVE! I'M PREGNANT!
HA HA HA! NOTHING TO WORRY ABOUT! I'VE BEEN THROUGH ALL THIS BEFORE, AND IT'S ALL GOING TO TURN OUT TO BE A DREAM!
DRU
AND SO ON...

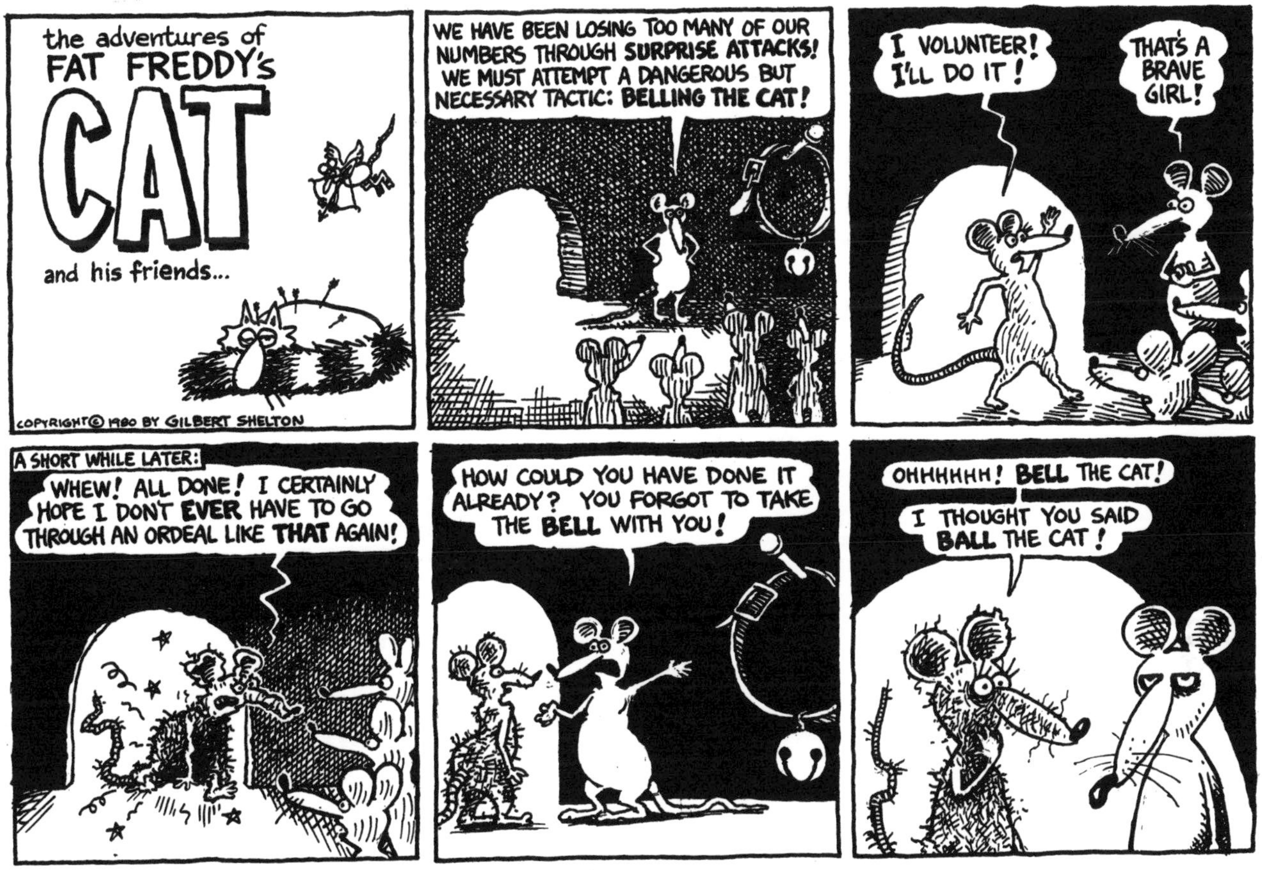
the adventures of
FAT FREDDY's
CAT
and his friends...
COPYRIGHT © 1980 BY GILBERT SHELTON
WE HAVE BEEN LOSING TOO MANY OF OUR NUMBERS THROUGH SURPRISE ATTACKS! WE MUST ATTEMPT A DANGEROUS BUT NECESSARY TACTIC: BELLING THE CAT!
I VOLUNTEER! I'LL DO IT!
THAT'S A BRAVE GIRL!
A SHORT WHILE LATER:
WHEW! ALL DONE! I CERTAINLY HOPE I DON'T EVER HAVE TO GO THROUGH AN ORDEAL LIKE THAT AGAIN!
HOW COULD YOU HAVE DONE IT ALREADY? YOU FORGOT TO TAKE THE BELL WITH YOU!
OHHHHHH! BELL THE CAT!
I THOUGHT YOU SAID BALL THE CAT!

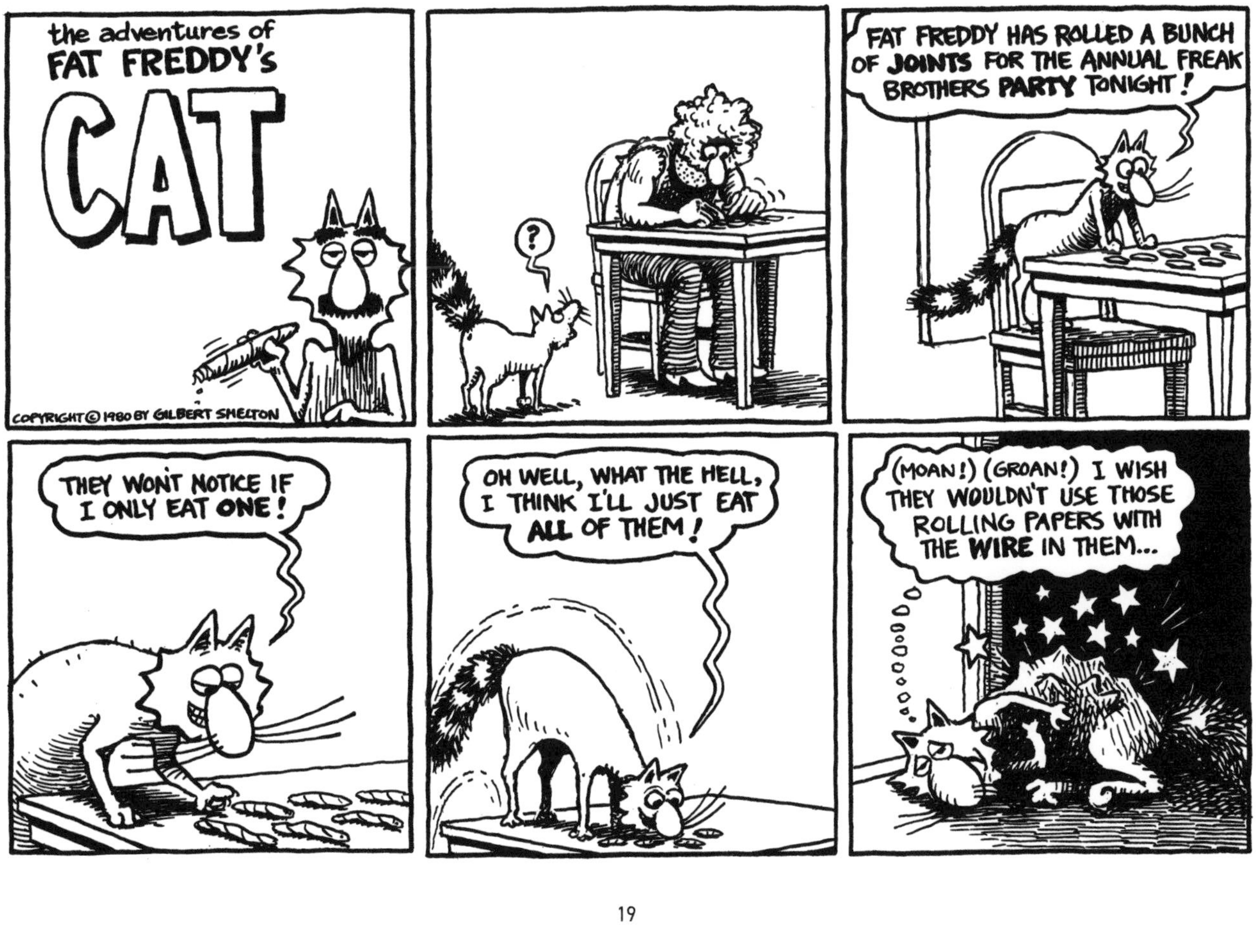
the adventures of
FAT FREDDY's
CAT
COPYRIGHT © 1980 BY GILBERT SHELTON
?
FAT FREDDY HAS ROLLED A BUNCH OF JOINTS FOR THE ANNUAL FREAK BROTHERS PARTY TONIGHT!
THEY WON'T NOTICE IF I ONLY EAT ONE!
OH WELL, WHAT THE HELL, I THINK I'LL JUST EAT ALL OF THEM!
(MOAN!) (GROAN!) I WISH THEY WOULDN'T USE THOSE ROLLING PAPERS WITH THE WIRE IN THEM...

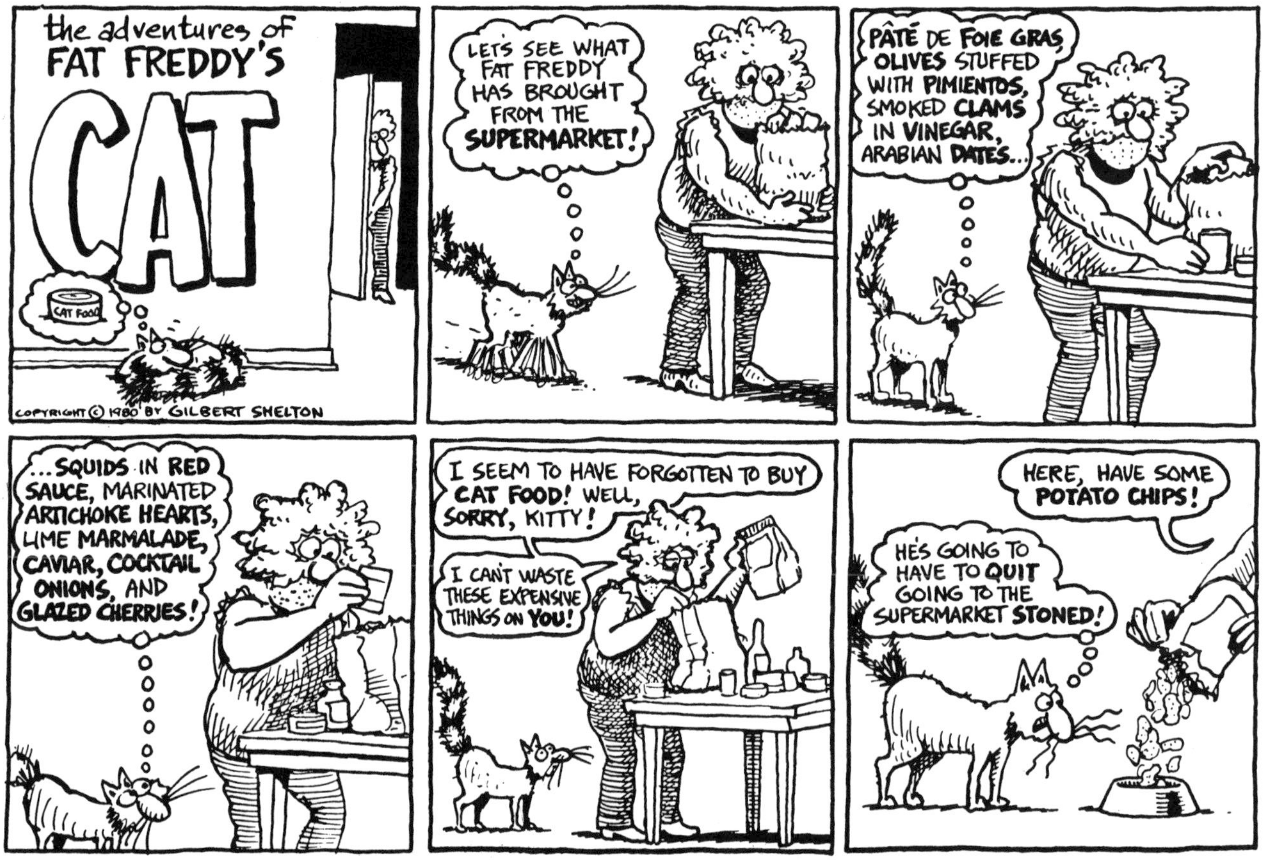

the adventures of
FAT FREDDY'S
CAT
CAT FOOD
COPYRIGHT © 1980 BY GILBERT SHELTON
LET'S SEE WHAT FAT FREDDY HAS BROUGHT FROM THE SUPERMARKET!
PÂTÉ DE FOIE GRAS, OLIVES STUFFED WITH PIMIENTOS, SMOKED CLAMS IN VINEGAR, ARABIAN DATES...
...SQUIDS IN RED SAUCE, MARINATED ARTICHOKE HEARTS, LIME MARMALADE, CAVIAR, COCKTAIL ONIONS, AND GLAZED CHERRIES!
I SEEM TO HAVE FORGOTTEN TO BUY CAT FOOD! WELL, SORRY, KITTY!
I CAN'T WASTE THESE EXPENSIVE THINGS ON YOU!
HERE, HAVE SOME POTATO CHIPS!
HE'S GOING TO HAVE TO QUIT GOING TO THE SUPERMARKET STONED!

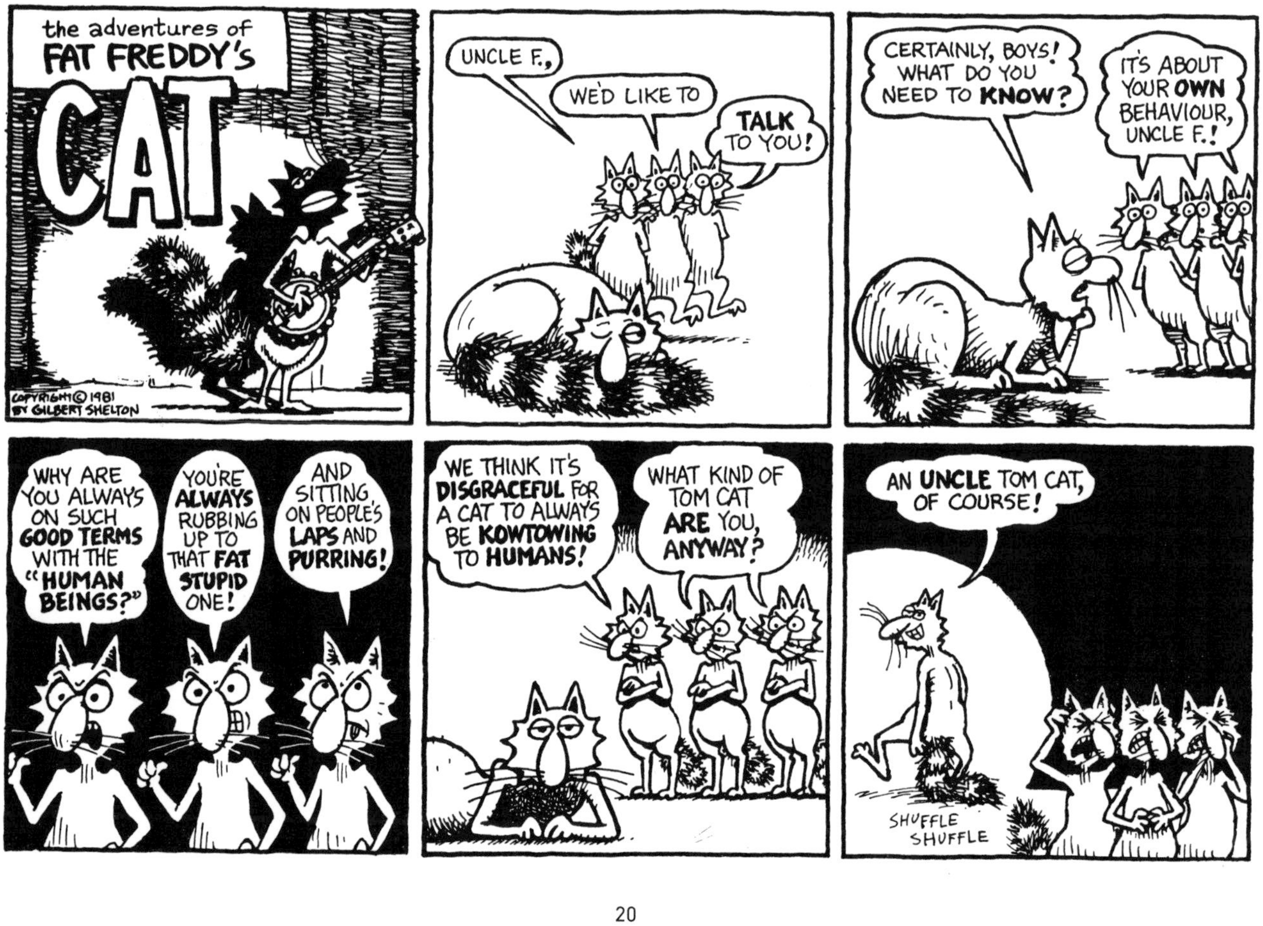

the adventures of
FAT FREDDY'S
CAT
COPYRIGHT © 1981 BY GILBERT SHELTON
UNCLE F.,
WE'D LIKE TO
TALK TO YOU!
CERTAINLY, BOYS! WHAT DO YOU NEED TO KNOW?
IT'S ABOUT YOUR OWN BEHAVIOUR, UNCLE F.!
WHY ARE YOU ALWAYS ON SUCH GOOD TERMS WITH THE "HUMAN BEINGS?"
YOU'RE ALWAYS RUBBING UP TO THAT FAT STUPID ONE!
AND SITTING ON PEOPLE'S LAPS AND PURRING!
WE THINK IT'S DISGRACEFUL FOR A CAT TO ALWAYS BE KOWTOWING TO HUMANS!
WHAT KIND OF TOM CAT ARE YOU, ANYWAY?
AN UNCLE TOM CAT, OF COURSE!
SHUFFLE
SHUFFLE

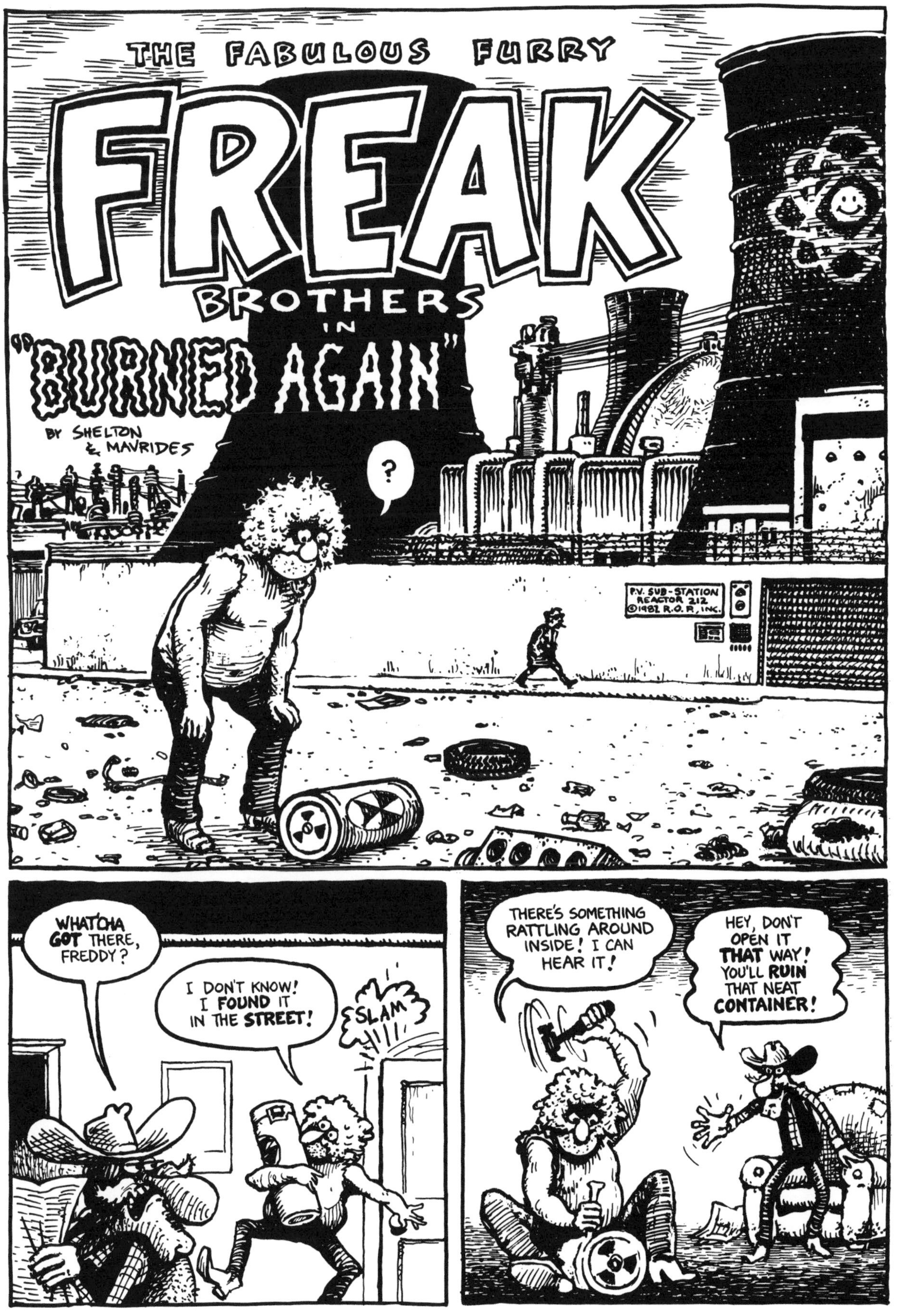
THE FABULOUS FURRY
FREAK
BROTHERS
IN
"BURNED AGAIN"
BY SHELTON & MAVRIDES
?
P.V. SUB-STATION REACTOR 212 ©1982 R.O.R., INC.
WHAT'CHA GOT THERE, FREDDY?
I DON'T KNOW! I FOUND IT IN THE STREET!
SLAM
THERE'S SOMETHING RATTLING AROUND INSIDE! I CAN HEAR IT!
HEY, DON'T OPEN IT THAT WAY! YOU'LL RUIN THAT NEAT CONTAINER!

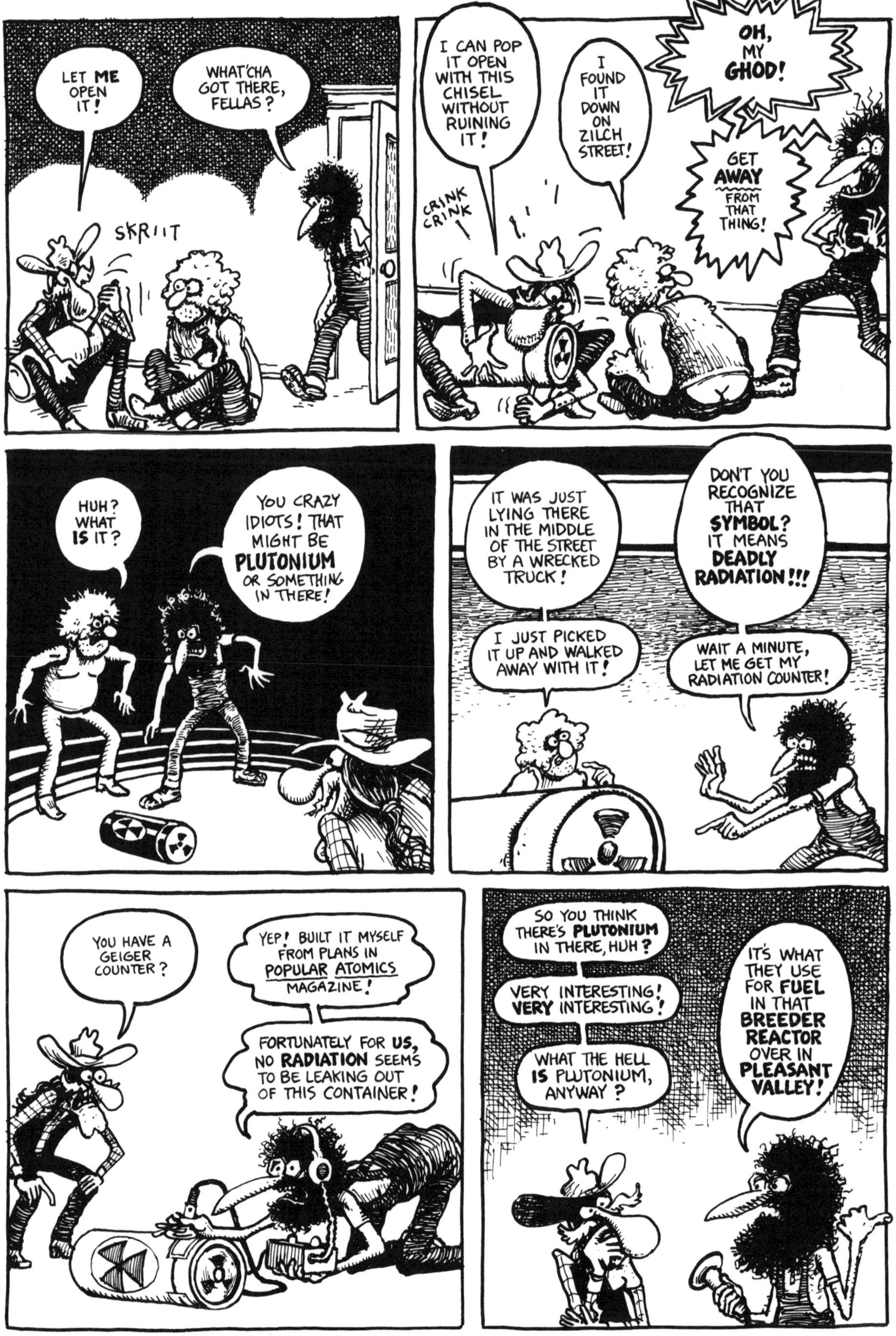
LET ME OPEN IT!
WHAT'CHA GOT THERE, FELLAS?
SKRIIT
I CAN POP IT OPEN WITH THIS CHISEL WITHOUT RUINING IT!
I FOUND IT DOWN ON ZILCH STREET!
CRINK CRINK
OH, MY GHOD!
GET AWAY FROM THAT THING!
HUH? WHAT IS IT?
YOU CRAZY IDIOTS! THAT MIGHT BE PLUTONIUM OR SOMETHING IN THERE!
IT WAS JUST LYING THERE IN THE MIDDLE OF THE STREET BY A WRECKED TRUCK!
I JUST PICKED IT UP AND WALKED AWAY WITH IT!
DON'T YOU RECOGNIZE THAT SYMBOL? IT MEANS DEADLY RADIATION!!!
WAIT A MINUTE, LET ME GET MY RADIATION COUNTER!
YOU HAVE A GEIGER COUNTER?
YEP! BUILT IT MYSELF FROM PLANS IN POPULAR ATOMICS MAGAZINE!
FORTUNATELY FOR US, NO RADIATION SEEMS TO BE LEAKING OUT OF THIS CONTAINER!
SO YOU THINK THERE'S PLUTONIUM IN THERE, HUH?
VERY INTERESTING! VERY INTERESTING!
WHAT THE HELL IS PLUTONIUM, ANYWAY?
IT'S WHAT THEY USE FOR FUEL IN THAT BREEDER REACTOR OVER IN PLEASANT VALLEY!

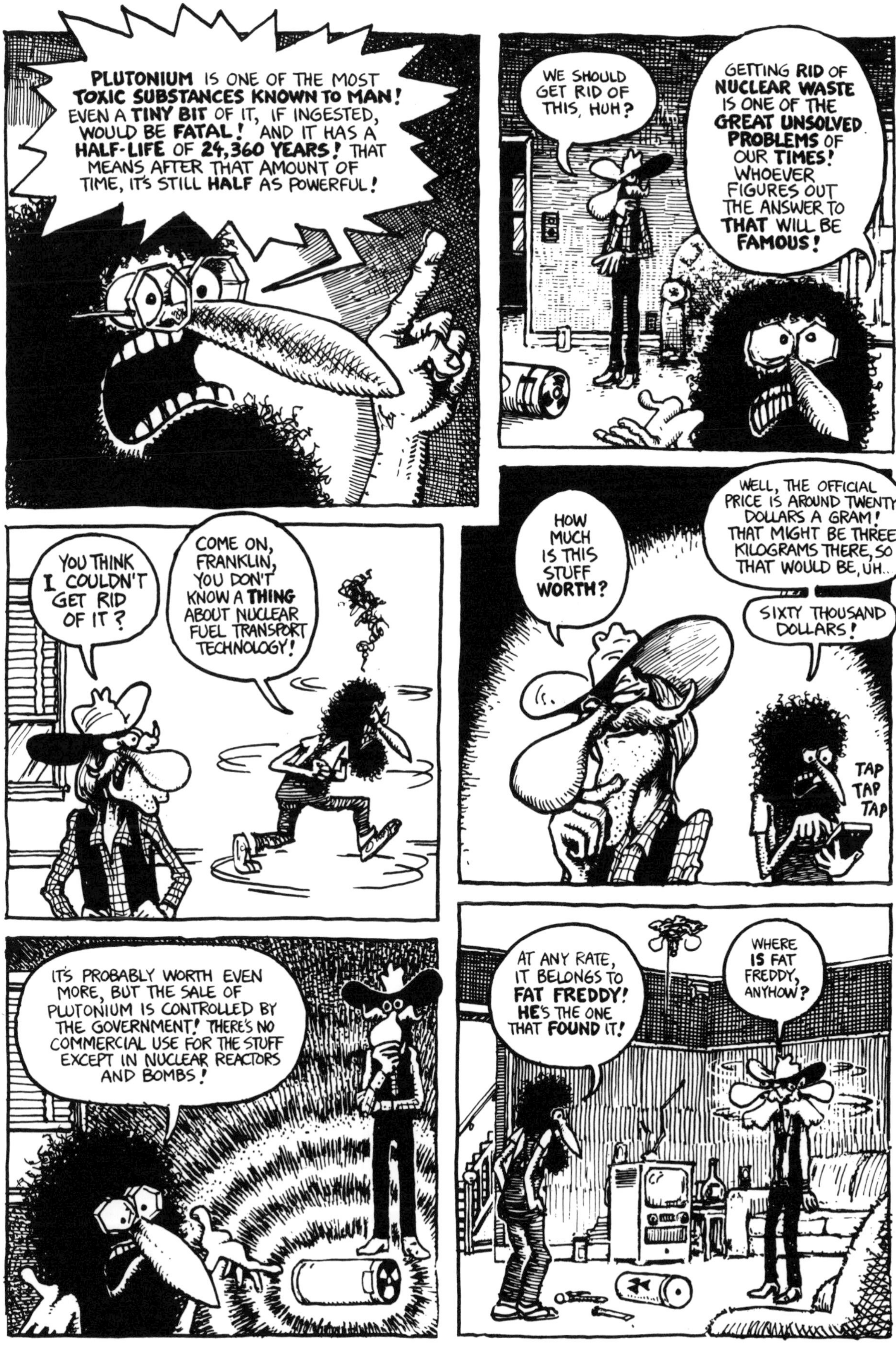
PLUTONIUM IS ONE OF THE MOST TOXIC SUBSTANCES KNOWN TO MAN! EVEN A TINY BIT OF IT, IF INGESTED, WOULD BE FATAL! AND IT HAS A HALF-LIFE OF 24,360 YEARS! THAT MEANS AFTER THAT AMOUNT OF TIME, IT'S STILL HALF AS POWERFUL!
WE SHOULD GET RID OF THIS, HUH?
GETTING RID OF NUCLEAR WASTE IS ONE OF THE GREAT UNSOLVED PROBLEMS OF OUR TIMES! WHOEVER FIGURES OUT THE ANSWER TO THAT WILL BE FAMOUS!
YOU THINK I COULDN'T GET RID OF IT?
COME ON, FRANKLIN, YOU DON'T KNOW A THING ABOUT NUCLEAR FUEL TRANSPORT TECHNOLOGY!
HOW MUCH IS THIS STUFF WORTH?
WELL, THE OFFICIAL PRICE IS AROUND TWENTY DOLLARS A GRAM! THAT MIGHT BE THREE KILOGRAMS THERE, SO THAT WOULD BE, UH...
TAP TAP TAP
SIXTY THOUSAND DOLLARS!
IT'S PROBABLY WORTH EVEN MORE, BUT THE SALE OF PLUTONIUM IS CONTROLLED BY THE GOVERNMENT! THERE'S NO COMMERCIAL USE FOR THE STUFF EXCEPT IN NUCLEAR REACTORS AND BOMBS!
AT ANY RATE, IT BELONGS TO FAT FREDDY! HE'S THE ONE THAT FOUND IT!
WHERE IS FAT FREDDY, ANYHOW?

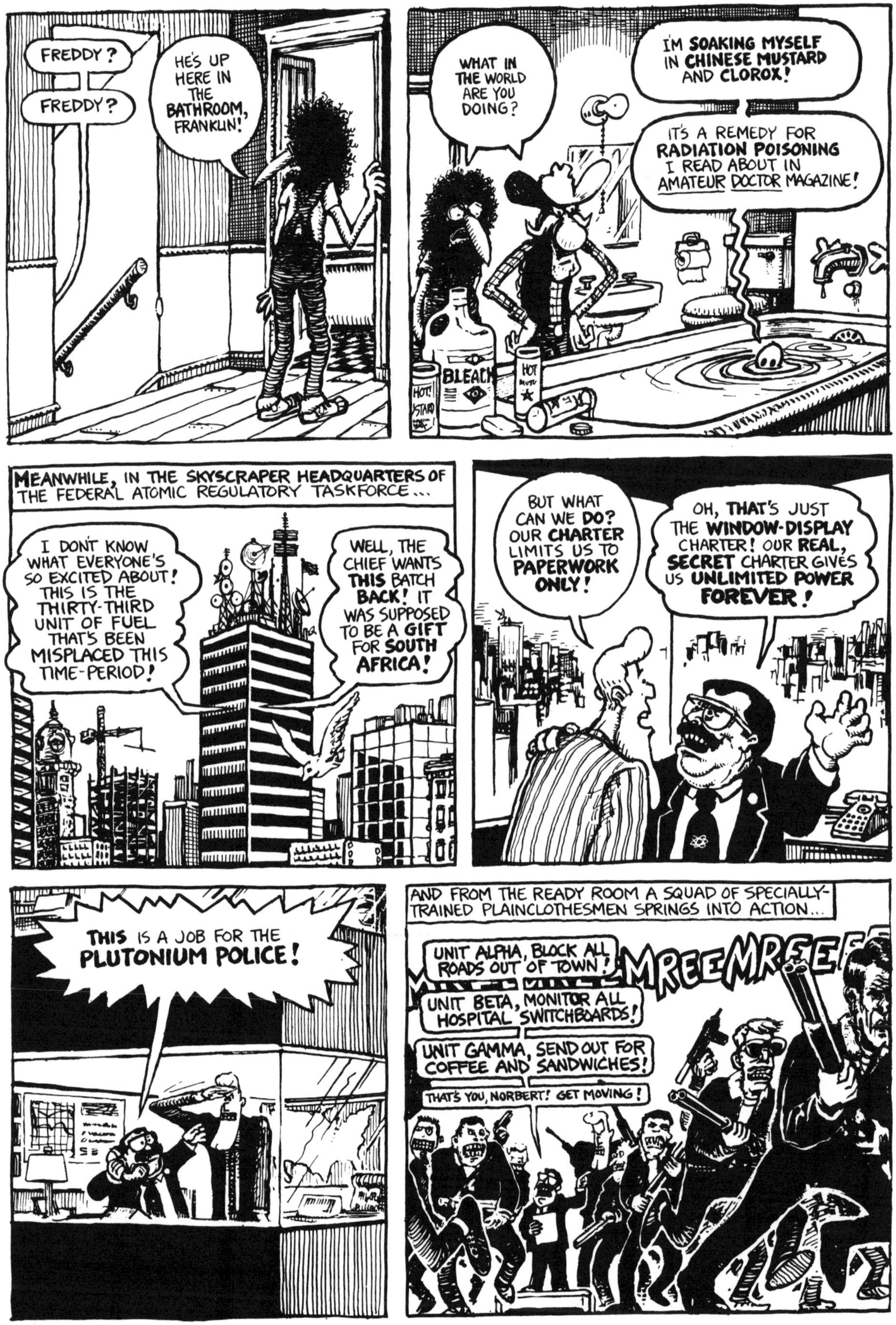
FREDDY?
FREDDY?
HE'S UP HERE IN THE BATHROOM, FRANKLIN!
WHAT IN THE WORLD ARE YOU DOING?
I'M SOAKING MYSELF IN CHINESE MUSTARD AND CLOROX!
IT'S A REMEDY FOR RADIATION POISONING I READ ABOUT IN AMATEUR DOCTOR MAGAZINE!
BLEACH
HOT
MEANWHILE, IN THE SKYSCRAPER HEADQUARTERS OF THE FEDERAL ATOMIC REGULATORY TASKFORCE...
I DON'T KNOW WHAT EVERYONE'S SO EXCITED ABOUT! THIS IS THE THIRTY-THIRD UNIT OF FUEL THAT'S BEEN MISPLACED THIS TIME-PERIOD!
WELL, THE CHIEF WANTS THIS BATCH BACK! IT WAS SUPPOSED TO BE A GIFT FOR SOUTH AFRICA!
BUT WHAT CAN WE DO? OUR CHARTER LIMITS US TO PAPERWORK ONLY!
OH, THAT'S JUST THE WINDOW-DISPLAY CHARTER! OUR REAL, SECRET CHARTER GIVES US UNLIMITED POWER FOREVER!
THIS IS A JOB FOR THE PLUTONIUM POLICE!
AND FROM THE READY ROOM A SQUAD OF SPECIALLY-TRAINED PLAINCLOTHESMEN SPRINGS INTO ACTION...
MREEMREE
UNIT ALPHA, BLOCK ALL ROADS OUT OF TOWN!
UNIT BETA, MONITOR ALL HOSPITAL SWITCHBOARDS!
UNIT GAMMA, SEND OUT FOR COFFEE AND SANDWICHES!
THAT'S YOU, NORBERT! GET MOVING!

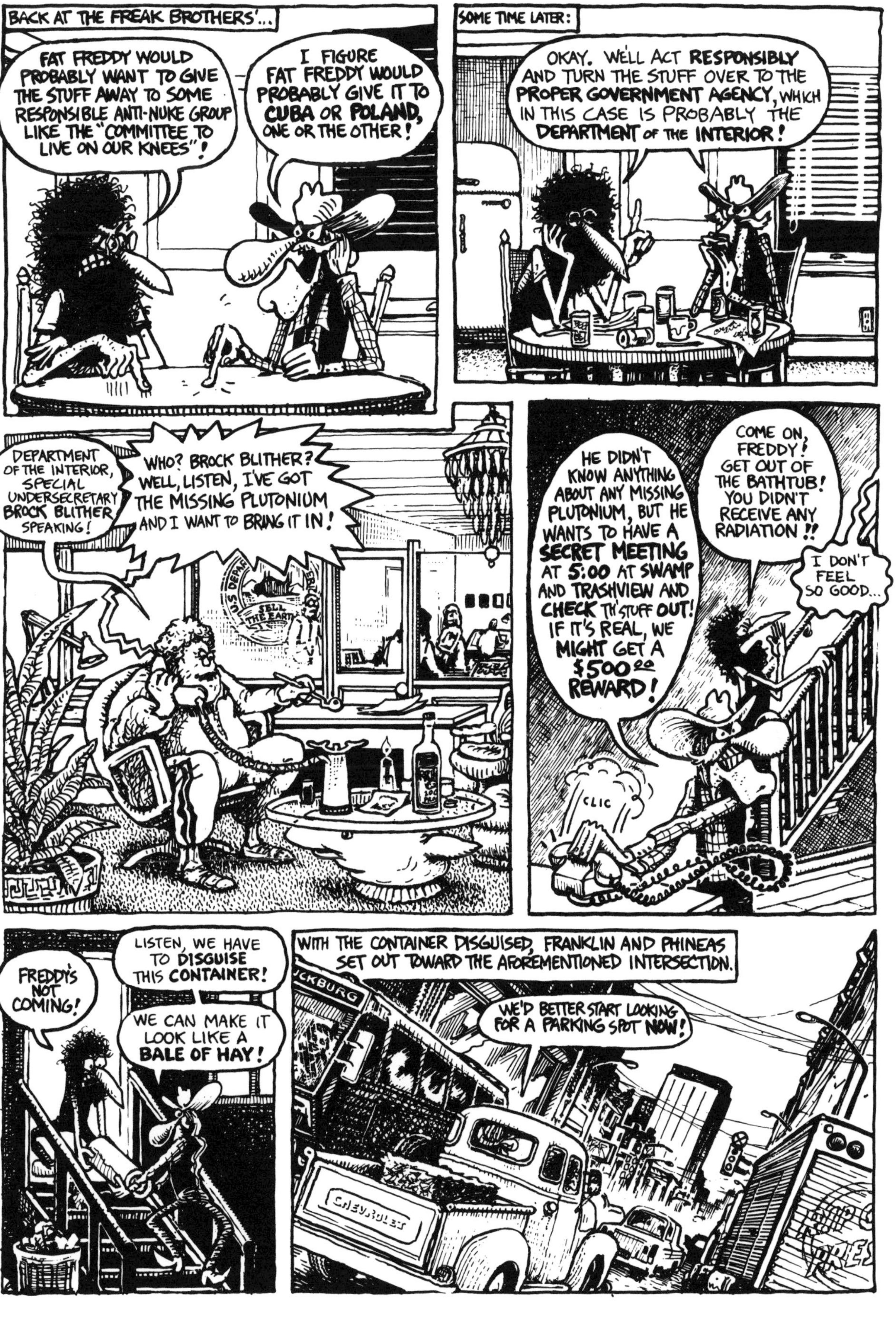

BACK AT THE FREAK BROTHERS'...
FAT FREDDY WOULD PROBABLY WANT TO GIVE THE STUFF AWAY TO SOME RESPONSIBLE ANTI-NUKE GROUP LIKE THE "COMMITTEE TO LIVE ON OUR KNEES"!
I FIGURE FAT FREDDY WOULD PROBABLY GIVE IT TO CUBA OR POLAND, ONE OR THE OTHER!
SOME TIME LATER:
OKAY. WE'LL ACT RESPONSIBLY AND TURN THE STUFF OVER TO THE PROPER GOVERNMENT AGENCY, WHICH IN THIS CASE IS PROBABLY THE DEPARTMENT OF THE INTERIOR!
DEPARTMENT OF THE INTERIOR, SPECIAL UNDERSECRETARY BROCK BLITHER SPEAKING!
WHO? BROCK BLITHER? WELL, LISTEN, I'VE GOT THE MISSING PLUTONIUM AND I WANT TO BRING IT IN!
SELL THE EARTH
HE DIDN'T KNOW ANYTHING ABOUT ANY MISSING PLUTONIUM, BUT HE WANTS TO HAVE A SECRET MEETING AT 5:00 AT SWAMP AND TRASHVIEW AND CHECK TH' STUFF OUT! IF IT'S REAL, WE MIGHT GET A $500.00 REWARD!
COME ON, FREDDY! GET OUT OF THE BATHTUB! YOU DIDN'T RECEIVE ANY RADIATION!!
I DON'T FEEL SO GOOD...
CLIC
FREDDY'S NOT COMING!
LISTEN, WE HAVE TO DISGUISE THIS CONTAINER!
WE CAN MAKE IT LOOK LIKE A BALE OF HAY!
WITH THE CONTAINER DISGUISED, FRANKLIN AND PHINEAS SET OUT TOWARD THE AFOREMENTIONED INTERSECTION.
WE'D BETTER START LOOKING FOR A PARKING SPOT NOW!
CHEVROLET

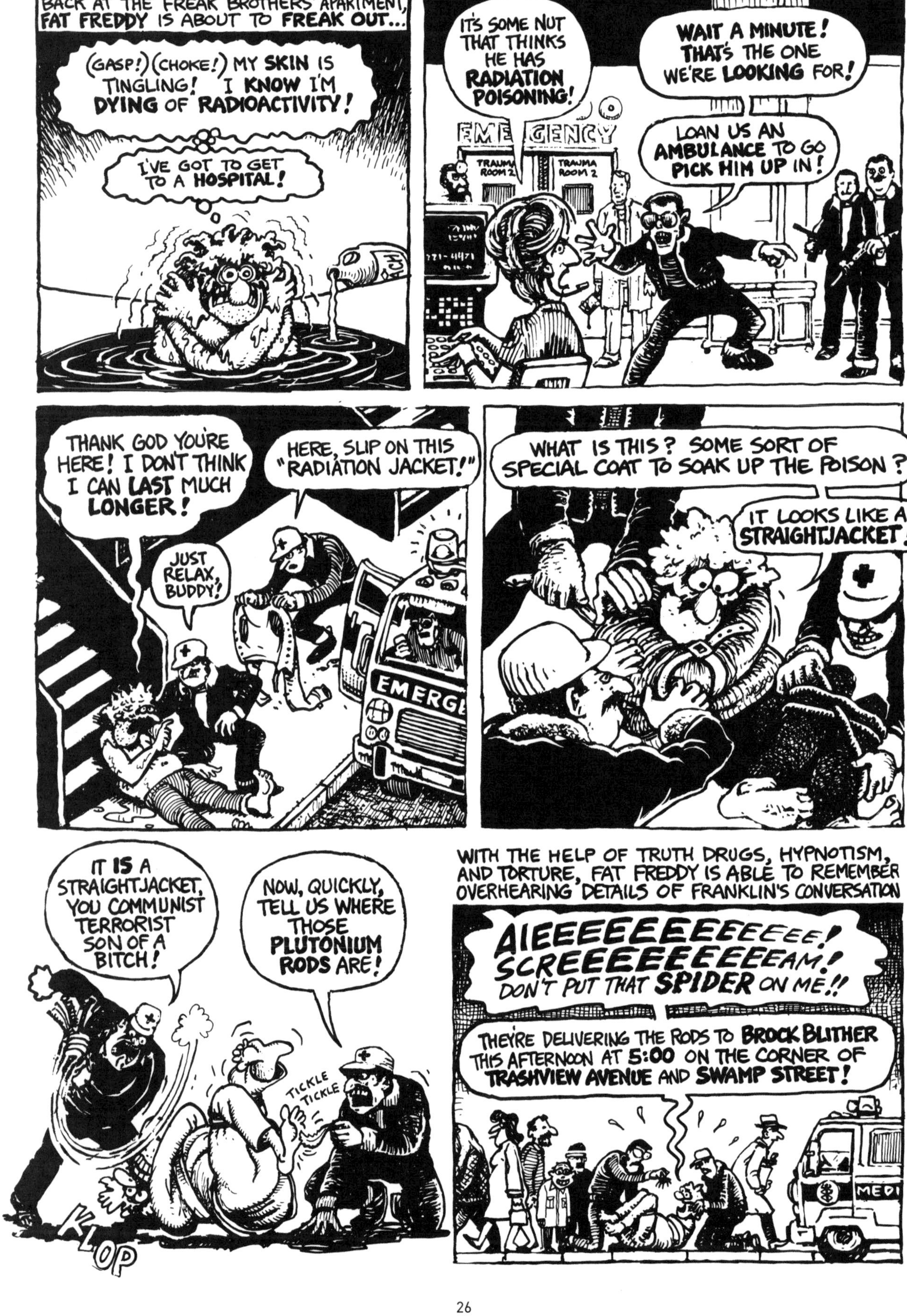
BACK AT THE FREAK BROTHERS' APARTMENT, FAT FREDDY IS ABOUT TO FREAK OUT...
(GASP!) (CHOKE!) MY SKIN IS TINGLING! I KNOW I'M DYING OF RADIOACTIVITY!
I'VE GOT TO GET TO A HOSPITAL!
IT'S SOME NUT THAT THINKS HE HAS RADIATION POISONING!
WAIT A MINUTE! THAT'S THE ONE WE'RE LOOKING FOR!
LOAN US AN AMBULANCE TO GO PICK HIM UP IN!
EMERGENCY
TRAUMA ROOM 2
TRAUMA ROOM 2
THANK GOD YOU'RE HERE! I DON'T THINK I CAN LAST MUCH LONGER!
HERE, SLIP ON THIS "RADIATION JACKET!"
JUST RELAX, BUDDY!
EMERGE
WHAT IS THIS? SOME SORT OF SPECIAL COAT TO SOAK UP THE POISON?
IT LOOKS LIKE A STRAIGHTJACKET!
IT IS A STRAIGHTJACKET, YOU COMMUNIST TERRORIST SON OF A BITCH!
NOW, QUICKLY, TELL US WHERE THOSE PLUTONIUM RODS ARE!
TICKLE TICKLE
KLOP
WITH THE HELP OF TRUTH DRUGS, HYPNOTISM, AND TORTURE, FAT FREDDY IS ABLE TO REMEMBER OVERHEARING DETAILS OF FRANKLIN'S CONVERSATION
AIEEEEEEEEEEEEEE! SCREEEEEEEEEEEAM! DON'T PUT THAT SPIDER ON ME!!
THEY'RE DELIVERING THE RODS TO BROCK BLITHER THIS AFTERNOON AT 5:00 ON THE CORNER OF TRASHVIEW AVENUE AND SWAMP STREET!
MEDI

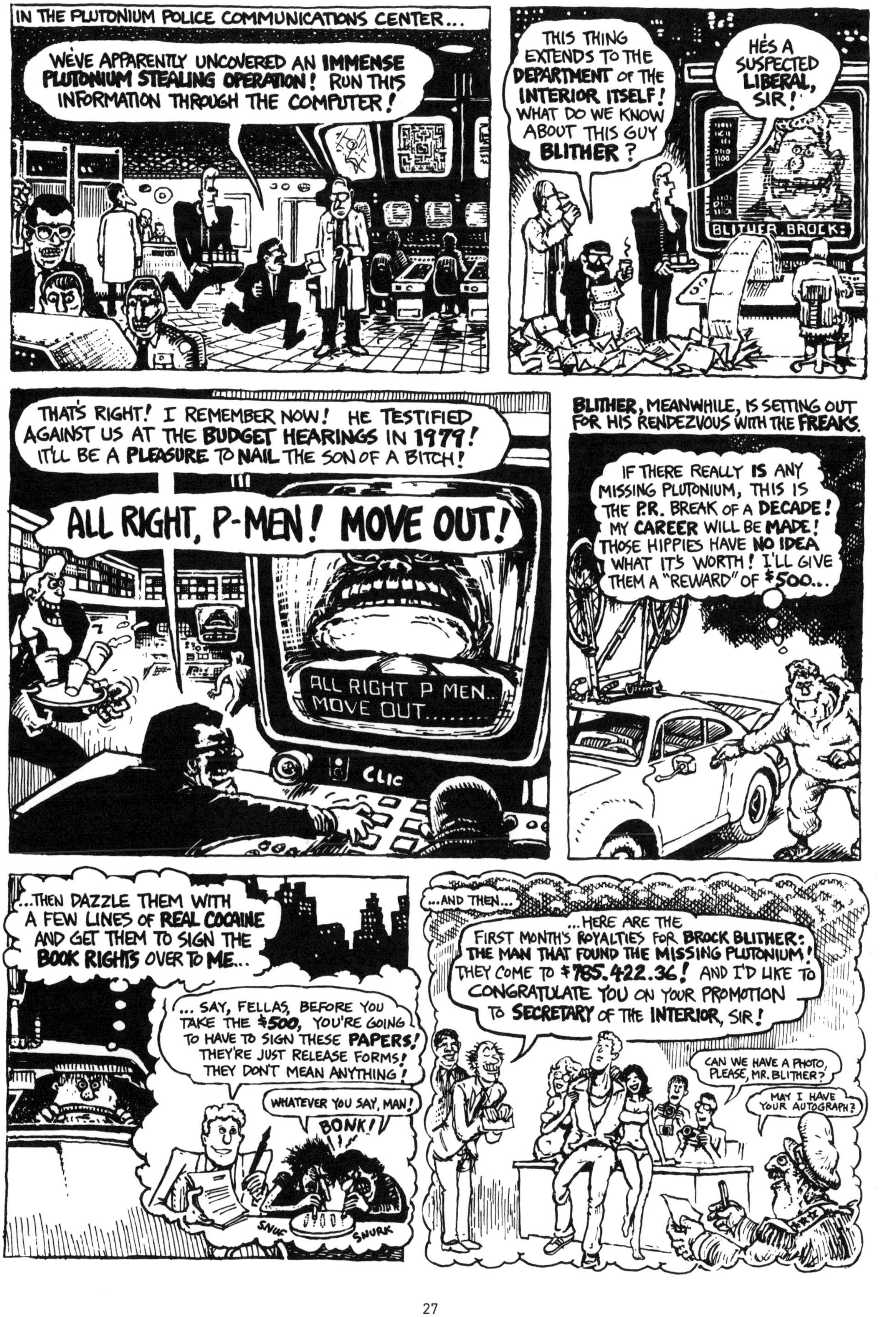
IN THE PLUTONIUM POLICE COMMUNICATIONS CENTER...
WE'VE APPARENTLY UNCOVERED AN IMMENSE PLUTONIUM STEALING OPERATION! RUN THIS INFORMATION THROUGH THE COMPUTER!
THIS THING EXTENDS TO THE DEPARTMENT OF THE INTERIOR ITSELF! WHAT DO WE KNOW ABOUT THIS GUY BLITHER?
HE'S A SUSPECTED LIBERAL, SIR!
BLITHER, BROCK:
THAT'S RIGHT! I REMEMBER NOW! HE TESTIFIED AGAINST US AT THE BUDGET HEARINGS IN 1979! IT'LL BE A PLEASURE TO NAIL THE SON OF A BITCH!
ALL RIGHT, P-MEN! MOVE OUT!
ALL RIGHT P MEN.. MOVE OUT.........
CLIC
BLITHER, MEANWHILE, IS SETTING OUT FOR HIS RENDEZVOUS WITH THE FREAKS.
IF THERE REALLY IS ANY MISSING PLUTONIUM, THIS IS THE P.R. BREAK OF A DECADE! MY CAREER WILL BE MADE! THOSE HIPPIES HAVE NO IDEA WHAT IT'S WORTH! I'LL GIVE THEM A "REWARD" OF $500...
...THEN DAZZLE THEM WITH A FEW LINES OF REAL COCAINE AND GET THEM TO SIGN THE BOOK RIGHTS OVER TO ME...
... SAY, FELLAS, BEFORE YOU TAKE THE $500, YOU'RE GOING TO HAVE TO SIGN THESE PAPERS! THEY'RE JUST RELEASE FORMS! THEY DON'T MEAN ANYTHING!
WHATEVER YOU SAY, MAN!
BONK!
SNUK
SNURK
...AND THEN...
...HERE ARE THE FIRST MONTH'S ROYALTIES FOR BROCK BLITHER: THE MAN THAT FOUND THE MISSING PLUTONIUM! THEY COME TO $785.422.36! AND I'D LIKE TO CONGRATULATE YOU ON YOUR PROMOTION TO SECRETARY OF THE INTERIOR, SIR!
CAN WE HAVE A PHOTO, PLEASE, MR. BLITHER?
MAY I HAVE YOUR AUTOGRAPH?

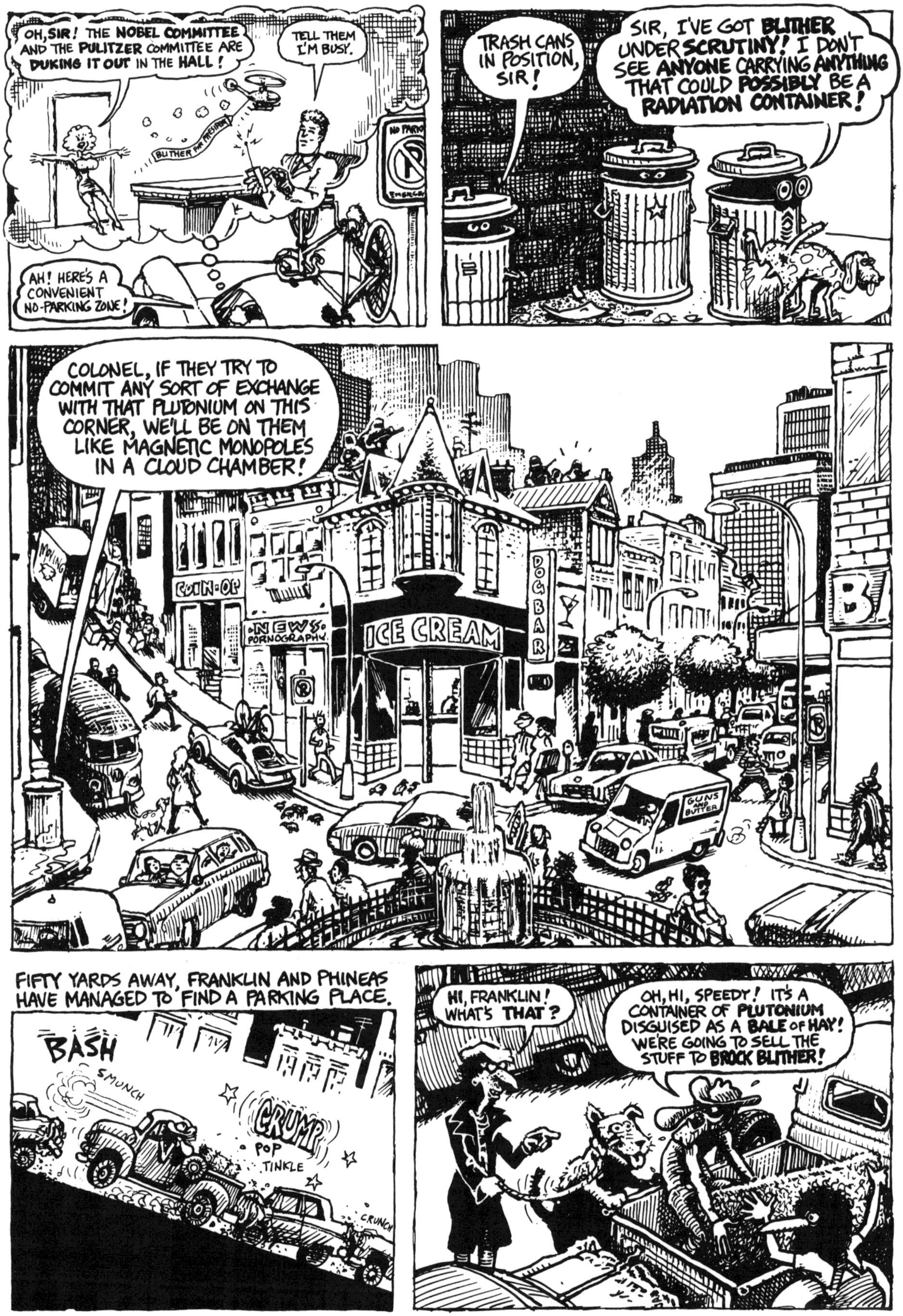
OH, SIR! THE NOBEL COMMITTEE AND THE PULITZER COMMITTEE ARE DUKING IT OUT IN THE HALL!
TELL THEM I'M BUSY.
AH! HERE'S A CONVENIENT NO-PARKING ZONE!
TRASH CANS IN POSITION, SIR!
SIR, I'VE GOT BLITHER UNDER SCRUTINY! I DON'T SEE ANYONE CARRYING ANYTHING THAT COULD POSSIBLY BE A RADIATION CONTAINER!
COLONEL, IF THEY TRY TO COMMIT ANY SORT OF EXCHANGE WITH THAT PLUTONIUM ON THIS CORNER, WE'LL BE ON THEM LIKE MAGNETIC MONOPOLES IN A CLOUD CHAMBER!
MOVING
COIN-OP
NEWS PORNOGRAPHY
ICE CREAM
DOG BAR
GUNS AND BUTTER
FIFTY YARDS AWAY, FRANKLIN AND PHINEAS HAVE MANAGED TO FIND A PARKING PLACE.
BASH
SMUNCH
CRUMP
POP
TINKLE
CRUNCH
HI, FRANKLIN! WHAT'S THAT?
OH, HI, SPEEDY! IT'S A CONTAINER OF PLUTONIUM DISGUISED AS A BALE OF HAY! WE'RE GOING TO SELL THE STUFF TO BROCK BLITHER!

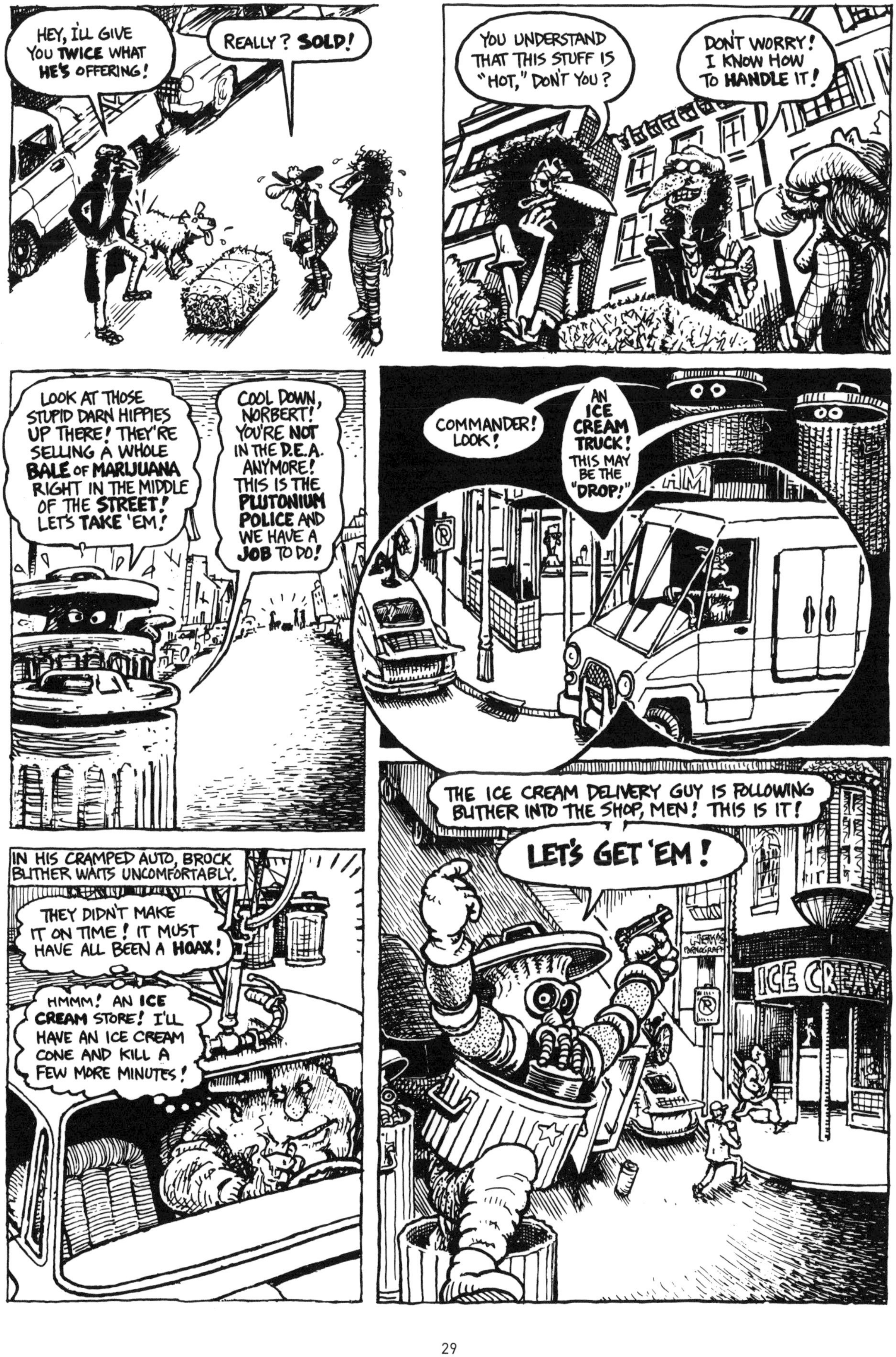

HEY, I'LL GIVE YOU TWICE WHAT HE'S OFFERING!
REALLY? SOLD!
YOU UNDERSTAND THAT THIS STUFF IS "HOT," DON'T YOU?
DON'T WORRY! I KNOW HOW TO HANDLE IT!
LOOK AT THOSE STUPID DARN HIPPIES UP THERE! THEY'RE SELLING A WHOLE BALE OF MARIJUANA RIGHT IN THE MIDDLE OF THE STREET! LET'S TAKE 'EM!
COOL DOWN, NORBERT! YOU'RE NOT IN THE D.E.A. ANYMORE! THIS IS THE PLUTONIUM POLICE AND WE HAVE A JOB TO DO!
COMMANDER! LOOK!
AN ICE CREAM TRUCK! THIS MAY BE THE "DROP!"
IN HIS CRAMPED AUTO, BROCK BLITHER WAITS UNCOMFORTABLY.
THEY DIDN'T MAKE IT ON TIME! IT MUST HAVE ALL BEEN A HOAX!
HMMM! AN ICE CREAM STORE! I'LL HAVE AN ICE CREAM CONE AND KILL A FEW MORE MINUTES!
THE ICE CREAM DELIVERY GUY IS FOLLOWING BLITHER INTO THE SHOP, MEN! THIS IS IT!
LET'S GET 'EM!

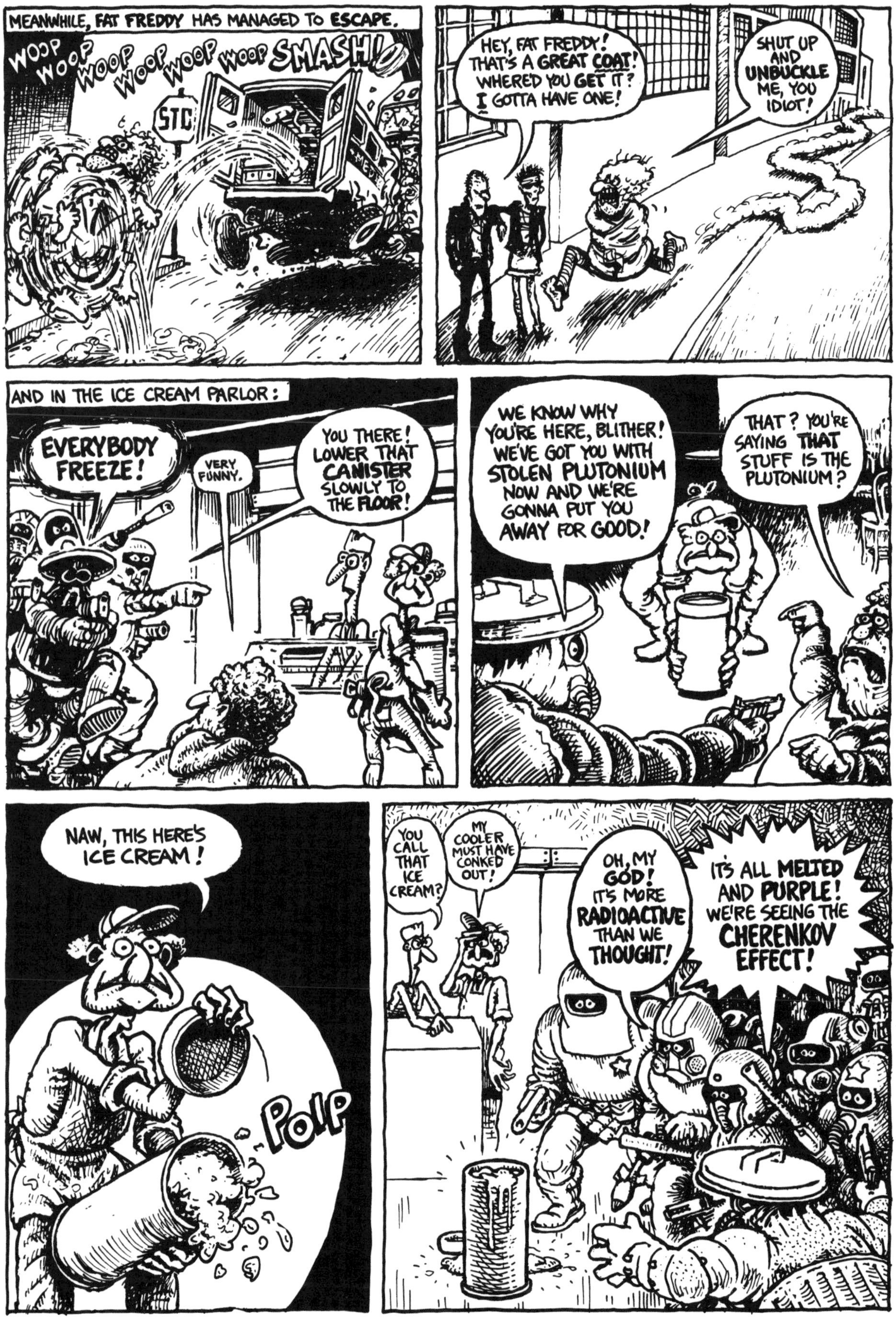
MEANWHILE, FAT FREDDY HAS MANAGED TO ESCAPE.
WOOP WOOP WOOP WOOP WOOP WOOP SMASH!
HEY, FAT FREDDY! THAT'S A GREAT COAT! WHERE'D YOU GET IT? I GOTTA HAVE ONE!
SHUT UP AND UNBUCKLE ME, YOU IDIOT!
AND IN THE ICE CREAM PARLOR:
EVERYBODY FREEZE!
VERY FUNNY.
YOU THERE! LOWER THAT CANISTER SLOWLY TO THE FLOOR!
WE KNOW WHY YOU'RE HERE, BLITHER! WE'VE GOT YOU WITH STOLEN PLUTONIUM NOW AND WE'RE GONNA PUT YOU AWAY FOR GOOD!
THAT? YOU'RE SAYING THAT STUFF IS THE PLUTONIUM?
NAW, THIS HERE'S ICE CREAM!
POIP
YOU CALL THAT ICE CREAM?
MY COOLER MUST HAVE CONKED OUT!
OH, MY GOD! IT'S MORE RADIOACTIVE THAN WE THOUGHT!
IT'S ALL MELTED AND PURPLE! WE'RE SEEING THE CHERENKOV EFFECT!

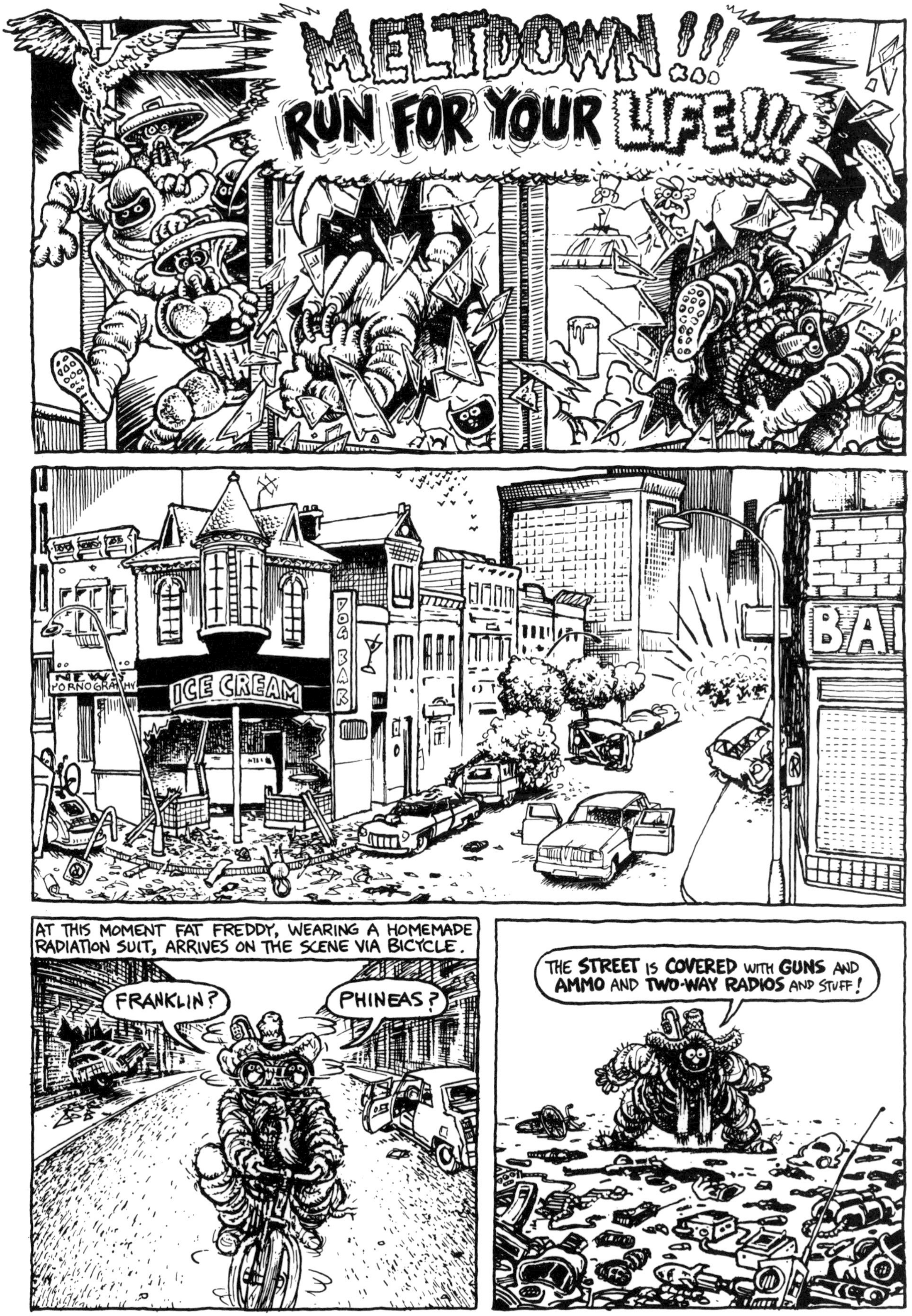
MELTDOWN!!!
RUN FOR YOUR LIFE!!!
NEWS
PORNOGRAPHY
ICE CREAM
DOG BAR
AT THIS MOMENT FAT FREDDY, WEARING A HOMEMADE RADIATION SUIT, ARRIVES ON THE SCENE VIA BICYCLE.
FRANKLIN?
PHINEAS?
THE STREET IS COVERED WITH GUNS AND AMMO AND TWO-WAY RADIOS AND STUFF!

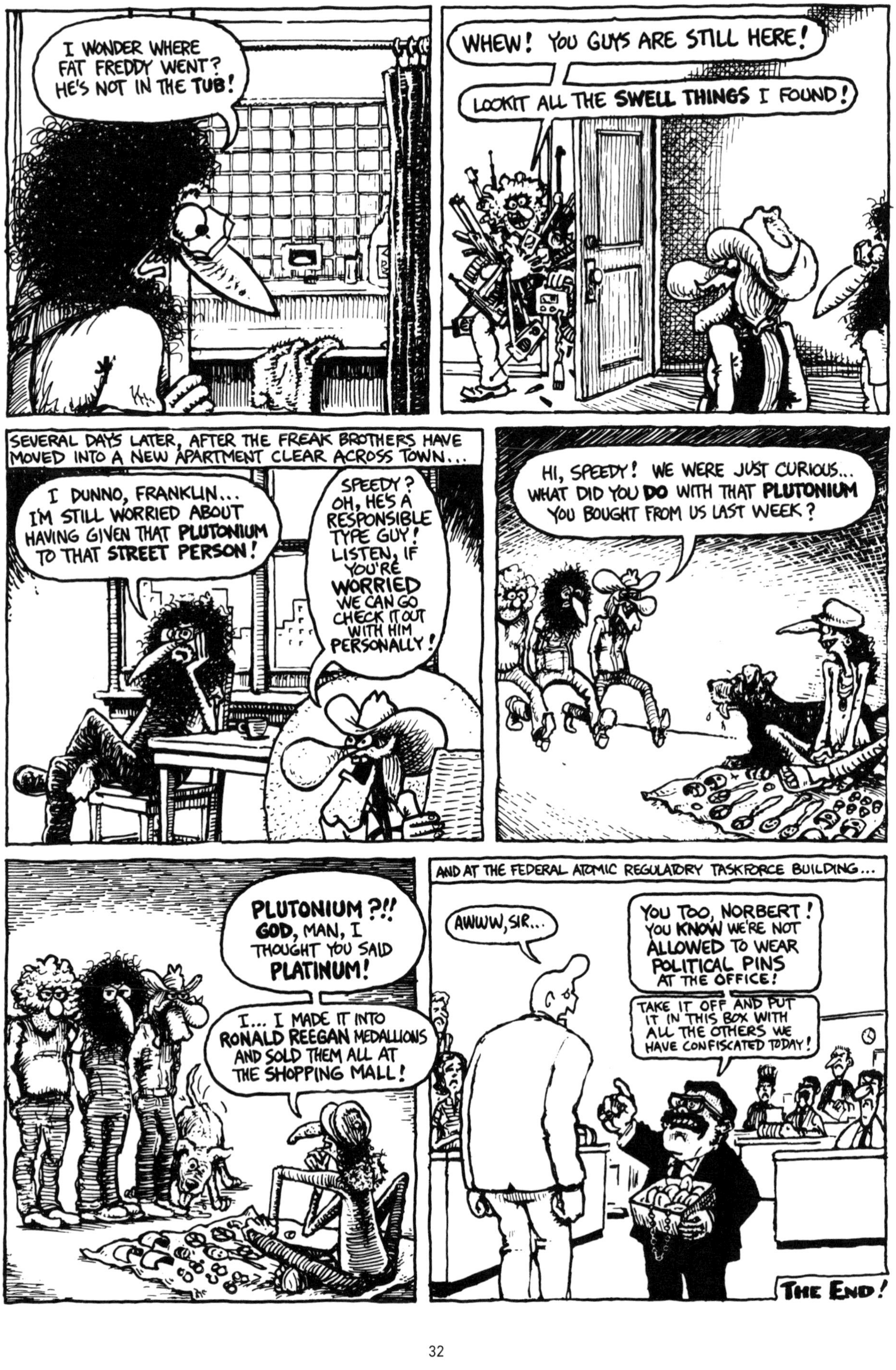
I WONDER WHERE FAT FREDDY WENT? HE'S NOT IN THE TUB!
WHEW! YOU GUYS ARE STILL HERE!
LOOKIT ALL THE SWELL THINGS I FOUND!
SEVERAL DAYS LATER, AFTER THE FREAK BROTHERS HAVE MOVED INTO A NEW APARTMENT CLEAR ACROSS TOWN...
I DUNNO, FRANKLIN... I'M STILL WORRIED ABOUT HAVING GIVEN THAT PLUTONIUM TO THAT STREET PERSON!
SPEEDY? OH, HE'S A RESPONSIBLE TYPE GUY! LISTEN, IF YOU'RE WORRIED WE CAN GO CHECK IT OUT WITH HIM PERSONALLY!
HI, SPEEDY! WE WERE JUST CURIOUS... WHAT DID YOU DO WITH THAT PLUTONIUM YOU BOUGHT FROM US LAST WEEK?
PLUTONIUM?!! GOD, MAN, I THOUGHT YOU SAID PLATINUM!
I... I MADE IT INTO RONALD REEGAN MEDALLIONS AND SOLD THEM ALL AT THE SHOPPING MALL!
AND AT THE FEDERAL ATOMIC REGULATORY TASKFORCE BUILDING...
AWWW, SIR...
YOU TOO, NORBERT! YOU KNOW WE'RE NOT ALLOWED TO WEAR POLITICAL PINS AT THE OFFICE!
TAKE IT OFF AND PUT IT IN THIS BOX WITH ALL THE OTHERS WE HAVE CONFISCATED TODAY!
THE END!

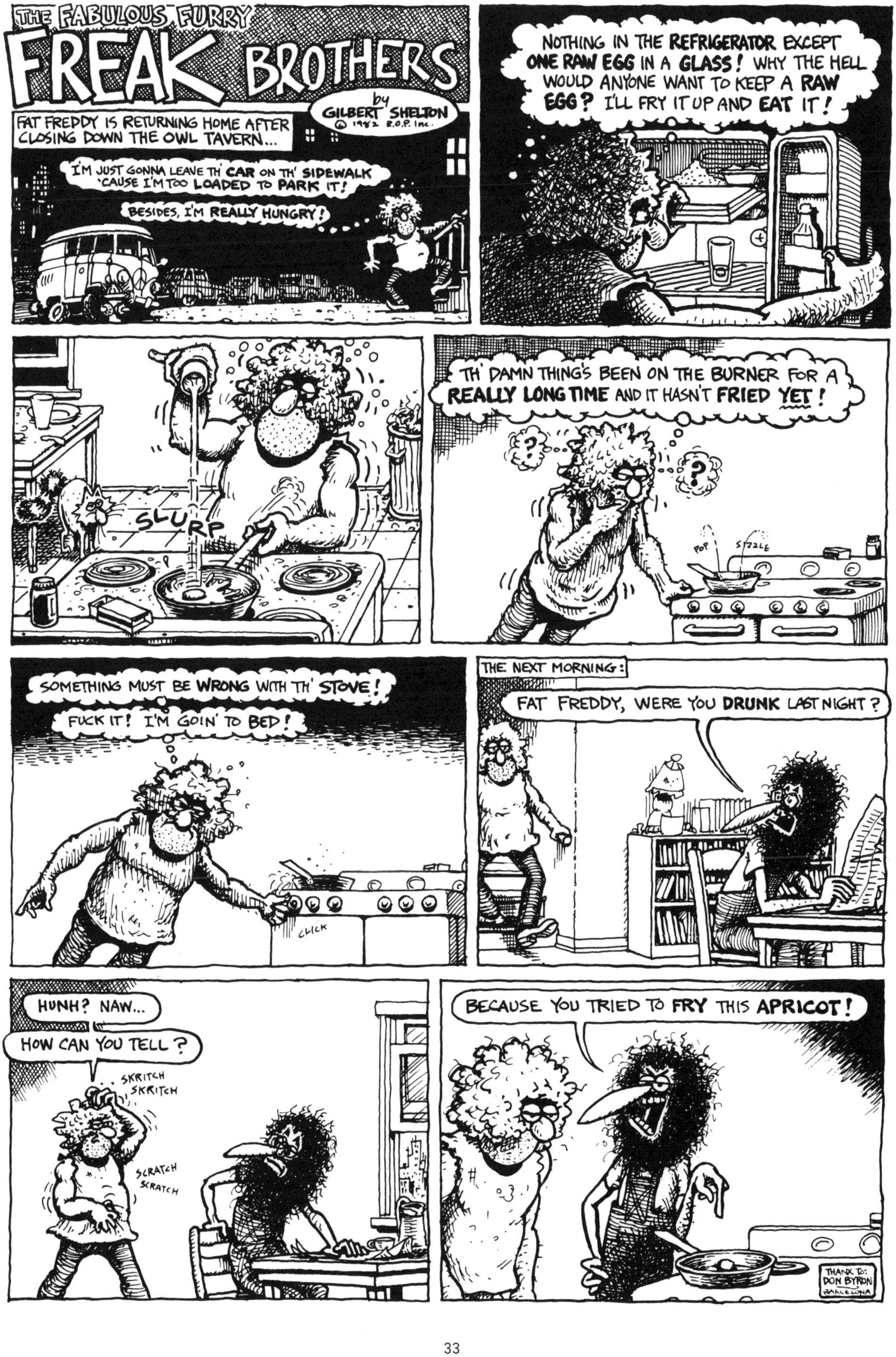
THE FABULOUS FURRY
FREAK BROTHERS
by GILBERT SHELTON
© 1982 R.O.P. Inc.
FAT FREDDY IS RETURNING HOME AFTER CLOSING DOWN THE OWL TAVERN...
I'M JUST GONNA LEAVE TH' CAR ON TH' SIDEWALK 'CAUSE I'M TOO LOADED TO PARK IT!
BESIDES, I'M REALLY HUNGRY!
NOTHING IN THE REFRIGERATOR EXCEPT ONE RAW EGG IN A GLASS! WHY THE HELL WOULD ANYONE WANT TO KEEP A RAW EGG? I'LL FRY IT UP AND EAT IT!
SLURP
TH' DAMN THING'S BEEN ON THE BURNER FOR A REALLY LONG TIME AND IT HASN'T FRIED YET!
POP
SIZZLE
SOMETHING MUST BE WRONG WITH TH' STOVE!
FUCK IT! I'M GOIN' TO BED!
CLICK
THE NEXT MORNING:
FAT FREDDY, WERE YOU DRUNK LAST NIGHT?
HUNH? NAW...
HOW CAN YOU TELL?
SKRITCH SKRITCH
SCRATCH SCRATCH
BECAUSE YOU TRIED TO FRY THIS APRICOT!
THANX TO: DON BYRON BARCELONA

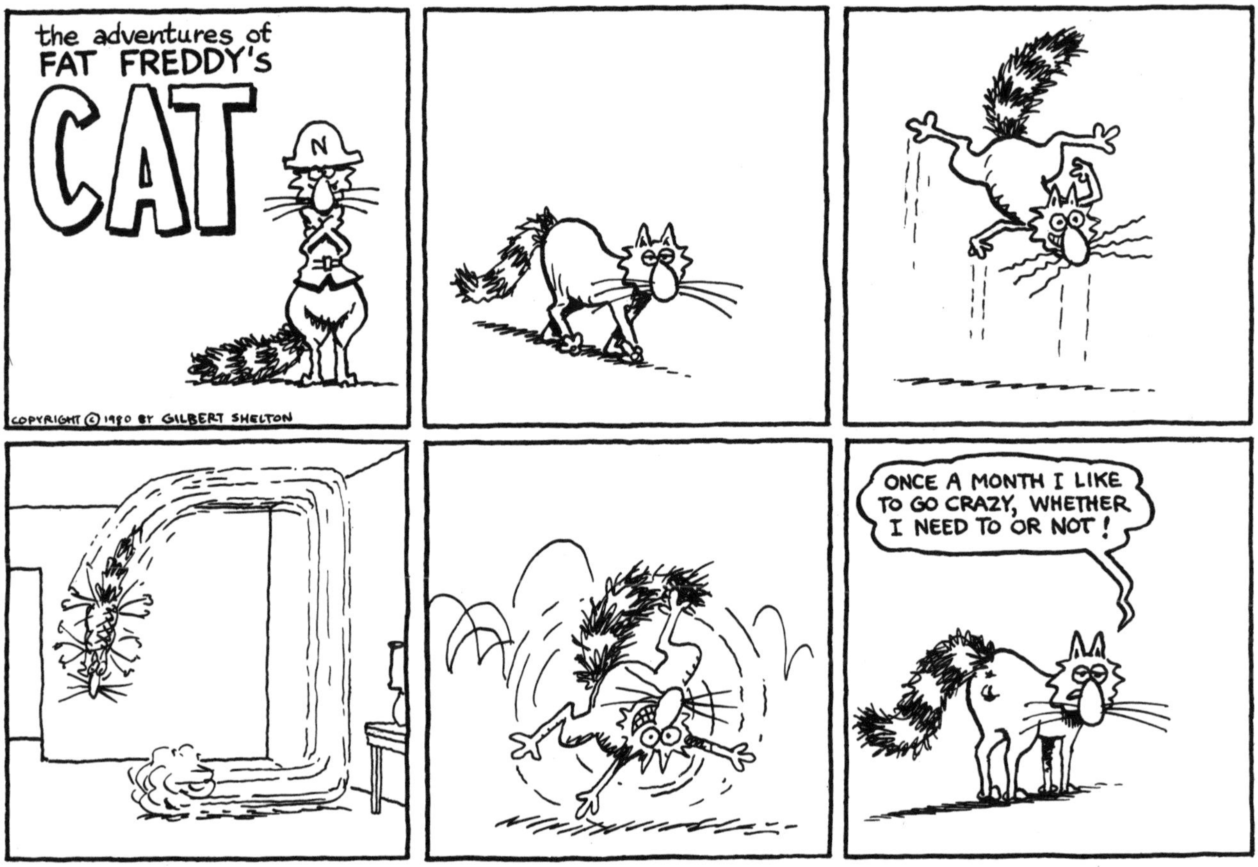
the adventures of
FAT FREDDY's
CAT
COPYRIGHT © 1980 BY GILBERT SHELTON
ONCE A MONTH I LIKE TO GO CRAZY, WHETHER I NEED TO OR NOT!

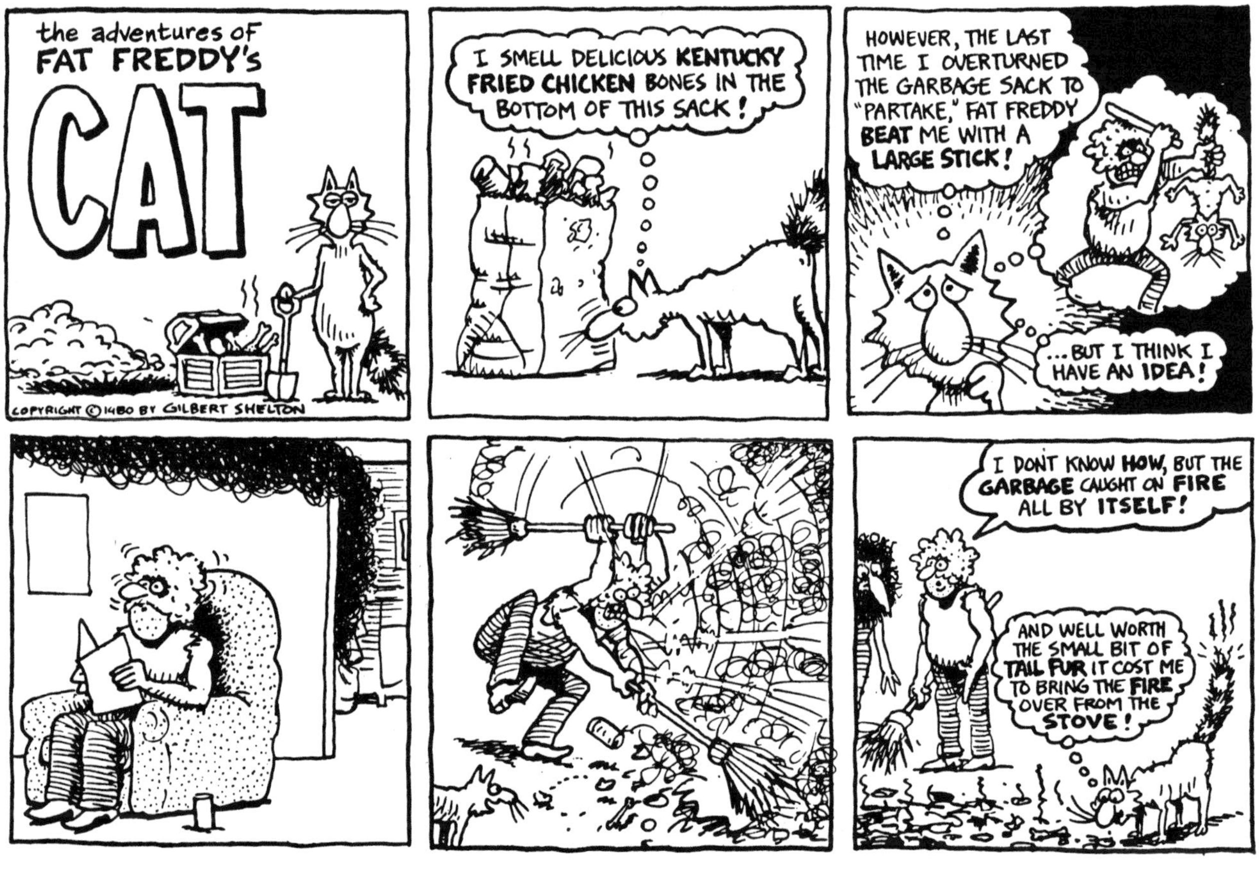
the adventures of
FAT FREDDY's
CAT
COPYRIGHT © 1980 BY GILBERT SHELTON
I SMELL DELICIOUS KENTUCKY FRIED CHICKEN BONES IN THE BOTTOM OF THIS SACK!
HOWEVER, THE LAST TIME I OVERTURNED THE GARBAGE SACK TO "PARTAKE," FAT FREDDY BEAT ME WITH A LARGE STICK!
...BUT I THINK I HAVE AN IDEA!
I DON'T KNOW HOW, BUT THE GARBAGE CAUGHT ON FIRE ALL BY ITSELF!
AND WELL WORTH THE SMALL BIT OF TAIL FUR IT COST ME TO BRING THE FIRE OVER FROM THE STOVE!

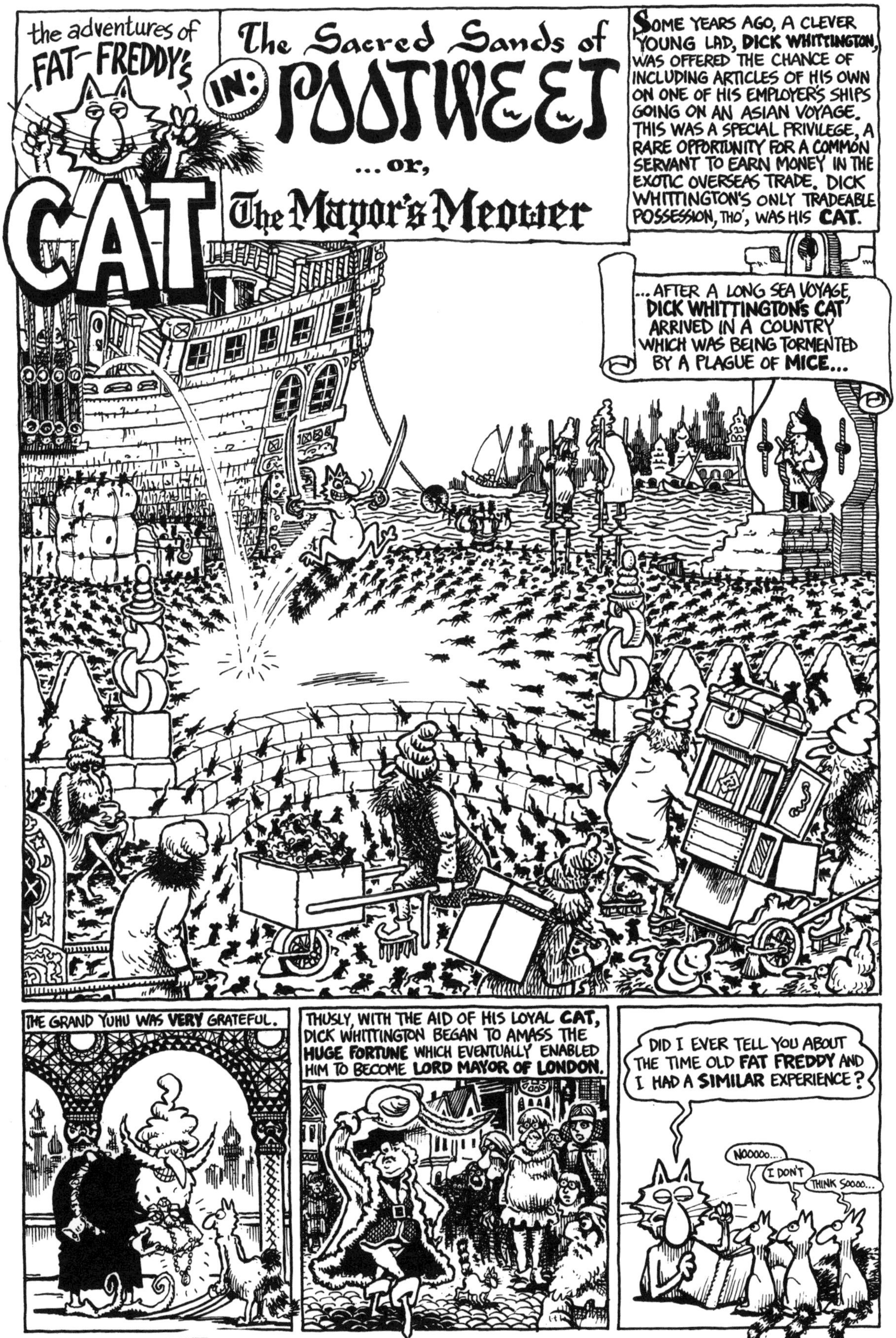
the adventures of
FAT-FREDDY'S
CAT
IN:
The Sacred Sands of
POOTWEET
...or,
The Mayor's Meower
SOME YEARS AGO, A CLEVER YOUNG LAD, DICK WHITTINGTON, WAS OFFERED THE CHANCE OF INCLUDING ARTICLES OF HIS OWN ON ONE OF HIS EMPLOYER'S SHIPS GOING ON AN ASIAN VOYAGE. THIS WAS A SPECIAL PRIVILEGE, A RARE OPPORTUNITY FOR A COMMON SERVANT TO EARN MONEY IN THE EXOTIC OVERSEAS TRADE. DICK WHITTINGTON'S ONLY TRADEABLE POSSESSION, THO', WAS HIS CAT.
...AFTER A LONG SEA VOYAGE, DICK WHITTINGTON'S CAT ARRIVED IN A COUNTRY WHICH WAS BEING TORMENTED BY A PLAGUE OF MICE...
THE GRAND YUHU WAS VERY GRATEFUL.
THUSLY, WITH THE AID OF HIS LOYAL CAT, DICK WHITTINGTON BEGAN TO AMASS THE HUGE FORTUNE WHICH EVENTUALLY ENABLED HIM TO BECOME LORD MAYOR OF LONDON.
DID I EVER TELL YOU ABOUT THE TIME OLD FAT FREDDY AND I HAD A SIMILAR EXPERIENCE?
NOOOOO...
I DON'T
THINK SOOOO...

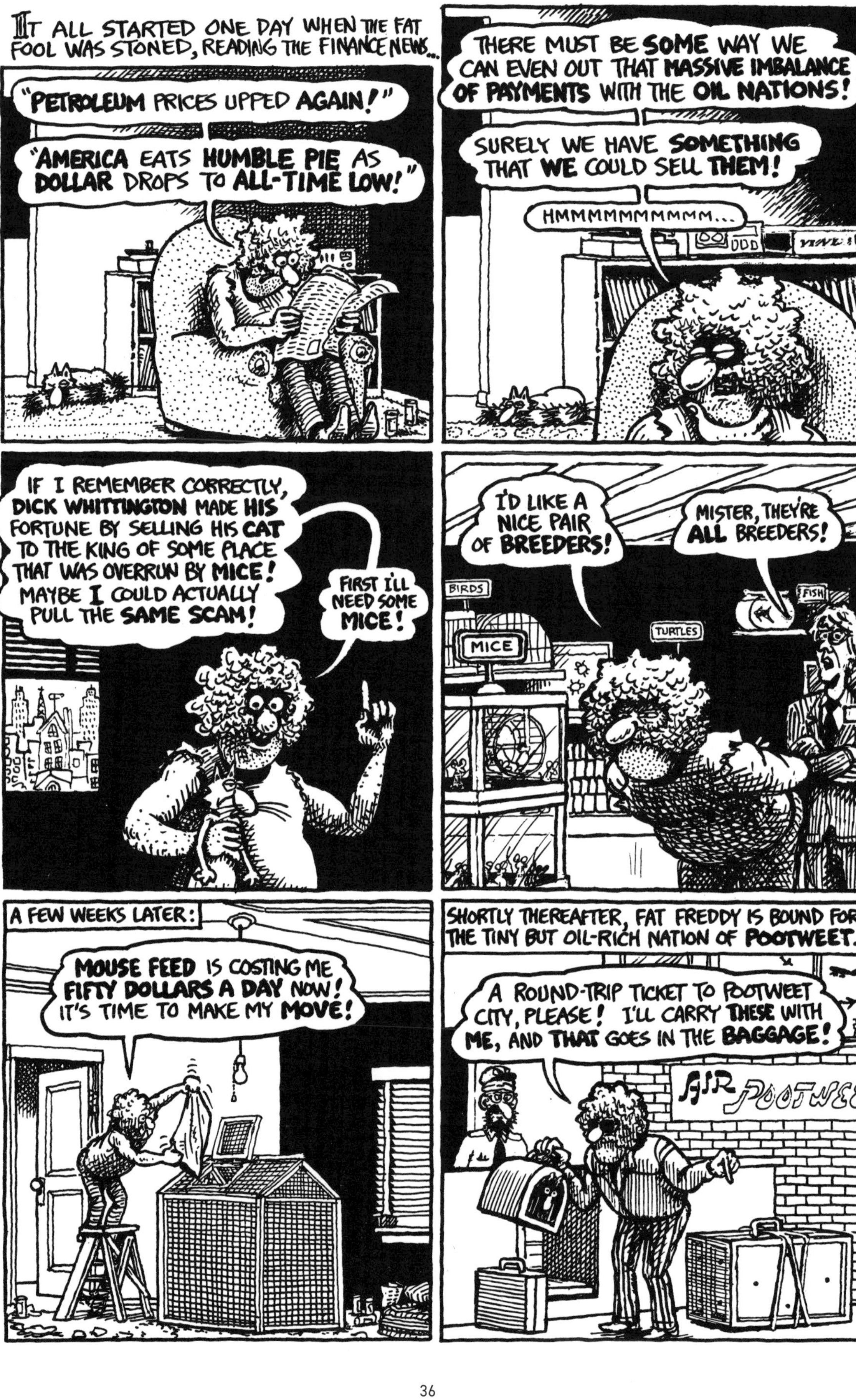
IT ALL STARTED ONE DAY WHEN THE FAT FOOL WAS STONED, READING THE FINANCE NEWS...
"PETROLEUM PRICES UPPED AGAIN!"
"AMERICA EATS HUMBLE PIE AS DOLLAR DROPS TO ALL-TIME LOW!"
THERE MUST BE SOME WAY WE CAN EVEN OUT THAT MASSIVE IMBALANCE OF PAYMENTS WITH THE OIL NATIONS!
SURELY WE HAVE SOMETHING THAT WE COULD SELL THEM!
HMMMMMMMMMM...
IF I REMEMBER CORRECTLY, DICK WHITTINGTON MADE HIS FORTUNE BY SELLING HIS CAT TO THE KING OF SOME PLACE THAT WAS OVERRUN BY MICE! MAYBE I COULD ACTUALLY PULL THE SAME SCAM!
FIRST I'LL NEED SOME MICE!
I'D LIKE A NICE PAIR OF BREEDERS!
MISTER, THEY'RE ALL BREEDERS!
BIRDS
FISH
MICE
TURTLES
A FEW WEEKS LATER:
MOUSE FEED IS COSTING ME FIFTY DOLLARS A DAY NOW! IT'S TIME TO MAKE MY MOVE!
SHORTLY THEREAFTER, FAT FREDDY IS BOUND FOR THE TINY BUT OIL-RICH NATION OF POOTWEET.
A ROUND-TRIP TICKET TO POOTWEET CITY, PLEASE! I'LL CARRY THESE WITH ME, AND THAT GOES IN THE BAGGAGE!
AIR POOTWEE

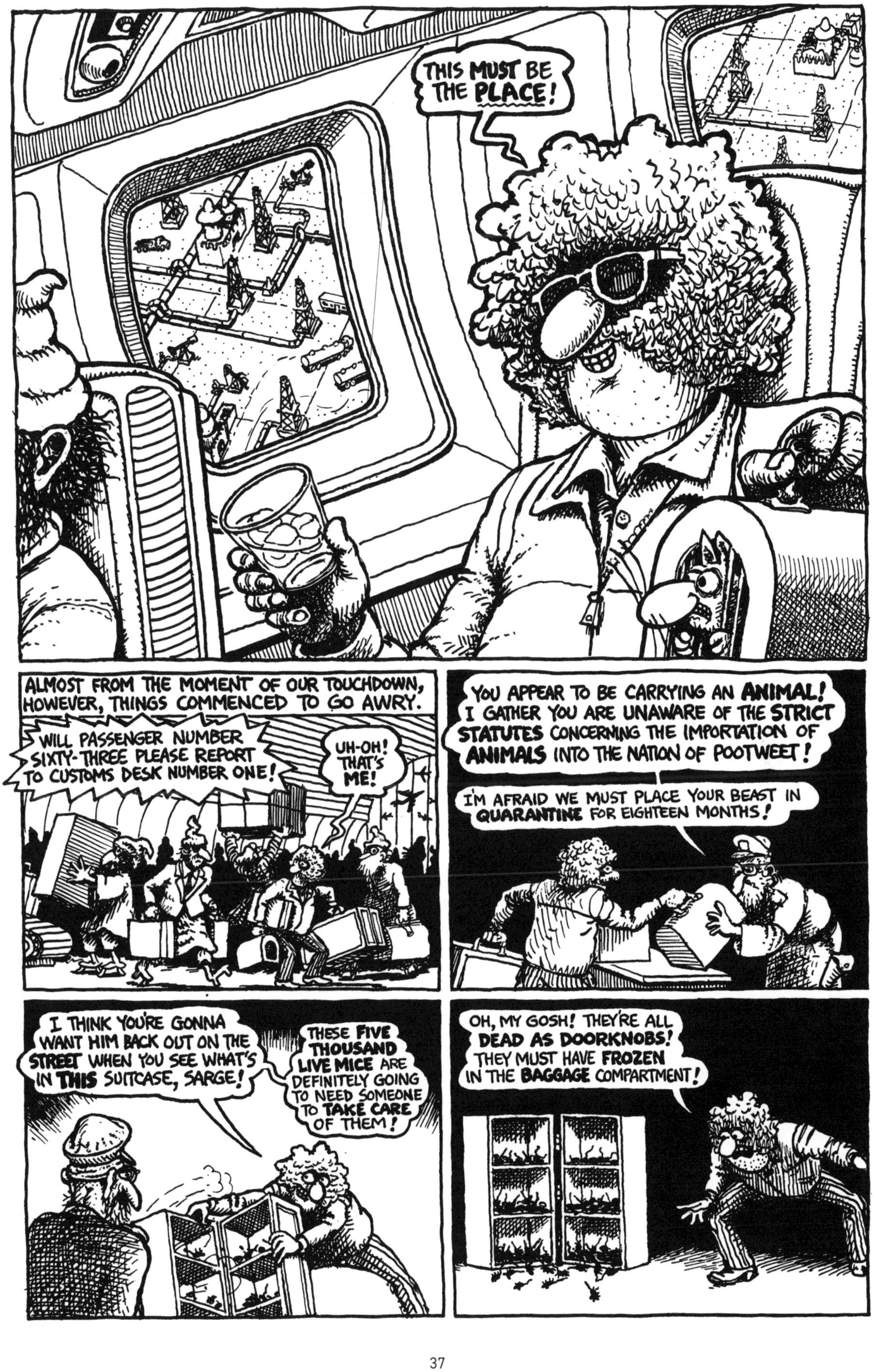
THIS MUST BE THE PLACE!
ALMOST FROM THE MOMENT OF OUR TOUCHDOWN, HOWEVER, THINGS COMMENCED TO GO AWRY.
WILL PASSENGER NUMBER SIXTY-THREE PLEASE REPORT TO CUSTOMS DESK NUMBER ONE!
UH-OH! THAT'S ME!
YOU APPEAR TO BE CARRYING AN ANIMAL! I GATHER YOU ARE UNAWARE OF THE STRICT STATUTES CONCERNING THE IMPORTATION OF ANIMALS INTO THE NATION OF POOTWEET!
I'M AFRAID WE MUST PLACE YOUR BEAST IN QUARANTINE FOR EIGHTEEN MONTHS!
I THINK YOU'RE GONNA WANT HIM BACK OUT ON THE STREET WHEN YOU SEE WHAT'S IN THIS SUITCASE, SARGE!
THESE FIVE THOUSAND LIVE MICE ARE DEFINITELY GOING TO NEED SOMEONE TO TAKE CARE OF THEM!
OH, MY GOSH! THEY'RE ALL DEAD AS DOORKNOBS! THEY MUST HAVE FROZEN IN THE BAGGAGE COMPARTMENT!

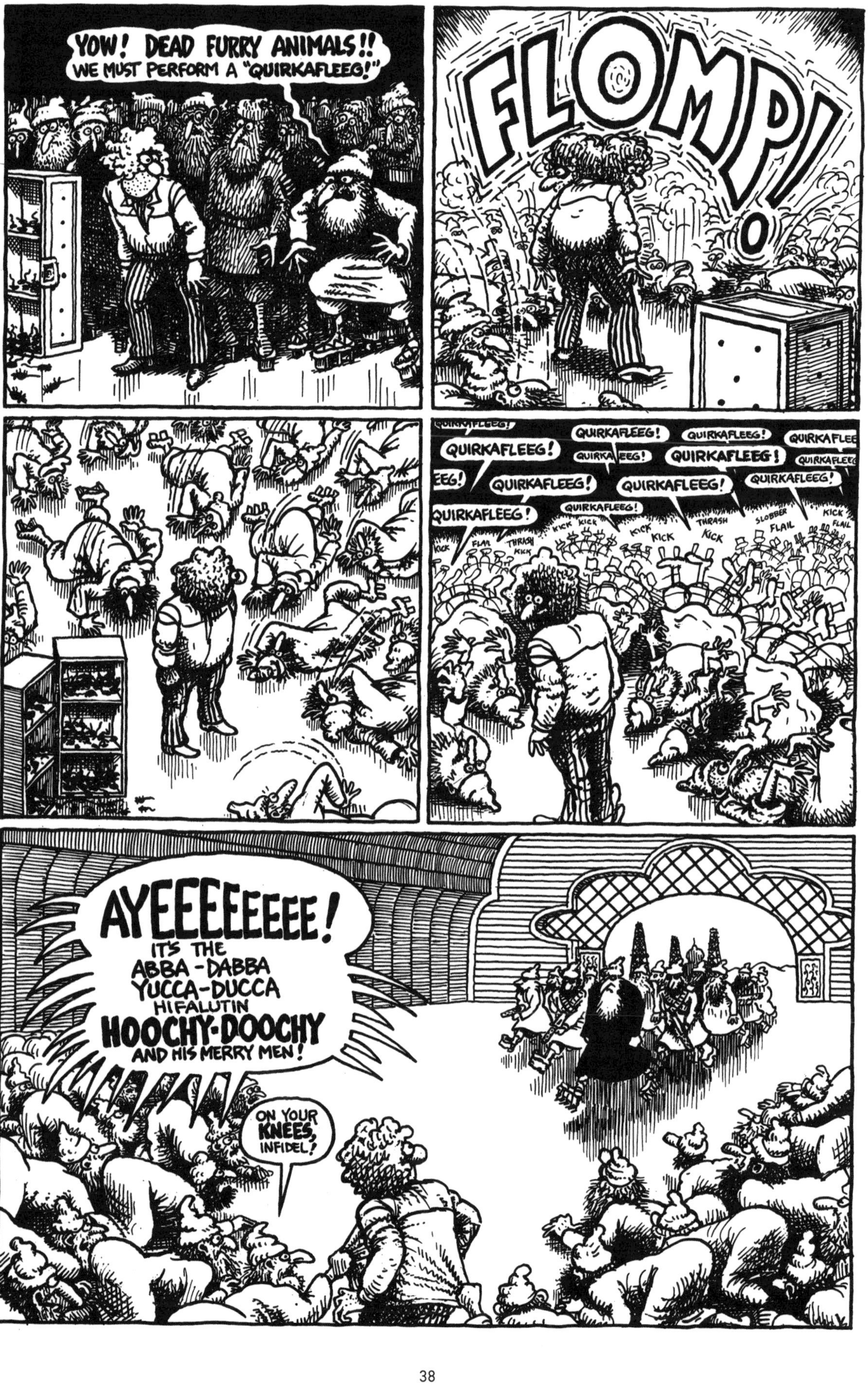
YOW! DEAD FURRY ANIMALS!! WE MUST PERFORM A "QUIRKAFLEEG!"
FLOMP!
QUIRKAFLEEG!
QUIRKAFLEEG!
QUIRKAFLEEG!
QUIRKAFLEEG!
QUIRKAFLEEG!
QUIRKAFLEEG!
QUIRKAFLEEG!
QUIRKAFLEEG!
QUIRKAFLEEG!
KICK
FLAIL
THRASH
KICK
KICK KICK
KICK
KICK
THRASH
KICK
SLOBBER
FLAIL
KICK
FLAIL
AYEEEEEEEE! IT'S THE ABBA-DABBA YUCCA-DUCCA HIFALUTIN HOOCHY-DOOCHY AND HIS MERRY MEN!
ON YOUR KNEES, INFIDEL!

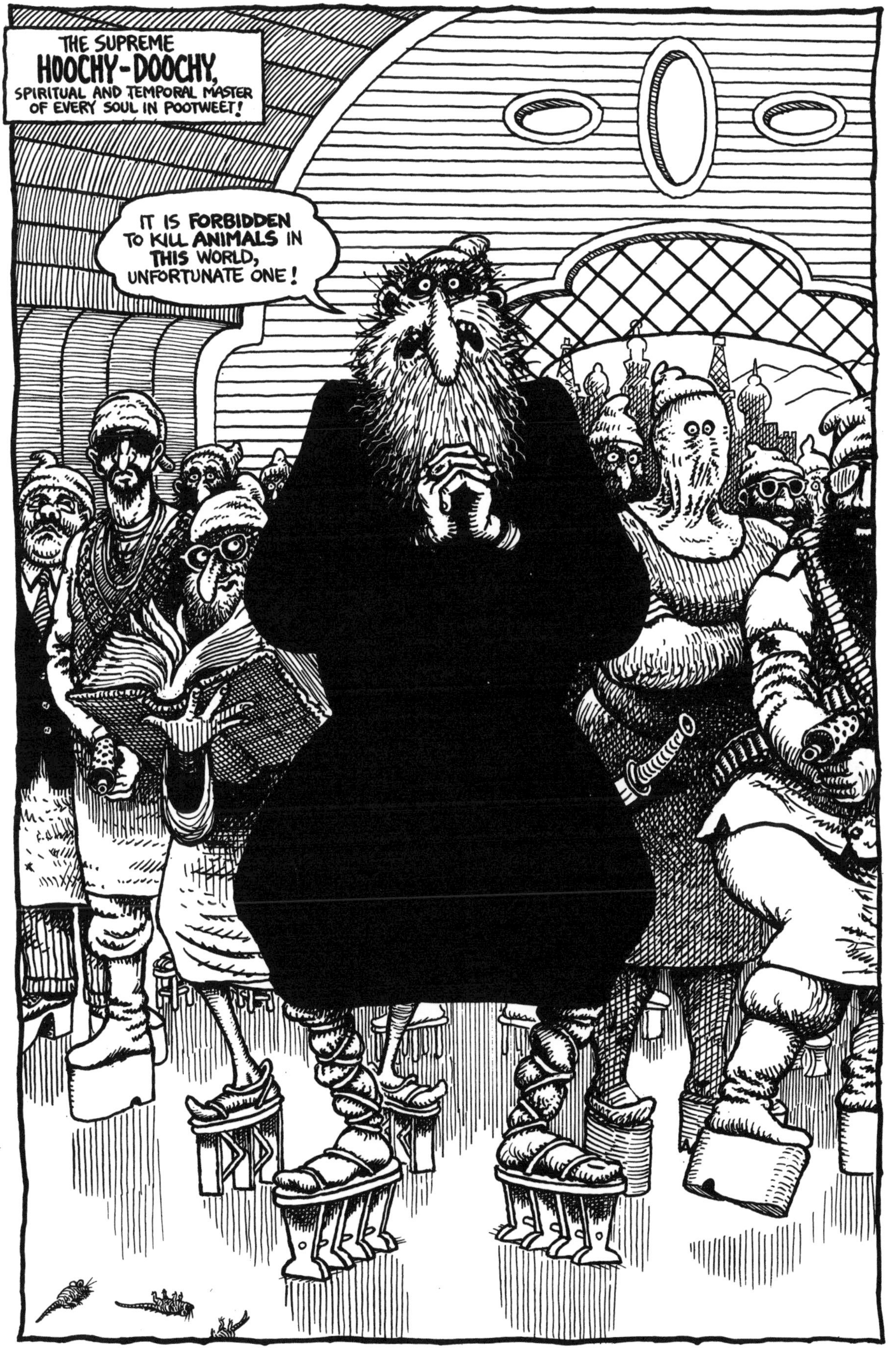
THE SUPREME HOOCHY-DOOCHY, SPIRITUAL AND TEMPORAL MASTER OF EVERY SOUL IN POOTWEET!
IT IS FORBIDDEN TO KILL ANIMALS IN THIS WORLD, UNFORTUNATE ONE!

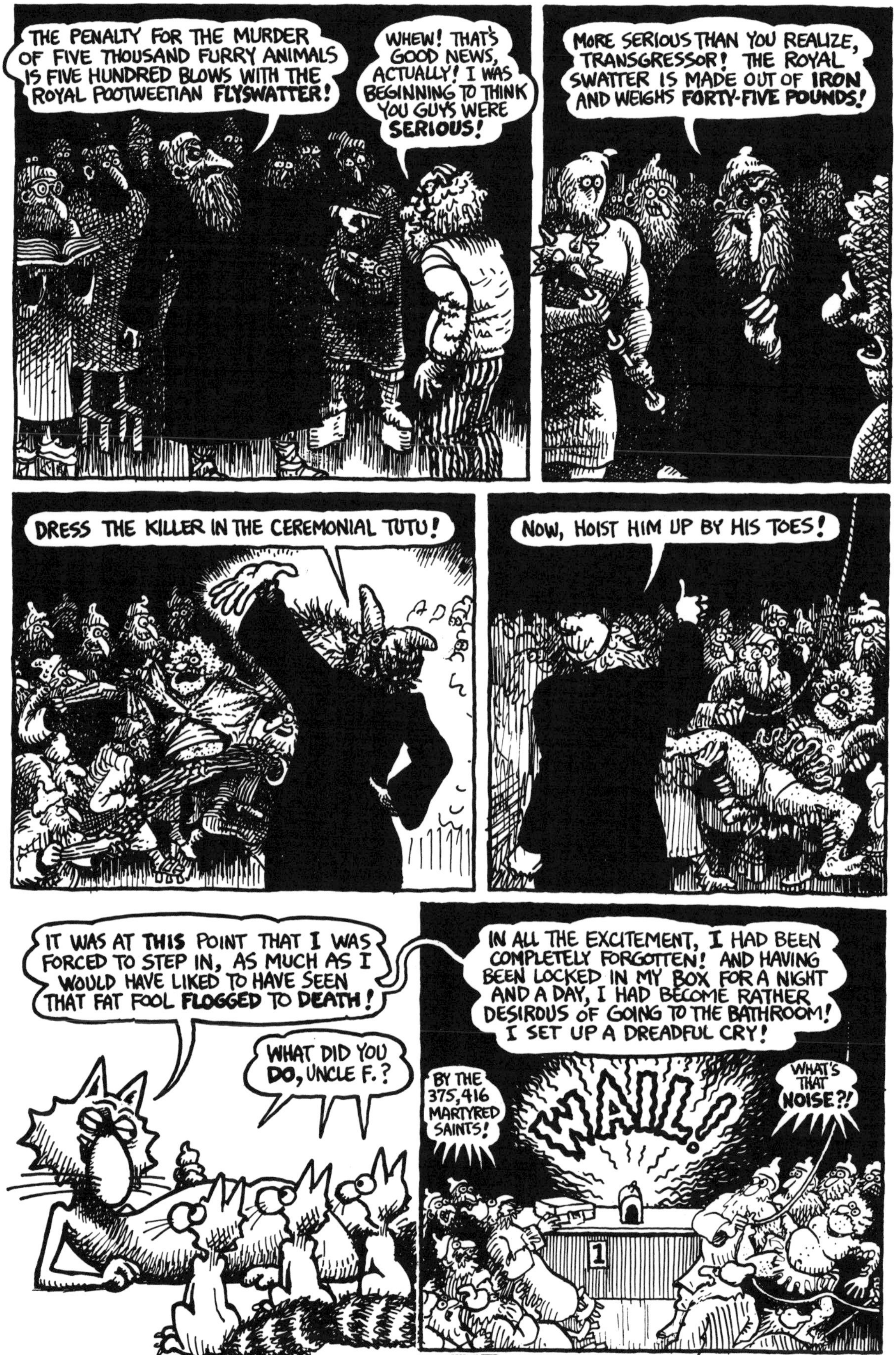
THE PENALTY FOR THE MURDER OF FIVE THOUSAND FURRY ANIMALS IS FIVE HUNDRED BLOWS WITH THE ROYAL POOTWEETIAN FLYSWATTER!
WHEW! THAT'S GOOD NEWS, ACTUALLY! I WAS BEGINNING TO THINK YOU GUYS WERE SERIOUS!
MORE SERIOUS THAN YOU REALIZE, TRANSGRESSOR! THE ROYAL SWATTER IS MADE OUT OF IRON AND WEIGHS FORTY-FIVE POUNDS!
DRESS THE KILLER IN THE CEREMONIAL TUTU!
NOW, HOIST HIM UP BY HIS TOES!
IT WAS AT THIS POINT THAT I WAS FORCED TO STEP IN, AS MUCH AS I WOULD HAVE LIKED TO HAVE SEEN THAT FAT FOOL FLOGGED TO DEATH!
WHAT DID YOU DO, UNCLE F.?
IN ALL THE EXCITEMENT, I HAD BEEN COMPLETELY FORGOTTEN! AND HAVING BEEN LOCKED IN MY BOX FOR A NIGHT AND A DAY, I HAD BECOME RATHER DESIROUS OF GOING TO THE BATHROOM! I SET UP A DREADFUL CRY!
BY THE 375,416 MARTYRED SAINTS!
WAIL!
WHAT'S THAT NOISE?!
1

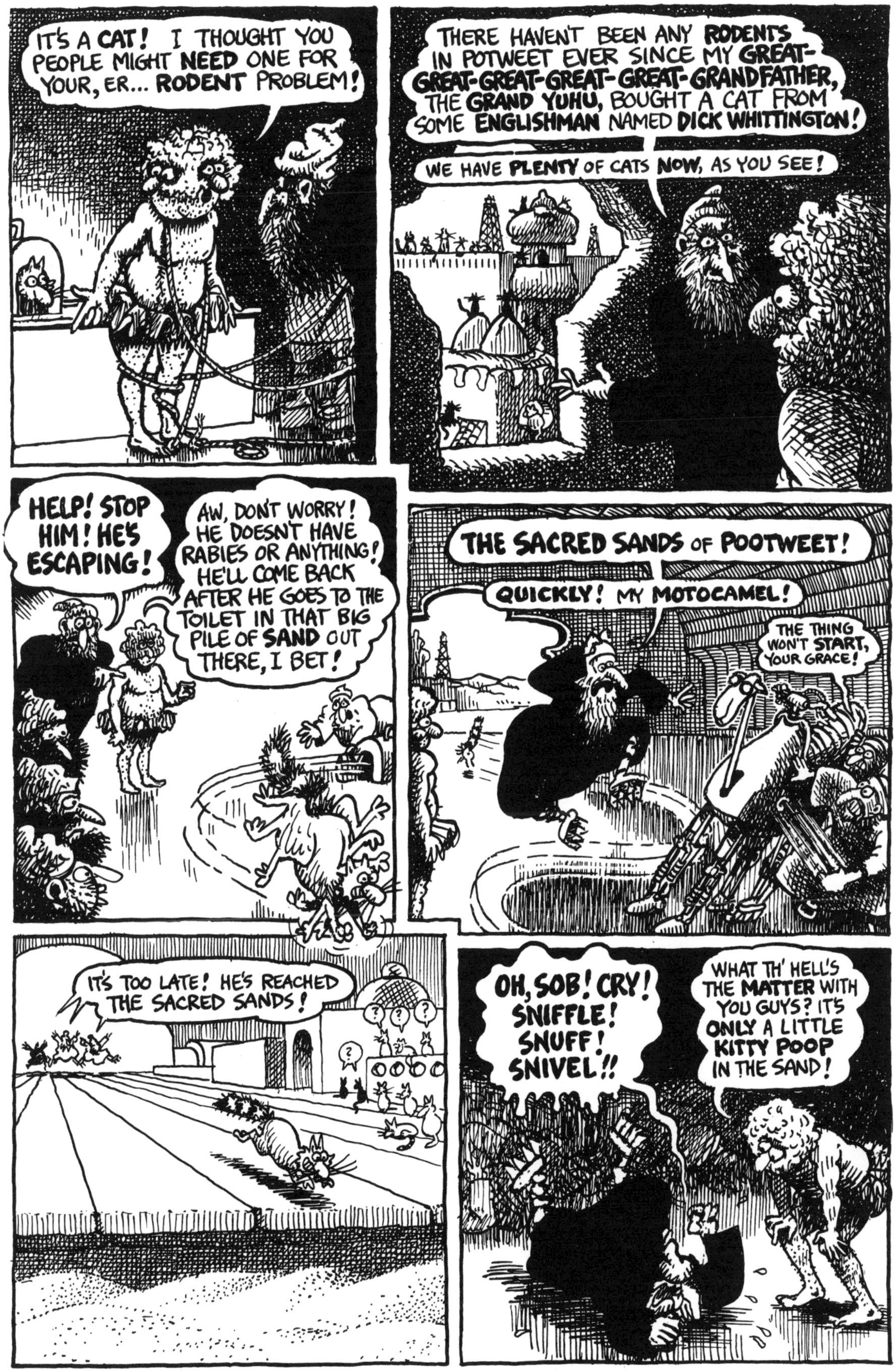
IT'S A CAT! I THOUGHT YOU PEOPLE MIGHT NEED ONE FOR YOUR, ER... RODENT PROBLEM!
THERE HAVEN'T BEEN ANY RODENTS IN POTWEET EVER SINCE MY GREAT-GREAT-GREAT-GREAT-GREAT-GRANDFATHER, THE GRAND YUHU, BOUGHT A CAT FROM SOME ENGLISHMAN NAMED DICK WHITTINGTON!
WE HAVE PLENTY OF CATS NOW, AS YOU SEE!
HELP! STOP HIM! HE'S ESCAPING!
AW, DON'T WORRY! HE DOESN'T HAVE RABIES OR ANYTHING! HE'LL COME BACK AFTER HE GOES TO THE TOILET IN THAT BIG PILE OF SAND OUT THERE, I BET!
THE SACRED SANDS OF POOTWEET!
QUICKLY! MY MOTOCAMEL!
THE THING WON'T START, YOUR GRACE!
IT'S TOO LATE! HE'S REACHED THE SACRED SANDS!
? ? ?
?
OH, SOB! CRY! SNIFFLE! SNUFF! SNIVEL!!
WHAT TH' HELL'S THE MATTER WITH YOU GUYS? IT'S ONLY A LITTLE KITTY POOP IN THE SAND!

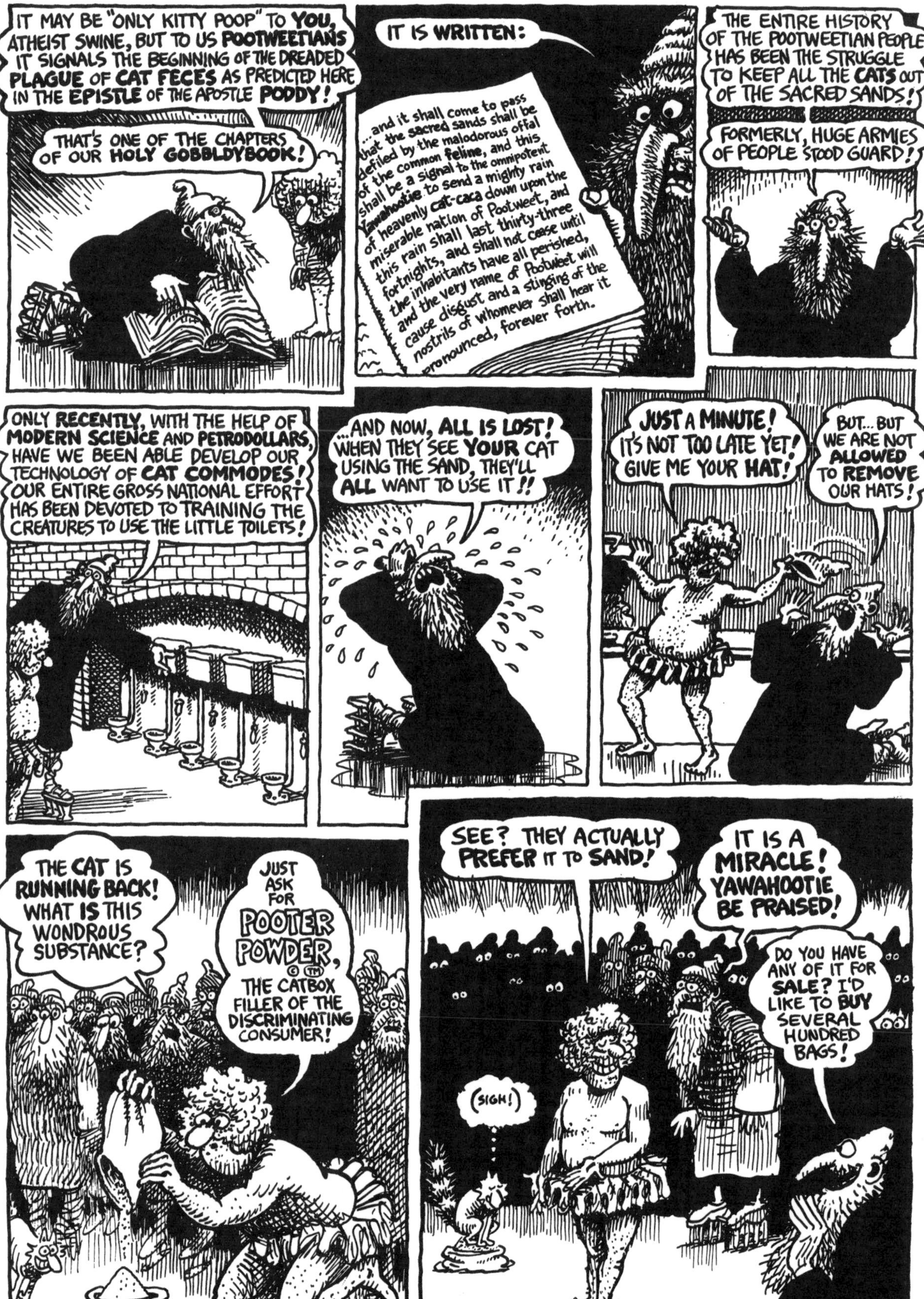
IT MAY BE "ONLY KITTY POOP" TO YOU, ATHEIST SWINE, BUT TO US POOTWEETIANS IT SIGNALS THE BEGINNING OF THE DREADED PLAGUE OF CAT FECES AS PREDICTED HERE IN THE EPISTLE OF THE APOSTLE PODDY!
THAT'S ONE OF THE CHAPTERS OF OUR HOLY GOBBLDYBOOK!
IT IS WRITTEN:
...and it shall come to pass that the sacred sands shall be defiled by the malodorous offal of the common feline, and this shall be a signal to the omnipotent Yawahootie to send a mighty rain of heavenly cat-caca down upon the miserable nation of Pootweet, and this rain shall last thirty-three fortnights, and shall not cease until the inhabitants have all perished, and the very name of Pootweet will cause disgust and a stinging of the nostrils of whomever shall hear it pronounced, forever forth.
THE ENTIRE HISTORY OF THE POOTWEETIAN PEOPLE HAS BEEN THE STRUGGLE TO KEEP ALL THE CATS OUT OF THE SACRED SANDS!
FORMERLY, HUGE ARMIES OF PEOPLE STOOD GUARD!
ONLY RECENTLY, WITH THE HELP OF MODERN SCIENCE AND PETRODOLLARS, HAVE WE BEEN ABLE DEVELOP OUR TECHNOLOGY OF CAT COMMODES! OUR ENTIRE GROSS NATIONAL EFFORT HAS BEEN DEVOTED TO TRAINING THE CREATURES TO USE THE LITTLE TOILETS!
...AND NOW, ALL IS LOST! WHEN THEY SEE YOUR CAT USING THE SAND, THEY'LL ALL WANT TO USE IT!!
JUST A MINUTE! IT'S NOT TOO LATE YET! GIVE ME YOUR HAT!
BUT... BUT WE ARE NOT ALLOWED TO REMOVE OUR HATS!
THE CAT IS RUNNING BACK! WHAT IS THIS WONDROUS SUBSTANCE?
JUST ASK FOR POOTER POWDER, © ™ THE CATBOX FILLER OF THE DISCRIMINATING CONSUMER!
SEE? THEY ACTUALLY PREFER IT TO SAND!
IT IS A MIRACLE! YAWAHOOTIE BE PRAISED!
DO YOU HAVE ANY OF IT FOR SALE? I'D LIKE TO BUY SEVERAL HUNDRED BAGS!
(SIGH!)

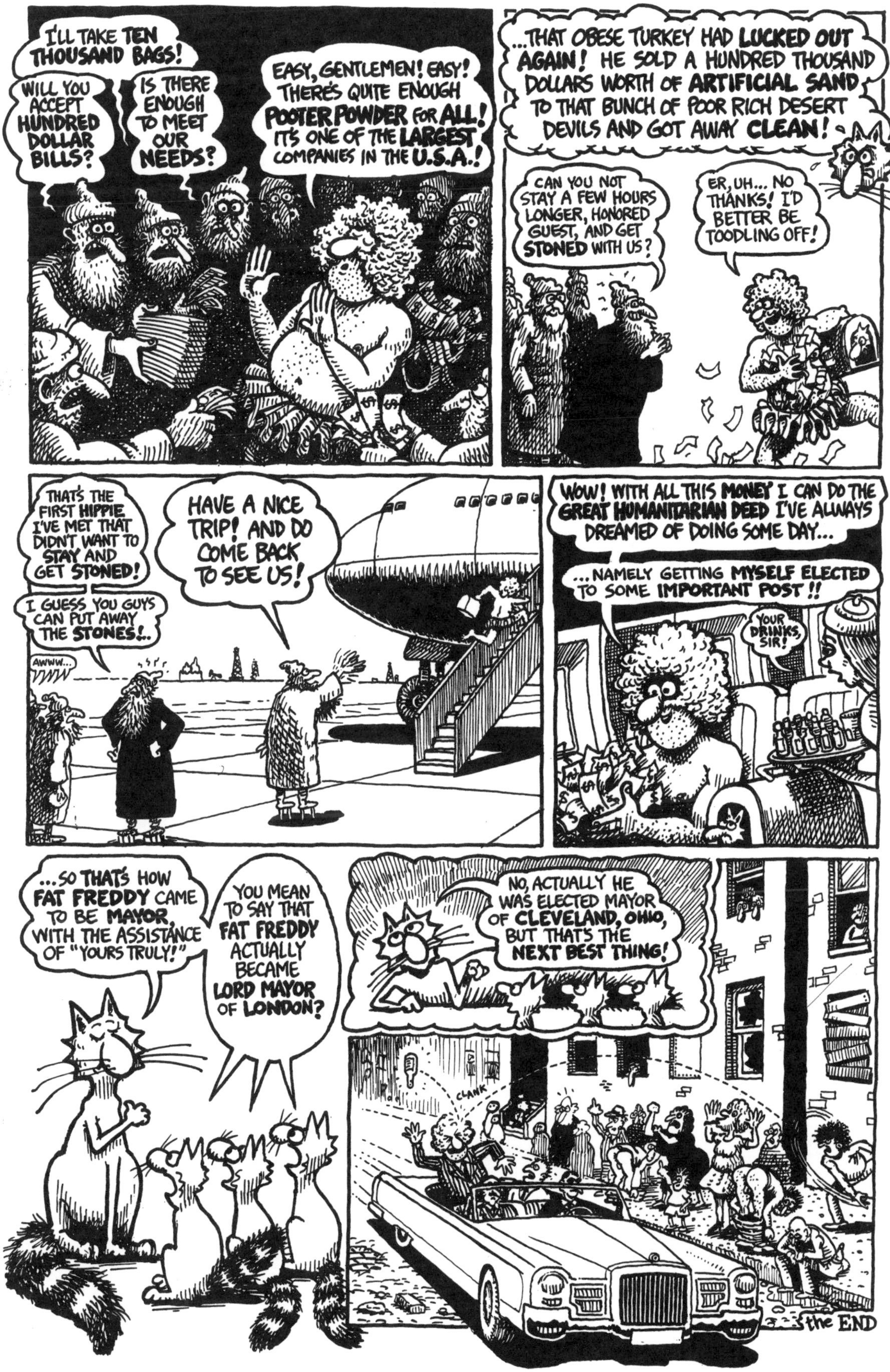

I'LL TAKE TEN THOUSAND BAGS!
WILL YOU ACCEPT HUNDRED DOLLAR BILLS?
IS THERE ENOUGH TO MEET OUR NEEDS?
EASY, GENTLEMEN! EASY! THERE'S QUITE ENOUGH POOTER POWDER FOR ALL! IT'S ONE OF THE LARGEST COMPANIES IN THE U.S.A.!
...THAT OBESE TURKEY HAD LUCKED OUT AGAIN! HE SOLD A HUNDRED THOUSAND DOLLARS WORTH OF ARTIFICIAL SAND TO THAT BUNCH OF POOR RICH DESERT DEVILS AND GOT AWAY CLEAN!
CAN YOU NOT STAY A FEW HOURS LONGER, HONORED GUEST, AND GET STONED WITH US?
ER, UH... NO THANKS! I'D BETTER BE TOODLING OFF!
THAT'S THE FIRST HIPPIE I'VE MET THAT DIDN'T WANT TO STAY AND GET STONED!
I GUESS YOU GUYS CAN PUT AWAY THE STONES!..
AWWW...
HAVE A NICE TRIP! AND DO COME BACK TO SEE US!
WOW! WITH ALL THIS MONEY I CAN DO THE GREAT HUMANITARIAN DEED I'VE ALWAYS DREAMED OF DOING SOME DAY...
...NAMELY GETTING MYSELF ELECTED TO SOME IMPORTANT POST!!
YOUR DRINKS, SIR!
...SO THAT'S HOW FAT FREDDY CAME TO BE MAYOR, WITH THE ASSISTANCE OF "YOURS TRULY!"
YOU MEAN TO SAY THAT FAT FREDDY ACTUALLY BECAME LORD MAYOR OF LONDON?
NO, ACTUALLY HE WAS ELECTED MAYOR OF CLEVELAND, OHIO, BUT THAT'S THE NEXT BEST THING!
CLANK
the END

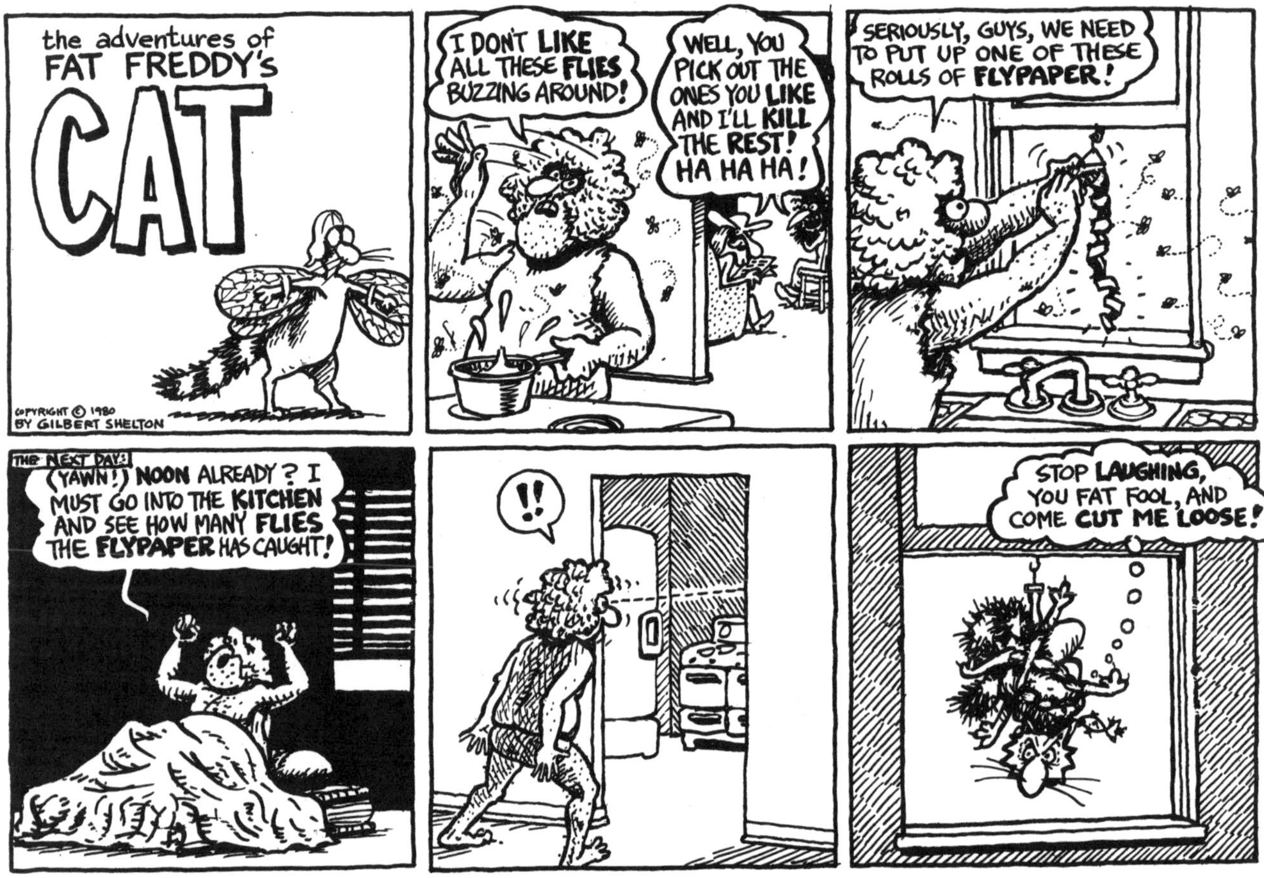

the adventures of
FAT FREDDY's
CAT
COPYRIGHT © 1980 BY GILBERT SHELTON
I DON'T LIKE ALL THESE FLIES BUZZING AROUND!
WELL, YOU PICK OUT THE ONES YOU LIKE AND I'LL KILL THE REST! HA HA HA!
SERIOUSLY, GUYS, WE NEED TO PUT UP ONE OF THESE ROLLS OF FLYPAPER!
THE NEXT DAY:
(YAWN!) NOON ALREADY? I MUST GO INTO THE KITCHEN AND SEE HOW MANY FLIES THE FLYPAPER HAS CAUGHT!
!!
STOP LAUGHING, YOU FAT FOOL, AND COME CUT ME LOOSE!

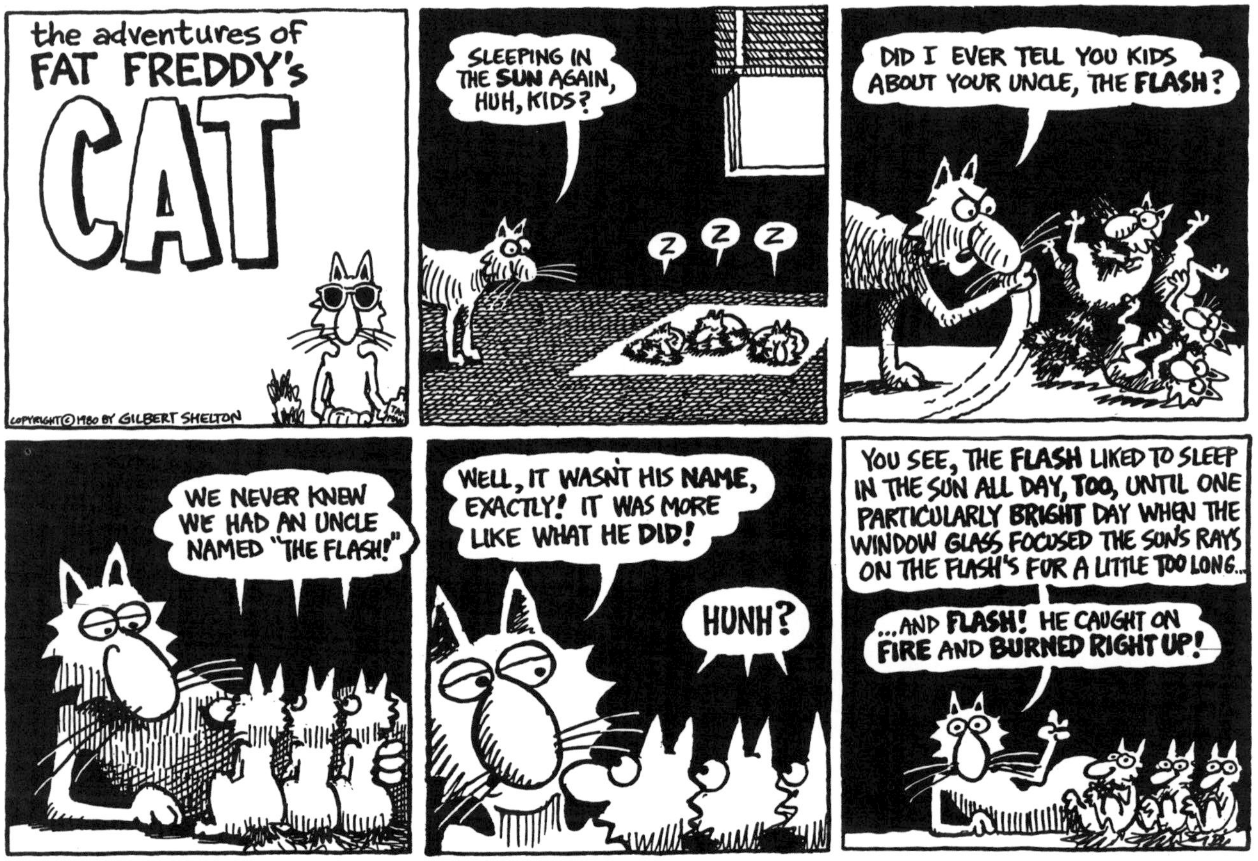

the adventures of
FAT FREDDY's
CAT
COPYRIGHT © 1980 BY GILBERT SHELTON
SLEEPING IN THE SUN AGAIN, HUH, KIDS?
Z Z Z
DID I EVER TELL YOU KIDS ABOUT YOUR UNCLE, THE FLASH?
WE NEVER KNEW WE HAD AN UNCLE NAMED "THE FLASH!"
WELL, IT WASN'T HIS NAME, EXACTLY! IT WAS MORE LIKE WHAT HE DID!
HUNH?
YOU SEE, THE FLASH LIKED TO SLEEP IN THE SUN ALL DAY, TOO, UNTIL ONE PARTICULARLY BRIGHT DAY WHEN THE WINDOW GLASS FOCUSED THE SUN'S RAYS ON THE FLASH'S FUR A LITTLE TOO LONG...
...AND FLASH! HE CAUGHT ON FIRE AND BURNED RIGHT UP!

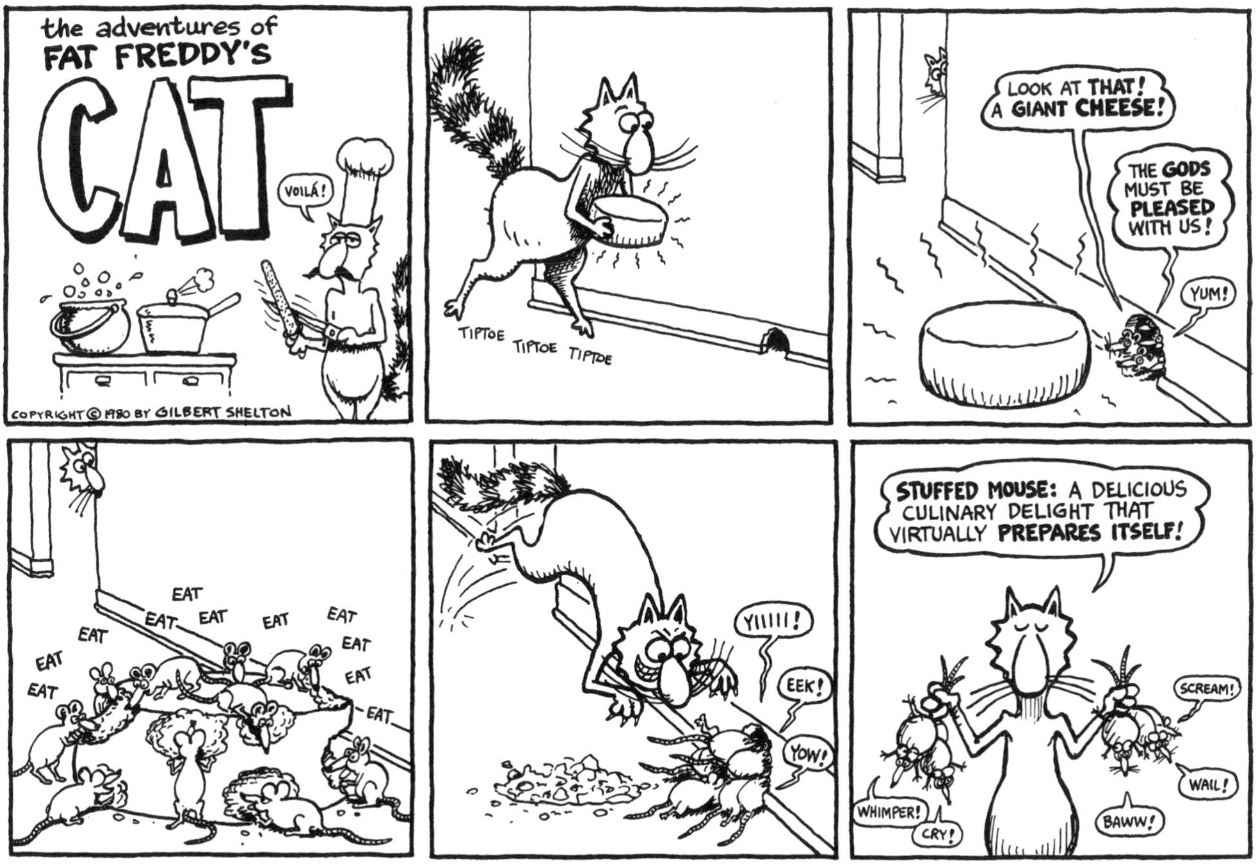
the adventures of
FAT FREDDY'S
CAT
VOILÁ!
COPYRIGHT © 1980 BY GILBERT SHELTON
TIPTOE TIPTOE TIPTOE
LOOK AT THAT! A GIANT CHEESE!
THE GODS MUST BE PLEASED WITH US!
YUM!
EAT
EAT
EAT
EAT
EAT
EAT
EAT
EAT
EAT
EAT
EAT
YIIIII!
EEK!
YOW!
STUFFED MOUSE: A DELICIOUS CULINARY DELIGHT THAT VIRTUALLY PREPARES ITSELF!
SCREAM!
WHIMPER!
CRY!
BAWW!
WAIL!

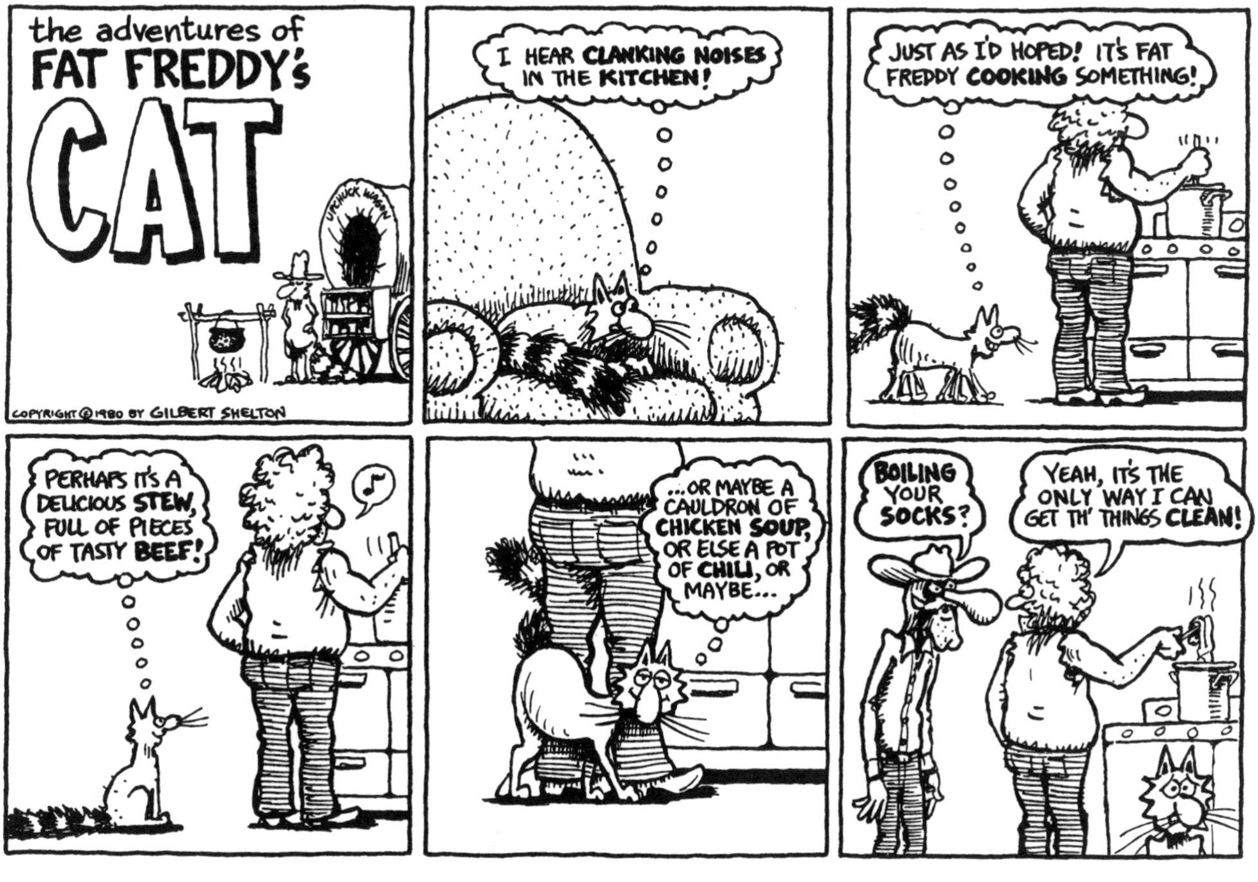
the adventures of
FAT FREDDY's
CAT
UPCHUCK WAGON
COPYRIGHT © 1980 BY GILBERT SHELTON
I HEAR CLANKING NOISES IN THE KITCHEN!
JUST AS I'D HOPED! IT'S FAT FREDDY COOKING SOMETHING!
PERHAPS IT'S A DELICIOUS STEW, FULL OF PIECES OF TASTY BEEF!
...OR MAYBE A CAULDRON OF CHICKEN SOUP, OR ELSE A POT OF CHILI, OR MAYBE...
BOILING YOUR SOCKS?
YEAH, IT'S THE ONLY WAY I CAN GET TH' THINGS CLEAN!

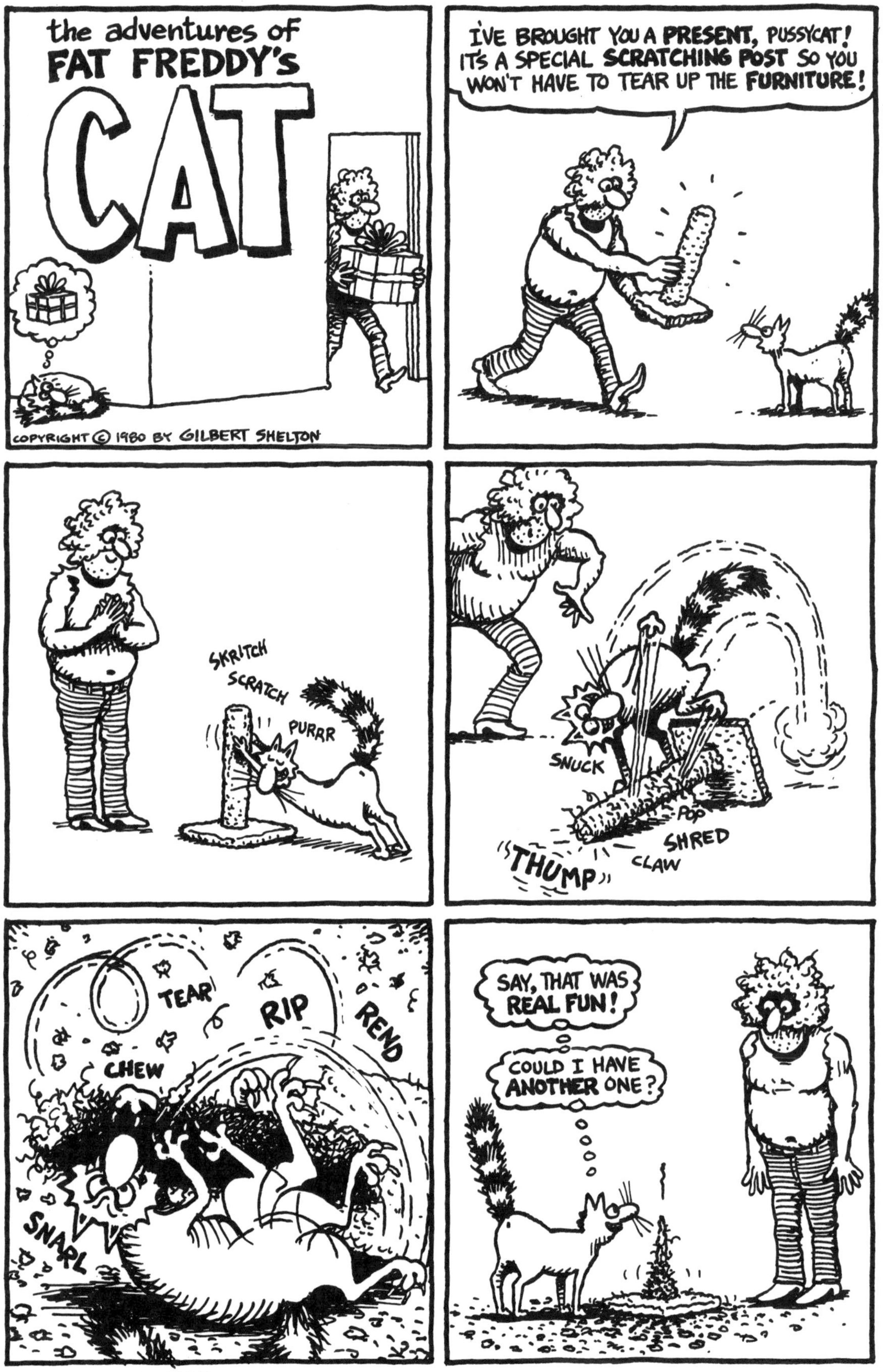
the adventures of
FAT FREDDY's
CAT
COPYRIGHT © 1980 BY GILBERT SHELTON
I'VE BROUGHT YOU A PRESENT, PUSSYCAT! IT'S A SPECIAL SCRATCHING POST SO YOU WON'T HAVE TO TEAR UP THE FURNITURE!
SKRITCH
SCRATCH
PURRR
SNUCK
POP
SHRED
CLAW
THUMP
TEAR
RIP
REND
CHEW
SNARL
SAY, THAT WAS REAL FUN!
COULD I HAVE ANOTHER ONE?

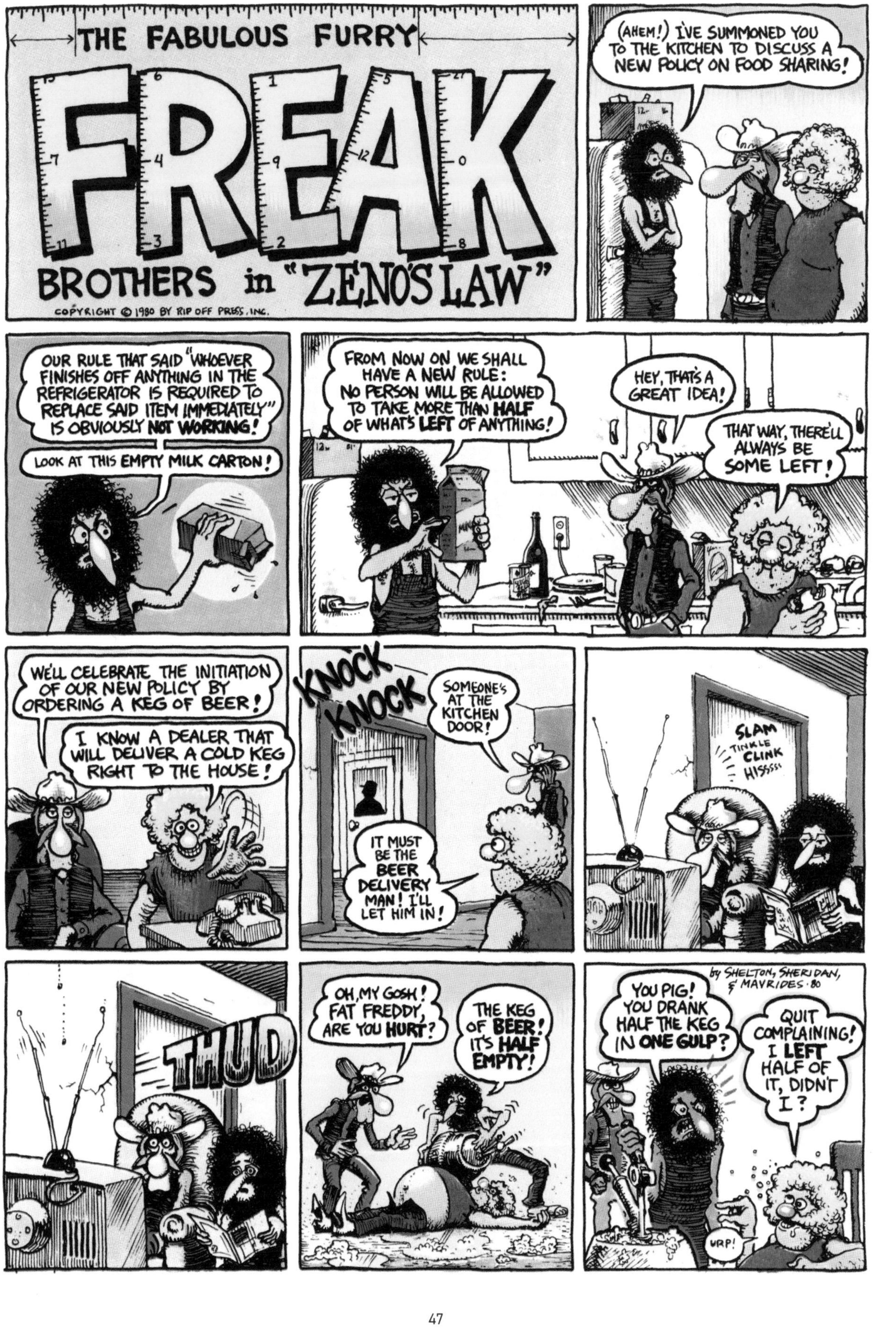
THE FABULOUS FURRY
FREAK
BROTHERS in "ZENO'S LAW"
COPYRIGHT © 1980 BY RIP OFF PRESS, INC.
(AHEM!) I'VE SUMMONED YOU TO THE KITCHEN TO DISCUSS A NEW POLICY ON FOOD SHARING!
OUR RULE THAT SAID "WHOEVER FINISHES OFF ANYTHING IN THE REFRIGERATOR IS REQUIRED TO REPLACE SAID ITEM IMMEDIATELY" IS OBVIOUSLY NOT WORKING!
LOOK AT THIS EMPTY MILK CARTON!
FROM NOW ON WE SHALL HAVE A NEW RULE: NO PERSON WILL BE ALLOWED TO TAKE MORE THAN HALF OF WHAT'S LEFT OF ANYTHING!
HEY, THAT'S A GREAT IDEA!
THAT WAY, THERE'LL ALWAYS BE SOME LEFT!
WE'LL CELEBRATE THE INITIATION OF OUR NEW POLICY BY ORDERING A KEG OF BEER!
I KNOW A DEALER THAT WILL DELIVER A COLD KEG RIGHT TO THE HOUSE!
KNOCK KNOCK
SOMEONE'S AT THE KITCHEN DOOR!
IT MUST BE THE BEER DELIVERY MAN! I'LL LET HIM IN!
SLAM
TINKLE
CLINK
HISSSSS
THUD
OH, MY GOSH! FAT FREDDY, ARE YOU HURT?
THE KEG OF BEER! IT'S HALF EMPTY!
by SHELTON, SHERIDAN, & MAVRIDES · 80
YOU PIG! YOU DRANK HALF THE KEG IN ONE GULP?
QUIT COMPLAINING! I LEFT HALF OF IT, DIDN'T I?
URP!

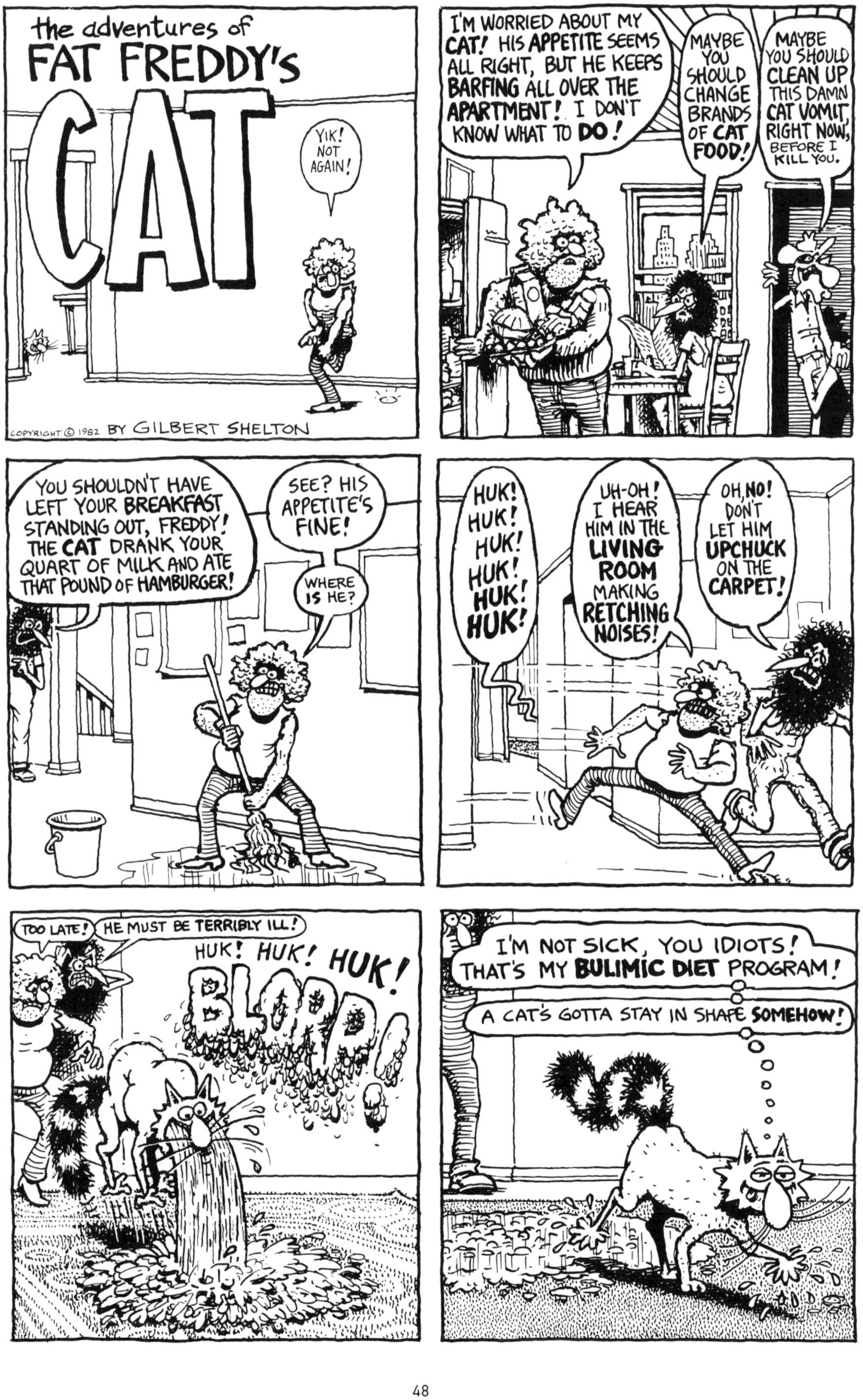
the adventures of
FAT FREDDY'S
CAT
YIK! NOT AGAIN!
COPYRIGHT © 1982 BY GILBERT SHELTON
I'M WORRIED ABOUT MY CAT! HIS APPETITE SEEMS ALL RIGHT, BUT HE KEEPS BARFING ALL OVER THE APARTMENT! I DON'T KNOW WHAT TO DO!
MAYBE YOU SHOULD CHANGE BRANDS OF CAT FOOD!
MAYBE YOU SHOULD CLEAN UP THIS DAMN CAT VOMIT, RIGHT NOW, BEFORE I KILL YOU.
YOU SHOULDN'T HAVE LEFT YOUR BREAKFAST STANDING OUT, FREDDY! THE CAT DRANK YOUR QUART OF MILK AND ATE THAT POUND OF HAMBURGER!
SEE? HIS APPETITE'S FINE!
WHERE IS HE?
HUK! HUK! HUK! HUK! HUK! HUK!
UH-OH! I HEAR HIM IN THE LIVING ROOM MAKING RETCHING NOISES!
OH, NO! DON'T LET HIM UPCHUCK ON THE CARPET!
TOO LATE!
HE MUST BE TERRIBLY ILL!
HUK! HUK! HUK!
BLOPP!
I'M NOT SICK, YOU IDIOTS! THAT'S MY BULIMIC DIET PROGRAM!
A CAT'S GOTTA STAY IN SHAPE SOMEHOW!

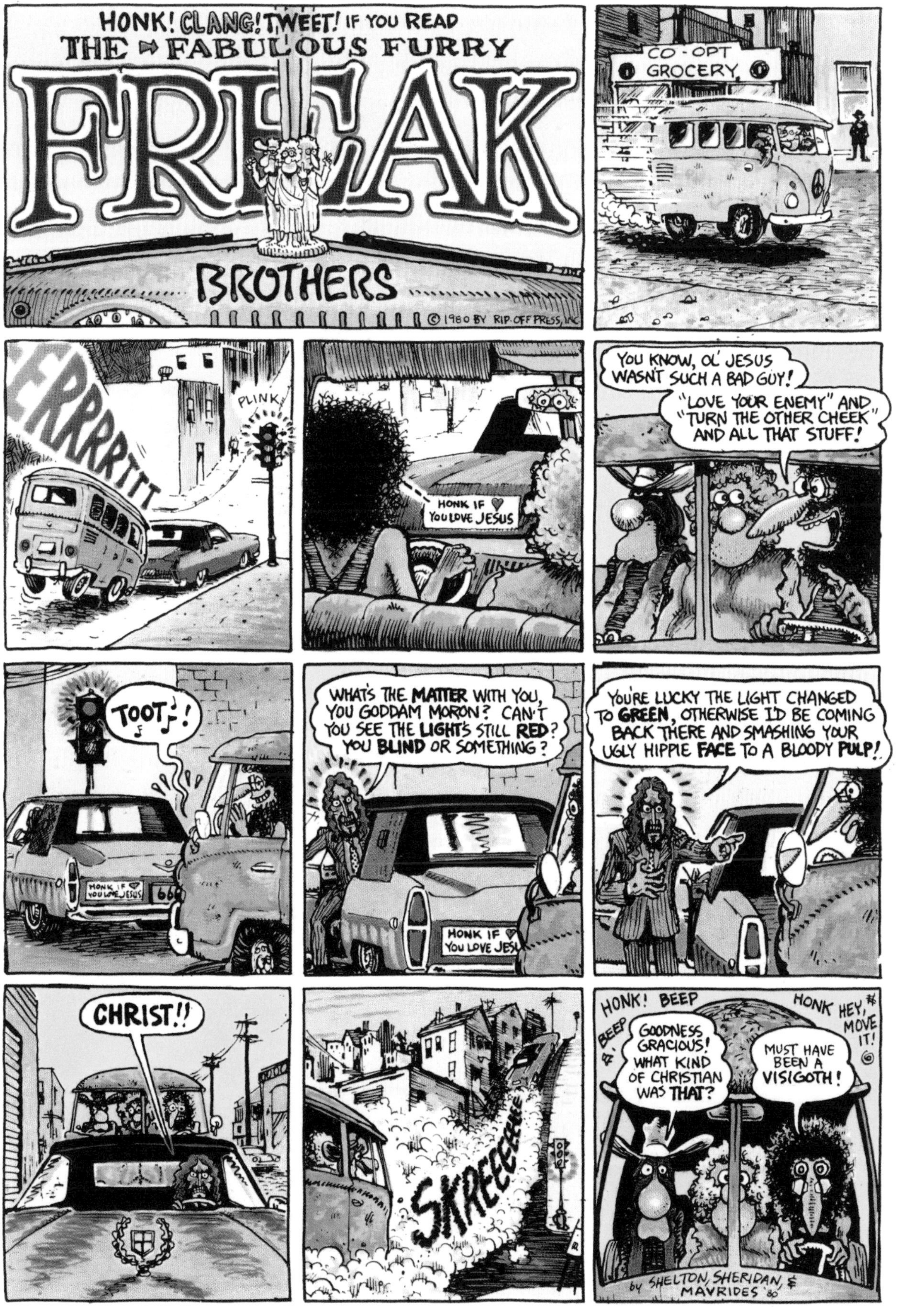
HONK! CLANG! TWEET! IF YOU READ
THE FABULOUS FURRY
FREAK
BROTHERS
© 1980 BY RIP-OFF PRESS, INC
CO-OPT GROCERY
ERRRRRTTT
PLINK
HONK IF ♥ YOU LOVE JESUS
YOU KNOW, OL' JESUS WASN'T SUCH A BAD GUY!
"LOVE YOUR ENEMY" AND "TURN THE OTHER CHEEK" AND ALL THAT STUFF!
TOOT!
HONK IF ♥ YOU LOVE JESUS
WHAT'S THE MATTER WITH YOU, YOU GODDAM MORON? CAN'T YOU SEE THE LIGHT'S STILL RED? YOU BLIND OR SOMETHING?
HONK IF ♥ YOU LOVE JES
YOU'RE LUCKY THE LIGHT CHANGED TO GREEN, OTHERWISE I'D BE COMING BACK THERE AND SMASHING YOUR UGLY HIPPIE FACE TO A BLOODY PULP!
CHRIST!!
SKREEEEEEE
HONK! BEEP
BEEP
HONK HEY, MOVE IT!
GOODNESS GRACIOUS! WHAT KIND OF CHRISTIAN WAS THAT?
MUST HAVE BEEN A VISIGOTH!
by SHELTON, SHERIDAN, & MAVRIDES '80

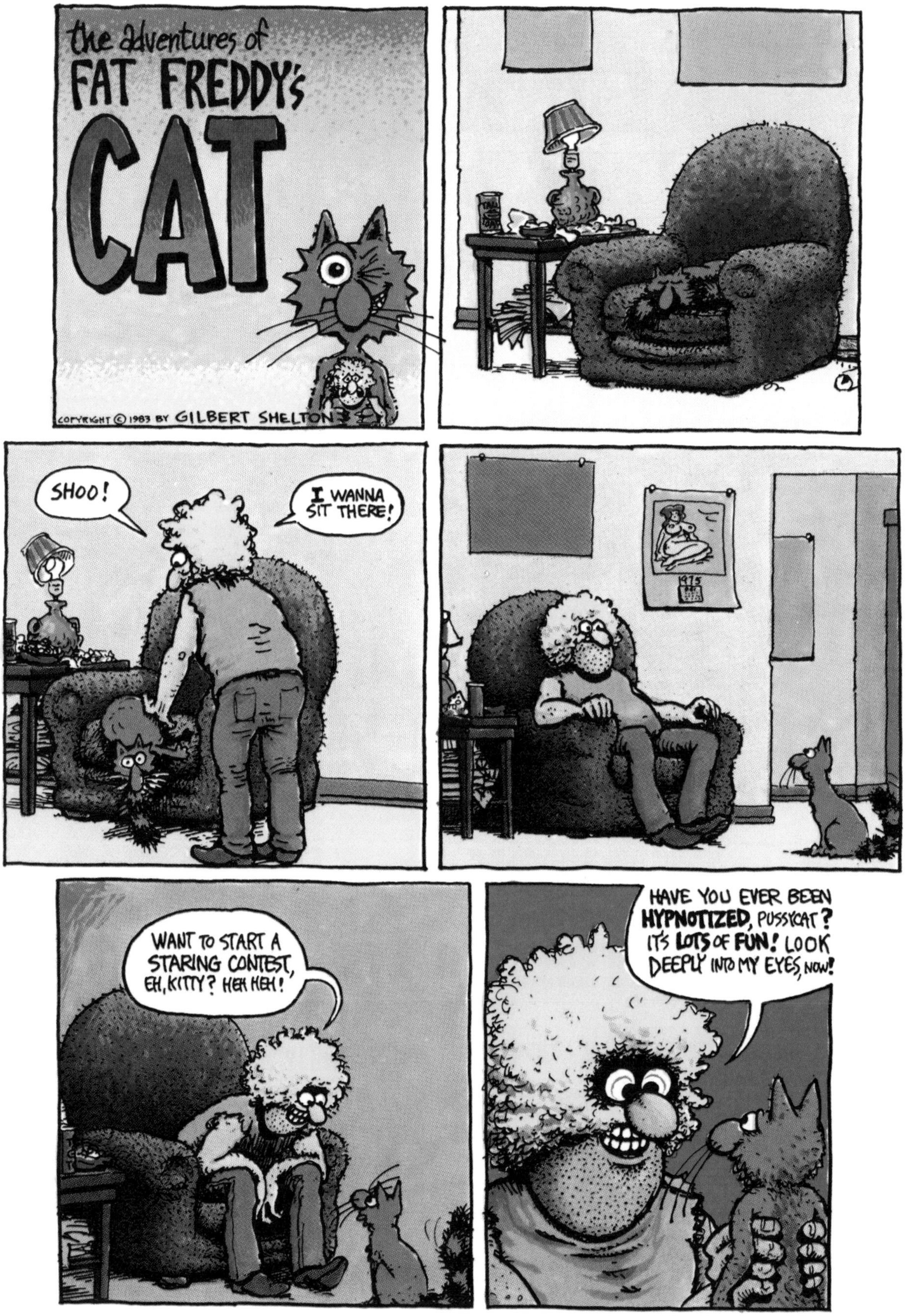
the adventures of
FAT FREDDY'S
CAT
COPYRIGHT © 1983 BY GILBERT SHELTON
SHOO!
I WANNA SIT THERE!
WANT TO START A STARING CONTEST, EH, KITTY? HEH HEH!
HAVE YOU EVER BEEN HYPNOTIZED, PUSSYCAT? IT'S LOTS OF FUN! LOOK DEEPLY INTO MY EYES, NOW!

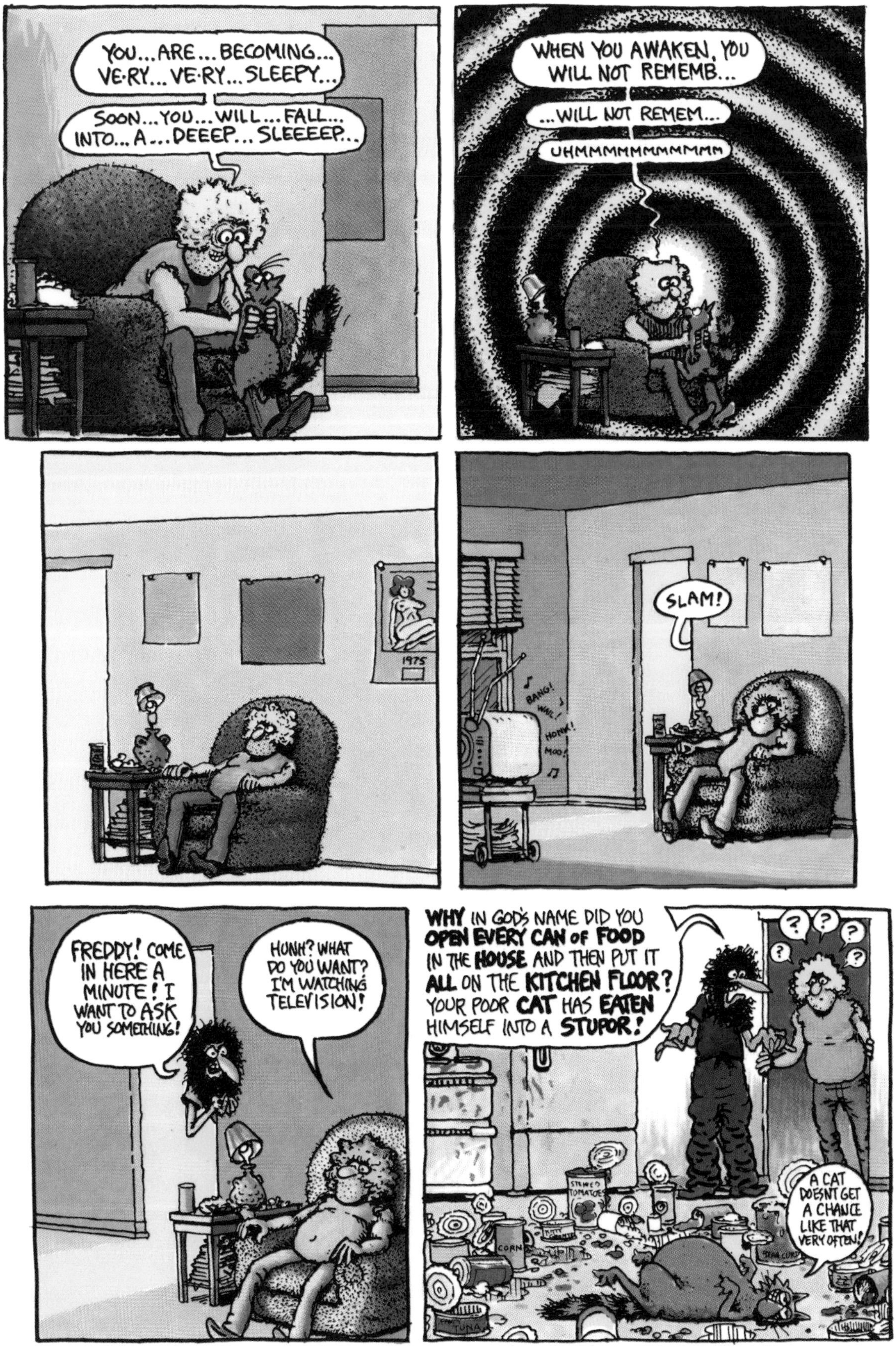

YOU... ARE... BECOMING... VE·RY... VE·RY... SLEEPY...
SOON... YOU... WILL... FALL... INTO... A... DEEEP... SLEEEEP...
WHEN YOU AWAKEN, YOU WILL NOT REMEMB...
...WILL NOT REMEM...
UHMMMMMMMMMMM
1975
SLAM!
BANG!
WAIL!
HONK!
MOO!
FREDDY! COME IN HERE A MINUTE! I WANT TO ASK YOU SOMETHING!
HUNH? WHAT DO YOU WANT? I'M WATCHING TELEVISION!
WHY IN GOD'S NAME DID YOU OPEN EVERY CAN OF FOOD IN THE HOUSE AND THEN PUT IT ALL ON THE KITCHEN FLOOR? YOUR POOR CAT HAS EATEN HIMSELF INTO A STUPOR!
? ? ? ? ?
STEWED TOMATOES
CORN
TUNA
A CAT DOESNT GET A CHANCE LIKE THAT VERY OFTEN!

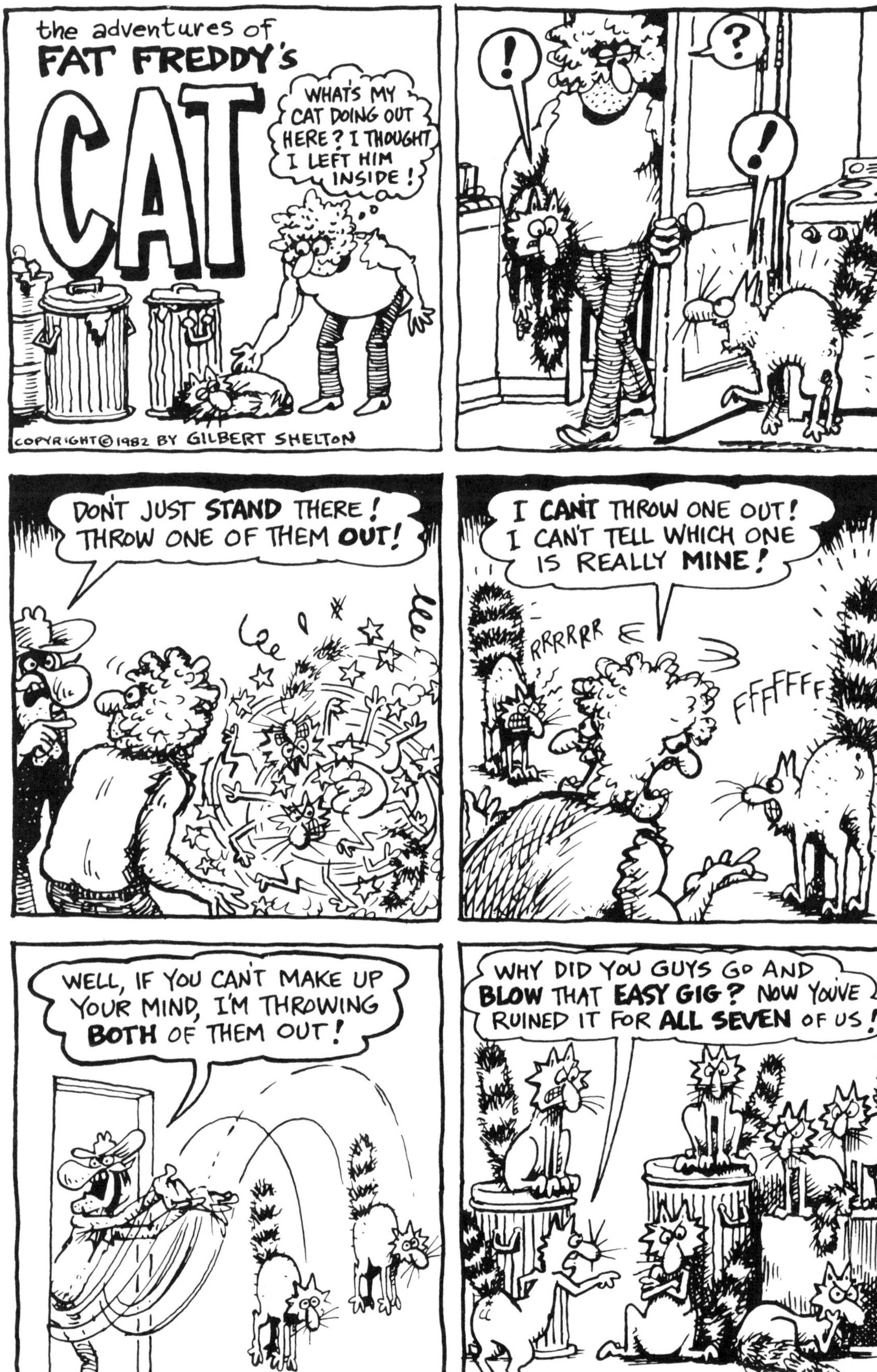
the adventures of
FAT FREDDY's
CAT
WHAT'S MY CAT DOING OUT HERE? I THOUGHT I LEFT HIM INSIDE!
COPYRIGHT © 1982 BY GILBERT SHELTON
!
?
!
DON'T JUST STAND THERE! THROW ONE OF THEM OUT!
I CAN'T THROW ONE OUT! I CAN'T TELL WHICH ONE IS REALLY MINE!
RRRRRR
FFFFFFF
WELL, IF YOU CAN'T MAKE UP YOUR MIND, I'M THROWING BOTH OF THEM OUT!
WHY DID YOU GUYS GO AND BLOW THAT EASY GIG? NOW YOU'VE RUINED IT FOR ALL SEVEN OF US!

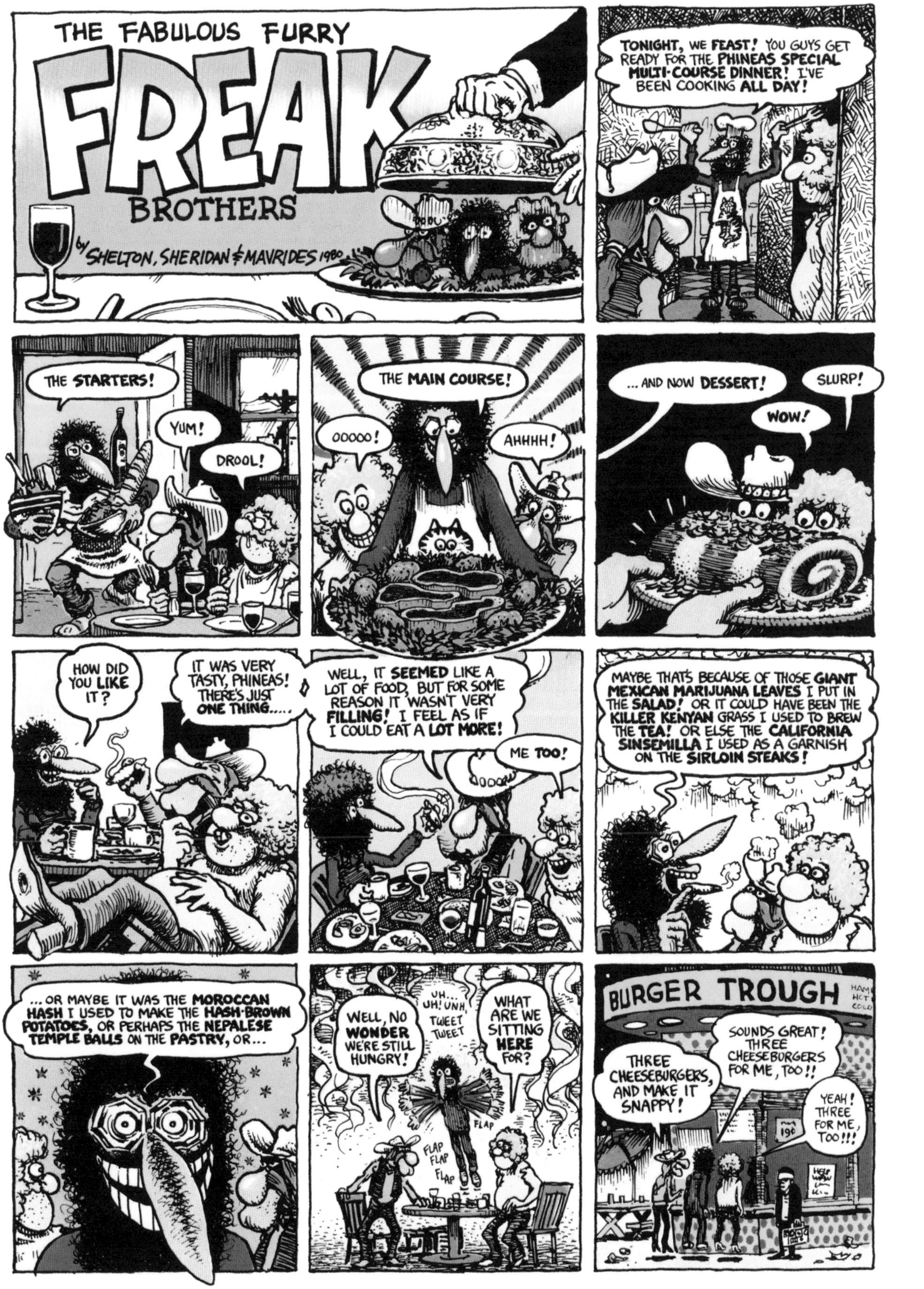
THE FABULOUS FURRY
FREAK
BROTHERS
by SHELTON, SHERIDAN & MAVRIDES 1980
TONIGHT, WE FEAST! YOU GUYS GET READY FOR THE PHINEAS SPECIAL MULTI-COURSE DINNER! I'VE BEEN COOKING ALL DAY!
THE STARTERS!
YUM!
DROOL!
THE MAIN COURSE!
OOOOO!
AHHHH!
...AND NOW DESSERT!
WOW!
SLURP!
HOW DID YOU LIKE IT?
IT WAS VERY TASTY, PHINEAS! THERE'S JUST ONE THING.....
WELL, IT SEEMED LIKE A LOT OF FOOD, BUT FOR SOME REASON IT WASN'T VERY FILLING! I FEEL AS IF I COULD EAT A LOT MORE!
ME TOO!
MAYBE THAT'S BECAUSE OF THOSE GIANT MEXICAN MARIJUANA LEAVES I PUT IN THE SALAD! OR IT COULD HAVE BEEN THE KILLER KENYAN GRASS I USED TO BREW THE TEA! OR ELSE THE CALIFORNIA SINSEMILLA I USED AS A GARNISH ON THE SIRLOIN STEAKS!
...OR MAYBE IT WAS THE MOROCCAN HASH I USED TO MAKE THE HASH-BROWN POTATOES, OR PERHAPS THE NEPALESE TEMPLE BALLS ON THE PASTRY, OR...
WELL, NO WONDER WE'RE STILL HUNGRY!
UH... UH! UNH
TWEET TWEET
WHAT ARE WE SITTING HERE FOR?
FLAP
FLAP FLAP FLAP
BURGER TROUGH
THREE CHEESEBURGERS, AND MAKE IT SNAPPY!
SOUNDS GREAT! THREE CHEESEBURGERS FOR ME, TOO!!
YEAH! THREE FOR ME, TOO!!!
19¢

FAT FREDDY
DEMONSTRATES
HOW TO USE ROLLING PAPERS

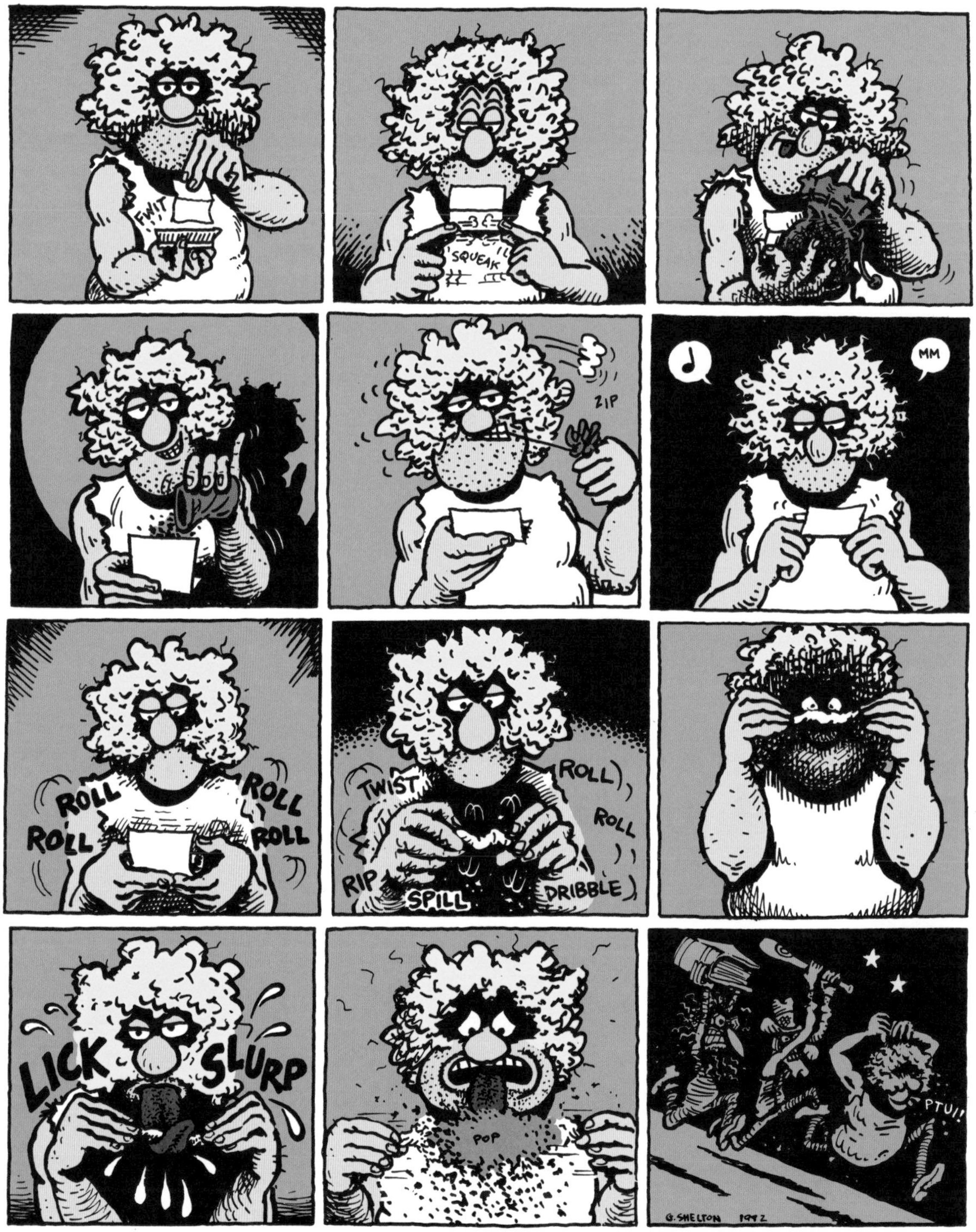
FWIT
SQUEAK
ZIP
♪
MM
ROLL
ROLL
ROLL
ROLL
TWIST
ROLL
ROLL
RIP
SPILL
DRIBBLE
LICK
SLURP
POP
PTUI!
G. SHELTON 1992

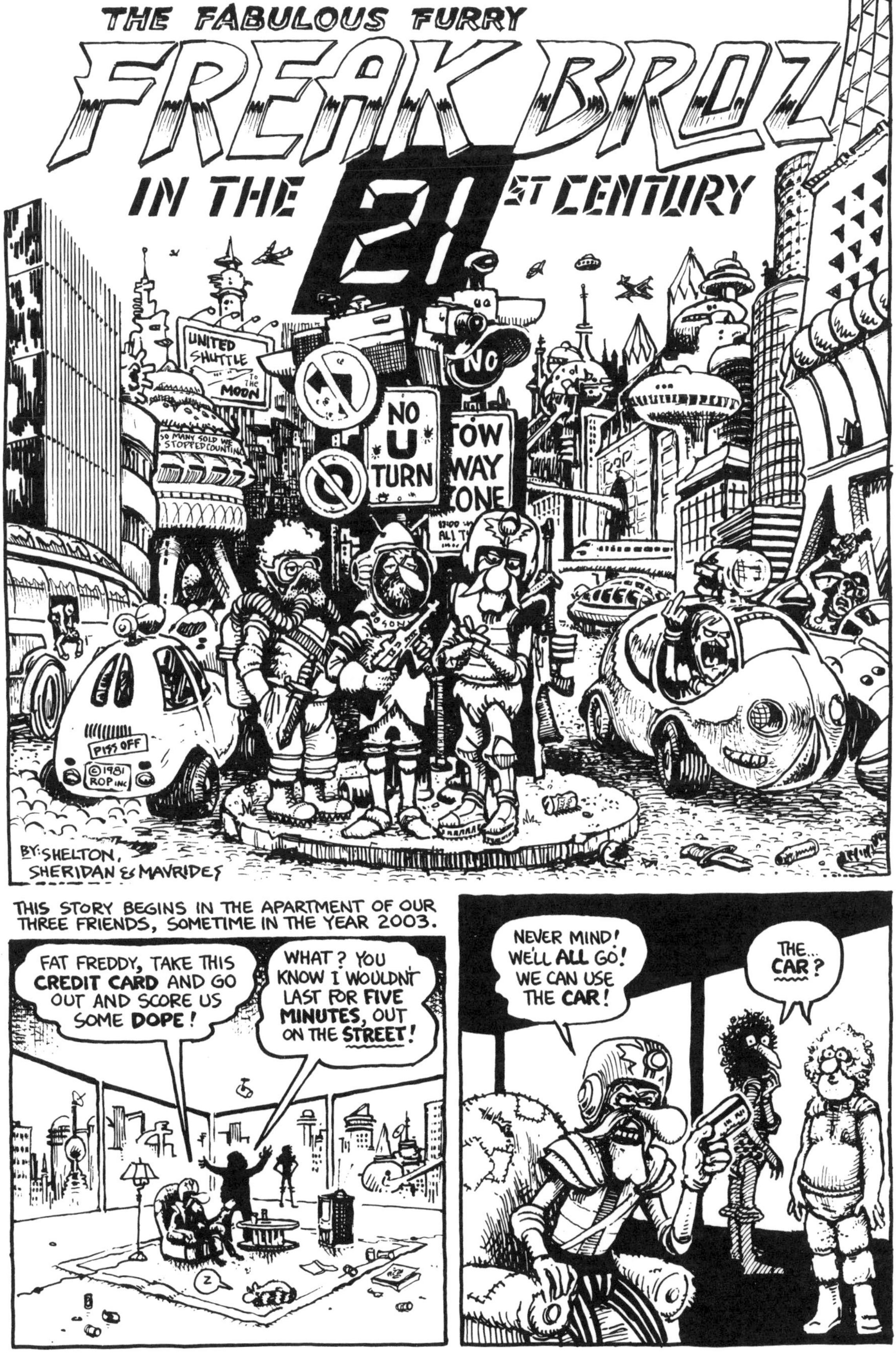
THE FABULOUS FURRY
FREAK BROZ
IN THE 21ST CENTURY
UNITED SHUTTLE TO THE MOON
SO MANY SOLD WE STOPPED COUNTING
NO
NO U TURN
TOW AWAY ZONE
PISS OFF
©1981 ROP INC
BY: SHELTON, SHERIDAN & MAVRIDES
THIS STORY BEGINS IN THE APARTMENT OF OUR THREE FRIENDS, SOMETIME IN THE YEAR 2003.
FAT FREDDY, TAKE THIS CREDIT CARD AND GO OUT AND SCORE US SOME DOPE!
WHAT? YOU KNOW I WOULDN'T LAST FOR FIVE MINUTES, OUT ON THE STREET!
Z
NEVER MIND! WE'LL ALL GO! WE CAN USE THE CAR!
THE... CAR?

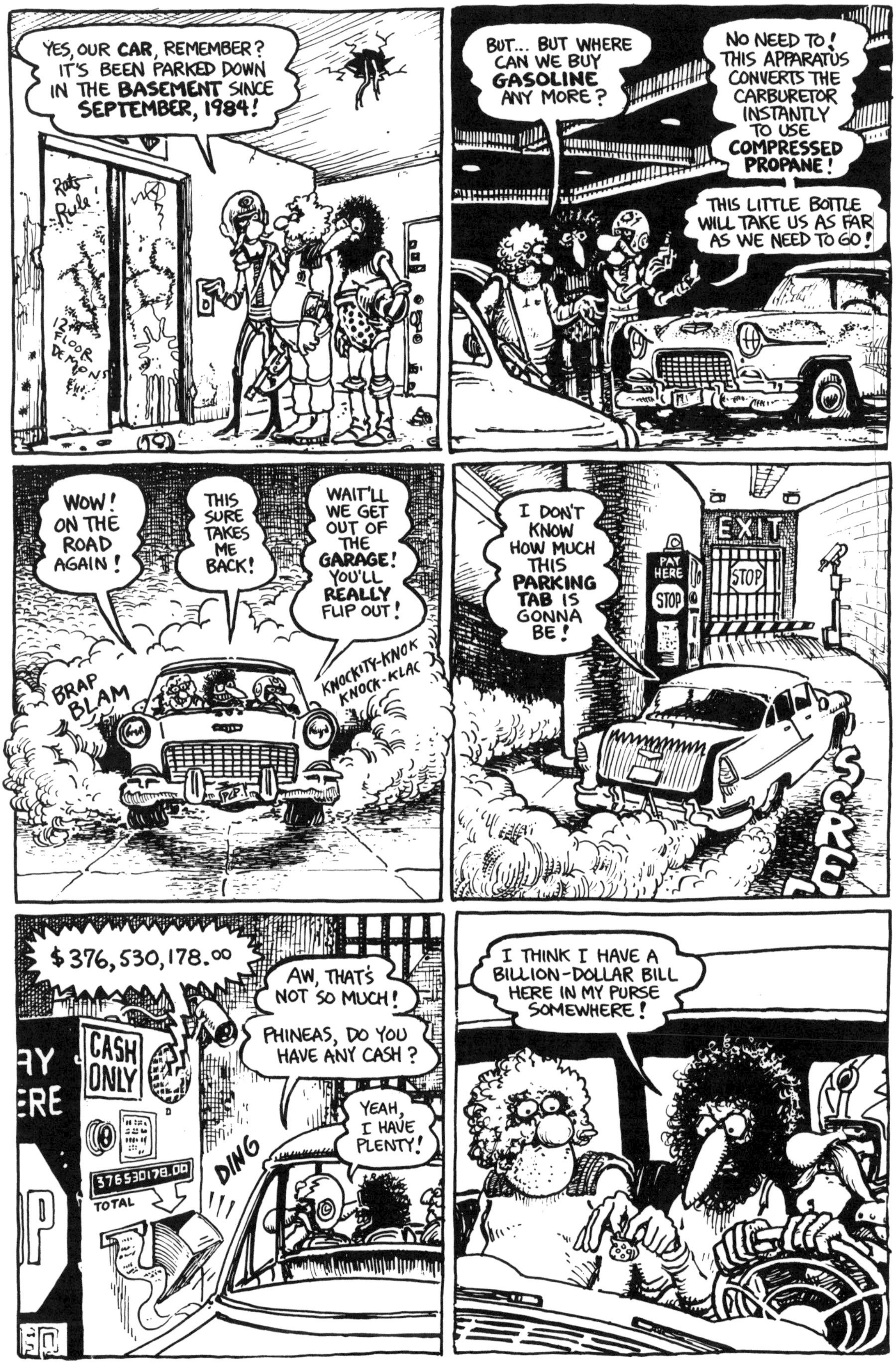

YES, OUR CAR, REMEMBER? IT'S BEEN PARKED DOWN IN THE BASEMENT SINCE SEPTEMBER, 1984!
Rats Rule!
12 FLOOR DEMONS
BUT... BUT WHERE CAN WE BUY GASOLINE ANY MORE?
NO NEED TO! THIS APPARATUS CONVERTS THE CARBURETOR INSTANTLY TO USE COMPRESSED PROPANE!
THIS LITTLE BOTTLE WILL TAKE US AS FAR AS WE NEED TO GO!
WOW! ON THE ROAD AGAIN!
THIS SURE TAKES ME BACK!
WAIT'LL WE GET OUT OF THE GARAGE! YOU'LL REALLY FLIP OUT!
BRAP BLAM
KNOCKITY-KNOK KNOCK-KLAC
I DON'T KNOW HOW MUCH THIS PARKING TAB IS GONNA BE!
EXIT
PAY HERE
STOP
STOP
SCRE
$376,530,178.00
AW, THAT'S NOT SO MUCH!
PHINEAS, DO YOU HAVE ANY CASH?
YEAH, I HAVE PLENTY!
CASH ONLY
376530178.00
TOTAL
DING
I THINK I HAVE A BILLION-DOLLAR BILL HERE IN MY PURSE SOMEWHERE!

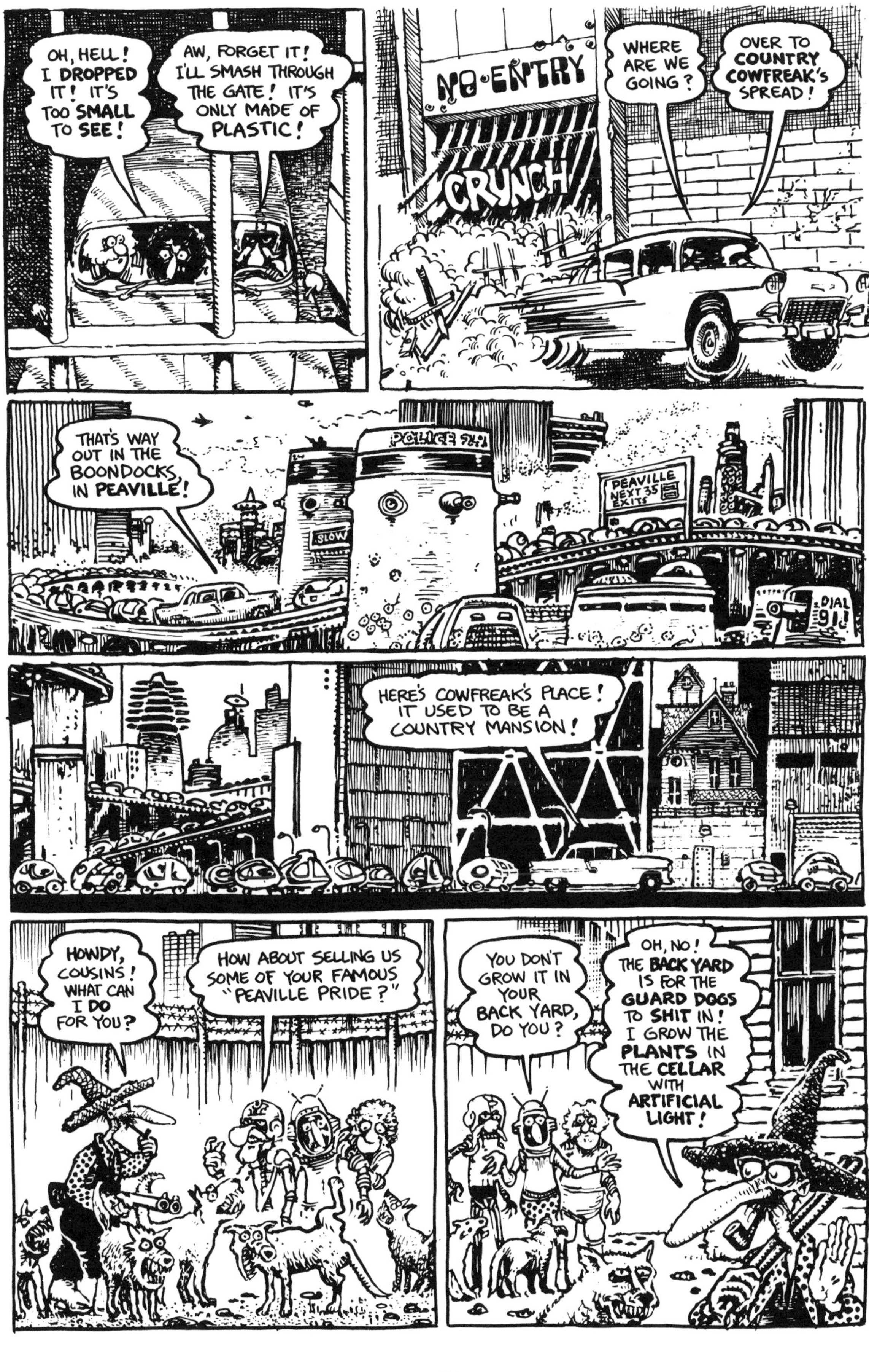
OH, HELL! I DROPPED IT! IT'S TOO SMALL TO SEE!
AW, FORGET IT! I'LL SMASH THROUGH THE GATE! IT'S ONLY MADE OF PLASTIC!
NO ENTRY
CRUNCH
WHERE ARE WE GOING?
OVER TO COUNTRY COWFREAK'S SPREAD!
THAT'S WAY OUT IN THE BOONDOCKS, IN PEAVILLE!
POLICE 911
SLOW
PEAVILLE NEXT 35 EXITS
DIAL 911
HERE'S COWFREAK'S PLACE! IT USED TO BE A COUNTRY MANSION!
HOWDY, COUSINS! WHAT CAN I DO FOR YOU?
HOW ABOUT SELLING US SOME OF YOUR FAMOUS "PEAVILLE PRIDE?"
YOU DON'T GROW IT IN YOUR BACK YARD, DO YOU?
OH, NO! THE BACK YARD IS FOR THE GUARD DOGS TO SHIT IN! I GROW THE PLANTS IN THE CELLAR WITH ARTIFICIAL LIGHT!

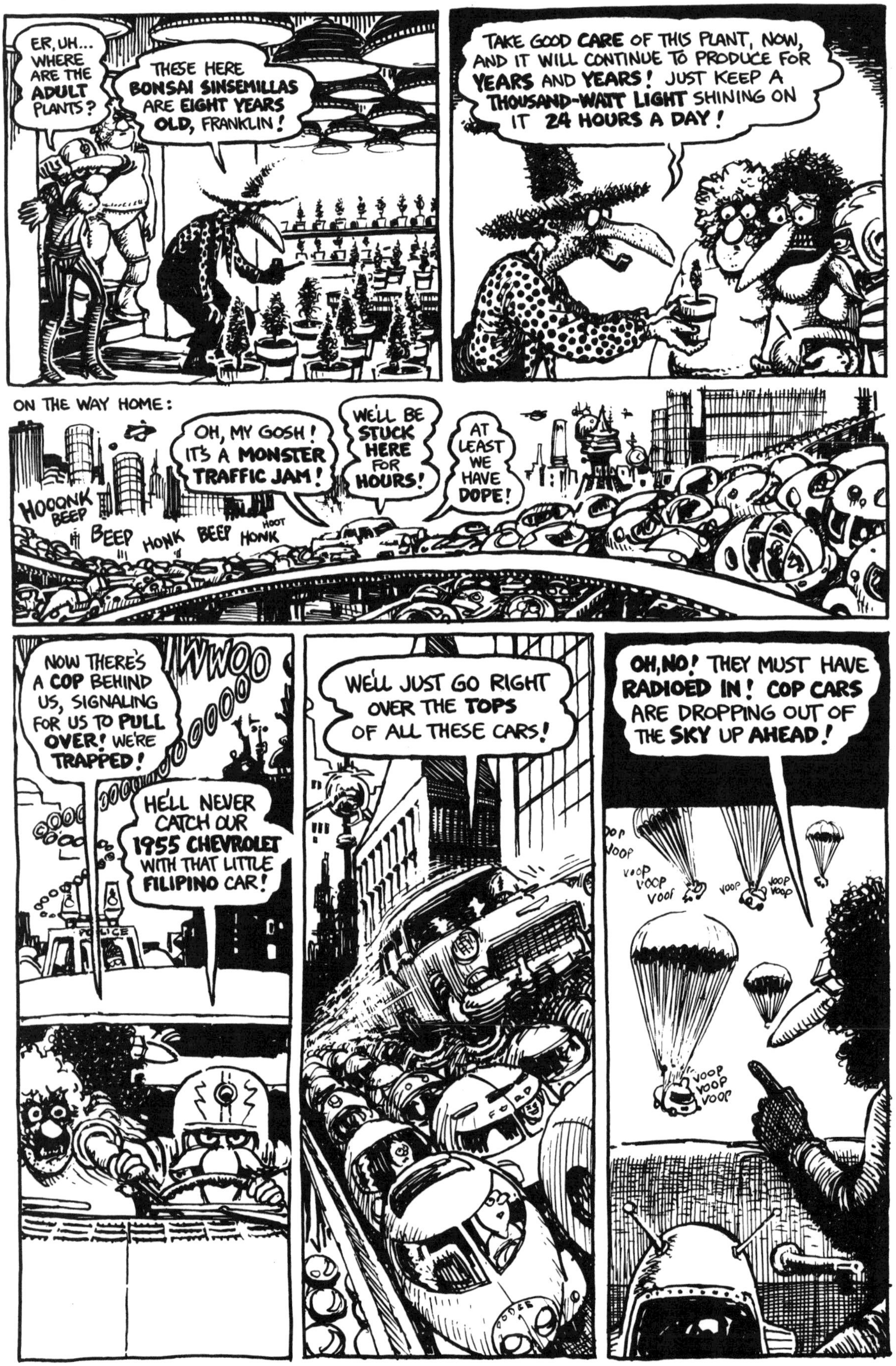
ER, UH... WHERE ARE THE ADULT PLANTS?
THESE HERE BONSAI SINSEMILLAS ARE EIGHT YEARS OLD, FRANKLIN!
TAKE GOOD CARE OF THIS PLANT, NOW, AND IT WILL CONTINUE TO PRODUCE FOR YEARS AND YEARS! JUST KEEP A THOUSAND-WATT LIGHT SHINING ON IT 24 HOURS A DAY!
ON THE WAY HOME:
OH, MY GOSH! IT'S A MONSTER TRAFFIC JAM!
WE'LL BE STUCK HERE FOR HOURS!
AT LEAST WE HAVE DOPE!
HOOONK BEEP
BEEP HONK BEEP HONK HOOT
NOW THERE'S A COP BEHIND US, SIGNALING FOR US TO PULL OVER! WE'RE TRAPPED!
HE'LL NEVER CATCH OUR 1955 CHEVROLET WITH THAT LITTLE FILIPINO CAR!
POLICE
WE'LL JUST GO RIGHT OVER THE TOPS OF ALL THESE CARS!
OH, NO! THEY MUST HAVE RADIOED IN! COP CARS ARE DROPPING OUT OF THE SKY UP AHEAD!
VOOP VOOP VOOP
VOOP VOOP VOOP

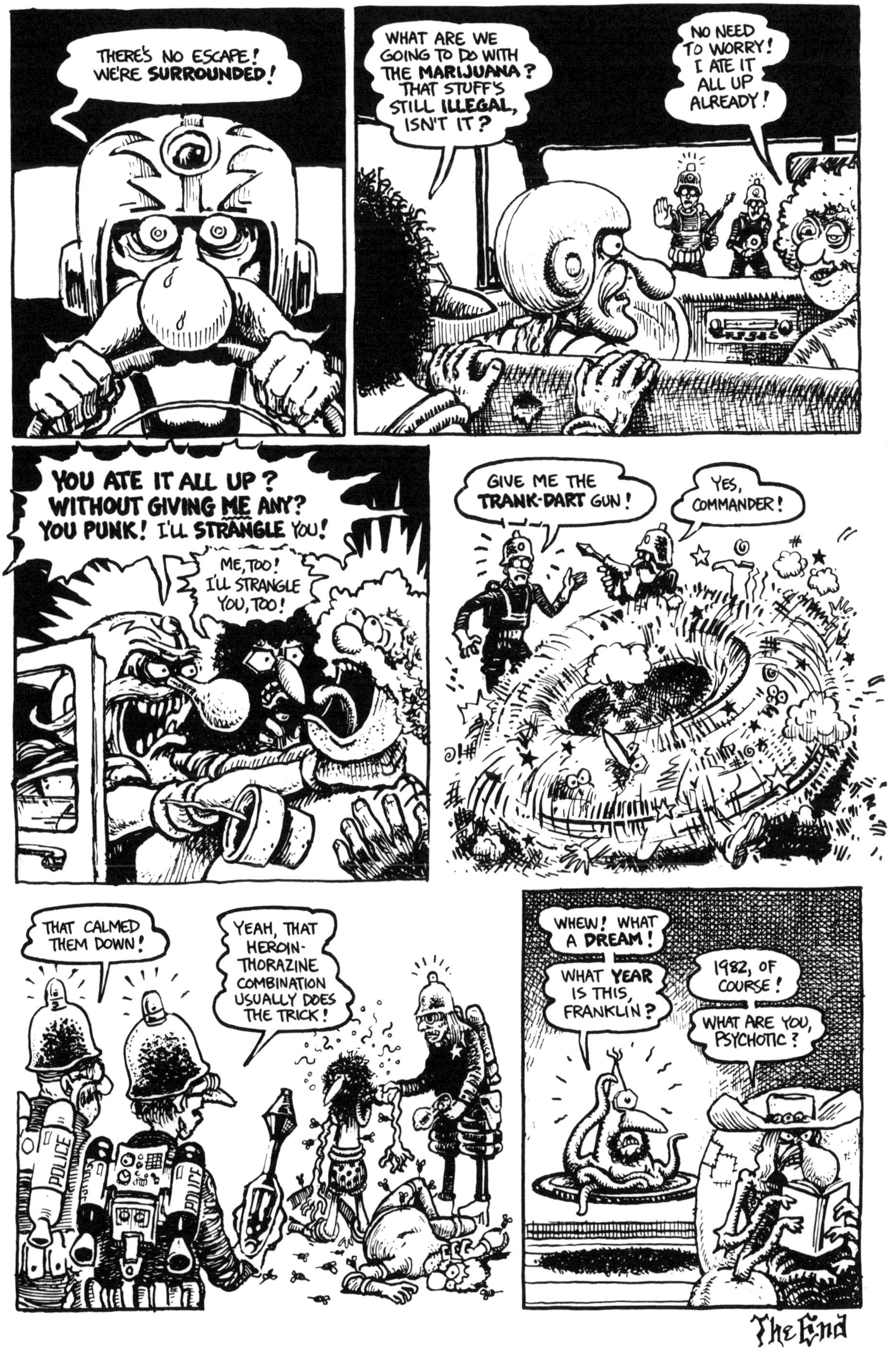
THERE'S NO ESCAPE! WE'RE SURROUNDED!
WHAT ARE WE GOING TO DO WITH THE MARIJUANA? THAT STUFF'S STILL ILLEGAL, ISN'T IT?
NO NEED TO WORRY! I ATE IT ALL UP ALREADY!
YOU ATE IT ALL UP? WITHOUT GIVING ME ANY? YOU PUNK! I'LL STRANGLE YOU!
ME, TOO! I'LL STRANGLE YOU, TOO!
GIVE ME THE TRANK-DART GUN!
YES, COMMANDER!
THAT CALMED THEM DOWN!
YEAH, THAT HEROIN-THORAZINE COMBINATION USUALLY DOES THE TRICK!
WHEW! WHAT A DREAM!
WHAT YEAR IS THIS, FRANKLIN?
1982, OF COURSE!
WHAT ARE YOU, PSYCHOTIC?
POLICE

The End

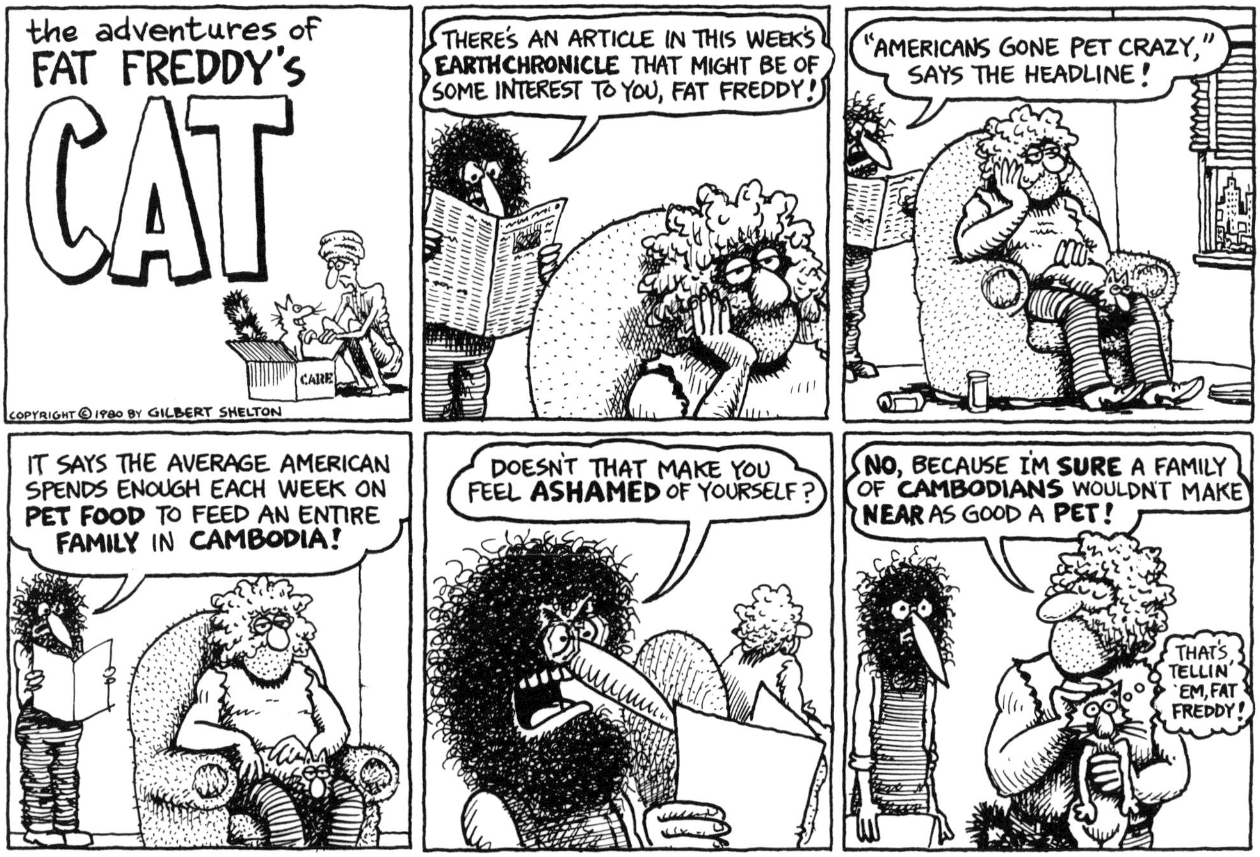
the adventures of
FAT FREDDY's
CAT
CARE
COPYRIGHT © 1980 BY GILBERT SHELTON
THERE'S AN ARTICLE IN THIS WEEK'S EARTHCHRONICLE THAT MIGHT BE OF SOME INTEREST TO YOU, FAT FREDDY!
"AMERICANS GONE PET CRAZY," SAYS THE HEADLINE!
IT SAYS THE AVERAGE AMERICAN SPENDS ENOUGH EACH WEEK ON PET FOOD TO FEED AN ENTIRE FAMILY IN CAMBODIA!
DOESN'T THAT MAKE YOU FEEL ASHAMED OF YOURSELF?
NO, BECAUSE I'M SURE A FAMILY OF CAMBODIANS WOULDN'T MAKE NEAR AS GOOD A PET!
THAT'S TELLIN' 'EM, FAT FREDDY!

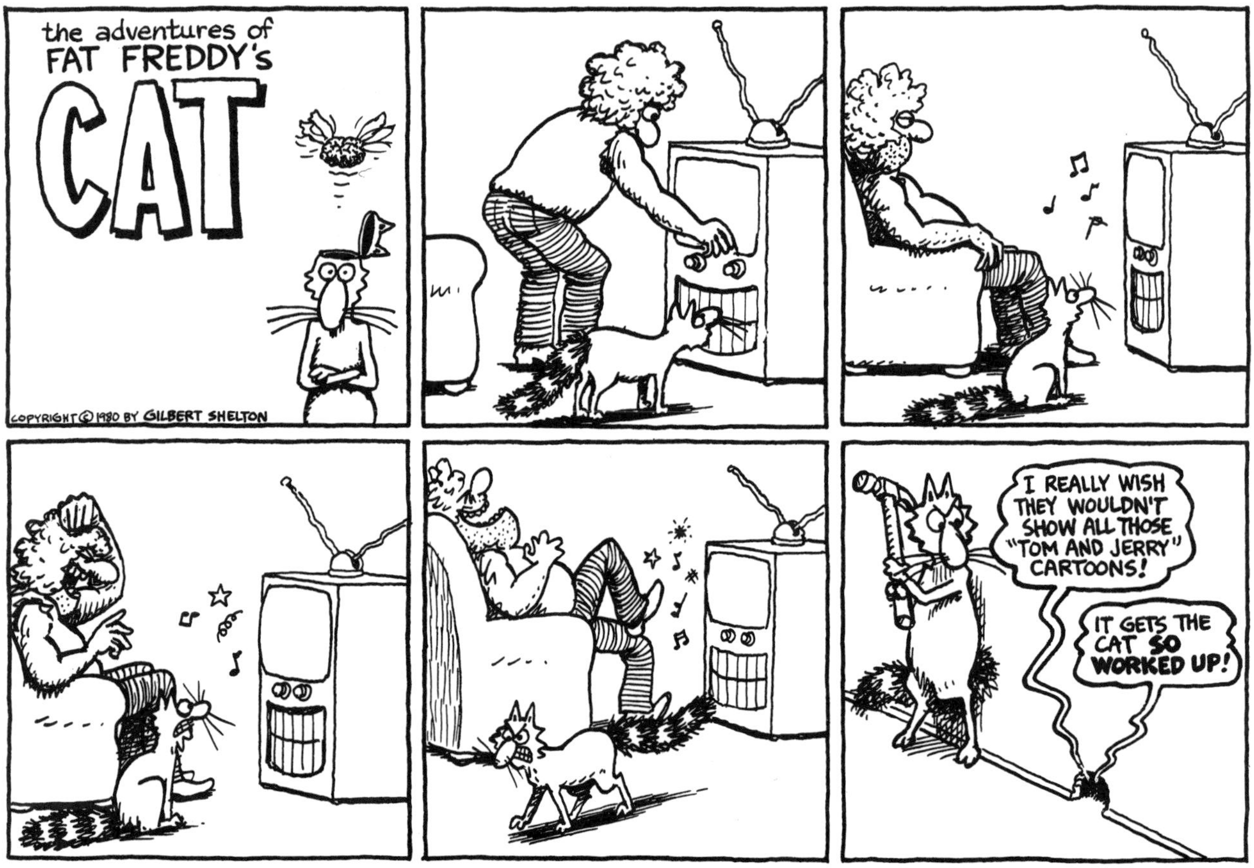
the adventures of
FAT FREDDY's
CAT
COPYRIGHT © 1980 BY GILBERT SHELTON
I REALLY WISH THEY WOULDN'T SHOW ALL THOSE "TOM AND JERRY" CARTOONS!
IT GETS THE CAT SO WORKED UP!

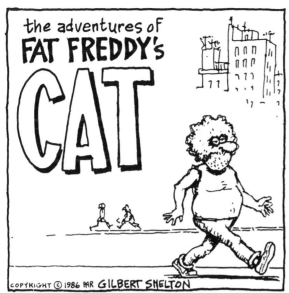

the adventures of
FAT FREDDY's
CAT

COPYRIGHT © 1986 PAR *GILBERT SHELTON*

WOW! THAT GUY HAS TRAINED HIS **CAT** TO RIDE AROUND ON HIS **SHOULDERS**! WHAT A SWELL WAY TO STRIKE UP **CONVERSATIONS** WITH THE **GIRLS**!

HEEERE, KITTY KITTY KITTY! I WANNA TEACH YOU A **TRICK**!

HMMM! I CAN TELL THIS IS GOING TO TAKE SOME **SERIOUS TEACHING**!

SEVERAL WEEKS LATER:

I SEE YOU FINALLY GOT YOUR **CAT** TO RIDE AROUND ON YOUR **SHOULDERS**!

YEAH, BUT THE GIRLS STILL WON'T TALK TO ME!

I BET THE S&M GUYS THINK IT'S CUTE, THOUGH!

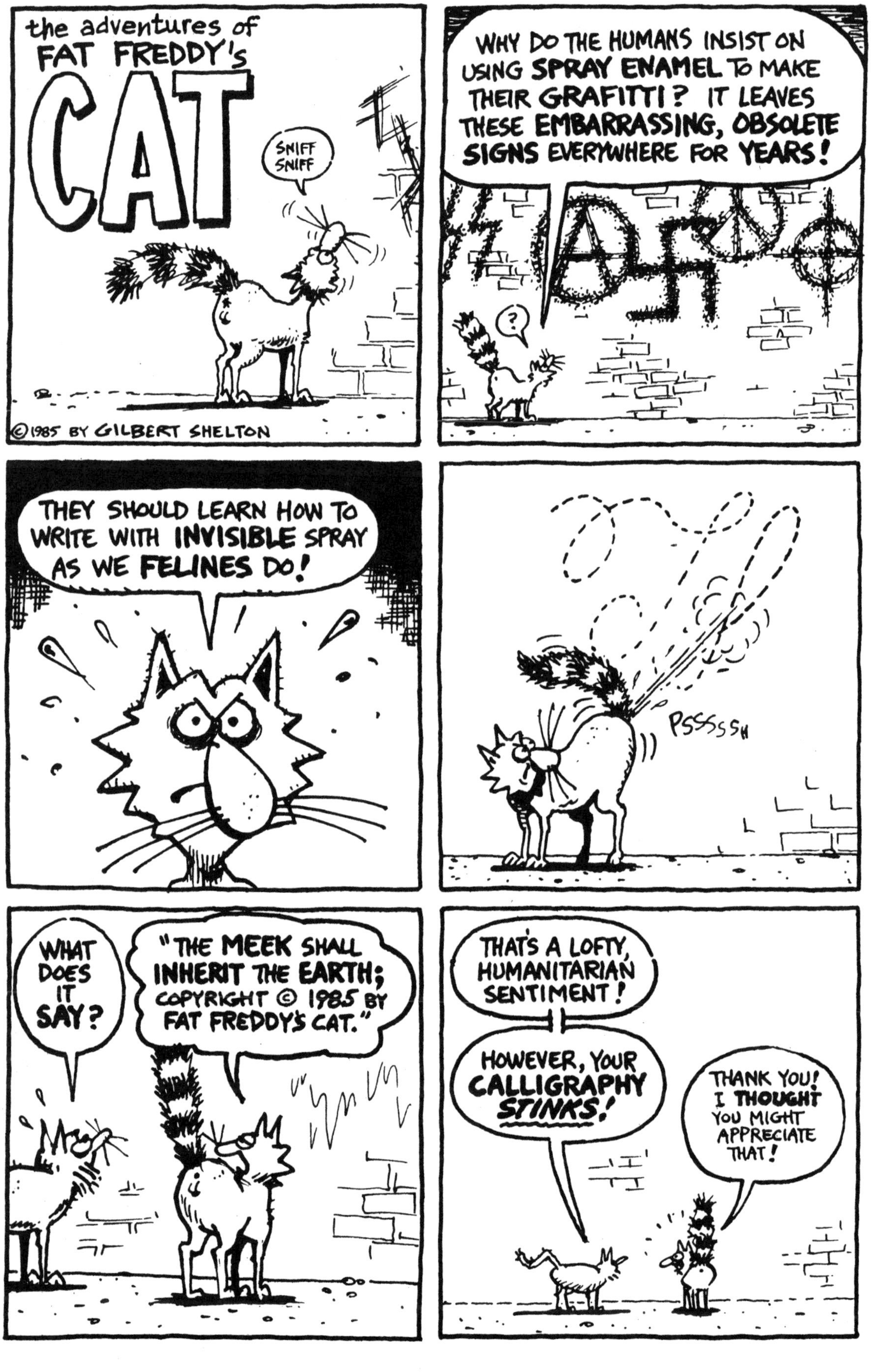
the adventures of
FAT FREDDY's
CAT
SNIFF SNIFF
©1985 BY GILBERT SHELTON
WHY DO THE HUMANS INSIST ON USING SPRAY ENAMEL TO MAKE THEIR GRAFITTI? IT LEAVES THESE EMBARRASSING, OBSOLETE SIGNS EVERYWHERE FOR YEARS!
?
THEY SHOULD LEARN HOW TO WRITE WITH INVISIBLE SPRAY AS WE FELINES DO!
PSSSSSH
WHAT DOES IT SAY?
"THE MEEK SHALL INHERIT THE EARTH; COPYRIGHT © 1985 BY FAT FREDDY'S CAT."
THAT'S A LOFTY, HUMANITARIAN SENTIMENT!
HOWEVER, YOUR CALLIGRAPHY STINKS!
THANK YOU! I THOUGHT YOU MIGHT APPRECIATE THAT!

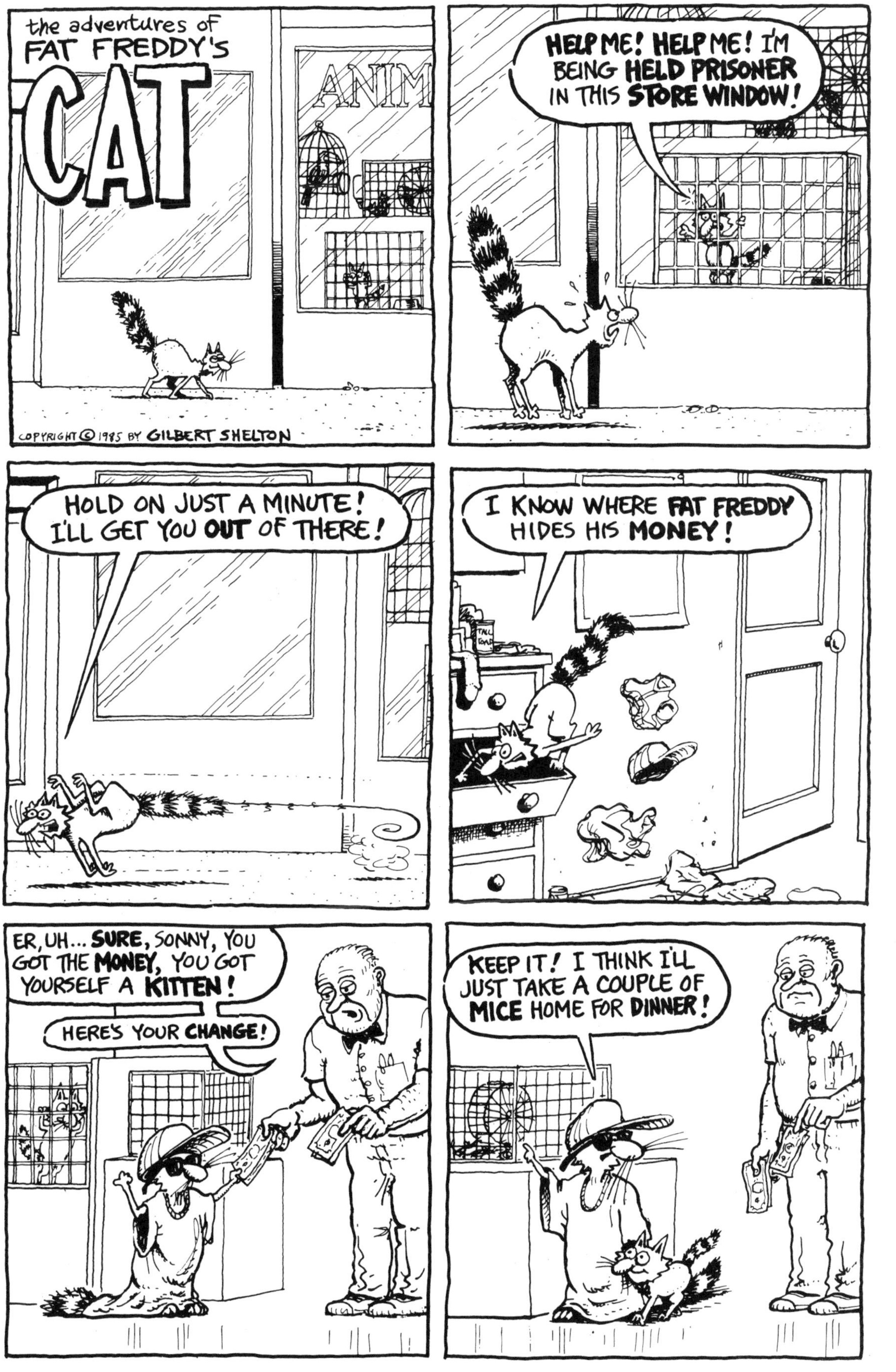
the adventures of
FAT FREDDY'S
CAT
COPYRIGHT © 1985 BY GILBERT SHELTON
ANIM
HELP ME! HELP ME! I'M BEING HELD PRISONER IN THIS STORE WINDOW!
HOLD ON JUST A MINUTE! I'LL GET YOU OUT OF THERE!
I KNOW WHERE FAT FREDDY HIDES HIS MONEY!
ER, UH... SURE, SONNY, YOU GOT THE MONEY, YOU GOT YOURSELF A KITTEN!
HERE'S YOUR CHANGE!
KEEP IT! I THINK I'LL JUST TAKE A COUPLE OF MICE HOME FOR DINNER!

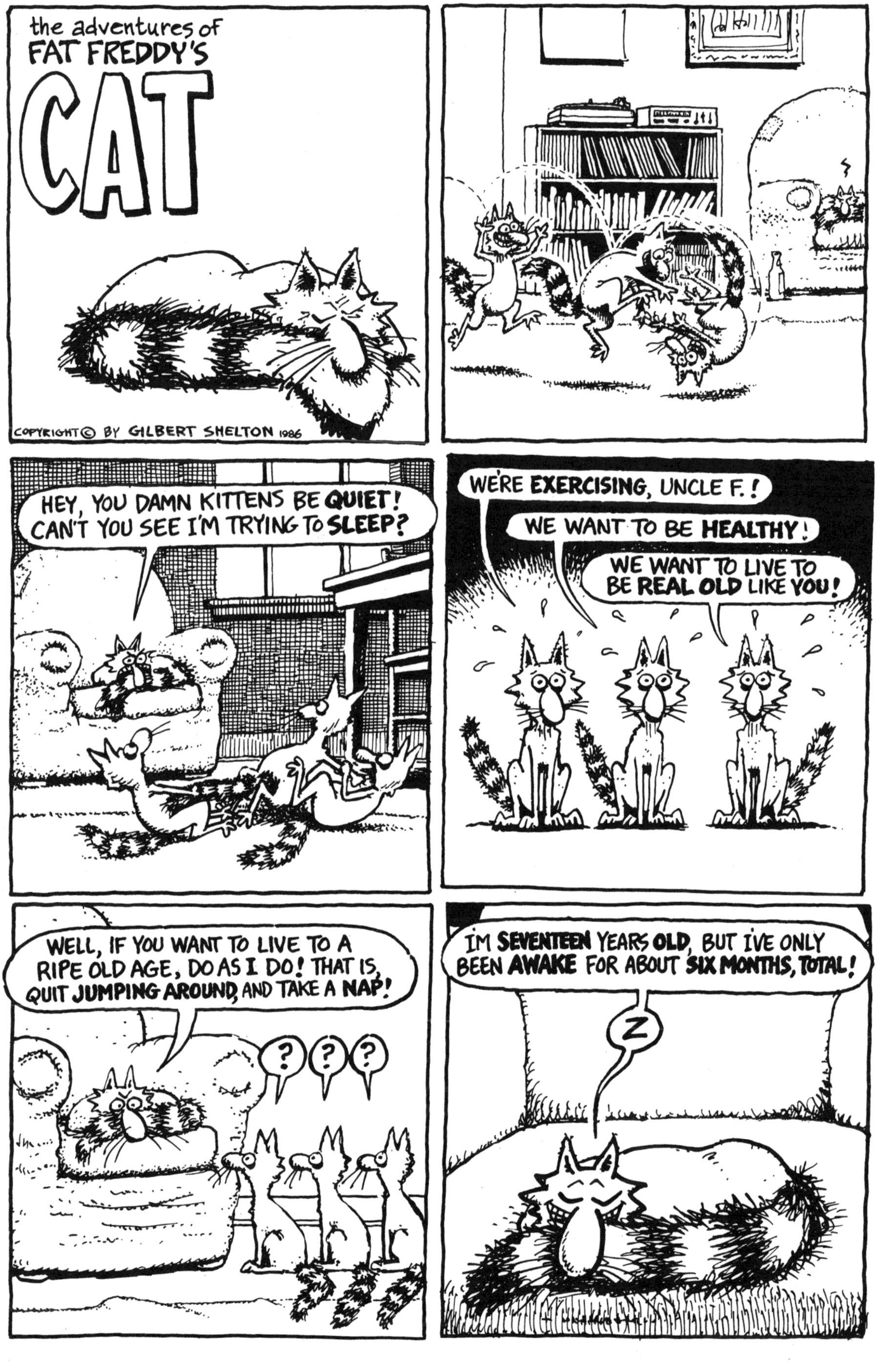
the adventures of
FAT FREDDY'S
CAT
COPYRIGHT © BY GILBERT SHELTON 1986
HEY, YOU DAMN KITTENS BE QUIET! CAN'T YOU SEE I'M TRYING TO SLEEP?
WE'RE EXERCISING, UNCLE F.!
WE WANT TO BE HEALTHY!
WE WANT TO LIVE TO BE REAL OLD LIKE YOU!
WELL, IF YOU WANT TO LIVE TO A RIPE OLD AGE, DO AS I DO! THAT IS, QUIT JUMPING AROUND, AND TAKE A NAP!
?
?
?
I'M SEVENTEEN YEARS OLD, BUT I'VE ONLY BEEN AWAKE FOR ABOUT SIX MONTHS, TOTAL!
Z

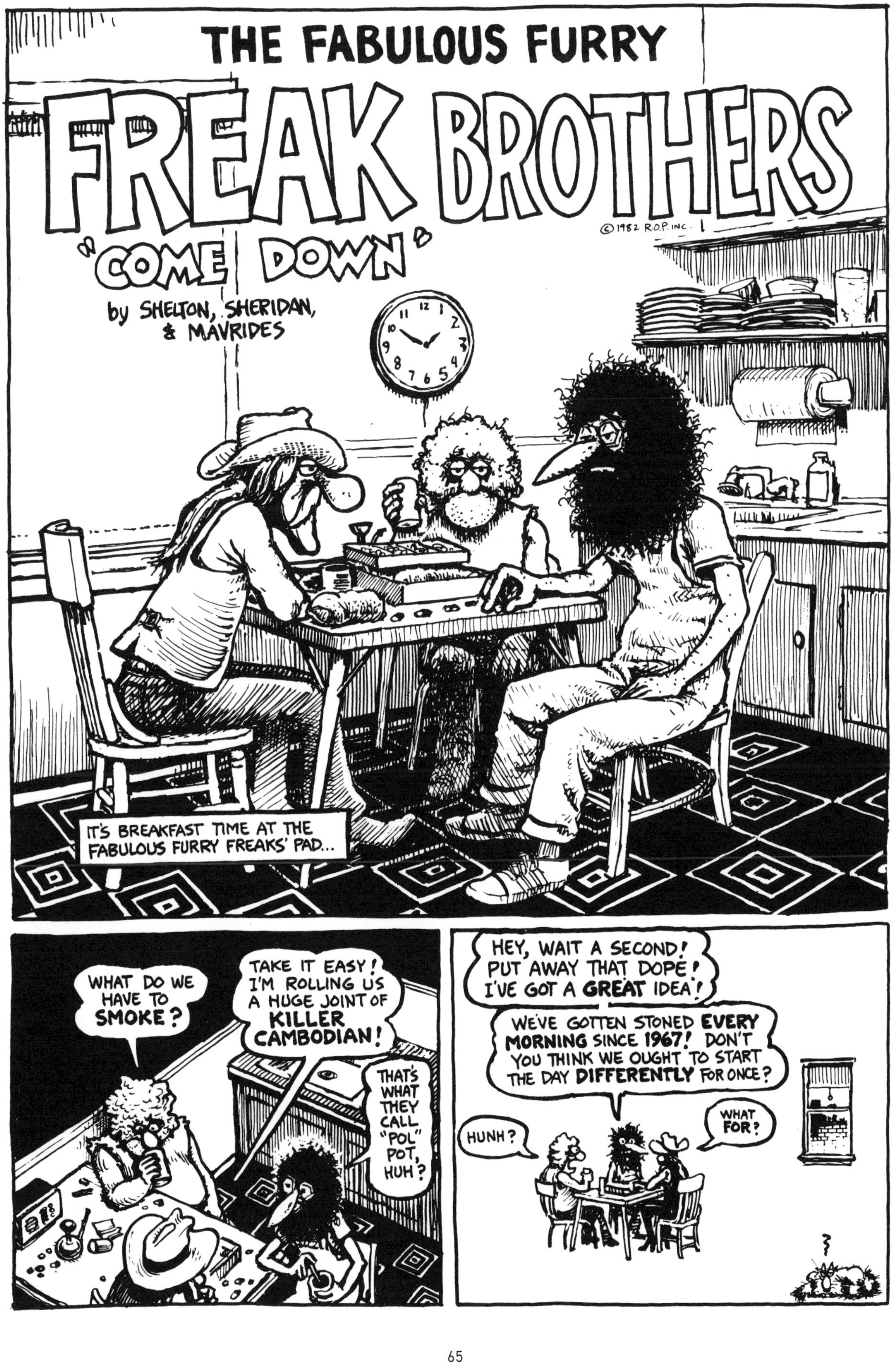
THE FABULOUS FURRY
FREAK BROTHERS
©1982 R.O.P. INC.
"COME DOWN"
by SHELTON, SHERIDAN, & MAVRIDES
IT'S BREAKFAST TIME AT THE FABULOUS FURRY FREAKS' PAD...
WHAT DO WE HAVE TO SMOKE?
TAKE IT EASY! I'M ROLLING US A HUGE JOINT OF KILLER CAMBODIAN!
THAT'S WHAT THEY CALL "POL" POT, HUH?
HEY, WAIT A SECOND! PUT AWAY THAT DOPE! I'VE GOT A GREAT IDEA!
WE'VE GOTTEN STONED EVERY MORNING SINCE 1967! DON'T YOU THINK WE OUGHT TO START THE DAY DIFFERENTLY FOR ONCE?
HUNH?
WHAT FOR?

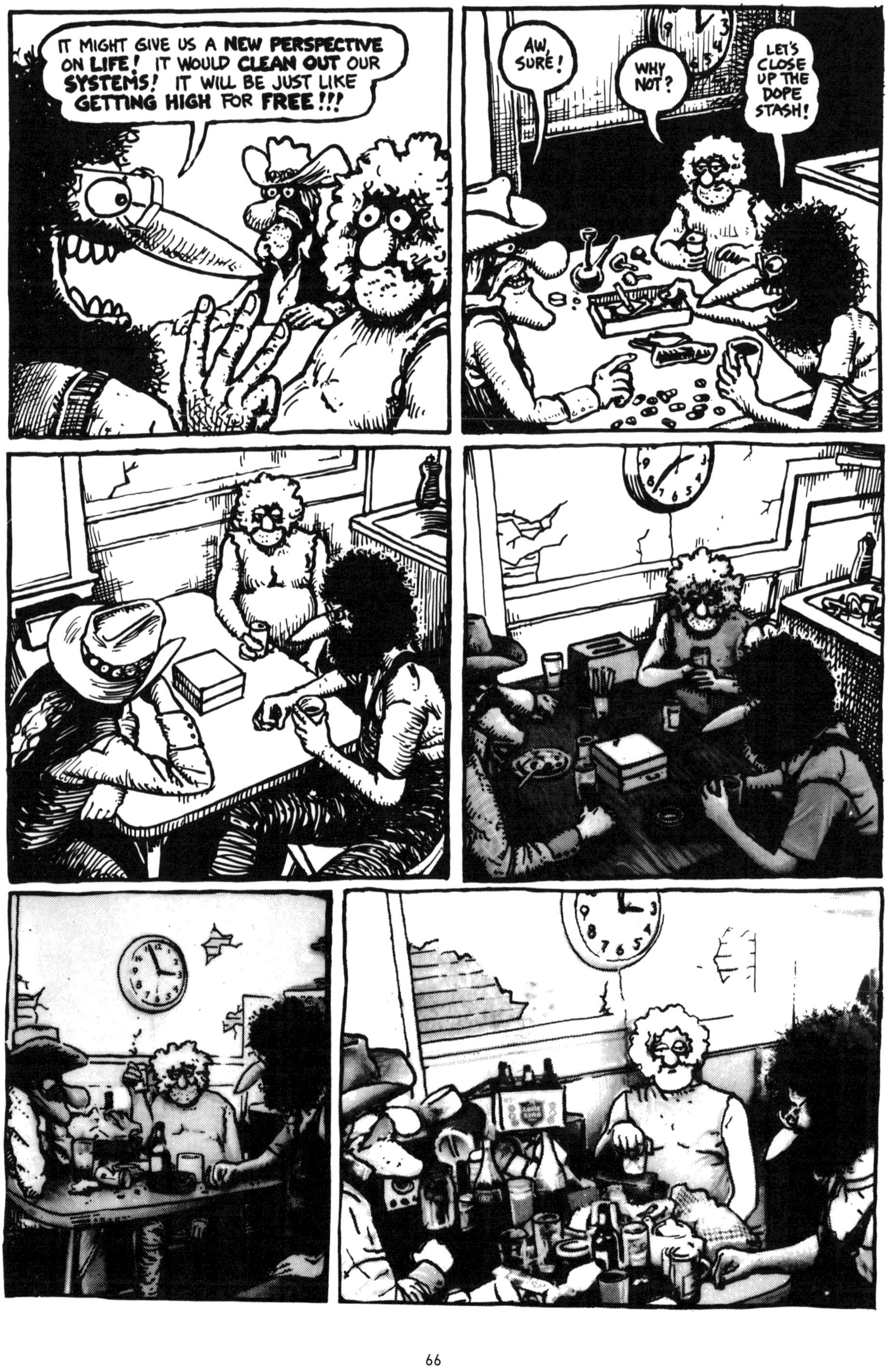
IT MIGHT GIVE US A NEW PERSPECTIVE ON LIFE! IT WOULD CLEAN OUT OUR SYSTEMS! IT WILL BE JUST LIKE GETTING HIGH FOR FREE!!!
AW, SURE!
WHY NOT?
LET'S CLOSE UP THE DOPE STASH!

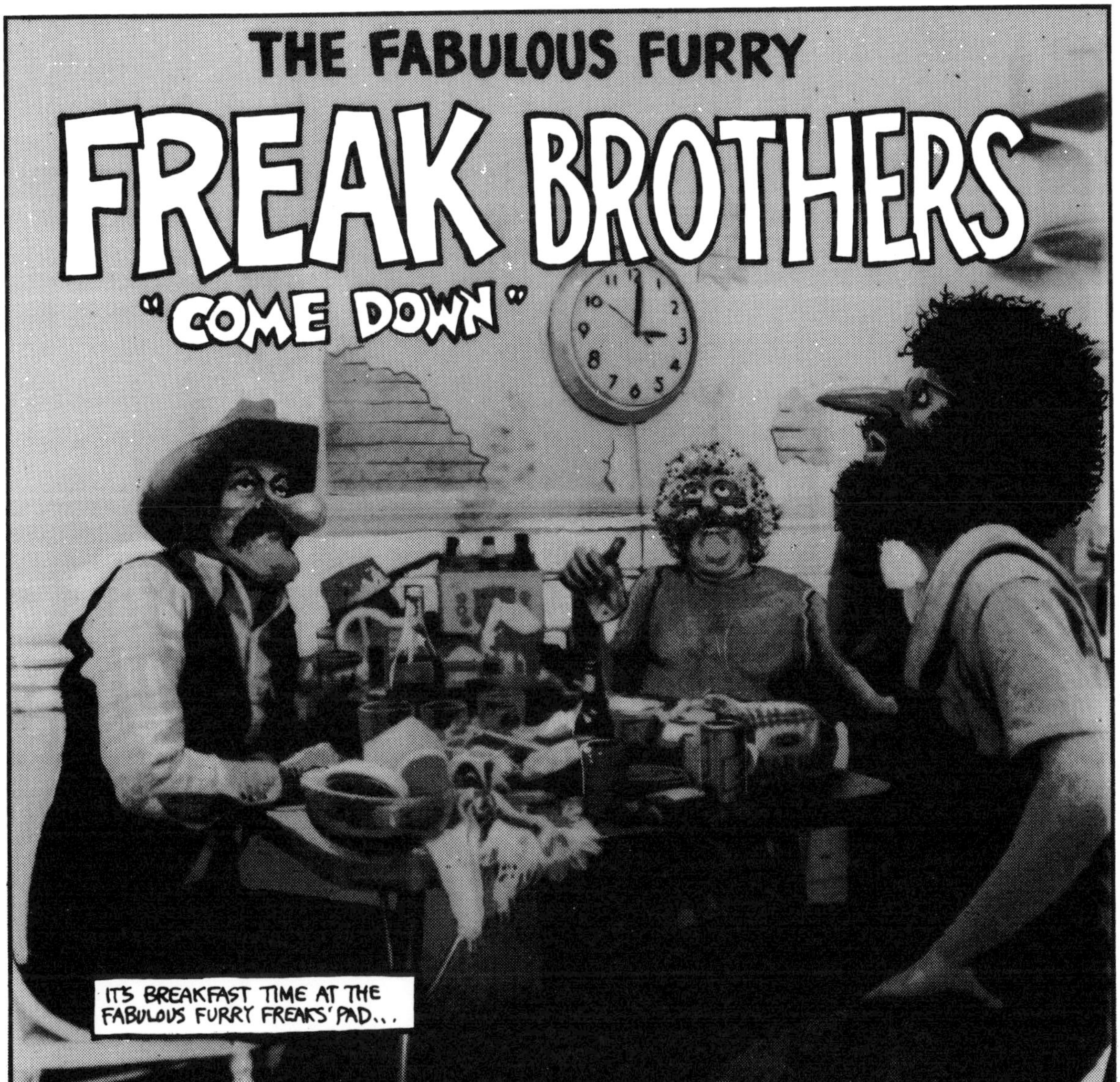
THE FABULOUS FURRY
FREAK BROTHERS
"COME DOWN"
IT'S BREAKFAST TIME AT THE FABULOUS FURRY FREAKS' PAD...

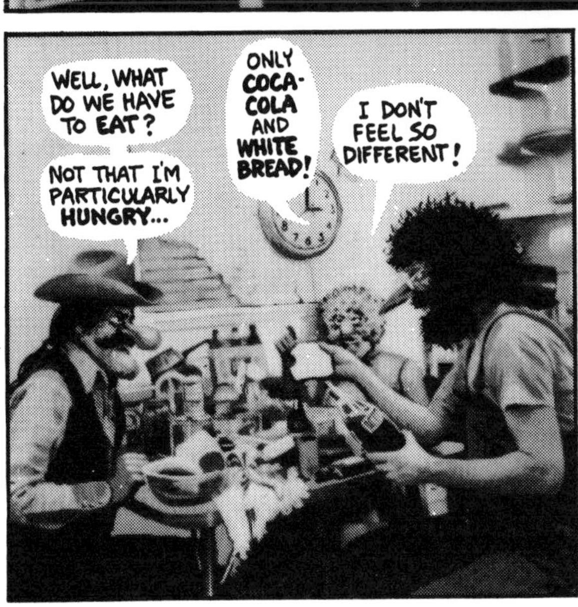
WELL, WHAT DO WE HAVE TO EAT?
NOT THAT I'M PARTICULARLY HUNGRY...
ONLY COCA-COLA AND WHITE BREAD!
I DON'T FEEL SO DIFFERENT!

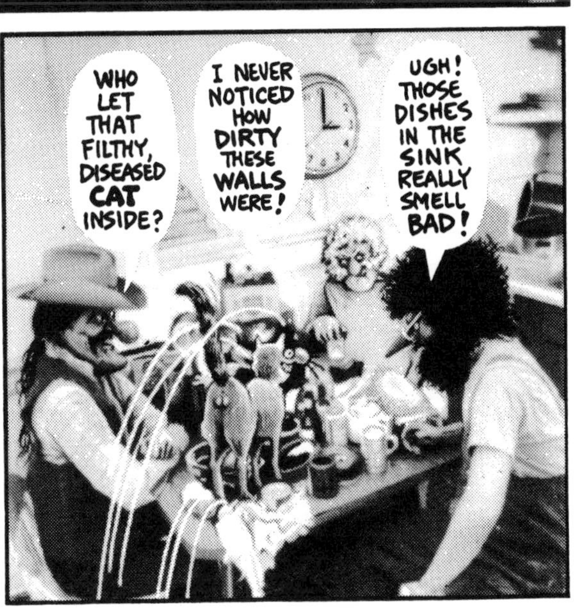
WHO LET THAT FILTHY, DISEASED CAT INSIDE?
I NEVER NOTICED HOW DIRTY THESE WALLS WERE!
UGH! THOSE DISHES IN THE SINK REALLY SMELL BAD!

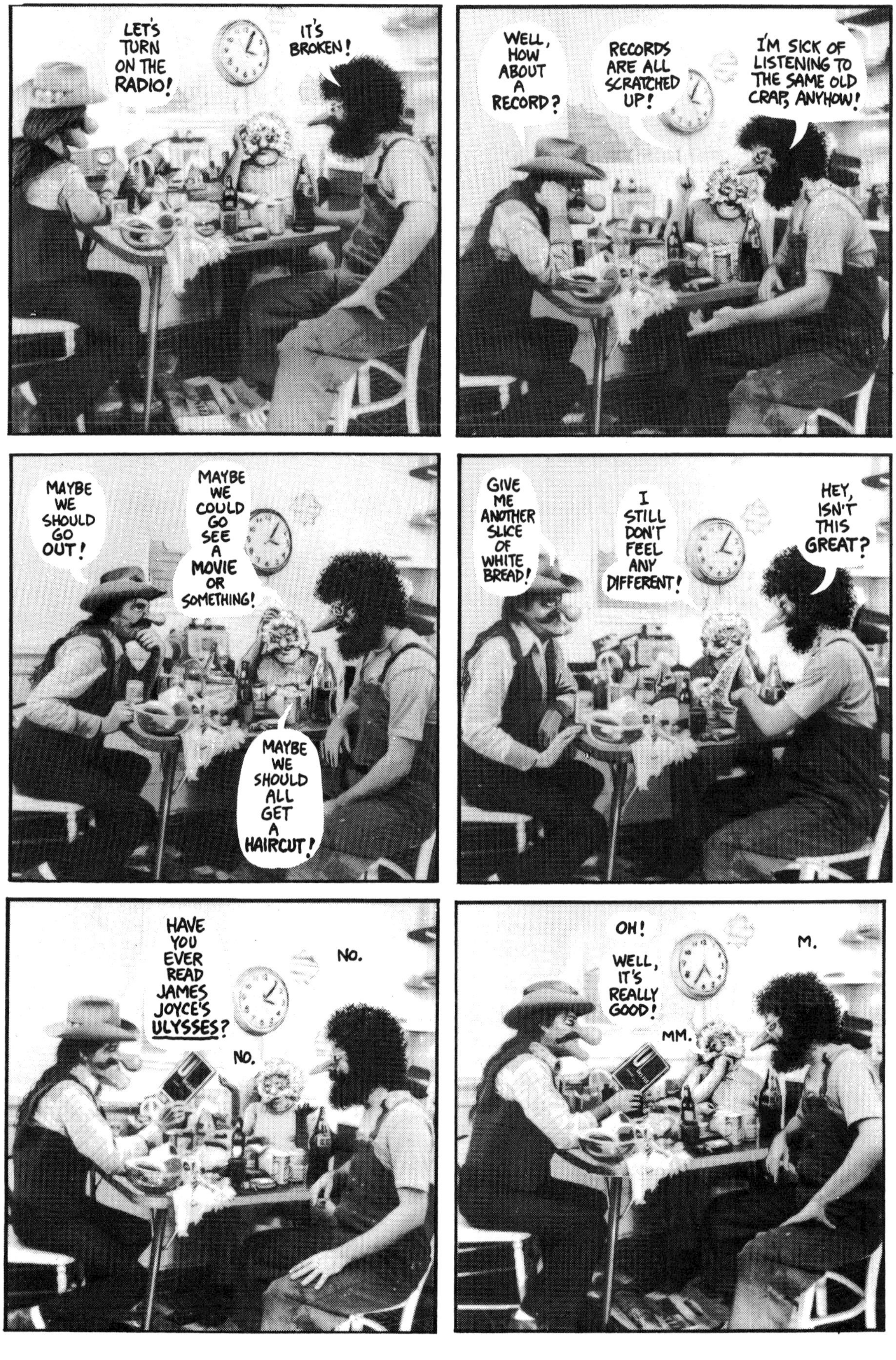

LET'S TURN ON THE RADIO!
IT'S BROKEN!
WELL, HOW ABOUT A RECORD?
RECORDS ARE ALL SCRATCHED UP!
I'M SICK OF LISTENING TO THE SAME OLD CRAP, ANYHOW!
MAYBE WE SHOULD GO OUT!
MAYBE WE COULD GO SEE A MOVIE OR SOMETHING!
MAYBE WE SHOULD ALL GET A HAIRCUT!
GIVE ME ANOTHER SLICE OF WHITE BREAD!
I STILL DON'T FEEL ANY DIFFERENT!
HEY, ISN'T THIS GREAT?
HAVE YOU EVER READ JAMES JOYCE'S ULYSSES?
NO.
NO.
OH!
WELL, IT'S REALLY GOOD!
M.
MM.

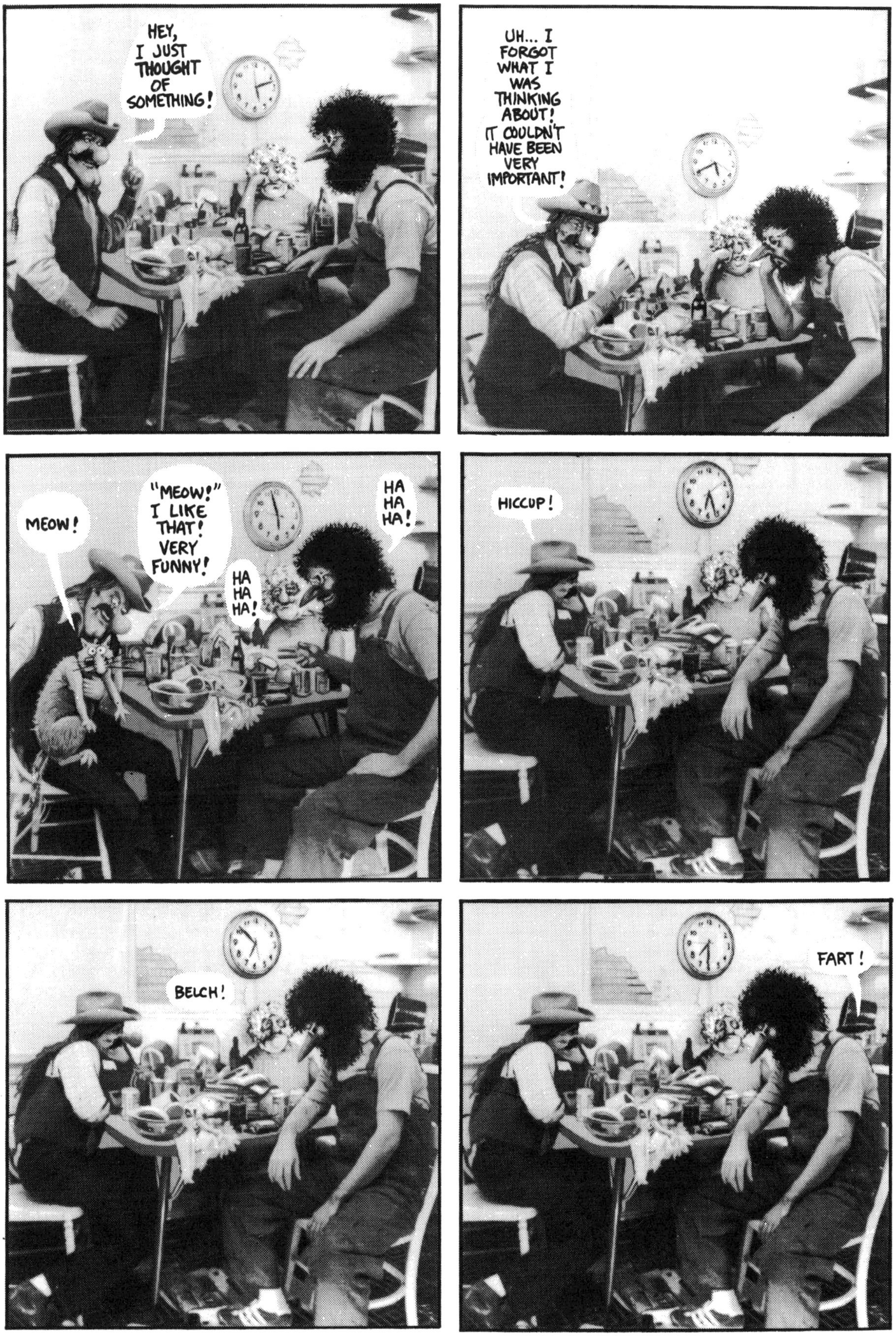
HEY, I JUST THOUGHT OF SOMETHING!
UH... I FORGOT WHAT I WAS THINKING ABOUT! IT COULDN'T HAVE BEEN VERY IMPORTANT!
MEOW!
"MEOW!" I LIKE THAT! VERY FUNNY!
HA HA HA!
HA HA HA!
HICCUP!
BELCH!
FART!

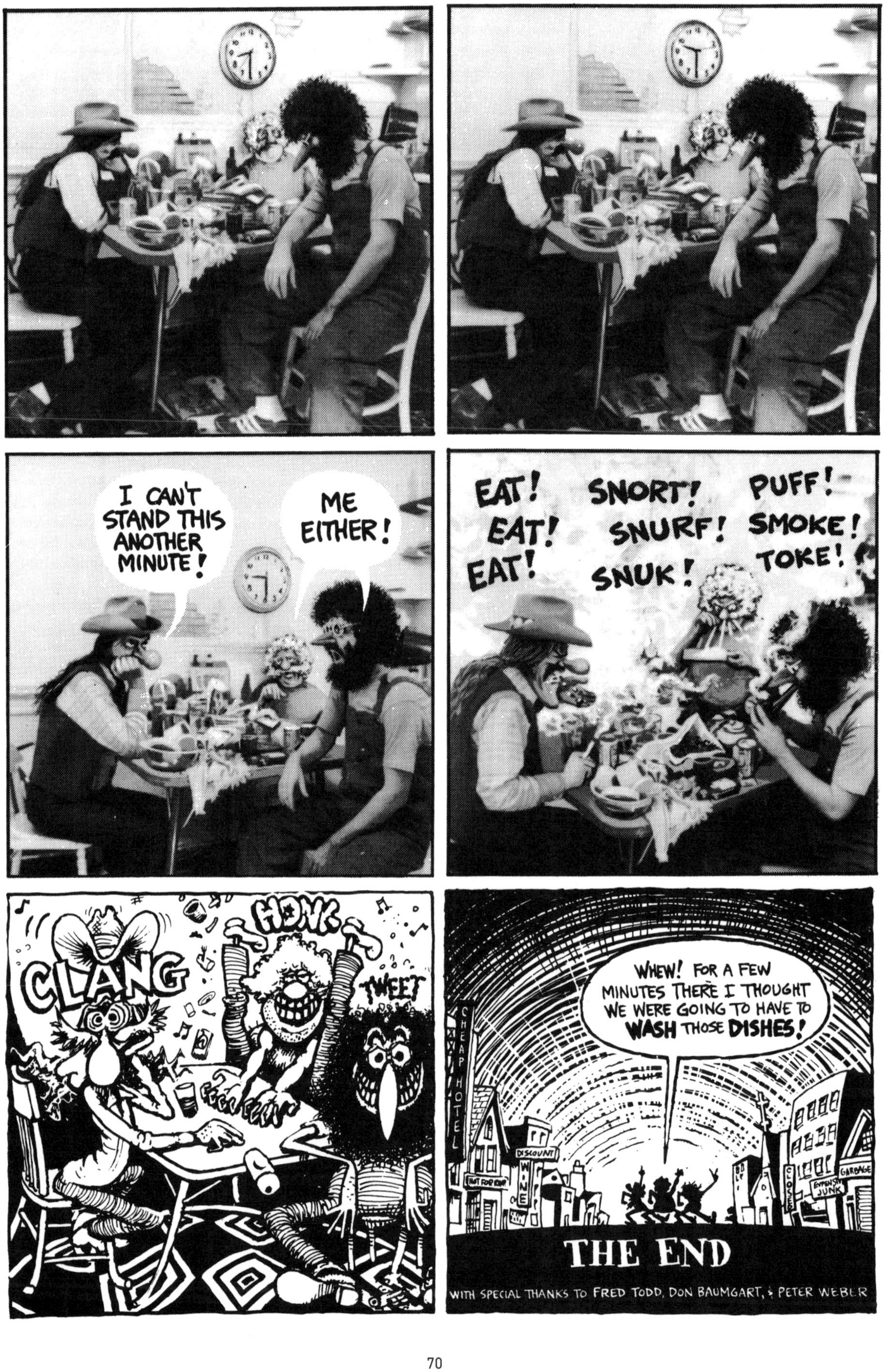
I CAN'T STAND THIS ANOTHER MINUTE!
ME EITHER!
EAT! EAT! EAT!
SNORT! SNURF! SNUK!
PUFF! SMOKE! TOKE!
CLANG
HONK
TWEET
WHEW! FOR A FEW MINUTES THERE I THOUGHT WE WERE GOING TO HAVE TO WASH THOSE DISHES!
CHEAP HOTEL
DISCOUNT
WINE
GARBAGE
JUNK
THE END
WITH SPECIAL THANKS TO FRED TODD, DON BAUMGART, & PETER WEBER

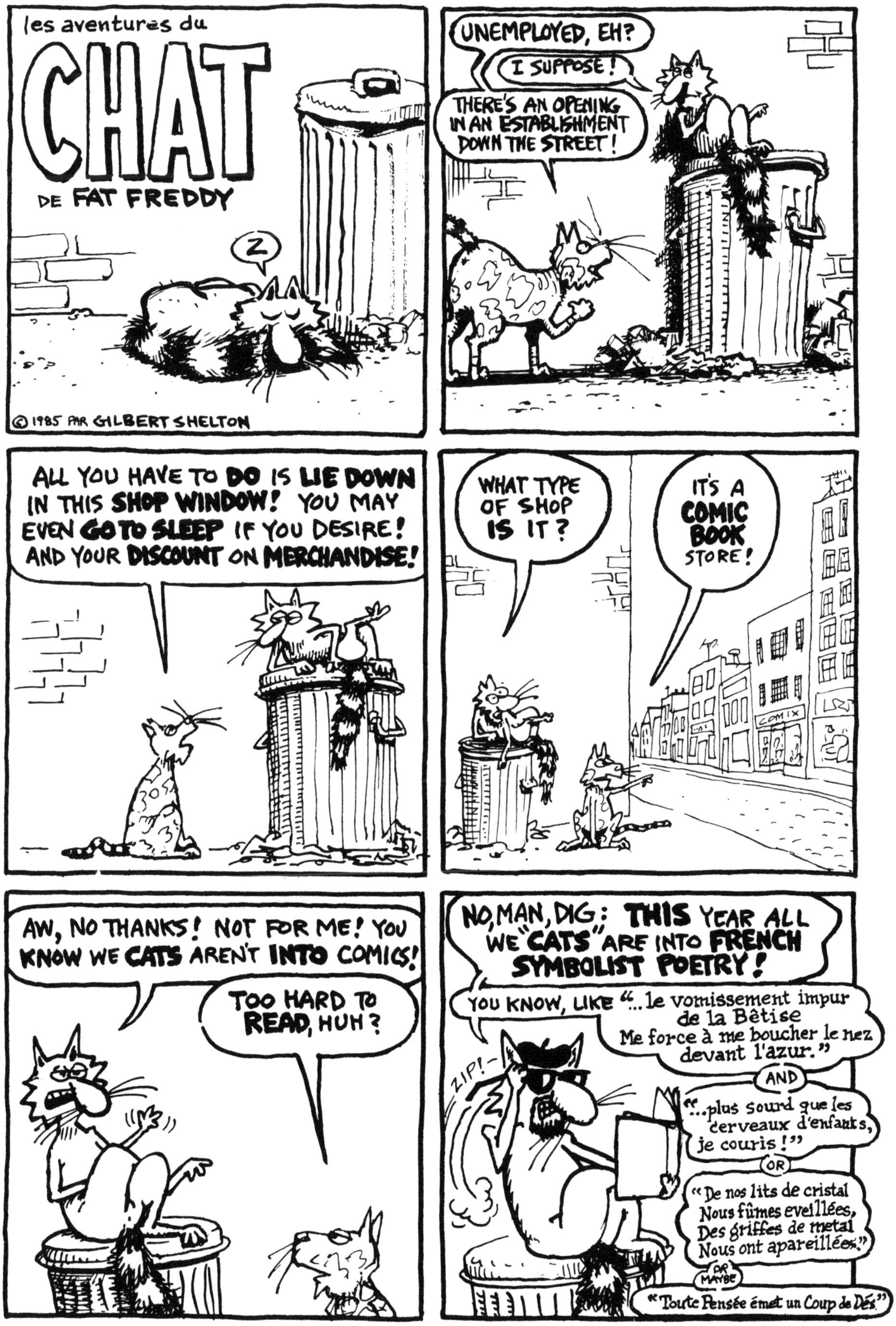

les aventures du
CHAT
DE FAT FREDDY
Z
© 1985 PAR GILBERT SHELTON
UNEMPLOYED, EH?
I SUPPOSE!
THERE'S AN OPENING IN AN ESTABLISHMENT DOWN THE STREET!
ALL YOU HAVE TO DO IS LIE DOWN IN THIS SHOP WINDOW! YOU MAY EVEN GO TO SLEEP IF YOU DESIRE! AND YOUR DISCOUNT ON MERCHANDISE!
WHAT TYPE OF SHOP IS IT?
IT'S A COMIC BOOK STORE!
COMIX
AW, NO THANKS! NOT FOR ME! YOU KNOW WE CATS AREN'T INTO COMICS!
TOO HARD TO READ, HUH?
NO, MAN, DIG: THIS YEAR ALL WE "CATS" ARE INTO FRENCH SYMBOLIST POETRY!
YOU KNOW, LIKE "...le vomissement impur de la Bêtise Me force à me boucher le nez devant l'azur."
AND
"...plus sourd que les cerveaux d'enfants, je couris!"
OR
"De nos lits de cristal Nous fûmes eveillées, Des griffes de metal Nous ont apareillées."
OR MAYBE
"Toute Pensée émet un Coup de Dés."
ZIP!

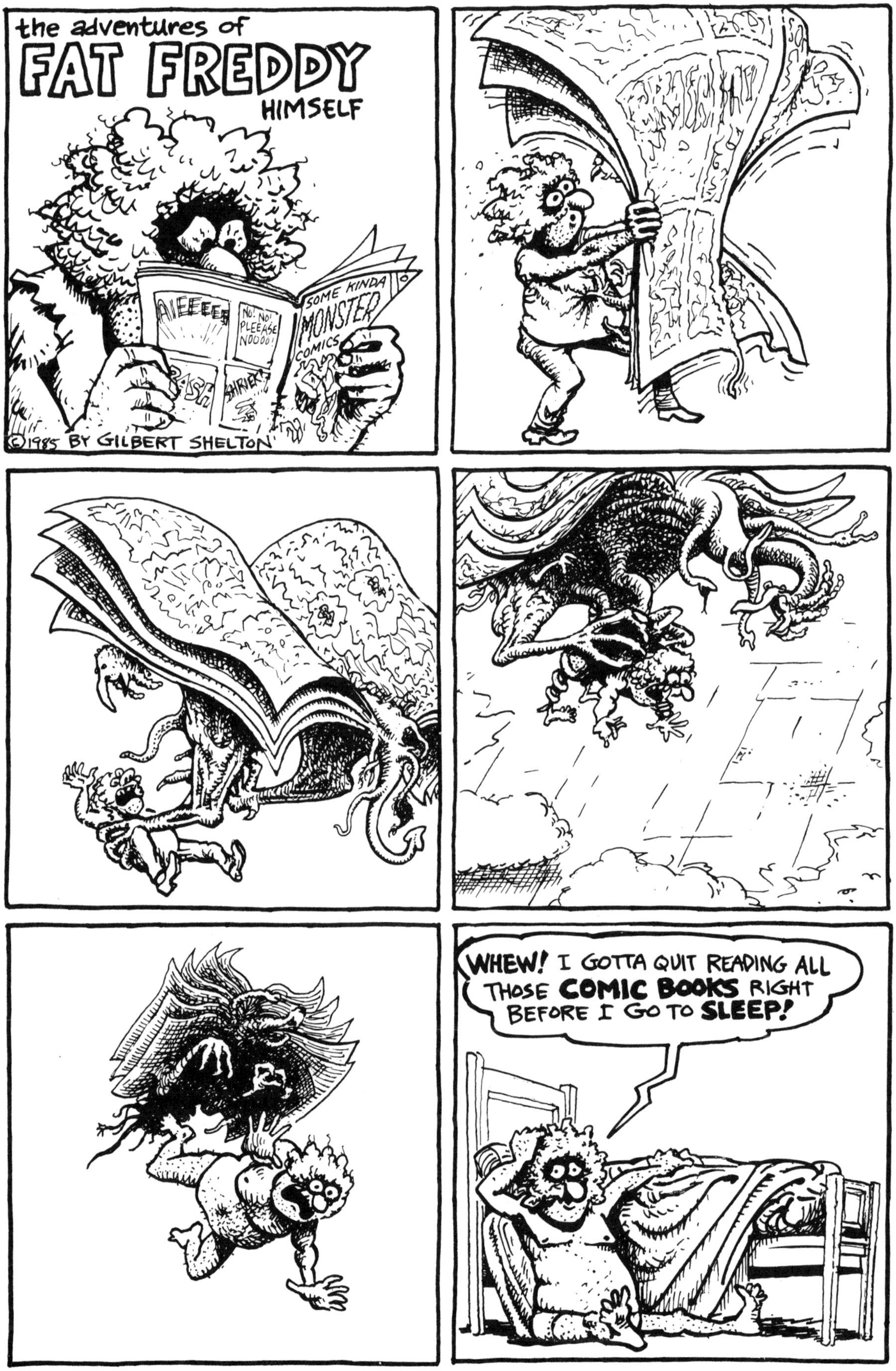
the adventures of
FAT FREDDY
HIMSELF
AIEEEEEE
NO! NO! PLEEASE NOOOO!
SOME KINDA MONSTER COMICS
BASH
SHRIEK
©1985 BY GILBERT SHELTON
WHEW! I GOTTA QUIT READING ALL THOSE COMIC BOOKS RIGHT BEFORE I GO TO SLEEP!

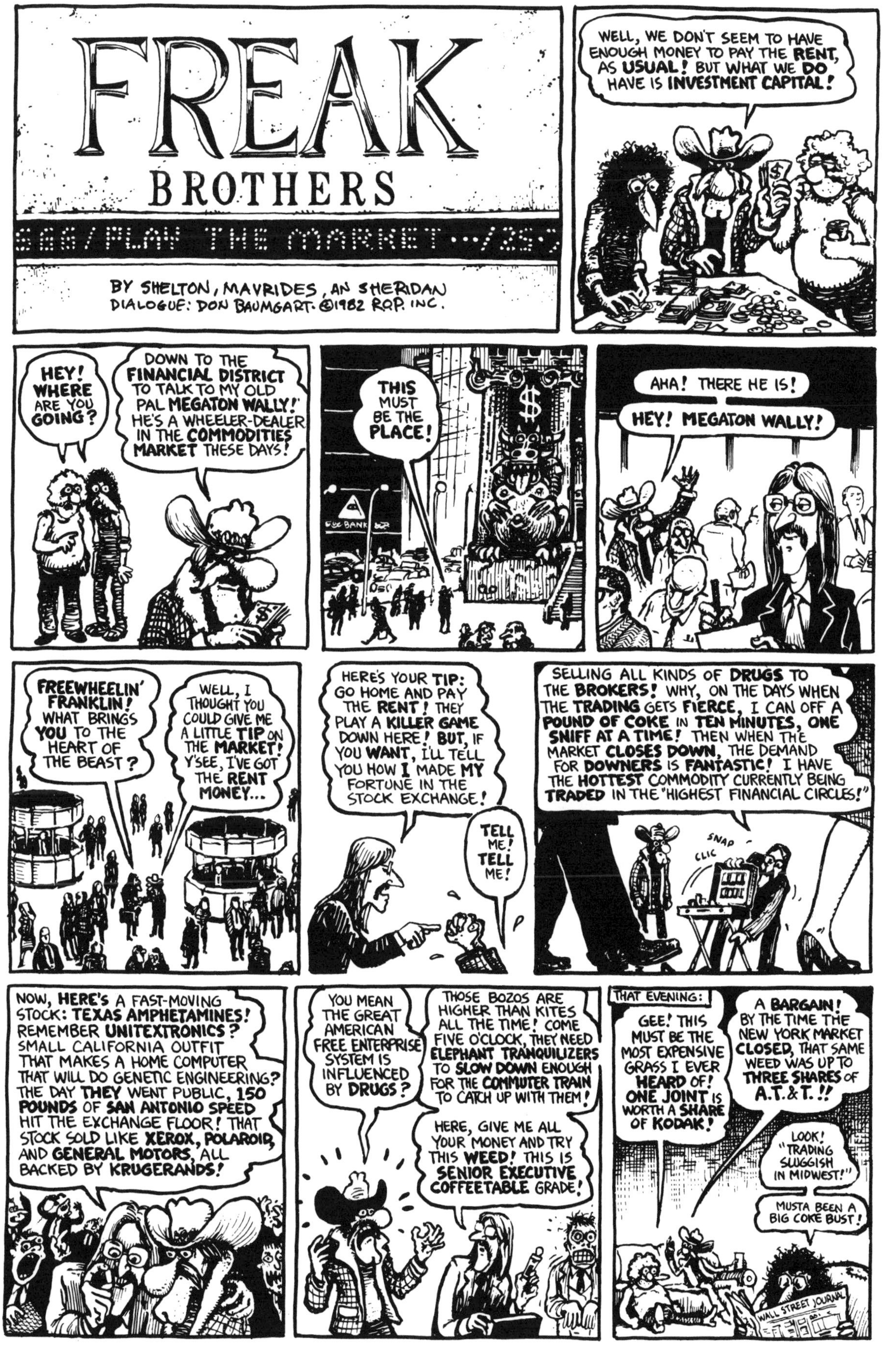

FREAK BROTHERS
PLAY THE MARKET
BY SHELTON, MAVRIDES, AN SHERIDAN
DIALOGUE: DON BAUMGART ©1982 R.O.P. INC.
WELL, WE DON'T SEEM TO HAVE ENOUGH MONEY TO PAY THE RENT, AS USUAL! BUT WHAT WE DO HAVE IS INVESTMENT CAPITAL!
HEY! WHERE ARE YOU GOING?
DOWN TO THE FINANCIAL DISTRICT TO TALK TO MY OLD PAL MEGATON WALLY! HE'S A WHEELER-DEALER IN THE COMMODITIES MARKET THESE DAYS!
THIS MUST BE THE PLACE!
BANK
AHA! THERE HE IS!
HEY! MEGATON WALLY!
FREEWHEELIN' FRANKLIN! WHAT BRINGS YOU TO THE HEART OF THE BEAST?
WELL, I THOUGHT YOU COULD GIVE ME A LITTLE TIP ON THE MARKET! Y'SEE, I'VE GOT THE RENT MONEY...
HERE'S YOUR TIP: GO HOME AND PAY THE RENT! THEY PLAY A KILLER GAME DOWN HERE! BUT, IF YOU WANT, I'LL TELL YOU HOW I MADE MY FORTUNE IN THE STOCK EXCHANGE!
TELL ME! TELL ME!
SELLING ALL KINDS OF DRUGS TO THE BROKERS! WHY, ON THE DAYS WHEN THE TRADING GETS FIERCE, I CAN OFF A POUND OF COKE IN TEN MINUTES, ONE SNIFF AT A TIME! THEN WHEN THE MARKET CLOSES DOWN, THE DEMAND FOR DOWNERS IS FANTASTIC! I HAVE THE HOTTEST COMMODITY CURRENTLY BEING TRADED IN THE "HIGHEST FINANCIAL CIRCLES!"
SNAP
CLIC
NOW, HERE'S A FAST-MOVING STOCK: TEXAS AMPHETAMINES! REMEMBER UNITEXTRONICS? SMALL CALIFORNIA OUTFIT THAT MAKES A HOME COMPUTER THAT WILL DO GENETIC ENGINEERING? THE DAY THEY WENT PUBLIC, 150 POUNDS OF SAN ANTONIO SPEED HIT THE EXCHANGE FLOOR! THAT STOCK SOLD LIKE XEROX, POLAROID, AND GENERAL MOTORS, ALL BACKED BY KRUGERANDS!
YOU MEAN THE GREAT AMERICAN FREE ENTERPRISE SYSTEM IS INFLUENCED BY DRUGS?
THOSE BOZOS ARE HIGHER THAN KITES ALL THE TIME! COME FIVE O'CLOCK, THEY NEED ELEPHANT TRANQUILIZERS TO SLOW DOWN ENOUGH FOR THE COMMUTER TRAIN TO CATCH UP WITH THEM!
HERE, GIVE ME ALL YOUR MONEY AND TRY THIS WEED! THIS IS SENIOR EXECUTIVE COFFEETABLE GRADE!
THAT EVENING:
GEE! THIS MUST BE THE MOST EXPENSIVE GRASS I EVER HEARD OF! ONE JOINT IS WORTH A SHARE OF KODAK!
A BARGAIN! BY THE TIME THE NEW YORK MARKET CLOSED, THAT SAME WEED WAS UP TO THREE SHARES OF A.T.&T.!!
LOOK! "TRADING SLUGGISH IN MIDWEST!"
MUSTA BEEN A BIG COKE BUST!
WALL STREET JOURNAL

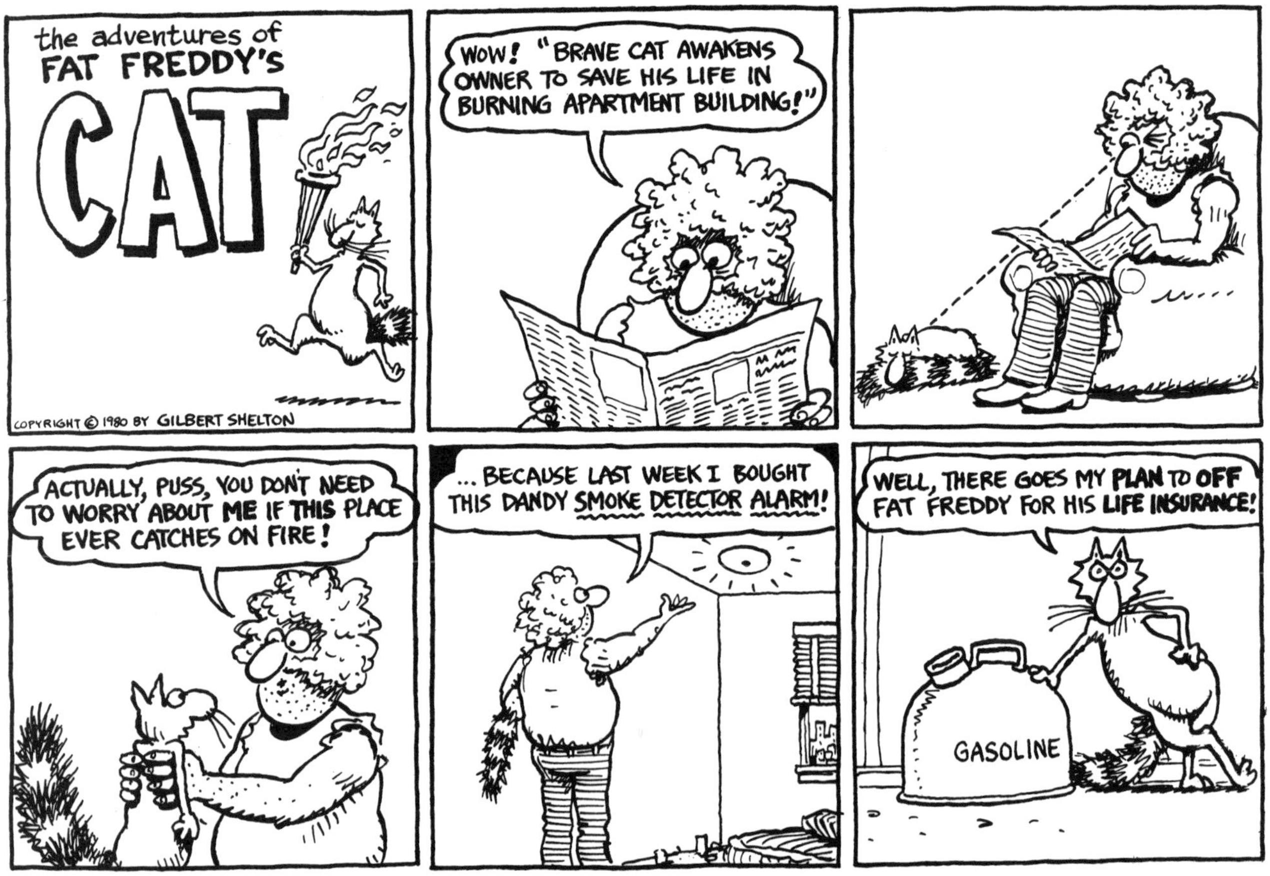
the adventures of
FAT FREDDY'S
CAT
COPYRIGHT © 1980 BY GILBERT SHELTON
WOW! "BRAVE CAT AWAKENS OWNER TO SAVE HIS LIFE IN BURNING APARTMENT BUILDING!"
ACTUALLY, PUSS, YOU DON'T NEED TO WORRY ABOUT ME IF THIS PLACE EVER CATCHES ON FIRE!
...BECAUSE LAST WEEK I BOUGHT THIS DANDY SMOKE DETECTOR ALARM!
WELL, THERE GOES MY PLAN TO OFF FAT FREDDY FOR HIS LIFE INSURANCE!
GASOLINE

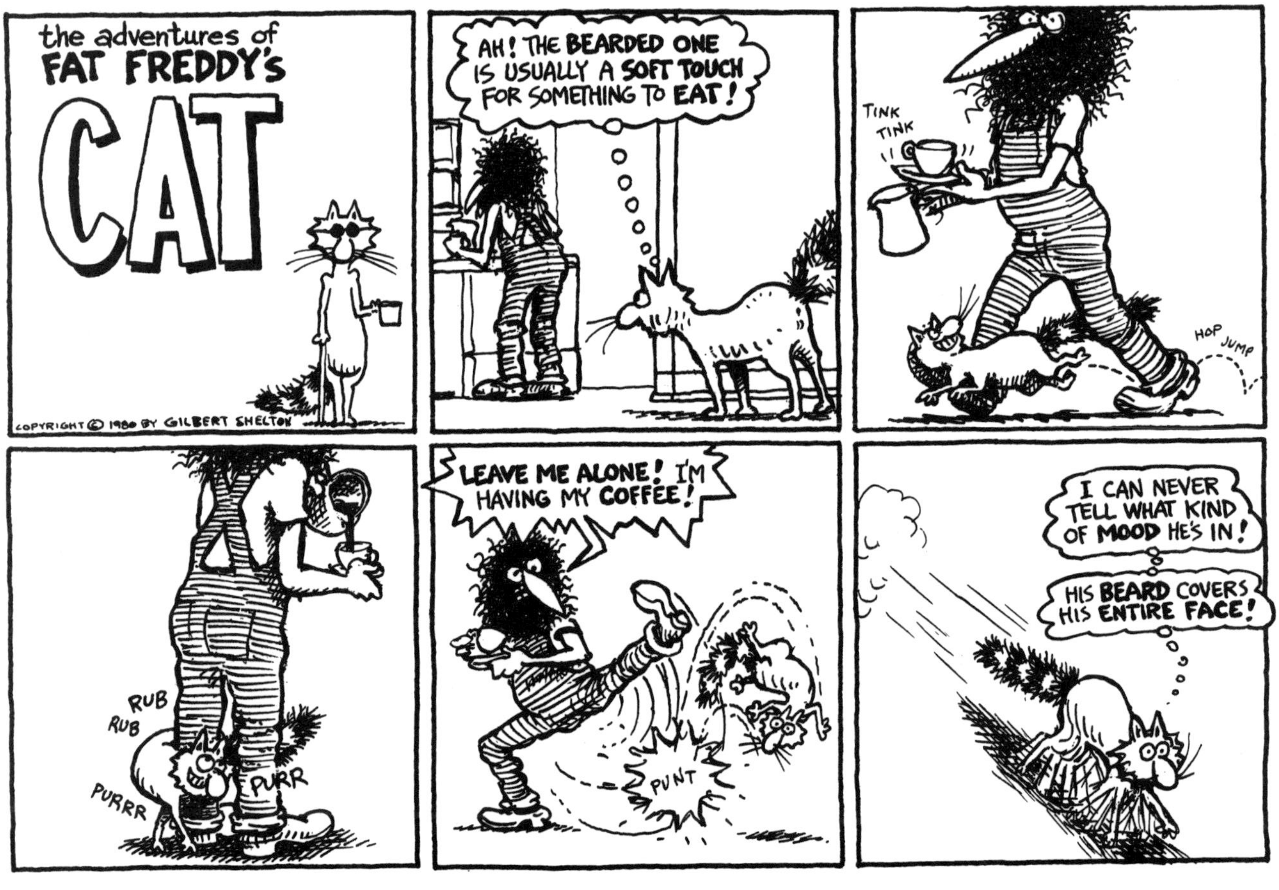
the adventures of
FAT FREDDY's
CAT
COPYRIGHT © 1980 BY GILBERT SHELTON
AH! THE BEARDED ONE IS USUALLY A SOFT TOUCH FOR SOMETHING TO EAT!
TINK
TINK
HOP
JUMP
RUB
RUB
PURRR
PURR
LEAVE ME ALONE! I'M HAVING MY COFFEE!
PUNT
I CAN NEVER TELL WHAT KIND OF MOOD HE'S IN!
HIS BEARD COVERS HIS ENTIRE FACE!

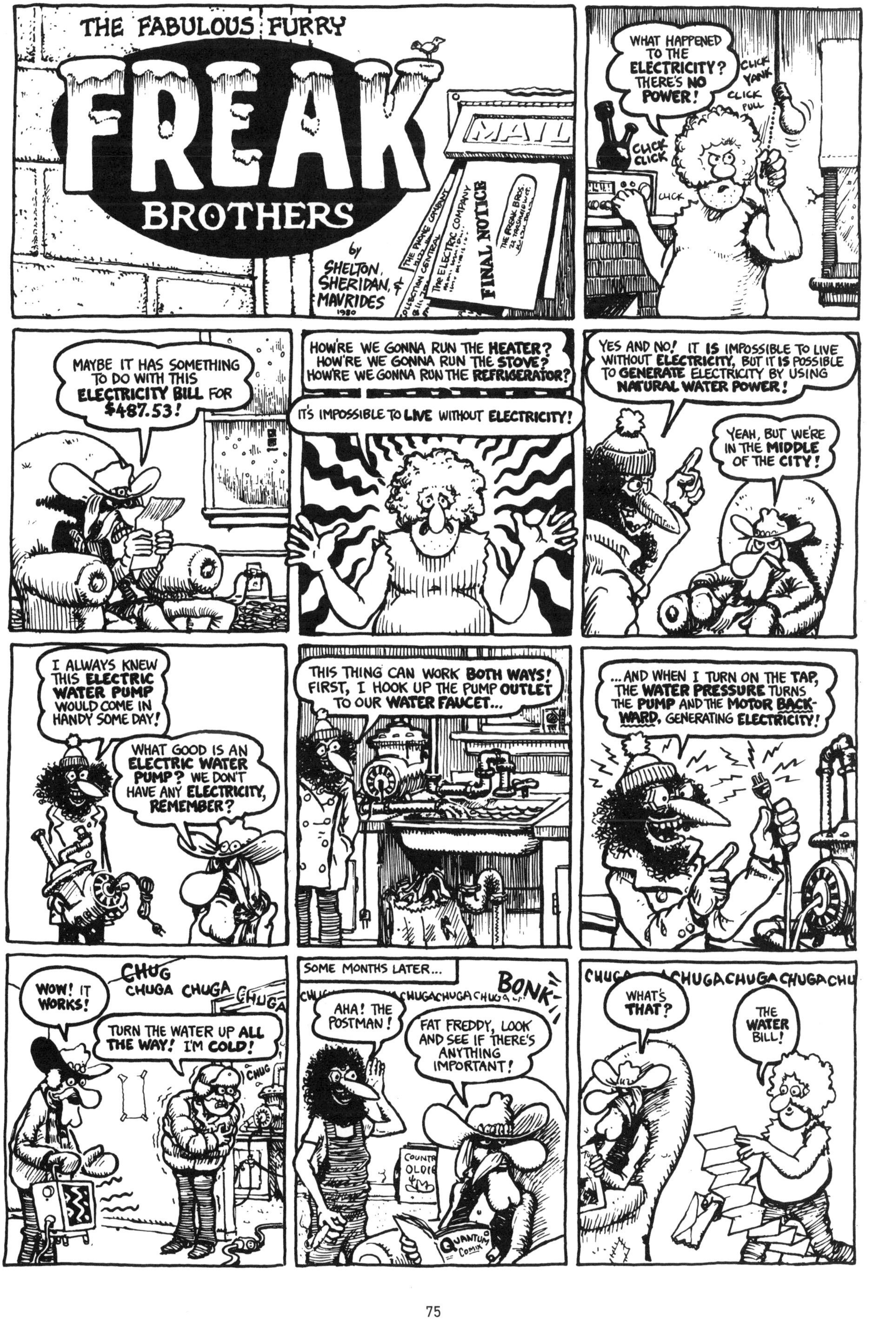

THE FABULOUS FURRY
FREAK
BROTHERS
by SHELTON, SHERIDAN, & MAVRIDES 1980
MAIL
THE PHONE COMPANY
COLLECTION CENTRAL
THE ELECTRIC COMPANY
FINAL NOTICE
WHAT HAPPENED TO THE ELECTRICITY? THERE'S NO POWER!
CLICK YANK
CLICK PULL
CLICK CLICK
CLICK
MAYBE IT HAS SOMETHING TO DO WITH THIS ELECTRICITY BILL FOR $487.53!
HOW'RE WE GONNA RUN THE HEATER? HOW'RE WE GONNA RUN THE STOVE? HOW'RE WE GONNA RUN THE REFRIGERATOR?
IT'S IMPOSSIBLE TO LIVE WITHOUT ELECTRICITY!
YES AND NO! IT IS IMPOSSIBLE TO LIVE WITHOUT ELECTRICITY, BUT IT IS POSSIBLE TO GENERATE ELECTRICITY BY USING NATURAL WATER POWER!
YEAH, BUT WE'RE IN THE MIDDLE OF THE CITY!
I ALWAYS KNEW THIS ELECTRIC WATER PUMP WOULD COME IN HANDY SOME DAY!
WHAT GOOD IS AN ELECTRIC WATER PUMP? WE DON'T HAVE ANY ELECTRICITY, REMEMBER?
THIS THING CAN WORK BOTH WAYS! FIRST, I HOOK UP THE PUMP OUTLET TO OUR WATER FAUCET...
...AND WHEN I TURN ON THE TAP, THE WATER PRESSURE TURNS THE PUMP AND THE MOTOR BACKWARD, GENERATING ELECTRICITY!
CHUG CHUGA CHUGA CHUGA
WOW! IT WORKS!
TURN THE WATER UP ALL THE WAY! I'M COLD!
CHUG
SOME MONTHS LATER...
BONK
AHA! THE POSTMAN!
FAT FREDDY, LOOK AND SEE IF THERE'S ANYTHING IMPORTANT!
QUANTUM COMIX
CHUGACHUGACHUGACHU
WHAT'S THAT?
THE WATER BILL!

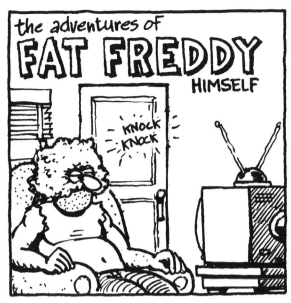

the adventures of
FAT FREDDY
HIMSELF
KNOCK KNOCK
YES?
GOOD AFTERNOON, SIR! I'M TAKING AN OPINION POLL! YOUR ANSWERS WILL BE HELD IN THE STRICTEST CONFIDENCE, OF COURSE!
GO AHEAD! SHOOT!
FIRST OF ALL, WHAT IS YOUR RELIGION?
MY RELIGION? ER, UH... I BELONG TO A LITTLE-KNOWN SECT, ONE THAT YOU'VE PROBABLY NEVER EVEN HEARD OF...
YES?
WE BELIEVE THAT SLEEPING IS A FORM OF PRAYER!
REALLY? HOW INTERESTING! COULD YOU TELL ME MORE?
CERTAINLY! WOULD YOU LIKE TO COME PRAY WITH ME TONIGHT?
GILBERT SHELTON

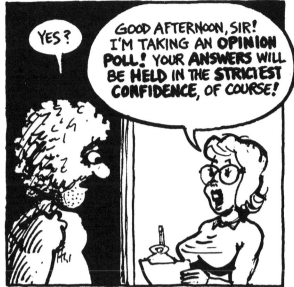

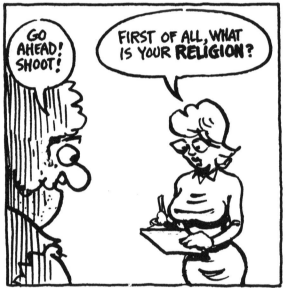

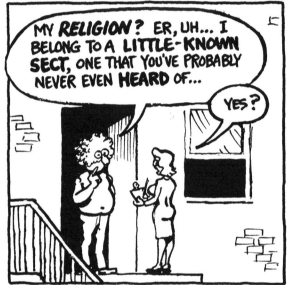

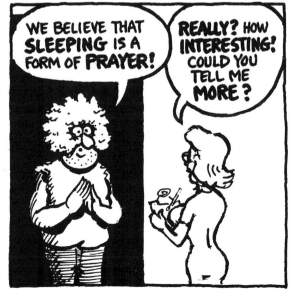

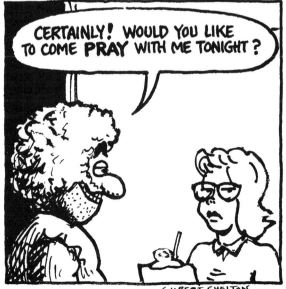

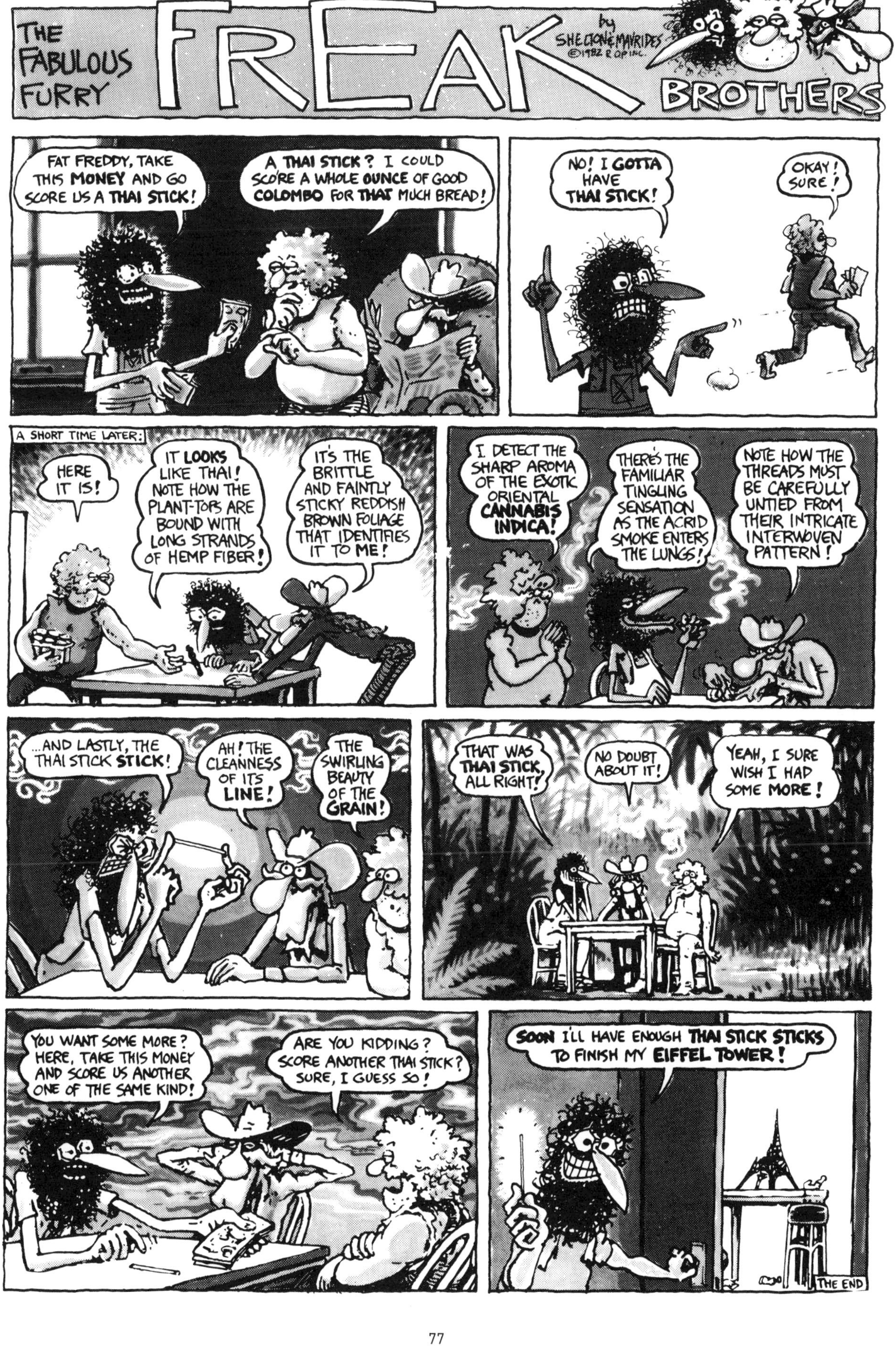

THE FABULOUS FURRY FREAK BROTHERS
by SHELTON & MAVRIDES ©1982 RIP OFF INC.
FAT FREDDY, TAKE THIS MONEY AND GO SCORE US A THAI STICK!
A THAI STICK? I COULD SCORE A WHOLE OUNCE OF GOOD COLOMBO FOR THAT MUCH BREAD!
NO! I GOTTA HAVE THAI STICK!
OKAY! SURE!
A SHORT TIME LATER:
HERE IT IS!
IT LOOKS LIKE THAI! NOTE HOW THE PLANT-TOPS ARE BOUND WITH LONG STRANDS OF HEMP FIBER!
IT'S THE BRITTLE AND FAINTLY STICKY REDDISH BROWN FOLIAGE THAT IDENTIFIES IT TO ME!
I DETECT THE SHARP AROMA OF THE EXOTIC ORIENTAL CANNABIS INDICA!
THERE'S THE FAMILIAR TINGLING SENSATION AS THE ACRID SMOKE ENTERS THE LUNGS!
NOTE HOW THE THREADS MUST BE CAREFULLY UNTIED FROM THEIR INTRICATE INTERWOVEN PATTERN!
...AND LASTLY, THE THAI STICK STICK!
AH! THE CLEANNESS OF ITS LINE!
THE SWIRLING BEAUTY OF THE GRAIN!
THAT WAS THAI STICK, ALL RIGHT!
NO DOUBT ABOUT IT!
YEAH, I SURE WISH I HAD SOME MORE!
YOU WANT SOME MORE? HERE, TAKE THIS MONEY AND SCORE US ANOTHER ONE OF THE SAME KIND!
ARE YOU KIDDING? SCORE ANOTHER THAI STICK? SURE, I GUESS SO!
SOON I'LL HAVE ENOUGH THAI STICK STICKS TO FINISH MY EIFFEL TOWER!
THE END

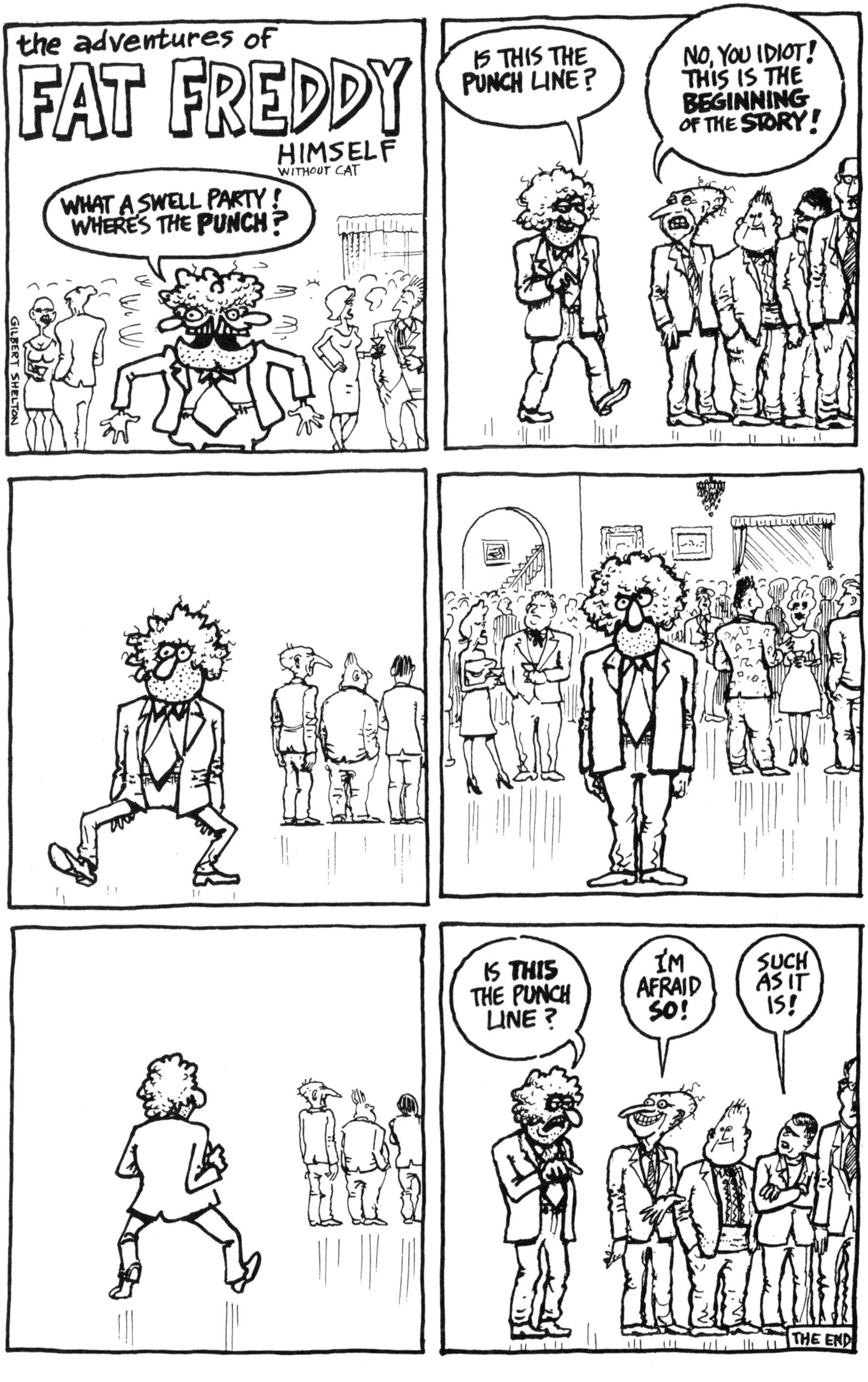
the adventures of
FAT FREDDY
HIMSELF
WITHOUT CAT
GILBERT SHELTON
WHAT A SWELL PARTY! WHERE'S THE PUNCH?
IS THIS THE PUNCH LINE?
NO, YOU IDIOT! THIS IS THE BEGINNING OF THE STORY!
IS THIS THE PUNCH LINE?
I'M AFRAID SO!
SUCH AS IT IS!
THE END

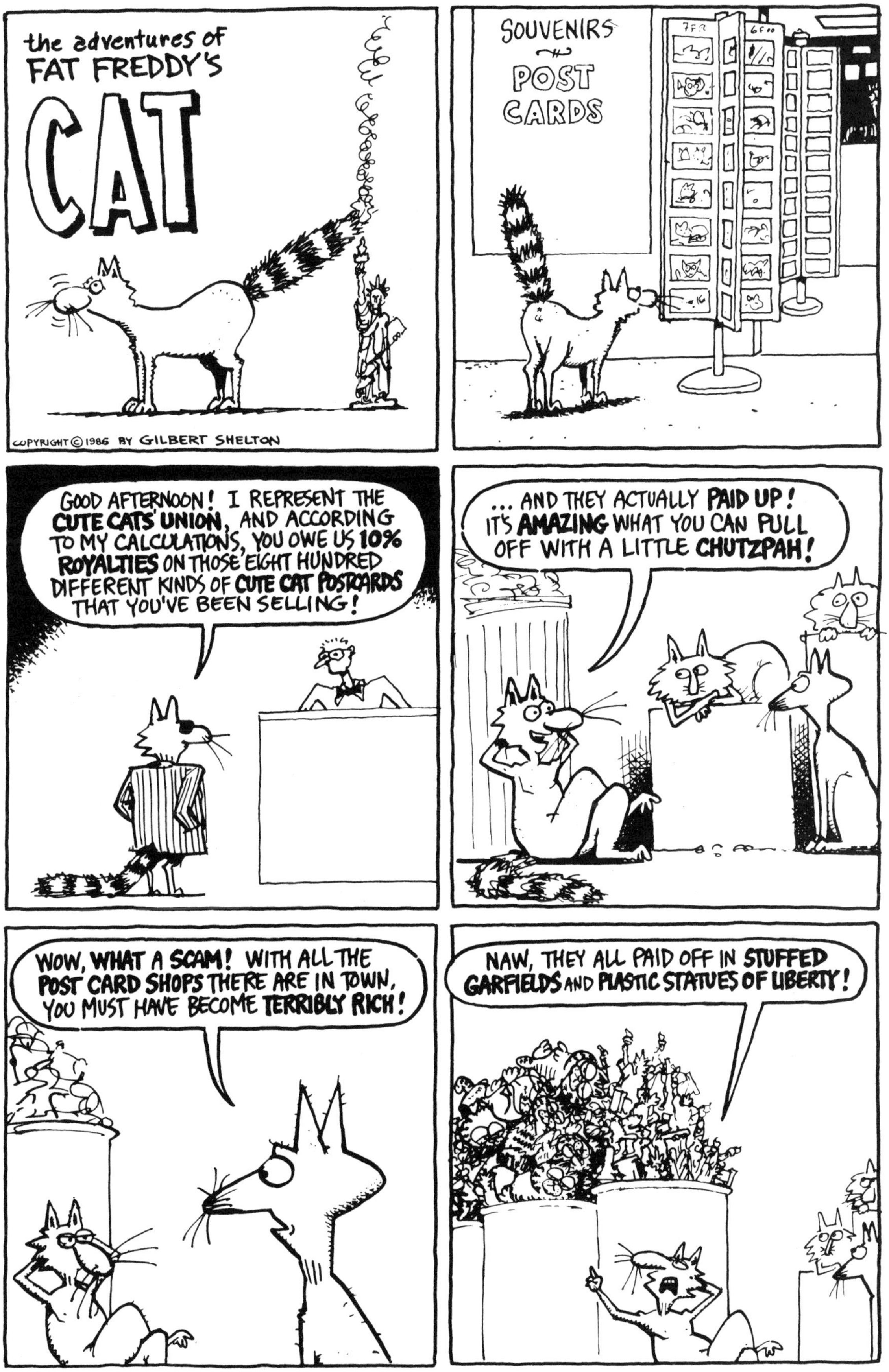
the adventures of
FAT FREDDY'S
CAT
COPYRIGHT © 1986 BY GILBERT SHELTON
SOUVENIRS
POST CARDS
GOOD AFTERNOON! I REPRESENT THE CUTE CATS' UNION, AND ACCORDING TO MY CALCULATIONS, YOU OWE US 10% ROYALTIES ON THOSE EIGHT HUNDRED DIFFERENT KINDS OF CUTE CAT POSTCARDS THAT YOU'VE BEEN SELLING!
... AND THEY ACTUALLY PAID UP! IT'S AMAZING WHAT YOU CAN PULL OFF WITH A LITTLE CHUTZPAH!
WOW, WHAT A SCAM! WITH ALL THE POST CARD SHOPS THERE ARE IN TOWN, YOU MUST HAVE BECOME TERRIBLY RICH!
NAW, THEY ALL PAID OFF IN STUFFED GARFIELDS AND PLASTIC STATUES OF LIBERTY!

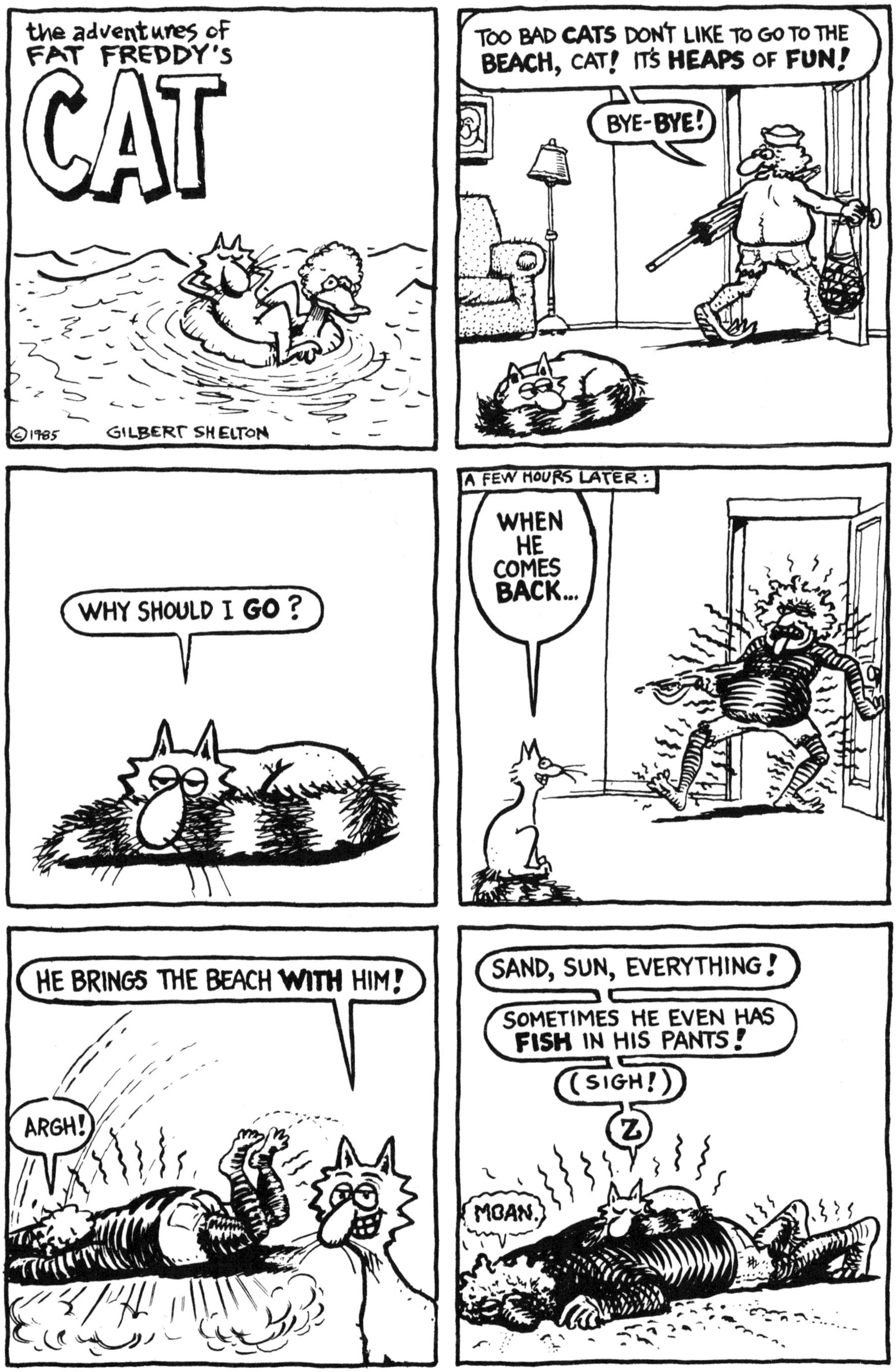
the adventures of FAT FREDDY's CAT
©1985 GILBERT SHELTON
TOO BAD CATS DON'T LIKE TO GO TO THE BEACH, CAT! IT'S HEAPS OF FUN!
BYE-BYE!
WHY SHOULD I GO?
A FEW HOURS LATER:
WHEN HE COMES BACK...
HE BRINGS THE BEACH WITH HIM!
ARGH!
SAND, SUN, EVERYTHING!
SOMETIMES HE EVEN HAS FISH IN HIS PANTS!
(SIGH!)
Z
MOAN.

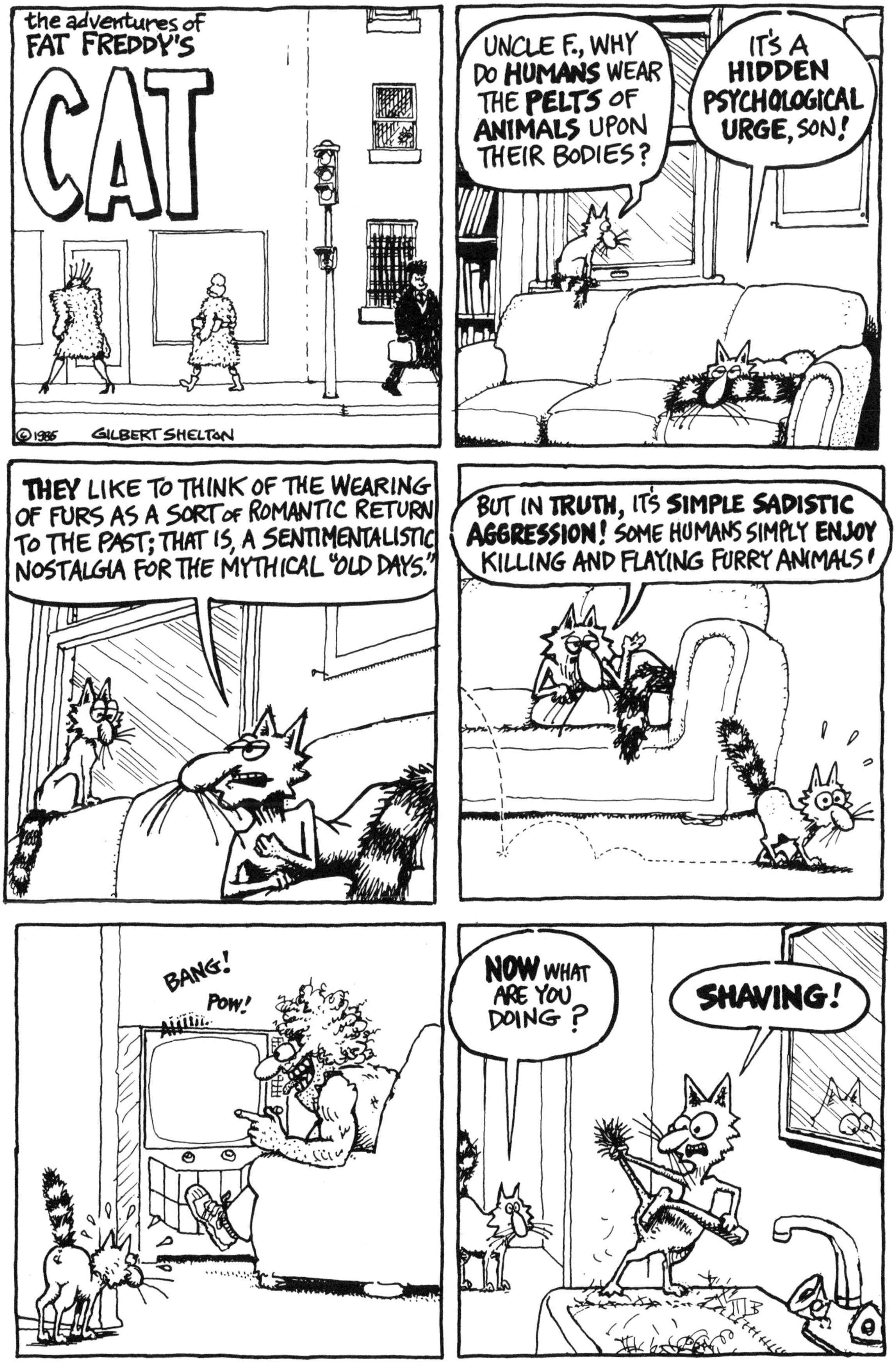
the adventures of
FAT FREDDY'S
CAT
© 1985 GILBERT SHELTON
UNCLE F., WHY DO HUMANS WEAR THE PELTS OF ANIMALS UPON THEIR BODIES?
IT'S A HIDDEN PSYCHOLOGICAL URGE, SON!
THEY LIKE TO THINK OF THE WEARING OF FURS AS A SORT OF ROMANTIC RETURN TO THE PAST; THAT IS, A SENTIMENTALISTIC NOSTALGIA FOR THE MYTHICAL "OLD DAYS."
BUT IN TRUTH, IT'S SIMPLE SADISTIC AGGRESSION! SOME HUMANS SIMPLY ENJOY KILLING AND FLAYING FURRY ANIMALS!
BANG!
POW!
NOW WHAT ARE YOU DOING?
SHAVING!

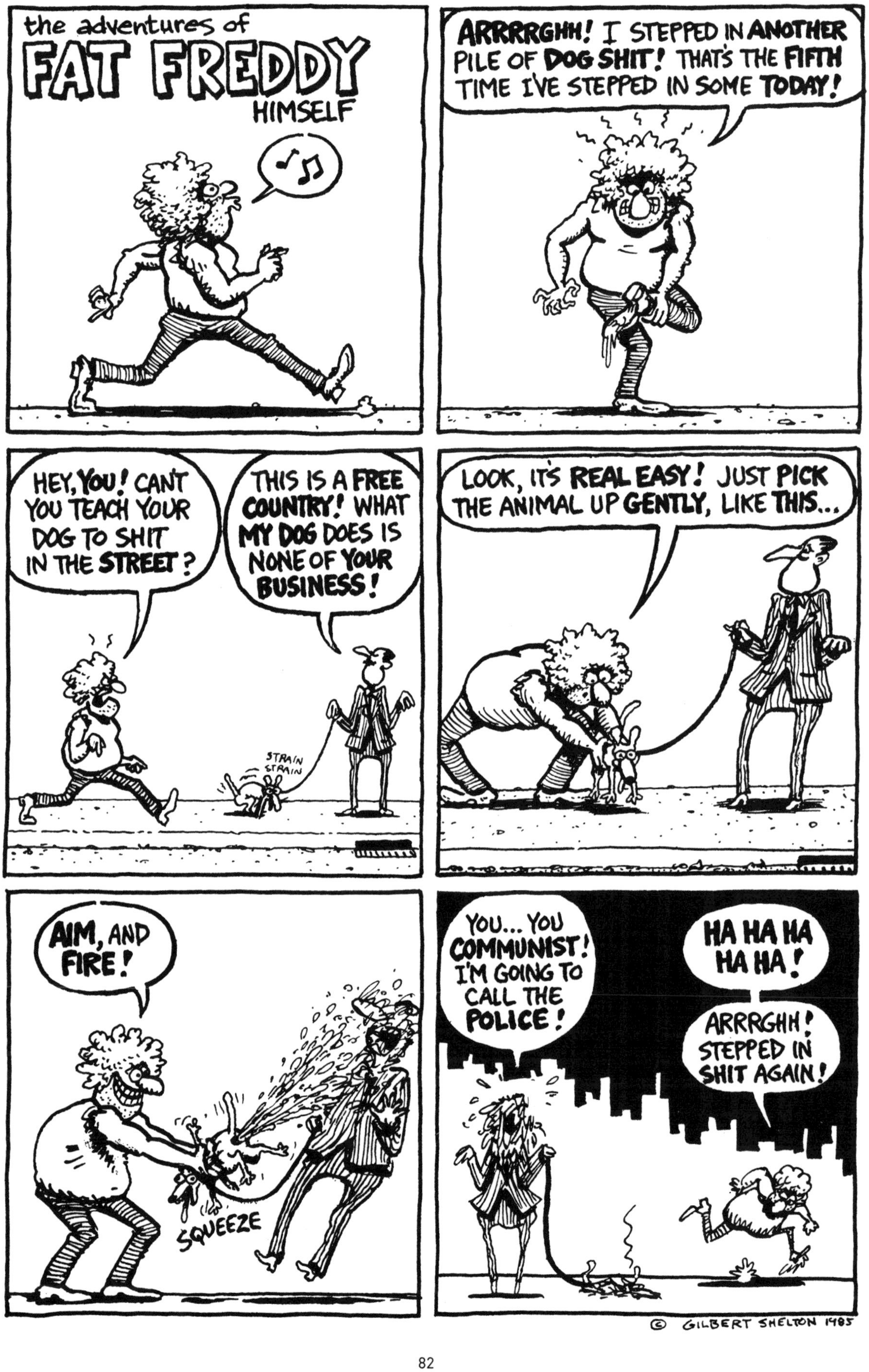
the adventures of
FAT FREDDY
HIMSELF
♪♫
ARRRRGHH! I STEPPED IN ANOTHER PILE OF DOG SHIT! THAT'S THE FIFTH TIME I'VE STEPPED IN SOME TODAY!
HEY, YOU! CAN'T YOU TEACH YOUR DOG TO SHIT IN THE STREET?
THIS IS A FREE COUNTRY! WHAT MY DOG DOES IS NONE OF YOUR BUSINESS!
STRAIN STRAIN
LOOK, IT'S REAL EASY! JUST PICK THE ANIMAL UP GENTLY, LIKE THIS...
AIM, AND FIRE!
SQUEEZE
YOU... YOU COMMUNIST! I'M GOING TO CALL THE POLICE!
HA HA HA HA HA!
ARRRGHH! STEPPED IN SHIT AGAIN!
© GILBERT SHELTON 1985

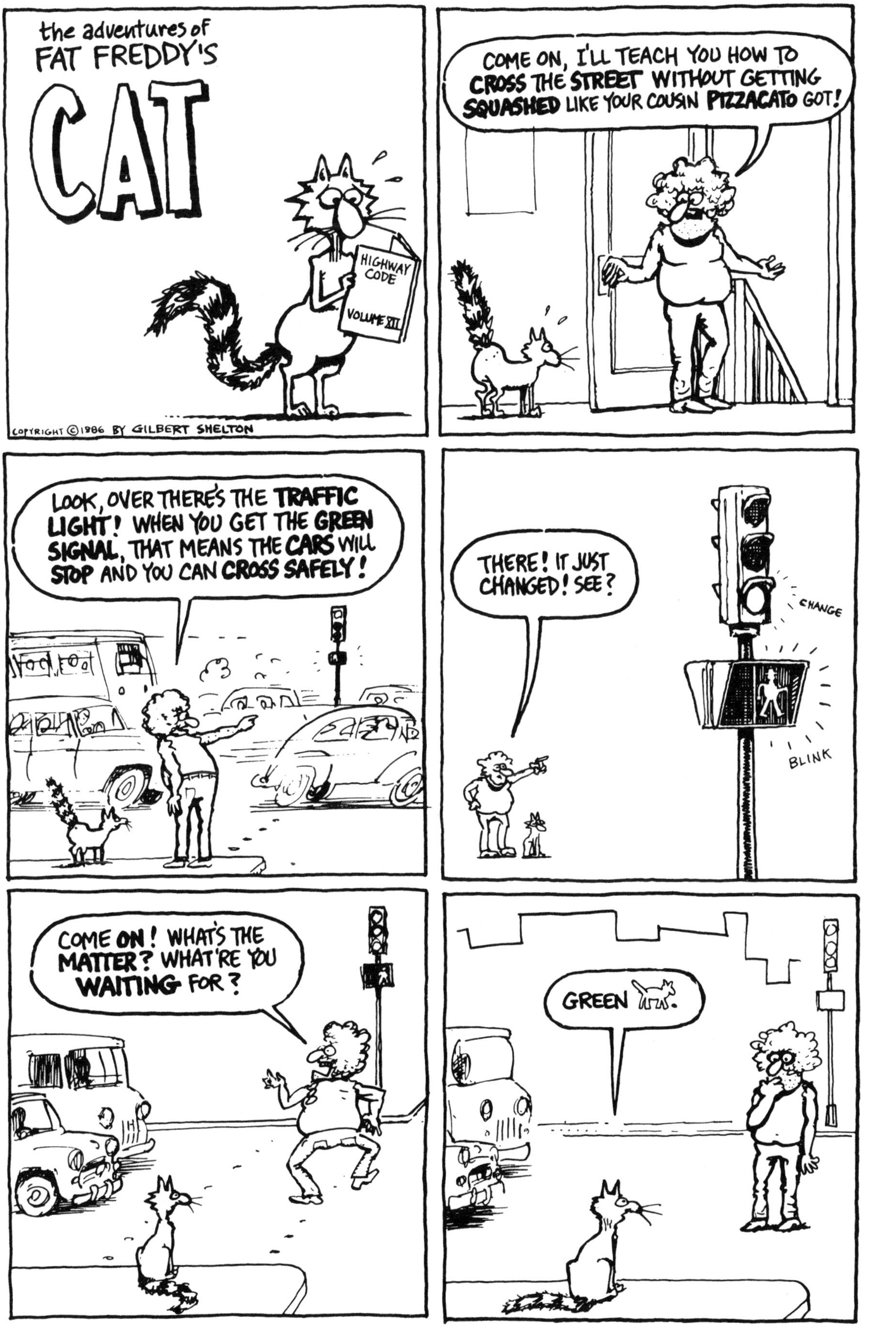

the adventures of
FAT FREDDY'S
CAT
HIGHWAY CODE
VOLUME XII
COPYRIGHT © 1986 BY GILBERT SHELTON
COME ON, I'LL TEACH YOU HOW TO CROSS THE STREET WITHOUT GETTING SQUASHED LIKE YOUR COUSIN PIZZACATO GOT!
LOOK, OVER THERE'S THE TRAFFIC LIGHT! WHEN YOU GET THE GREEN SIGNAL, THAT MEANS THE CARS WILL STOP AND YOU CAN CROSS SAFELY!
THERE! IT JUST CHANGED! SEE?
CHANGE
BLINK
COME ON! WHAT'S THE MATTER? WHAT'RE YOU WAITING FOR?
GREEN

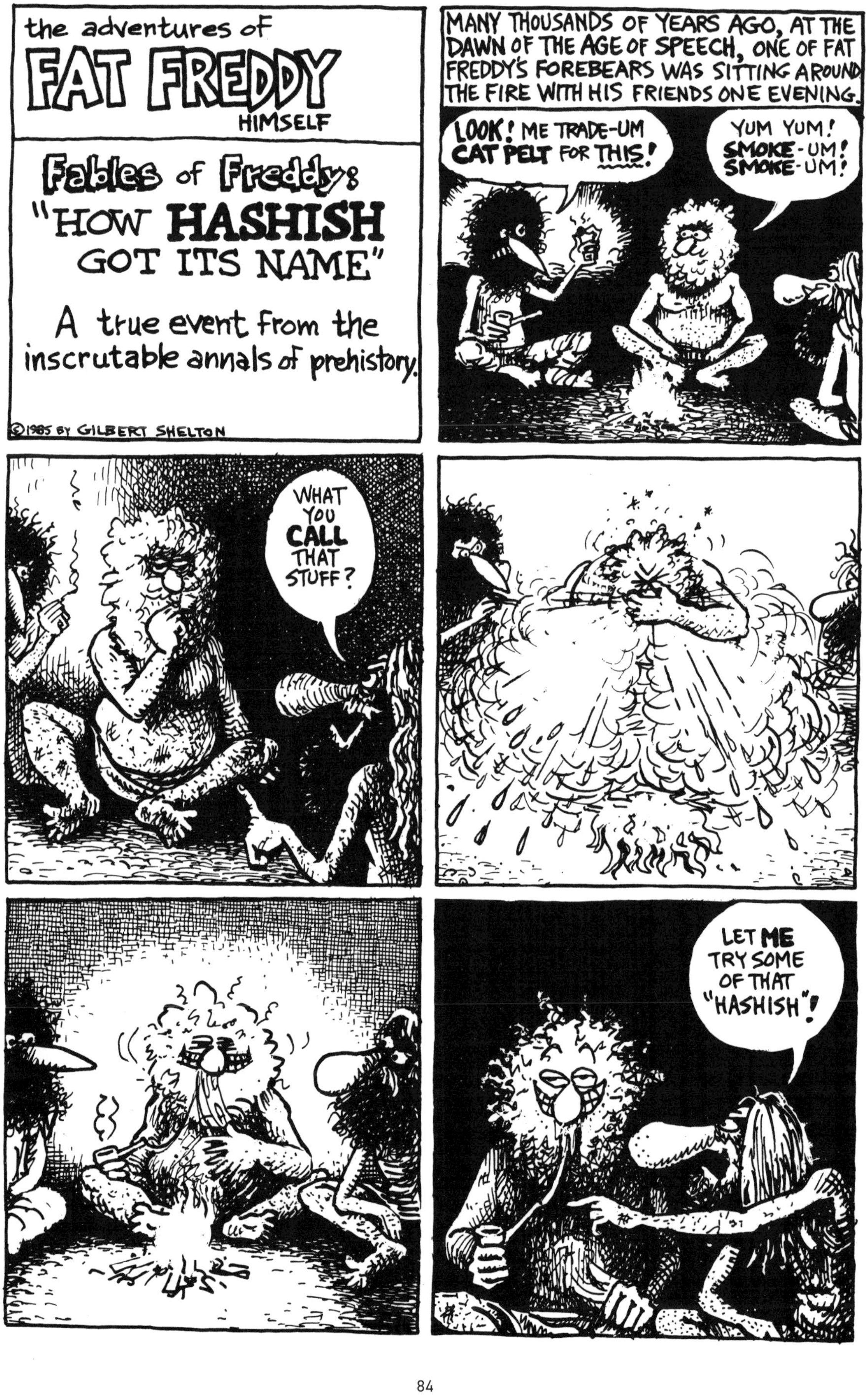

the adventures of
FAT FREDDY
HIMSELF
Fables of Freddy: "HOW HASHISH GOT ITS NAME"
A true event from the inscrutable annals of prehistory.
©1985 BY GILBERT SHELTON
MANY THOUSANDS OF YEARS AGO, AT THE DAWN OF THE AGE OF SPEECH, ONE OF FAT FREDDY'S FOREBEARS WAS SITTING AROUND THE FIRE WITH HIS FRIENDS ONE EVENING.
LOOK! ME TRADE-UM CAT PELT FOR THIS!
YUM YUM! SMOKE-UM! SMOKE-UM!
WHAT YOU CALL THAT STUFF?
LET ME TRY SOME OF THAT "HASHISH"!

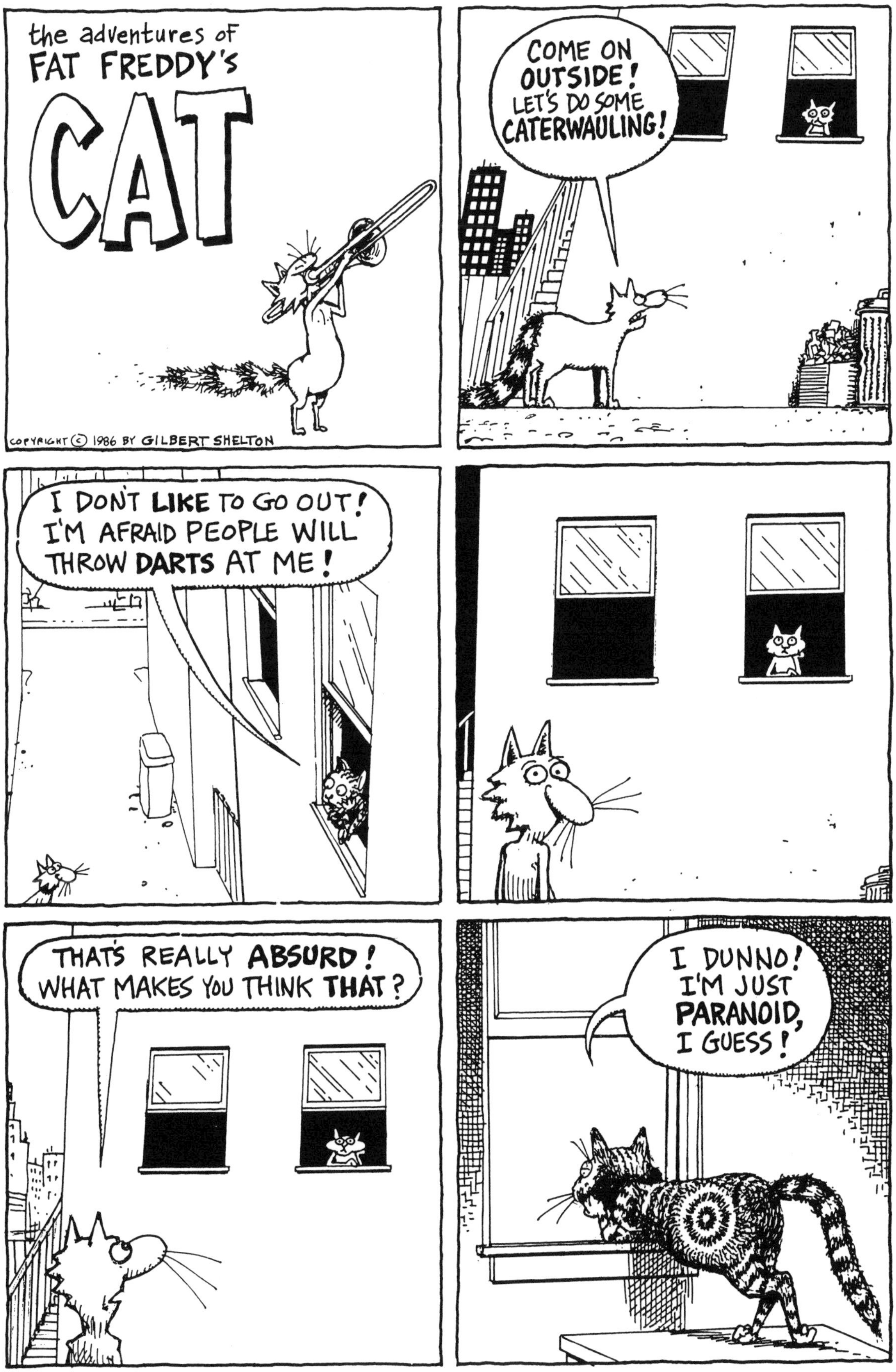
the adventures of
FAT FREDDY'S
CAT
COPYRIGHT © 1986 BY GILBERT SHELTON
COME ON OUTSIDE! LET'S DO SOME CATERWAULING!
I DON'T LIKE TO GO OUT! I'M AFRAID PEOPLE WILL THROW DARTS AT ME!
THAT'S REALLY ABSURD! WHAT MAKES YOU THINK THAT?
I DUNNO! I'M JUST PARANOID, I GUESS!

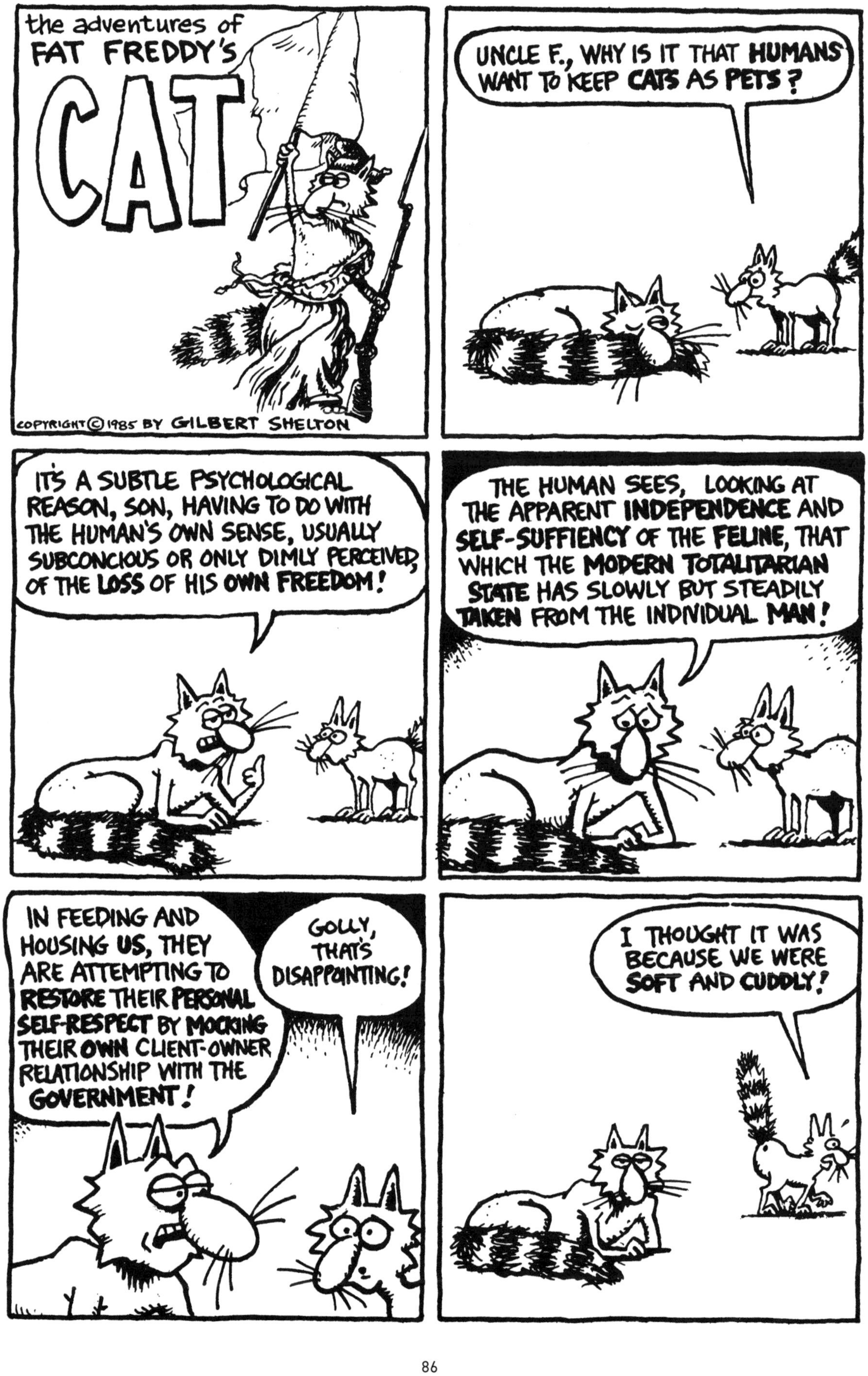
the adventures of FAT FREDDY'S CAT
COPYRIGHT © 1985 BY GILBERT SHELTON
UNCLE F., WHY IS IT THAT HUMANS WANT TO KEEP CATS AS PETS?
IT'S A SUBTLE PSYCHOLOGICAL REASON, SON, HAVING TO DO WITH THE HUMAN'S OWN SENSE, USUALLY SUBCONCIOUS OR ONLY DIMLY PERCEIVED, OF THE LOSS OF HIS OWN FREEDOM!
THE HUMAN SEES, LOOKING AT THE APPARENT INDEPENDENCE AND SELF-SUFFIENCY OF THE FELINE, THAT WHICH THE MODERN TOTALITARIAN STATE HAS SLOWLY BUT STEADILY TAKEN FROM THE INDIVIDUAL MAN!
IN FEEDING AND HOUSING US, THEY ARE ATTEMPTING TO RESTORE THEIR PERSONAL SELF-RESPECT BY MOCKING THEIR OWN CLIENT-OWNER RELATIONSHIP WITH THE GOVERNMENT!
GOLLY, THAT'S DISAPPOINTING!
I THOUGHT IT WAS BECAUSE WE WERE SOFT AND CUDDLY!

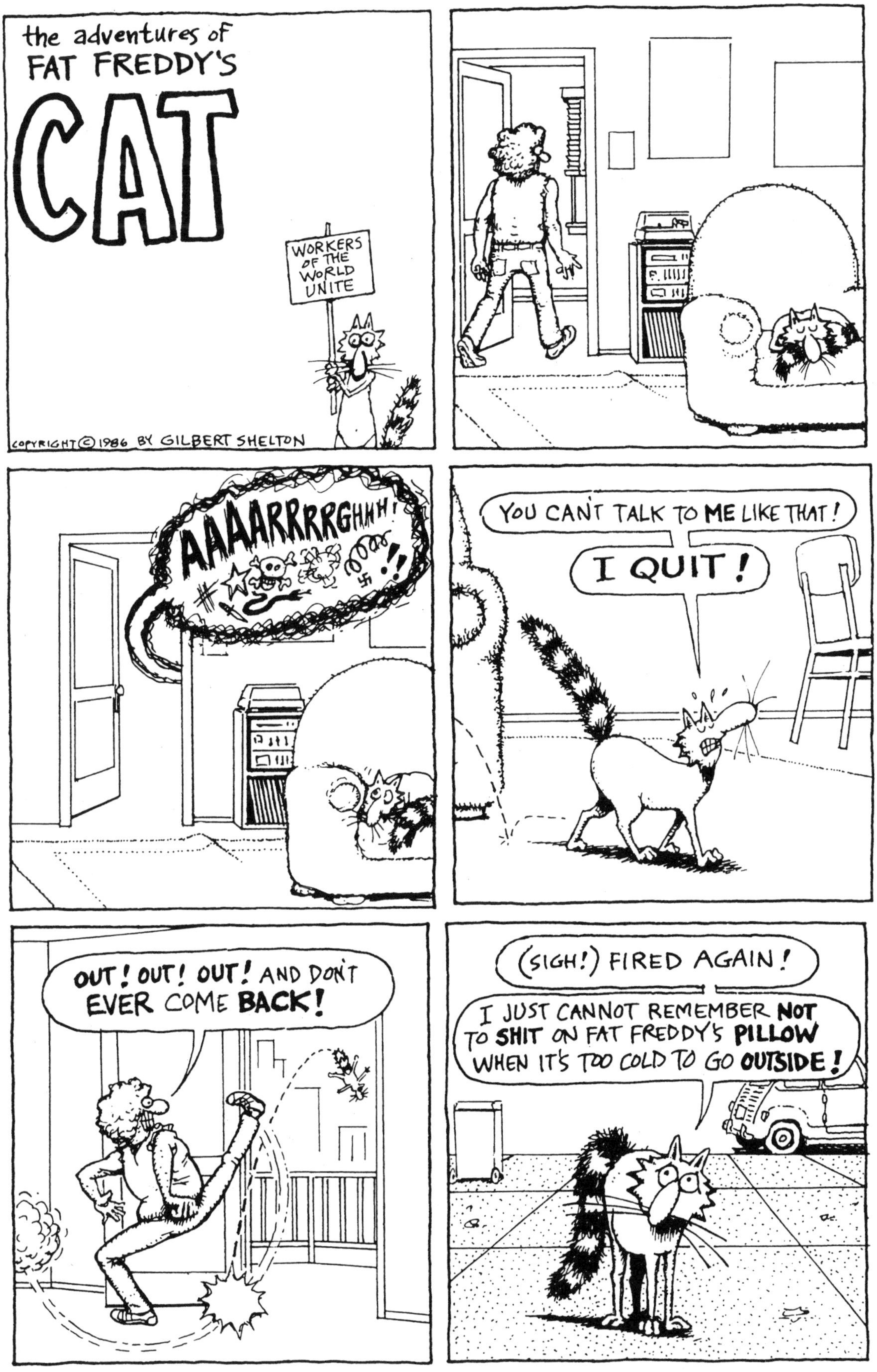
the adventures of
FAT FREDDY'S
CAT
WORKERS OF THE WORLD UNITE
COPYRIGHT © 1986 BY GILBERT SHELTON
AAAARRRRGHHH!
YOU CAN'T TALK TO ME LIKE THAT!
I QUIT!
OUT! OUT! OUT! AND DON'T EVER COME BACK!
(SIGH!) FIRED AGAIN!
I JUST CANNOT REMEMBER NOT TO SHIT ON FAT FREDDY'S PILLOW WHEN IT'S TOO COLD TO GO OUTSIDE!

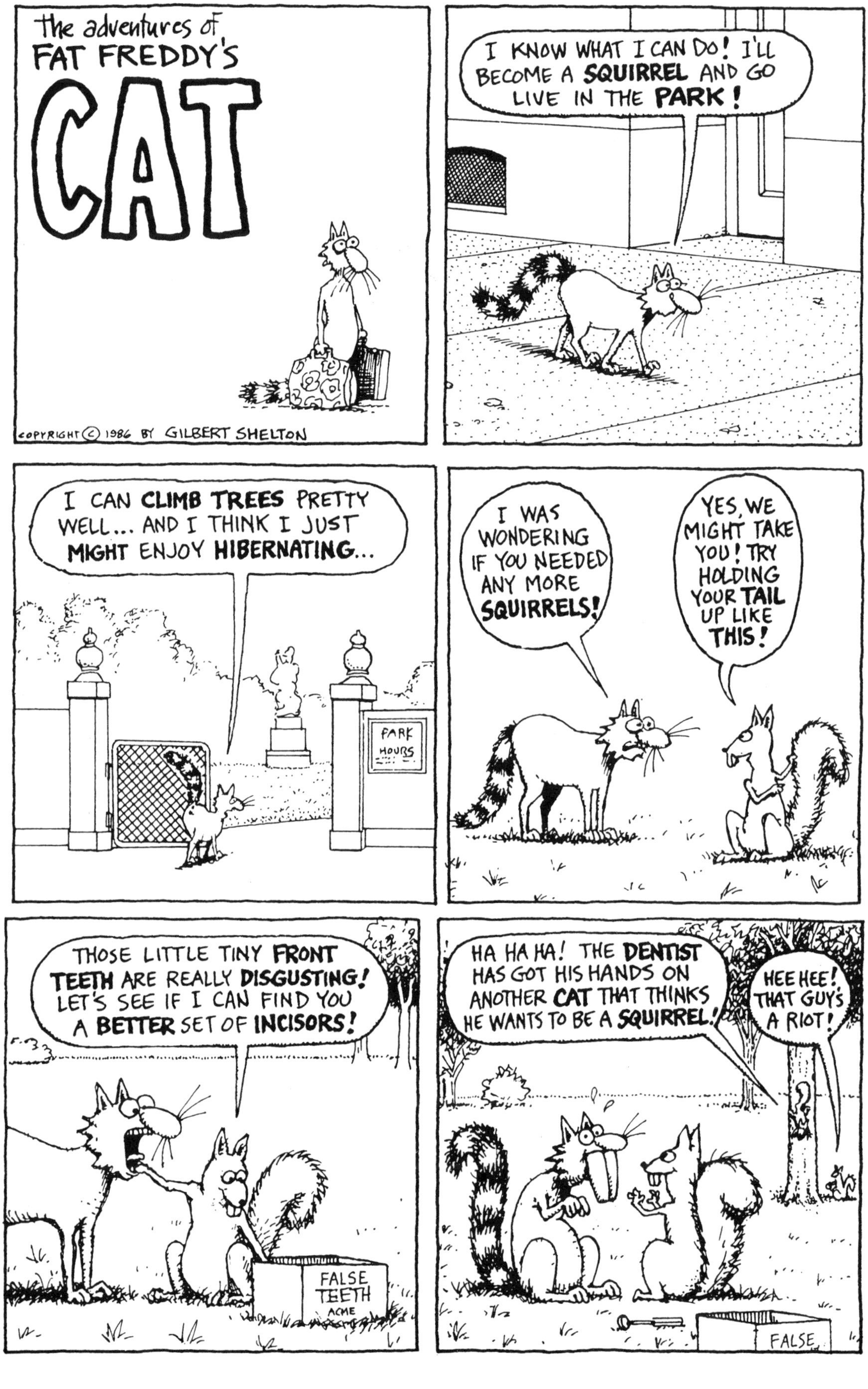
the adventures of
FAT FREDDY'S
CAT
COPYRIGHT © 1986 BY GILBERT SHELTON
I KNOW WHAT I CAN DO! I'LL BECOME A SQUIRREL AND GO LIVE IN THE PARK!
I CAN CLIMB TREES PRETTY WELL... AND I THINK I JUST MIGHT ENJOY HIBERNATING...
PARK HOURS
I WAS WONDERING IF YOU NEEDED ANY MORE SQUIRRELS!
YES, WE MIGHT TAKE YOU! TRY HOLDING YOUR TAIL UP LIKE THIS!
THOSE LITTLE TINY FRONT TEETH ARE REALLY DISGUSTING! LET'S SEE IF I CAN FIND YOU A BETTER SET OF INCISORS!
FALSE TEETH
ACME
HA HA HA! THE DENTIST HAS GOT HIS HANDS ON ANOTHER CAT THAT THINKS HE WANTS TO BE A SQUIRREL!
HEE HEE! THAT GUY'S A RIOT!
FALSE

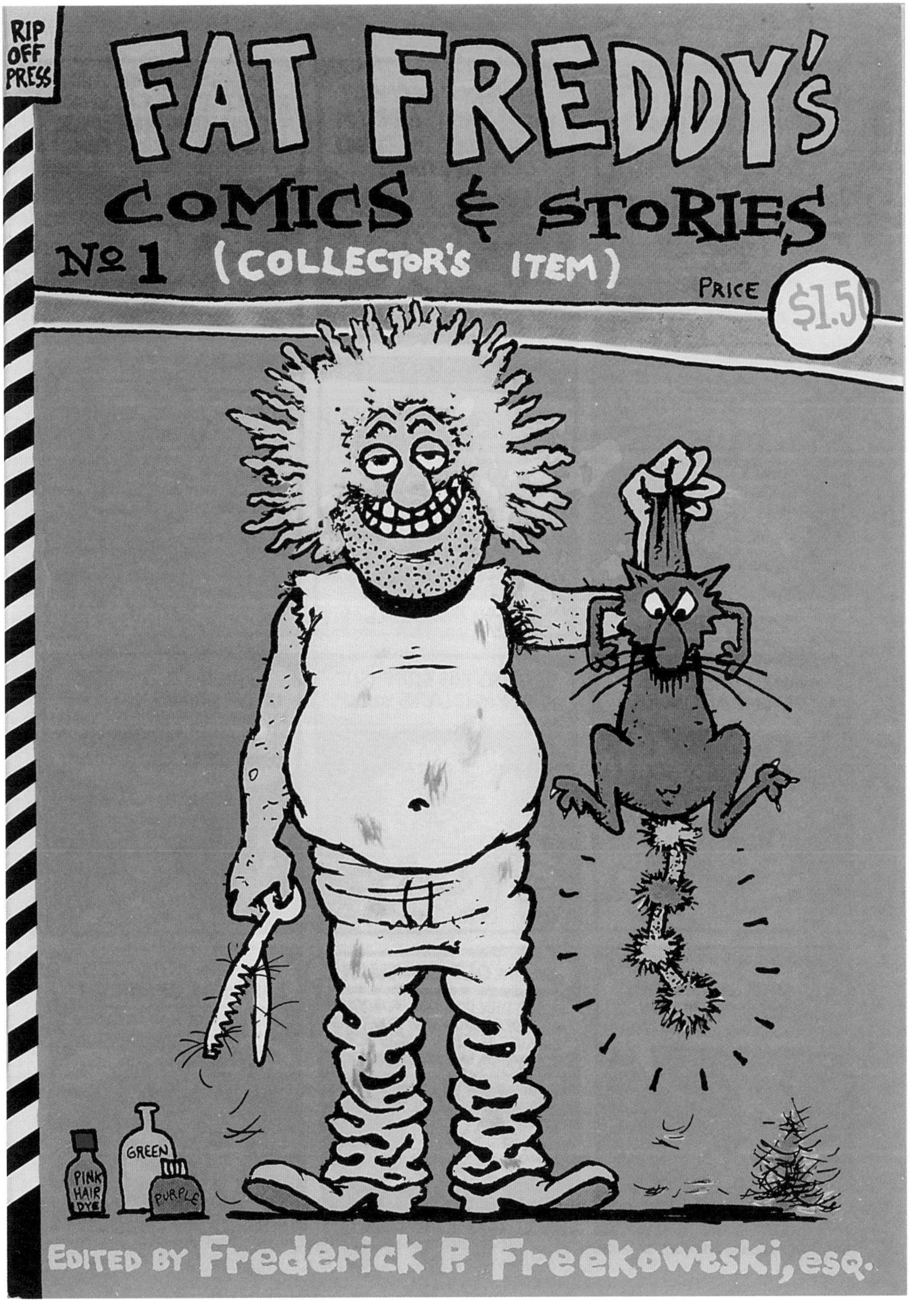
RIP OFF PRESS
FAT FREDDY'S
COMICS & STORIES
Nº 1 (COLLECTOR'S ITEM)
PRICE $1.50
PINK HAIR DYE
GREEN
PURPLE
EDITED BY Frederick P. Freekowtski, esq.

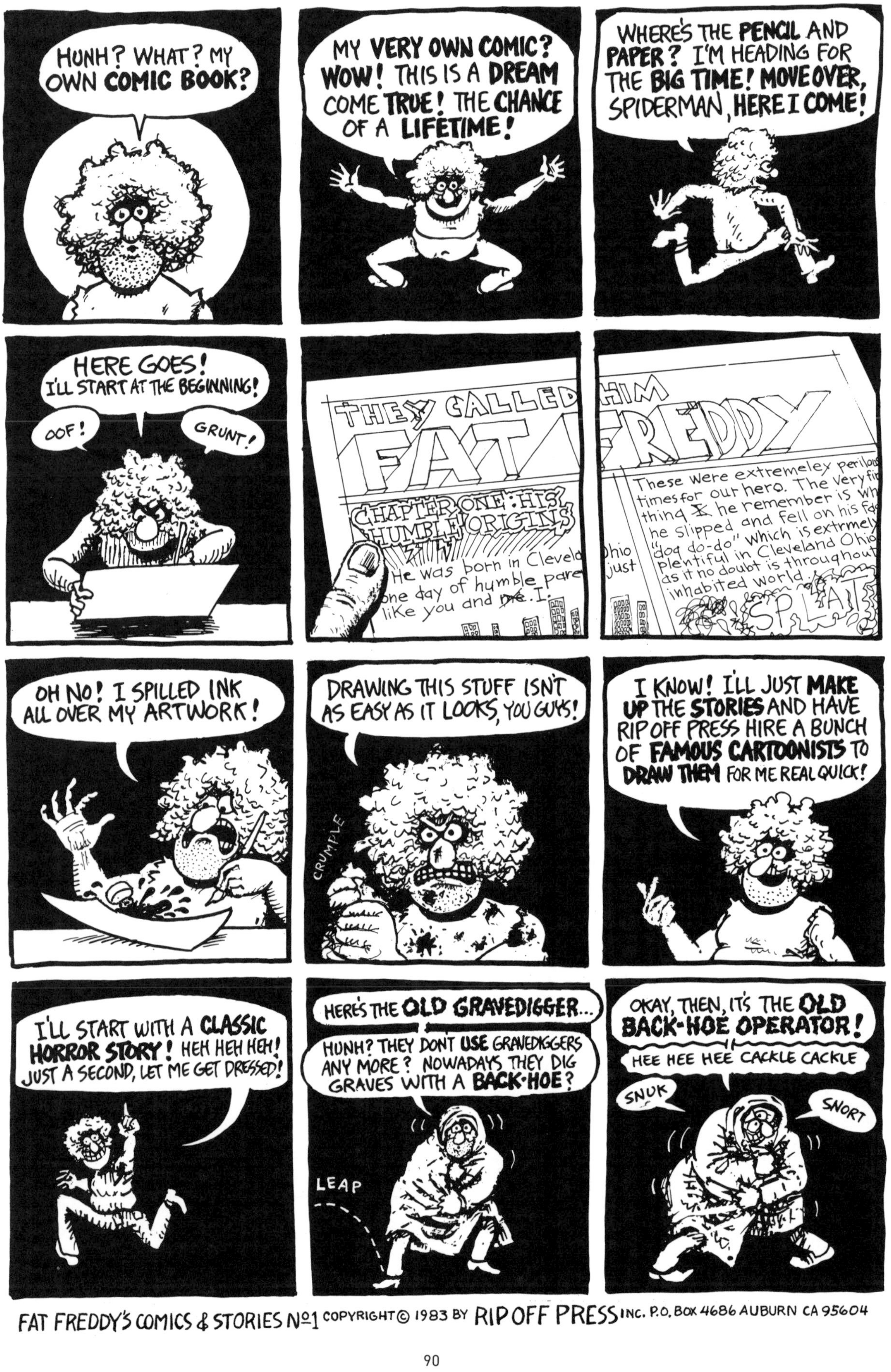
HUNH? WHAT? MY OWN COMIC BOOK?
MY VERY OWN COMIC? WOW! THIS IS A DREAM COME TRUE! THE CHANCE OF A LIFETIME!
WHERE'S THE PENCIL AND PAPER? I'M HEADING FOR THE BIG TIME! MOVE OVER, SPIDERMAN, HERE I COME!
HERE GOES! I'LL START AT THE BEGINNING!
OOF!
GRUNT!
THEY CALLED HIM FAT FREDDY
CHAPTER ONE: HIS HUMBLE ORIGINS
He was born in Cleveland Ohio just one day of humble parents like you and me. I.
These were extremeley perilous times for our hero. The very first thing he remember is when he slipped and fell on his face "dog do-do" which is extrmely plentiful in Cleveland Ohio as it no doubt is throughout the inhabited world.
SPLAT
OH NO! I SPILLED INK ALL OVER MY ARTWORK!
DRAWING THIS STUFF ISN'T AS EASY AS IT LOOKS, YOU GUYS!
CRUMPLE
I KNOW! I'LL JUST MAKE UP THE STORIES AND HAVE RIP OFF PRESS HIRE A BUNCH OF FAMOUS CARTOONISTS TO DRAW THEM FOR ME REAL QUICK!
I'LL START WITH A CLASSIC HORROR STORY! HEH HEH HEH! JUST A SECOND, LET ME GET DRESSED!
LEAP
HERE'S THE OLD GRAVEDIGGER...
HUNH? THEY DONT USE GRAVEDIGGERS ANY MORE? NOWADAYS THEY DIG GRAVES WITH A BACK-HOE?
OKAY, THEN, IT'S THE OLD BACK-HOE OPERATOR!
HEE HEE HEE CACKLE CACKLE
SNUK
SNORT

RETURN WITH US NOW TO THOSE *THRILLING DAYS OF YESTERYEAR,* WHEN *MEN* WERE *MEN* AND *COMIC BOOKS* WERE *COMIC BOOKS*, AND *GOD FORBID* THAT EVER THE *TWAIN* SHOULD *MEET.* AFTER ALL, *GROWNUPS* DON'T READ ***COMIC BOOKS***, *RIGHT?* IN FACT, *GROWN MEN* DON'T READ *ANYTHING AT ALL* IN *OUR* CULTURE. IF YOU EVER *SEE* ONE SNEAKING A LOOK AT ANYTHING OTHER THAN THE *SPORTS SECTION*, YOU CAN BE SURE HE'S EITHER A *GEEK*, A *WIMP*, OR A *WOOSIE*, OR ELSE A *LITTLE KID DRESSED UP* LIKE AN ADULT. *SO*, WIPE THE *SNOT* OFF YOUR LITTLE NOSE AND *JOIN* US NOW FOR A THRILLING OLD-TIME *HORROR STORY*, ONE OF THE GENERIC CLASSICS...

TALES FROM THE OLD BACK-HOE OPERATOR!

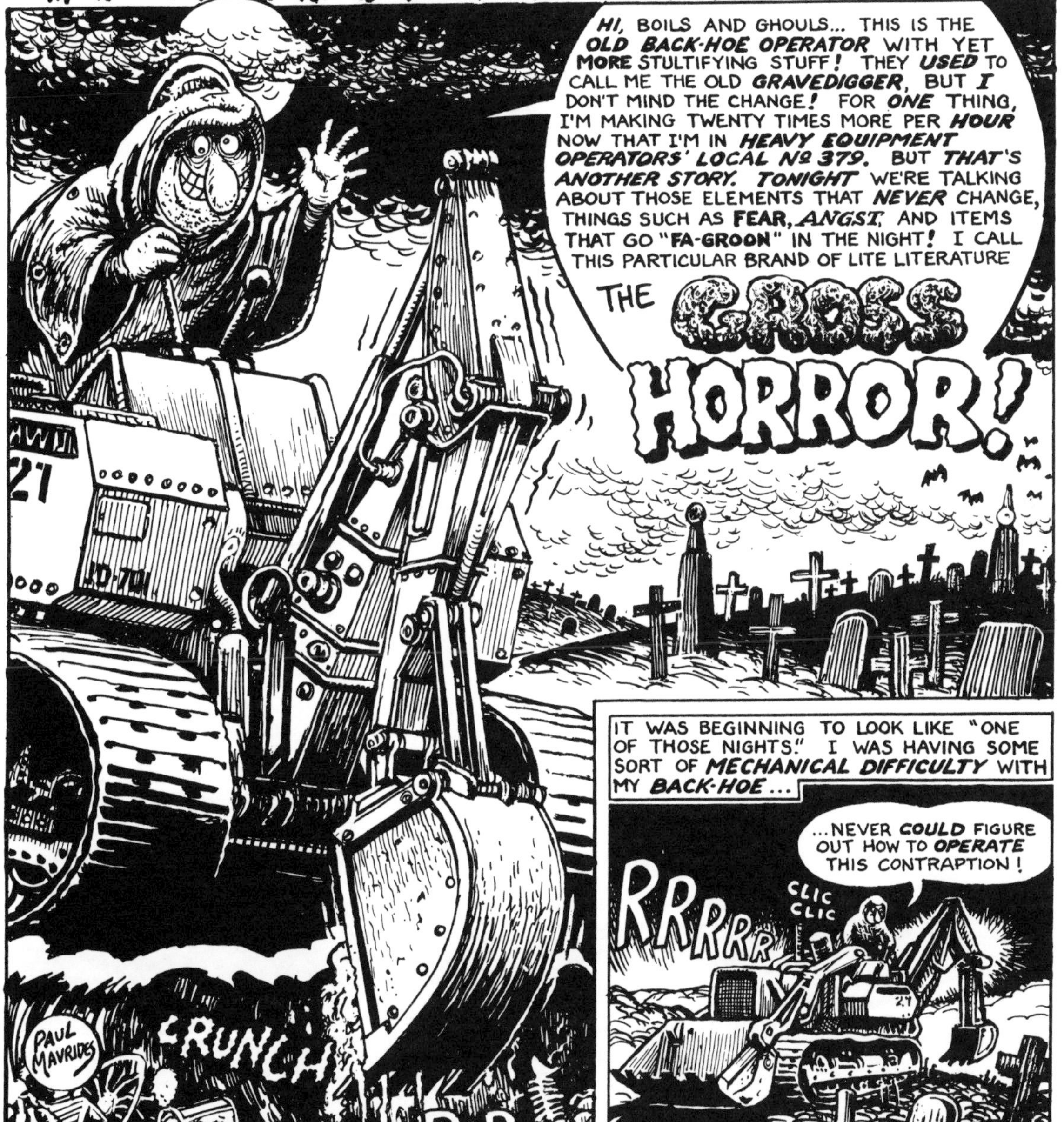

HI, BOILS AND GHOULS... THIS IS THE OLD BACK-HOE OPERATOR WITH YET MORE STULTIFYING STUFF! THEY USED TO CALL ME THE OLD GRAVEDIGGER, BUT I DON'T MIND THE CHANGE! FOR ONE THING, I'M MAKING TWENTY TIMES MORE PER HOUR NOW THAT I'M IN HEAVY EQUIPMENT OPERATORS' LOCAL № 379. BUT THAT'S ANOTHER STORY. TONIGHT WE'RE TALKING ABOUT THOSE ELEMENTS THAT NEVER CHANGE, THINGS SUCH AS FEAR, ANGST, AND ITEMS THAT GO "FA-GROON" IN THE NIGHT! I CALL THIS PARTICULAR BRAND OF LITE LITERATURE
THE GROSS HORROR!
PAUL MAVRIDES
CRUNCH
POP
IT WAS BEGINNING TO LOOK LIKE "ONE OF THOSE NIGHTS." I WAS HAVING SOME SORT OF MECHANICAL DIFFICULTY WITH MY BACK-HOE...
...NEVER COULD FIGURE OUT HOW TO OPERATE THIS CONTRAPTION!
RRRRRR
CLIC CLIC
©1983 R.O.P. INC.

ARTISTS (IN ORDER OF APPEARANCE): GILBERT SHELTON, PAUL MAVRIDES, HAL ROBINS, JACK JACKSON, SPAIN RODRIGUEZ, GUY COLWELL, S. CLAY WILSON, & TED RICHARDS. STORYBOARDS & LETTERING: SHELTON.

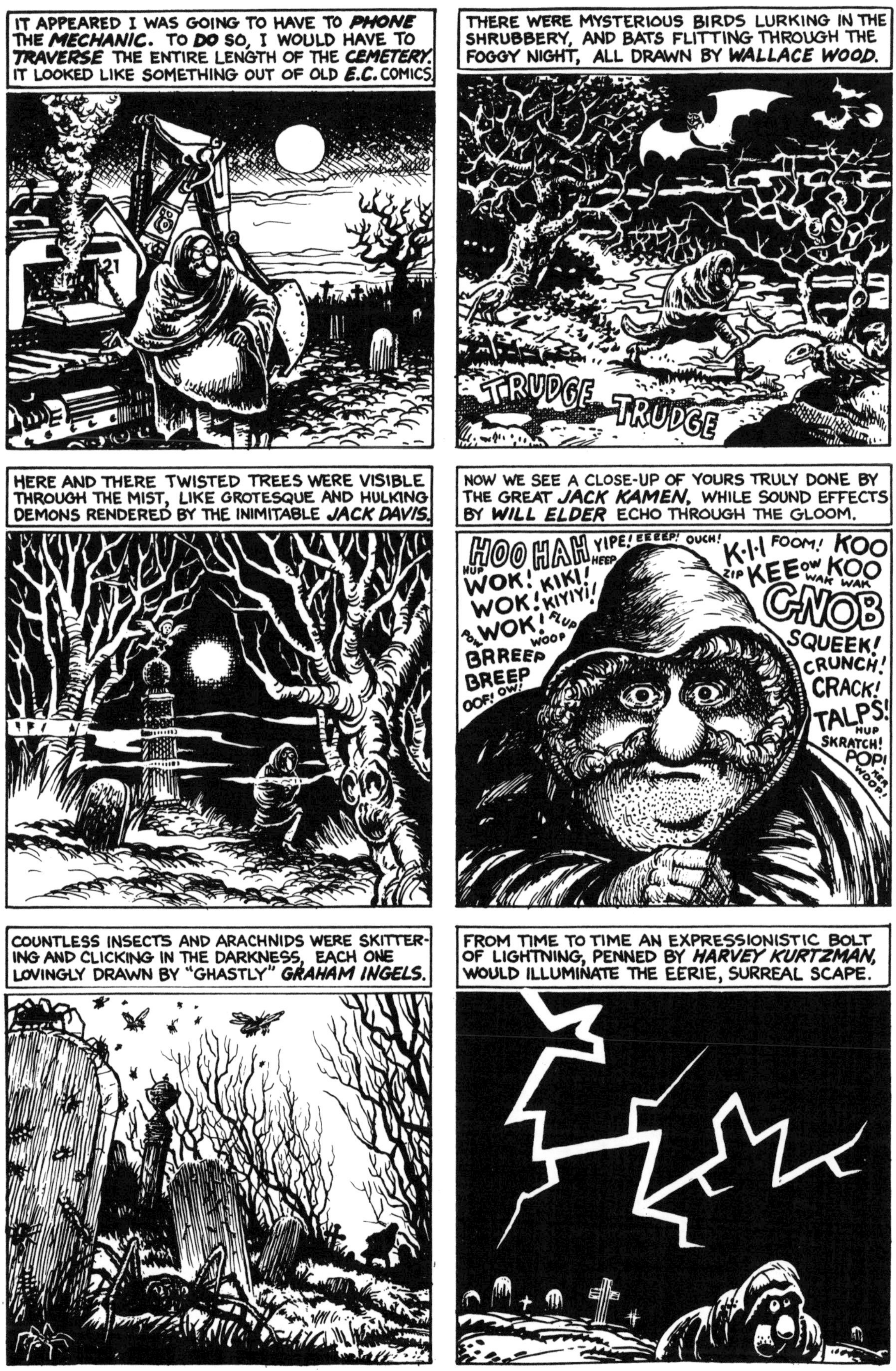
IT APPEARED I WAS GOING TO HAVE TO PHONE THE MECHANIC. TO DO SO, I WOULD HAVE TO TRAVERSE THE ENTIRE LENGTH OF THE CEMETERY. IT LOOKED LIKE SOMETHING OUT OF OLD E.C. COMICS.
21
THERE WERE MYSTERIOUS BIRDS LURKING IN THE SHRUBBERY, AND BATS FLITTING THROUGH THE FOGGY NIGHT, ALL DRAWN BY WALLACE WOOD.
TRUDGE
TRUDGE
HERE AND THERE TWISTED TREES WERE VISIBLE THROUGH THE MIST, LIKE GROTESQUE AND HULKING DEMONS RENDERED BY THE INIMITABLE JACK DAVIS.
NOW WE SEE A CLOSE-UP OF YOURS TRULY DONE BY THE GREAT JACK KAMEN, WHILE SOUND EFFECTS BY WILL ELDER ECHO THROUGH THE GLOOM.
HOO HAH
YIPE! EEEEP! OUCH!
HEEP
HUP
WOK! KIKI!
WOK! KIYIYI!
POW WOK! FLUP
WOOP
BRREEP
BREEP
OOF! OW!
K·I·I FOOM! KOO
ZIP KEE OW KOO
WAK WAK
C-NOB
SQUEEK!
CRUNCH!
CRACK!
TALPS!
HUP
SKRATCH!
POP!
KER WOOP!
COUNTLESS INSECTS AND ARACHNIDS WERE SKITTERING AND CLICKING IN THE DARKNESS, EACH ONE LOVINGLY DRAWN BY "GHASTLY" GRAHAM INGELS.
FROM TIME TO TIME AN EXPRESSIONISTIC BOLT OF LIGHTNING, PENNED BY HARVEY KURTZMAN, WOULD ILLUMINATE THE EERIE, SURREAL SCAPE.

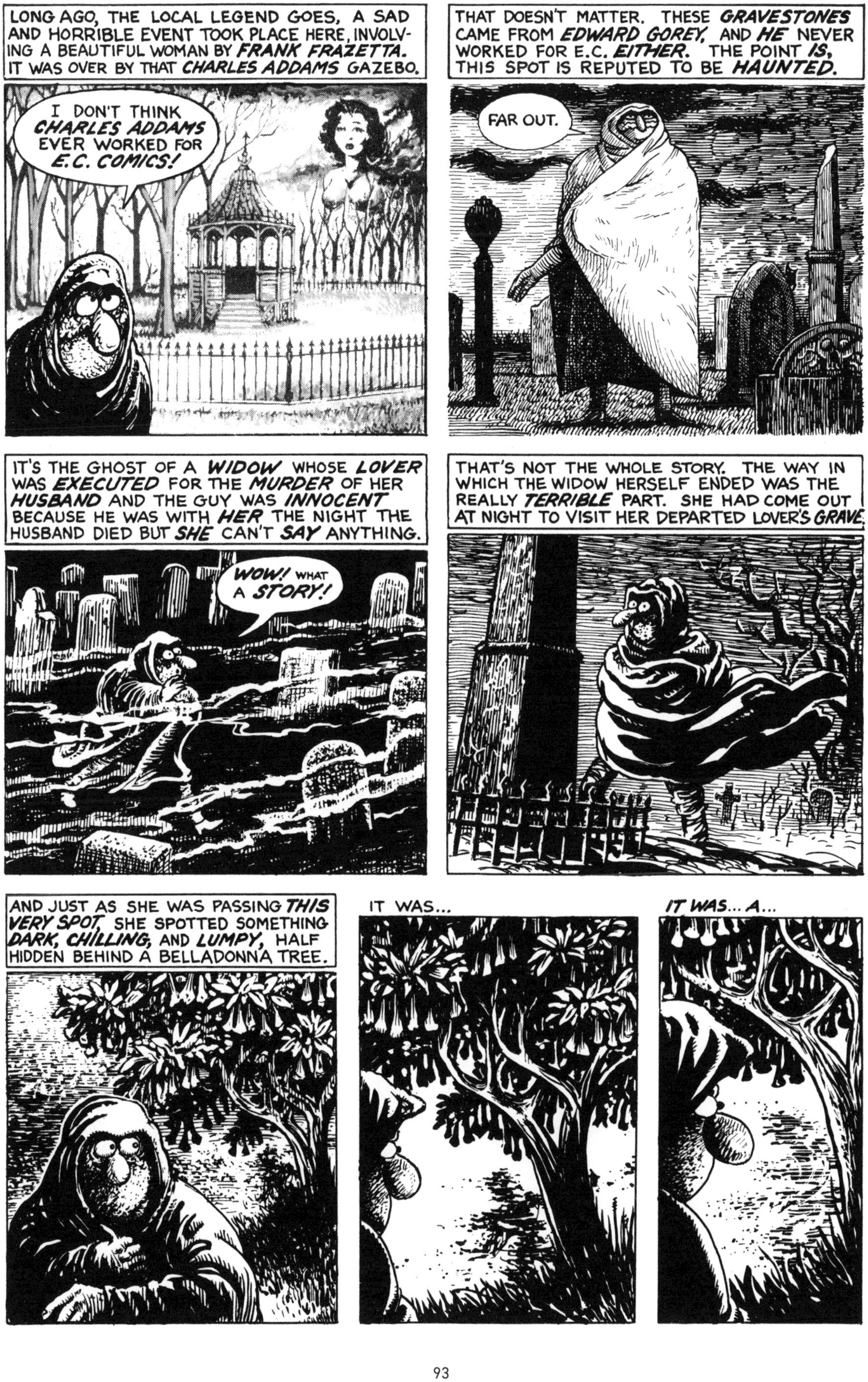

LONG AGO, THE LOCAL LEGEND GOES, A SAD AND HORRIBLE EVENT TOOK PLACE HERE, INVOLVING A BEAUTIFUL WOMAN BY FRANK FRAZETTA. IT WAS OVER BY THAT CHARLES ADDAMS GAZEBO.
I DON'T THINK CHARLES ADDAMS EVER WORKED FOR E.C. COMICS!
THAT DOESN'T MATTER. THESE GRAVESTONES CAME FROM EDWARD GOREY, AND HE NEVER WORKED FOR E.C. EITHER. THE POINT IS, THIS SPOT IS REPUTED TO BE HAUNTED.
FAR OUT.
IT'S THE GHOST OF A WIDOW WHOSE LOVER WAS EXECUTED FOR THE MURDER OF HER HUSBAND AND THE GUY WAS INNOCENT BECAUSE HE WAS WITH HER THE NIGHT THE HUSBAND DIED BUT SHE CAN'T SAY ANYTHING.
WOW! WHAT A STORY!
THAT'S NOT THE WHOLE STORY. THE WAY IN WHICH THE WIDOW HERSELF ENDED WAS THE REALLY TERRIBLE PART. SHE HAD COME OUT AT NIGHT TO VISIT HER DEPARTED LOVER'S GRAVE.
AND JUST AS SHE WAS PASSING THIS VERY SPOT, SHE SPOTTED SOMETHING DARK, CHILLING, AND LUMPY, HALF HIDDEN BEHIND A BELLADONNA TREE.
IT WAS...
IT WAS... A...

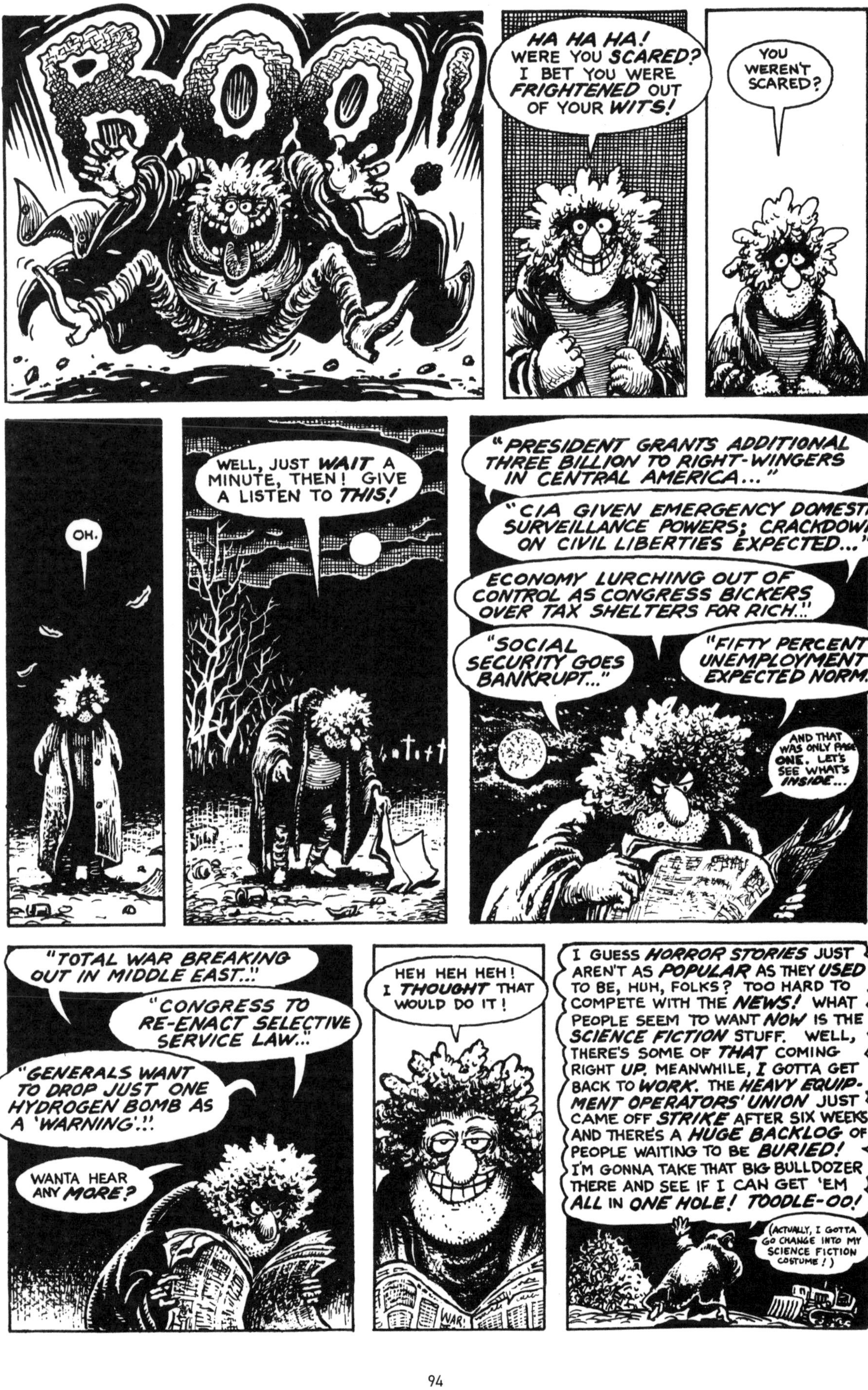
BOO!
HA HA HA! WERE YOU SCARED? I BET YOU WERE FRIGHTENED OUT OF YOUR WITS!
YOU WEREN'T SCARED?
OH.
WELL, JUST WAIT A MINUTE, THEN! GIVE A LISTEN TO THIS!
"PRESIDENT GRANTS ADDITIONAL THREE BILLION TO RIGHT-WINGERS IN CENTRAL AMERICA..."
"CIA GIVEN EMERGENCY DOMESTIC SURVEILLANCE POWERS; CRACKDOWN ON CIVIL LIBERTIES EXPECTED..."
ECONOMY LURCHING OUT OF CONTROL AS CONGRESS BICKERS OVER TAX SHELTERS FOR RICH..."
"SOCIAL SECURITY GOES BANKRUPT..."
"FIFTY PERCENT UNEMPLOYMENT EXPECTED NORM..."
AND THAT WAS ONLY PAGE ONE. LET'S SEE WHAT'S INSIDE...
"TOTAL WAR BREAKING OUT IN MIDDLE EAST..!"
"CONGRESS TO RE-ENACT SELECTIVE SERVICE LAW..."
"GENERALS WANT TO DROP JUST ONE HYDROGEN BOMB AS A 'WARNING'.!!
WANTA HEAR ANY MORE?
HEH HEH HEH! I THOUGHT THAT WOULD DO IT!
WAR!
I GUESS HORROR STORIES JUST AREN'T AS POPULAR AS THEY USED TO BE, HUH, FOLKS? TOO HARD TO COMPETE WITH THE NEWS! WHAT PEOPLE SEEM TO WANT NOW IS THE SCIENCE FICTION STUFF. WELL, THERE'S SOME OF THAT COMING RIGHT UP. MEANWHILE, I GOTTA GET BACK TO WORK. THE HEAVY EQUIPMENT OPERATORS' UNION JUST CAME OFF STRIKE AFTER SIX WEEKS AND THERE'S A HUGE BACKLOG OF PEOPLE WAITING TO BE BURIED! I'M GONNA TAKE THAT BIG BULLDOZER THERE AND SEE IF I CAN GET 'EM ALL IN ONE HOLE! TOODLE-OO!
(ACTUALLY, I GOTTA GO CHANGE INTO MY SCIENCE FICTION COSTUME!)

DA-DUMMMMMMMMM!!! REAL LOUD, SERIOUS-SOUNDING ORCHESTRA MUSIC. ***BOOM BOOM BOOM*** POO POO POO POO POO PEEP PEEP PEEP PEEP TINKLE BUZZ ***CRASH!*** VIOLINS AND MOOG SYNTHESIZERS AND ALL THOSE THINGS. IT'S MILLIONS OF YEARS IN THE FUTURE. ***BILLIONS*** OF YEARS. AND IT SEEMS THAT ALL THE EVIL AND UGLY FORCES IN THE UNIVERSE HAVE FORMED A ***GREAT CONSPIRACY*** TO ***WIPE OUT*** ALL THE ***NICE FOLKS*** BACK ON ***EARTH.*** ONLY ***ONE HUMAN BEING*** STANDS IN THE PATH OF THESE FIENDS AND MURDERERS, AND THIS MAN IS NONE OTHER THAN OUR OLD FRIEND ***FANTASTIC FREDDY,*** OTHERWISE KNOWN AS...

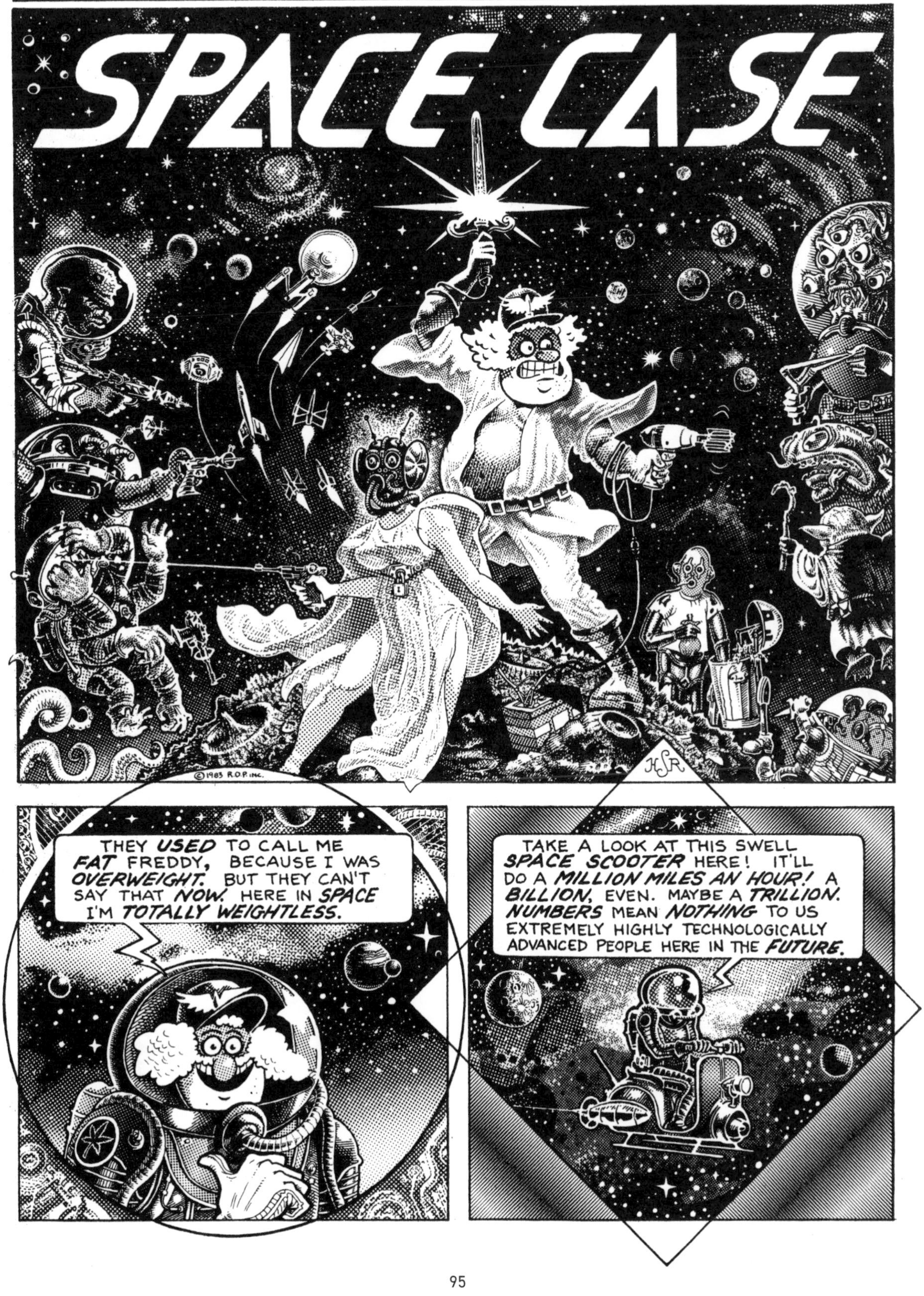
SPACE CASE
©1983 R.O.P. inc.
THEY USED TO CALL ME FAT FREDDY, BECAUSE I WAS OVERWEIGHT. BUT THEY CAN'T SAY THAT NOW. HERE IN SPACE I'M TOTALLY WEIGHTLESS.
TAKE A LOOK AT THIS SWELL SPACE SCOOTER HERE! IT'LL DO A MILLION MILES AN HOUR! A BILLION, EVEN. MAYBE A TRILLION. NUMBERS MEAN NOTHING TO US EXTREMELY HIGHLY TECHNOLOGICALLY ADVANCED PEOPLE HERE IN THE FUTURE.

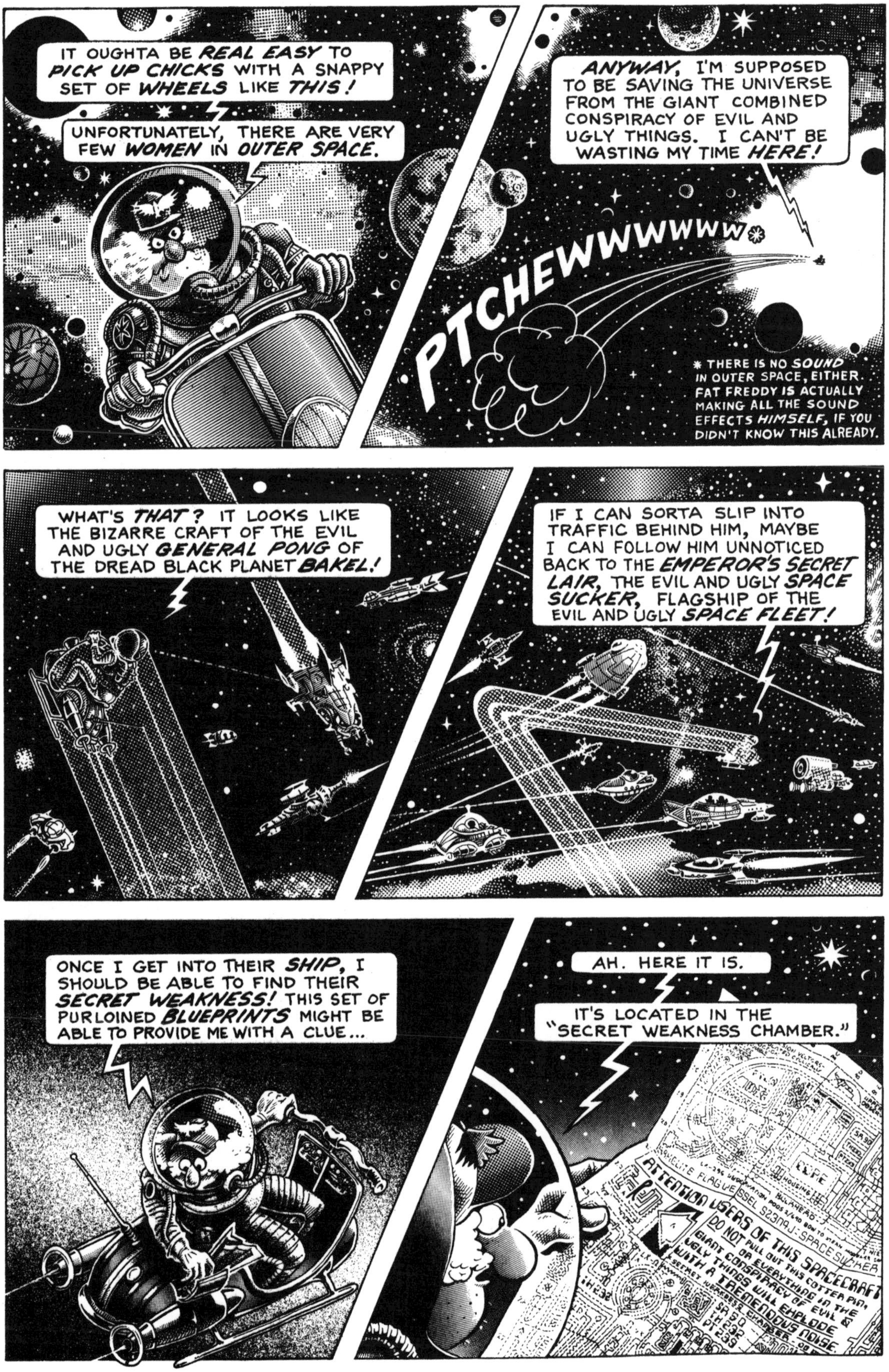

IT OUGHTA BE REAL EASY TO PICK UP CHICKS WITH A SNAPPY SET OF WHEELS LIKE THIS!
UNFORTUNATELY, THERE ARE VERY FEW WOMEN IN OUTER SPACE.
ANYWAY, I'M SUPPOSED TO BE SAVING THE UNIVERSE FROM THE GIANT COMBINED CONSPIRACY OF EVIL AND UGLY THINGS. I CAN'T BE WASTING MY TIME HERE!
PTCHEWWWWWWW*
* THERE IS NO SOUND IN OUTER SPACE, EITHER. FAT FREDDY IS ACTUALLY MAKING ALL THE SOUND EFFECTS HIMSELF, IF YOU DIDN'T KNOW THIS ALREADY.
WHAT'S THAT? IT LOOKS LIKE THE BIZARRE CRAFT OF THE EVIL AND UGLY GENERAL PONG OF THE DREAD BLACK PLANET BAKEL!
IF I CAN SORTA SLIP INTO TRAFFIC BEHIND HIM, MAYBE I CAN FOLLOW HIM UNNOTICED BACK TO THE EMPEROR'S SECRET LAIR, THE EVIL AND UGLY SPACE SUCKER, FLAGSHIP OF THE EVIL AND UGLY SPACE FLEET!
ONCE I GET INTO THEIR SHIP, I SHOULD BE ABLE TO FIND THEIR SECRET WEAKNESS! THIS SET OF PURLOINED BLUEPRINTS MIGHT BE ABLE TO PROVIDE ME WITH A CLUE...
AH. HERE IT IS.
IT'S LOCATED IN THE "SECRET WEAKNESS CHAMBER."
ATTENTION USERS OF THIS SPACECRAFT
DO NOT PULL OUT THIS COTTER PIN, OR EVERYTHING IN THE GIANT CONSPIRACY OF EVIL & UGLY THINGS WILL EXPLODE WITH A TREMENDOUS NOISE.
SSEL S23N9J-SPACESUCKER
HOUSING
SECRET WEAKNESS CHAMBER

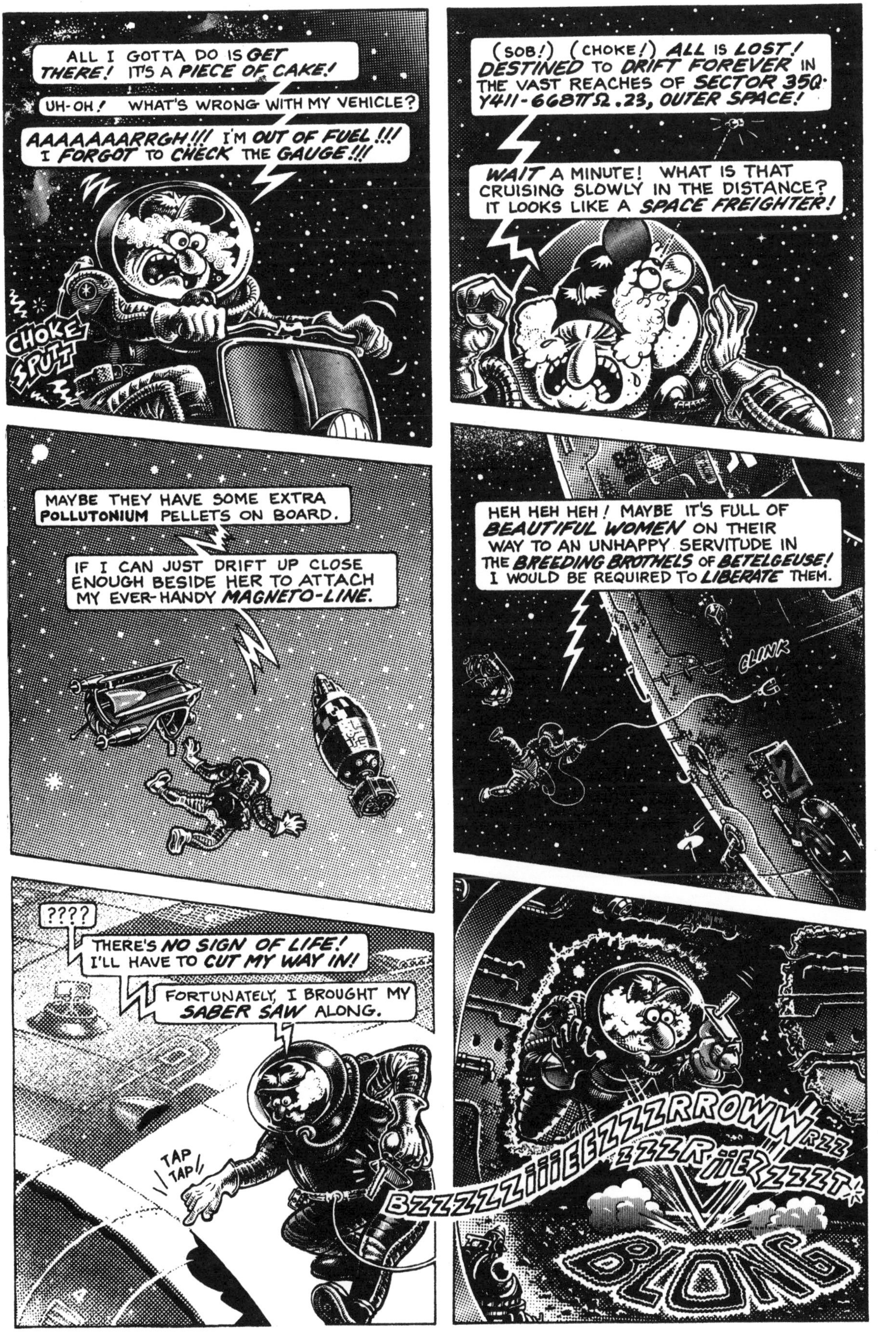
ALL I GOTTA DO IS GET THERE! IT'S A PIECE OF CAKE!
UH-OH! WHAT'S WRONG WITH MY VEHICLE?
AAAAAAARRGH!!! I'M OUT OF FUEL!!! I FORGOT TO CHECK THE GAUGE!!!
CHOKE
SPUTT
(SOB!) (CHOKE!) ALL IS LOST! DESTINED TO DRIFT FOREVER IN THE VAST REACHES OF SECTOR 35Q-Y411-668πΩ.23, OUTER SPACE!
WAIT A MINUTE! WHAT IS THAT CRUISING SLOWLY IN THE DISTANCE? IT LOOKS LIKE A SPACE FREIGHTER!
MAYBE THEY HAVE SOME EXTRA POLLUTONIUM PELLETS ON BOARD.
IF I CAN JUST DRIFT UP CLOSE ENOUGH BESIDE HER TO ATTACH MY EVER-HANDY MAGNETO-LINE.
HEH HEH HEH! MAYBE IT'S FULL OF BEAUTIFUL WOMEN ON THEIR WAY TO AN UNHAPPY SERVITUDE IN THE BREEDING BROTHELS OF BETELGEUSE! I WOULD BE REQUIRED TO LIBERATE THEM.
CLINK
????
THERE'S NO SIGN OF LIFE! I'LL HAVE TO CUT MY WAY IN!
FORTUNATELY, I BROUGHT MY SABER SAW ALONG.
TAP TAP
BLONG

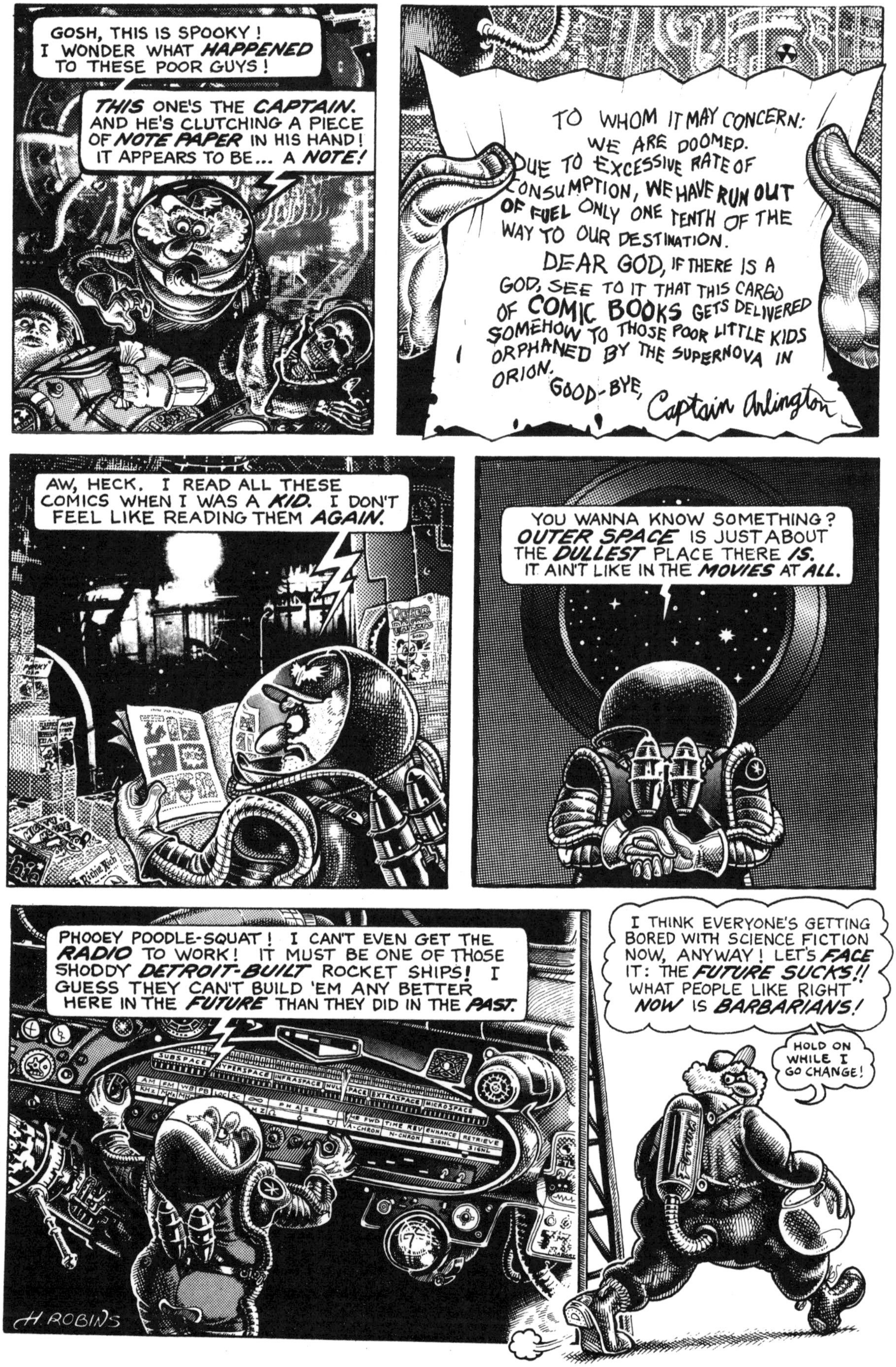
GOSH, THIS IS SPOOKY! I WONDER WHAT HAPPENED TO THESE POOR GUYS!
THIS ONE'S THE CAPTAIN. AND HE'S CLUTCHING A PIECE OF NOTE PAPER IN HIS HAND! IT APPEARS TO BE... A NOTE!
TO WHOM IT MAY CONCERN: WE ARE DOOMED. DUE TO EXCESSIVE RATE OF CONSUMPTION, WE HAVE RUN OUT OF FUEL ONLY ONE TENTH OF THE WAY TO OUR DESTINATION.
DEAR GOD, IF THERE IS A GOD, SEE TO IT THAT THIS CARGO OF COMIC BOOKS GETS DELIVERED SOMEHOW TO THOSE POOR LITTLE KIDS ORPHANED BY THE SUPERNOVA IN ORION.
GOOD-BYE, Captain Arlington
AW, HECK. I READ ALL THESE COMICS WHEN I WAS A KID. I DON'T FEEL LIKE READING THEM AGAIN.
YOU WANNA KNOW SOMETHING? OUTER SPACE IS JUST ABOUT THE DULLEST PLACE THERE IS. IT AIN'T LIKE IN THE MOVIES AT ALL.
PHOOEY POODLE-SQUAT! I CAN'T EVEN GET THE RADIO TO WORK! IT MUST BE ONE OF THOSE SHODDY DETROIT-BUILT ROCKET SHIPS! I GUESS THEY CAN'T BUILD 'EM ANY BETTER HERE IN THE FUTURE THAN THEY DID IN THE PAST.
SUBSPACE HYPERSPACE INFRASPACE EXTRASPACE MICROSPACE
PHASE
TIME REV ENHANCE RETRIEVE
A-CHRON N-CHRON SIGNL SIGNL
H. ROBINS
I THINK EVERYONE'S GETTING BORED WITH SCIENCE FICTION NOW, ANYWAY! LET'S FACE IT: THE FUTURE SUCKS!! WHAT PEOPLE LIKE RIGHT NOW IS BARBARIANS!
HOLD ON WHILE I GO CHANGE!

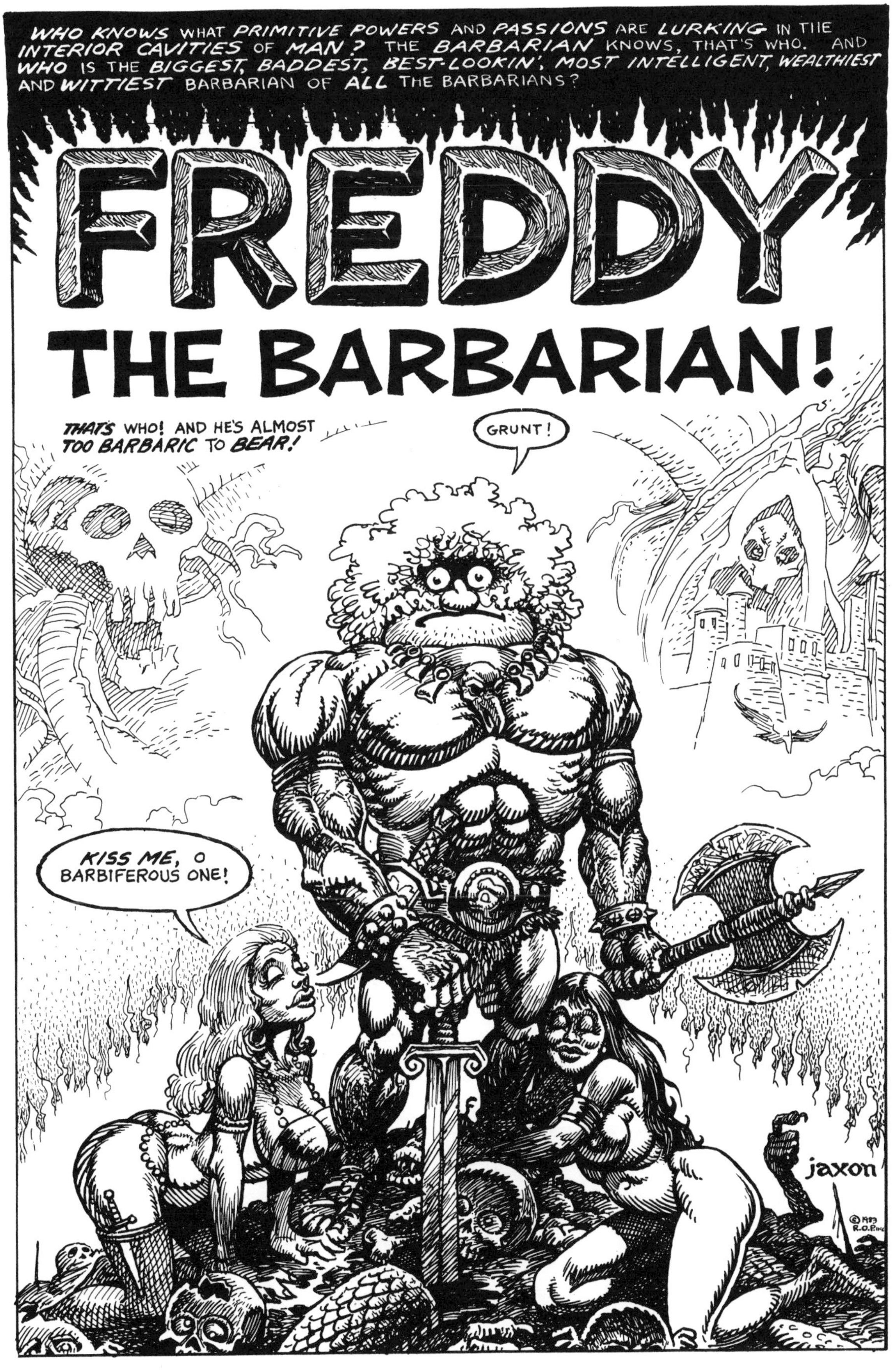
WHO KNOWS WHAT PRIMITIVE POWERS AND PASSIONS ARE LURKING IN THE INTERIOR CAVITIES OF MAN? THE BARBARIAN KNOWS, THAT'S WHO. AND WHO IS THE BIGGEST, BADDEST, BEST-LOOKIN', MOST INTELLIGENT, WEALTHIEST AND WITTIEST BARBARIAN OF ALL THE BARBARIANS?
FREDDY
THE BARBARIAN!
THAT'S WHO! AND HE'S ALMOST TOO BARBARIC TO BEAR!
GRUNT!
KISS ME, O BARBIFEROUS ONE!
jaxon

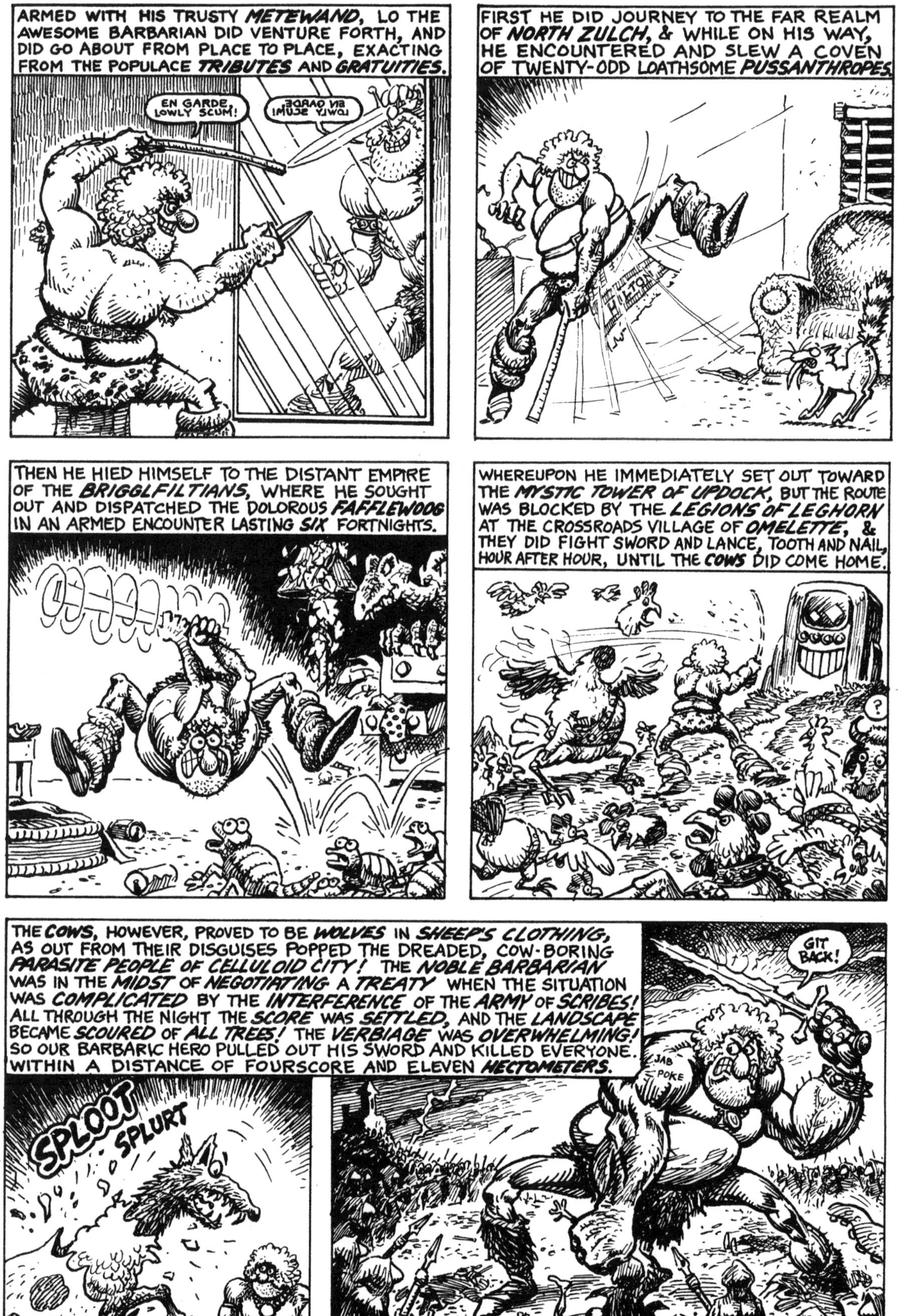
ARMED WITH HIS TRUSTY METEWAND, LO THE AWESOME BARBARIAN DID VENTURE FORTH, AND DID GO ABOUT FROM PLACE TO PLACE, EXACTING FROM THE POPULACE TRIBUTES AND GRATUITIES.
EN GARDE, LOWLY SCUM!
FIRST HE DID JOURNEY TO THE FAR REALM OF NORTH ZULCH, & WHILE ON HIS WAY, HE ENCOUNTERED AND SLEW A COVEN OF TWENTY-ODD LOATHSOME PUSSANTHROPES.
THEN HE HIED HIMSELF TO THE DISTANT EMPIRE OF THE BRIGGLFILTIANS, WHERE HE SOUGHT OUT AND DISPATCHED THE DOLOROUS FAFFLEWOOG IN AN ARMED ENCOUNTER LASTING SIX FORTNIGHTS.
WHEREUPON HE IMMEDIATELY SET OUT TOWARD THE MYSTIC TOWER OF UPDOCK, BUT THE ROUTE WAS BLOCKED BY THE LEGIONS OF LEGHORN AT THE CROSSROADS VILLAGE OF OMELETTE, & THEY DID FIGHT SWORD AND LANCE, TOOTH AND NAIL, HOUR AFTER HOUR, UNTIL THE COWS DID COME HOME.
?
THE COWS, HOWEVER, PROVED TO BE WOLVES IN SHEEP'S CLOTHING, AS OUT FROM THEIR DISGUISES POPPED THE DREADED, COW-BORING PARASITE PEOPLE OF CELLULOID CITY! THE NOBLE BARBARIAN WAS IN THE MIDST OF NEGOTIATING A TREATY WHEN THE SITUATION WAS COMPLICATED BY THE INTERFERENCE OF THE ARMY OF SCRIBES! ALL THROUGH THE NIGHT THE SCORE WAS SETTLED, AND THE LANDSCAPE BECAME SCOURED OF ALL TREES! THE VERBIAGE WAS OVERWHELMING! SO OUR BARBARIC HERO PULLED OUT HIS SWORD AND KILLED EVERYONE WITHIN A DISTANCE OF FOURSCORE AND ELEVEN HECTOMETERS.
GIT BACK!
JAB
POKE
SPLOOT
SPLURT

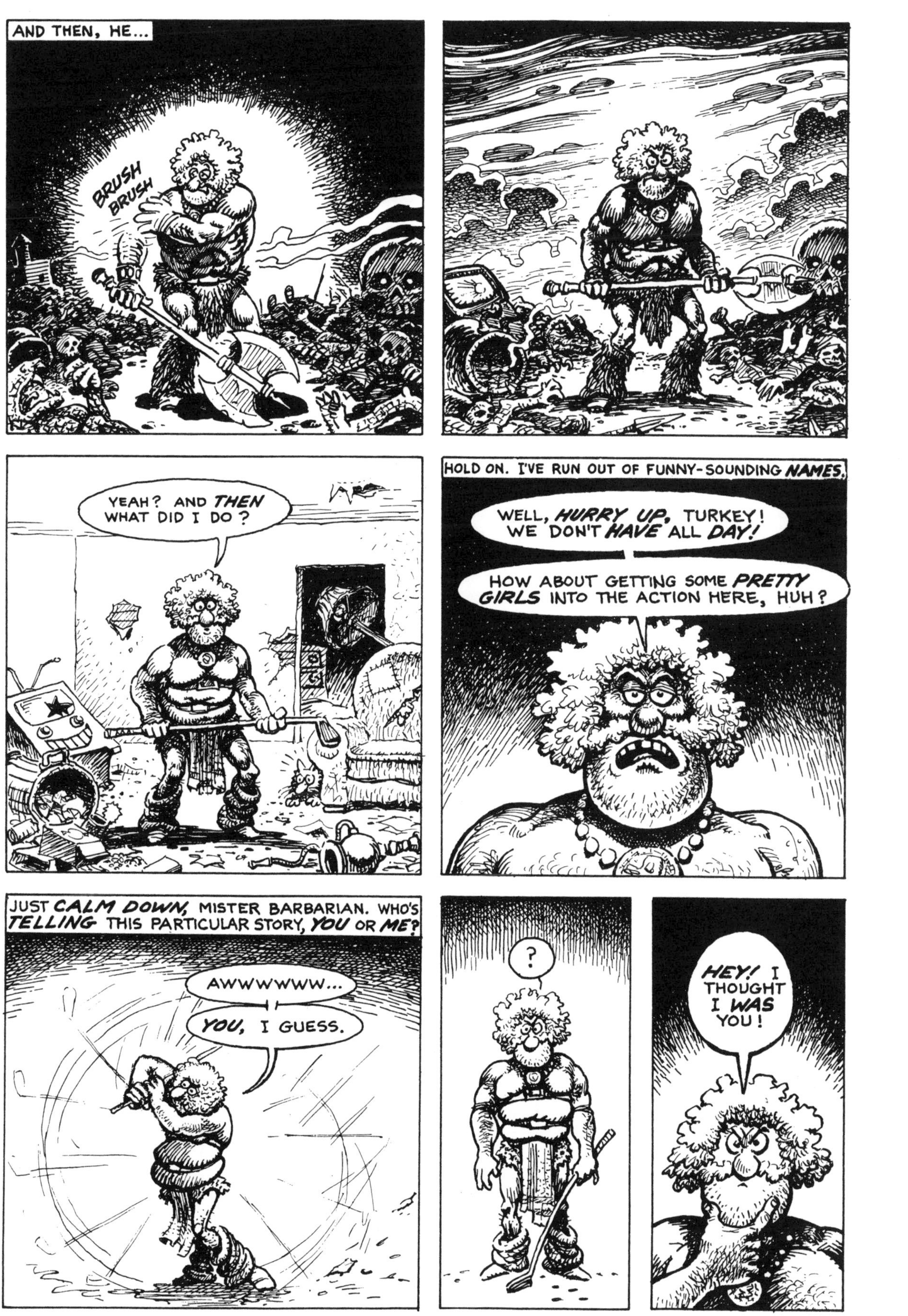
AND THEN, HE...
BRUSH BRUSH
YEAH? AND THEN WHAT DID I DO?
HOLD ON. I'VE RUN OUT OF FUNNY-SOUNDING NAMES.
WELL, HURRY UP, TURKEY! WE DON'T HAVE ALL DAY!
HOW ABOUT GETTING SOME PRETTY GIRLS INTO THE ACTION HERE, HUH?
JUST CALM DOWN, MISTER BARBARIAN. WHO'S TELLING THIS PARTICULAR STORY, YOU OR ME?
AWWWWWW...
YOU, I GUESS.
?
HEY! I THOUGHT I WAS YOU!

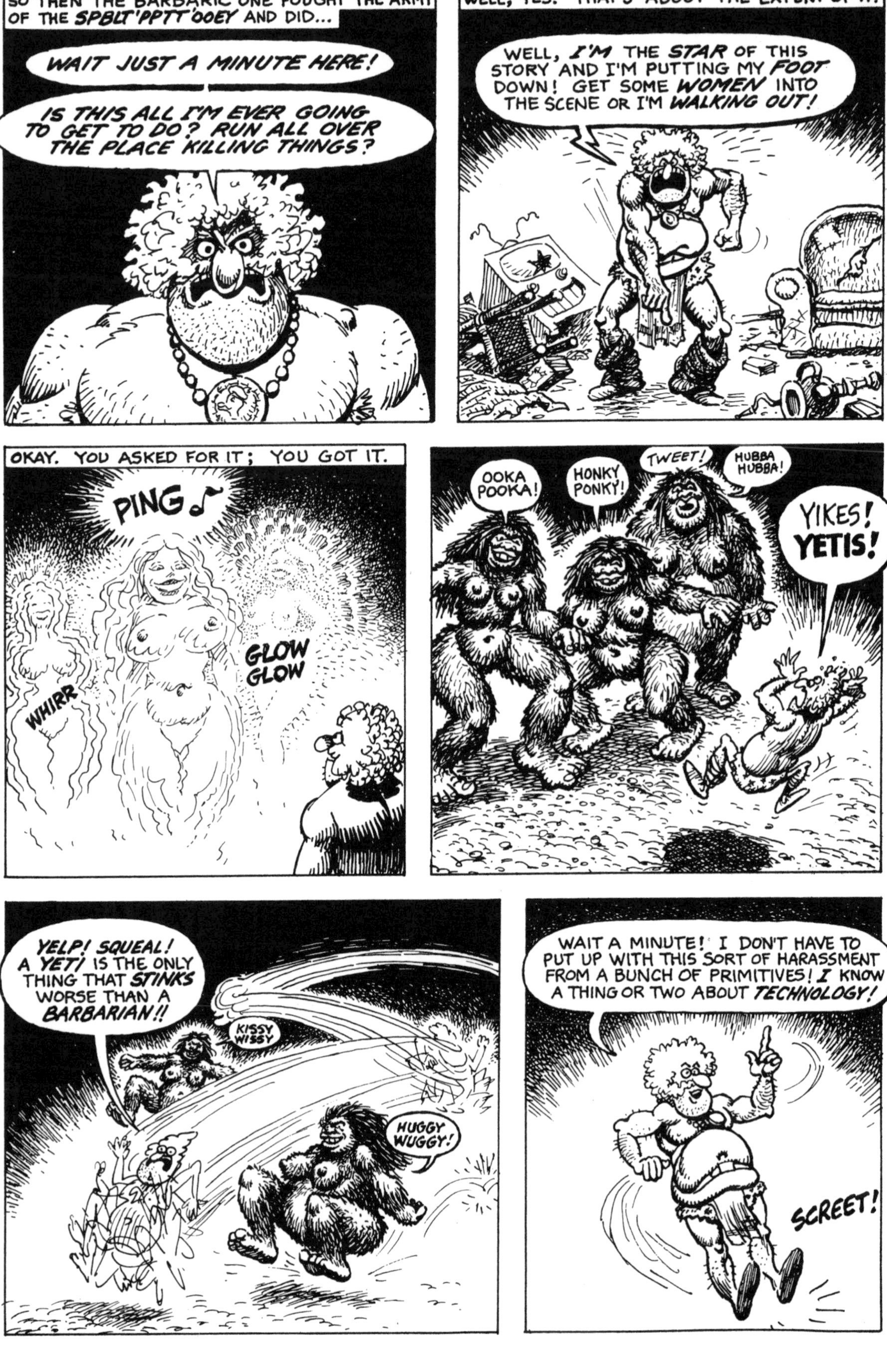
SO THEN THE BARBARIC ONE FOUGHT THE ARMY OF THE SPBLT'PPTT'OOEY AND DID...
WAIT JUST A MINUTE HERE!
IS THIS ALL I'M EVER GOING TO GET TO DO? RUN ALL OVER THE PLACE KILLING THINGS?
WELL, YES. THAT'S ABOUT THE EXTENT OF IT.
WELL, I'M THE STAR OF THIS STORY AND I'M PUTTING MY FOOT DOWN! GET SOME WOMEN INTO THE SCENE OR I'M WALKING OUT!
OKAY. YOU ASKED FOR IT; YOU GOT IT.
PING
GLOW GLOW
WHIRR
OOKA POOKA!
HONKY PONKY!
TWEET!
HUBBA HUBBA!
YIKES! YETIS!
YELP! SQUEAL! A YETI IS THE ONLY THING THAT STINKS WORSE THAN A BARBARIAN!!
KISSY WISSY
HUGGY WUGGY!
WAIT A MINUTE! I DON'T HAVE TO PUT UP WITH THIS SORT OF HARASSMENT FROM A BUNCH OF PRIMITIVES! I KNOW A THING OR TWO ABOUT TECHNOLOGY!
SCREET!

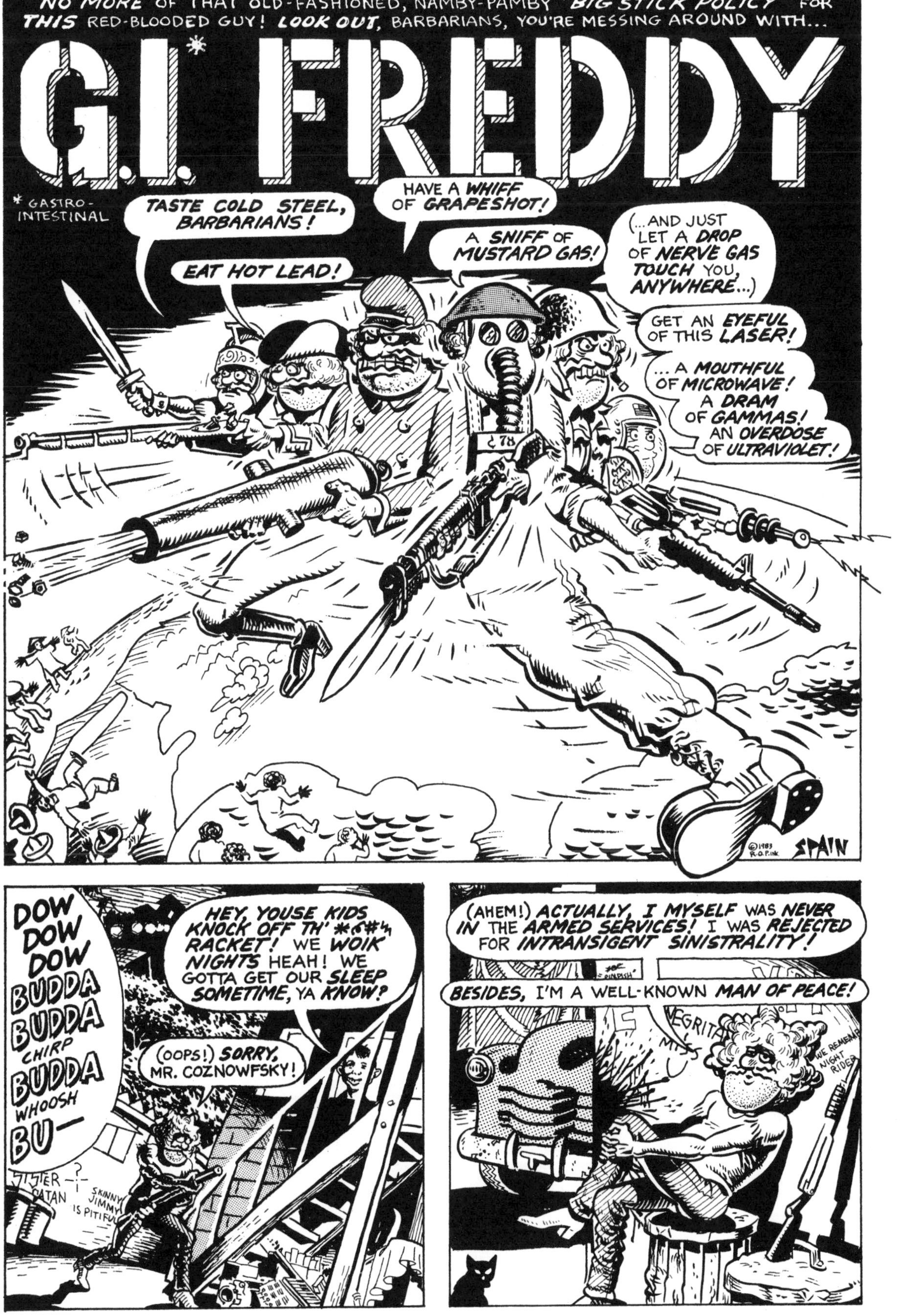
NO MORE OF THAT OLD-FASHIONED, NAMBY-PAMBY "BIG STICK POLICY" FOR THIS RED-BLOODED GUY! LOOK OUT, BARBARIANS, YOU'RE MESSING AROUND WITH...
G.I.* FREDDY
* GASTRO-INTESTINAL
TASTE COLD STEEL, BARBARIANS!
EAT HOT LEAD!
HAVE A WHIFF OF GRAPESHOT!
A SNIFF OF MUSTARD GAS!
(...AND JUST LET A DROP OF NERVE GAS TOUCH YOU, ANYWHERE...)
GET AN EYEFUL OF THIS LASER!
...A MOUTHFUL OF MICROWAVE! A DRAM OF GAMMAS! AN OVERDOSE OF ULTRAVIOLET!
¢78
©1983 R.O.P. INK
SPAIN
DOW DOW DOW DOW BUDDA BUDDA CHIRP BUDDA WHOOSH BU—
HEY, YOUSE KIDS KNOCK OFF TH' *&#% RACKET! WE WOIK NIGHTS HEAH! WE GOTTA GET OUR SLEEP SOMETIME, YA KNOW?
(OOPS!) SORRY, MR. COZNOWFSKY!
SISTER SATAN
SKINNY JIMMY IS PITIFUL
(AHEM!) ACTUALLY, I MYSELF WAS NEVER IN THE ARMED SERVICES! I WAS REJECTED FOR INTRANSIGENT SINISTRALITY!
BESIDES, I'M A WELL-KNOWN MAN OF PEACE!
WE REMEMB NIGHT RIDER

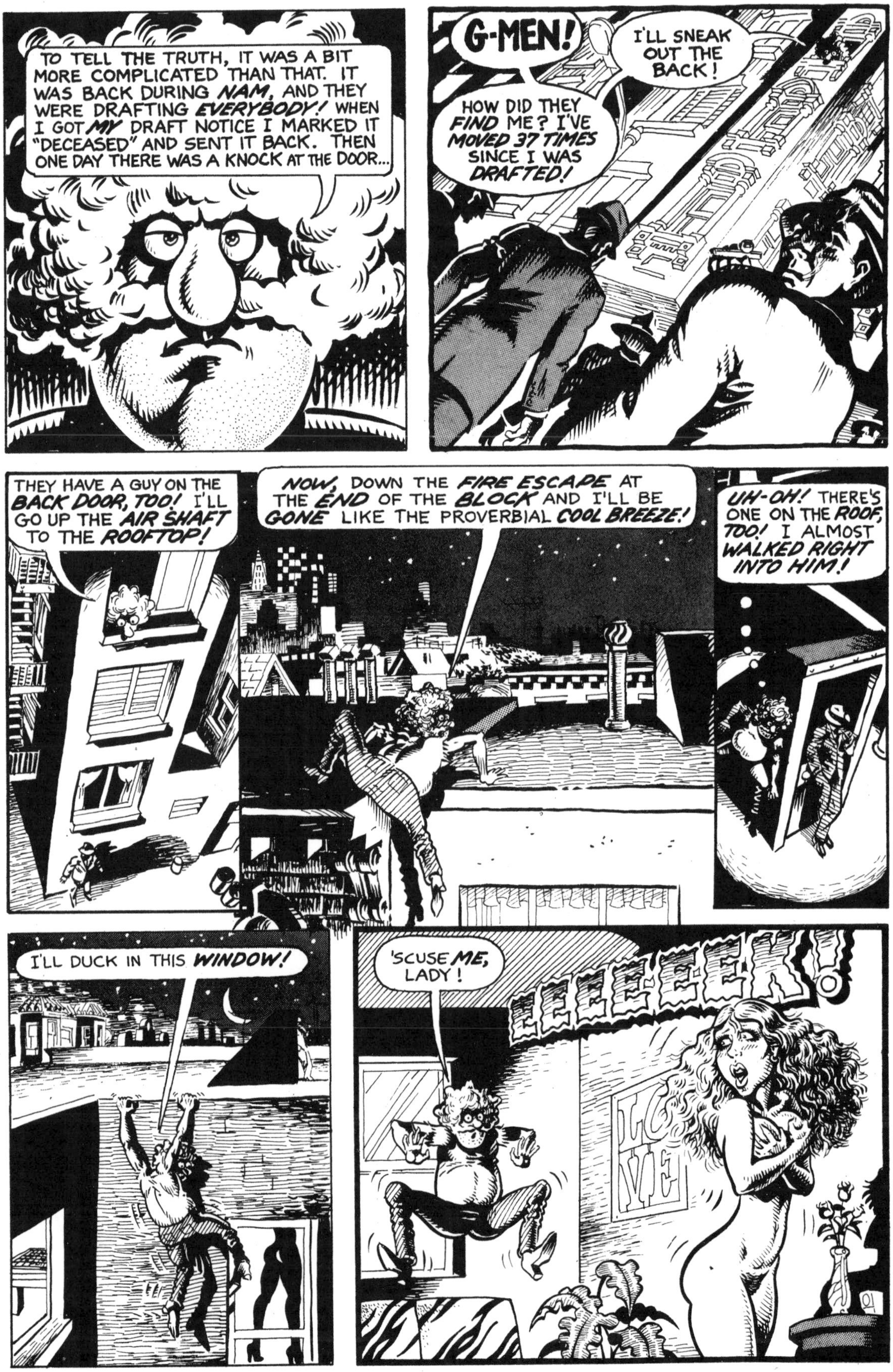
TO TELL THE TRUTH, IT WAS A BIT MORE COMPLICATED THAN THAT. IT WAS BACK DURING NAM, AND THEY WERE DRAFTING EVERYBODY! WHEN I GOT MY DRAFT NOTICE I MARKED IT "DECEASED" AND SENT IT BACK. THEN ONE DAY THERE WAS A KNOCK AT THE DOOR...
G-MEN!
HOW DID THEY FIND ME? I'VE MOVED 37 TIMES SINCE I WAS DRAFTED!
I'LL SNEAK OUT THE BACK!
THEY HAVE A GUY ON THE BACK DOOR, TOO! I'LL GO UP THE AIR SHAFT TO THE ROOFTOP!
NOW, DOWN THE FIRE ESCAPE AT THE END OF THE BLOCK AND I'LL BE GONE LIKE THE PROVERBIAL COOL BREEZE!
UH-OH! THERE'S ONE ON THE ROOF, TOO! I ALMOST WALKED RIGHT INTO HIM!
I'LL DUCK IN THIS WINDOW!
'SCUSE ME, LADY!
EEEEEEK!

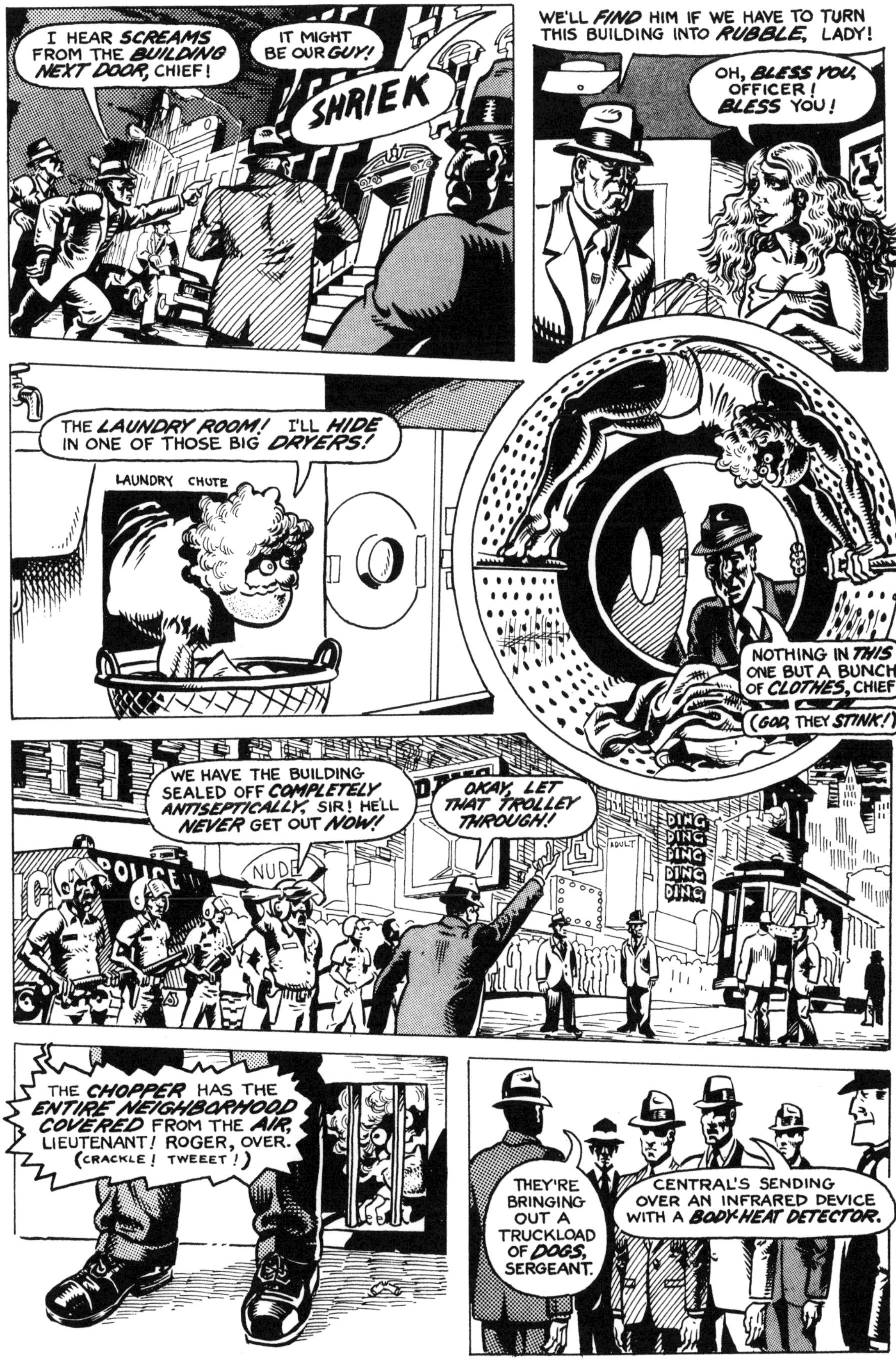
I HEAR SCREAMS FROM THE BUILDING NEXT DOOR, CHIEF!
IT MIGHT BE OUR GUY!
SHRIEK
WE'LL FIND HIM IF WE HAVE TO TURN THIS BUILDING INTO RUBBLE, LADY!
OH, BLESS YOU, OFFICER! BLESS YOU!
THE LAUNDRY ROOM! I'LL HIDE IN ONE OF THOSE BIG DRYERS!
LAUNDRY CHUTE
NOTHING IN THIS ONE BUT A BUNCH OF CLOTHES, CHIEF!
(GOD, THEY STINK!)
WE HAVE THE BUILDING SEALED OFF COMPLETELY ANTISEPTICALLY, SIR! HE'LL NEVER GET OUT NOW!
OKAY, LET THAT TROLLEY THROUGH!
POLICE
NUDE
ADULT
DING DING DING DING DING
THE CHOPPER HAS THE ENTIRE NEIGHBORHOOD COVERED FROM THE AIR, LIEUTENANT! ROGER, OVER.
(CRACKLE! TWEEET!)
THEY'RE BRINGING OUT A TRUCKLOAD OF DOGS, SERGEANT.
CENTRAL'S SENDING OVER AN INFRARED DEVICE WITH A BODY-HEAT DETECTOR.

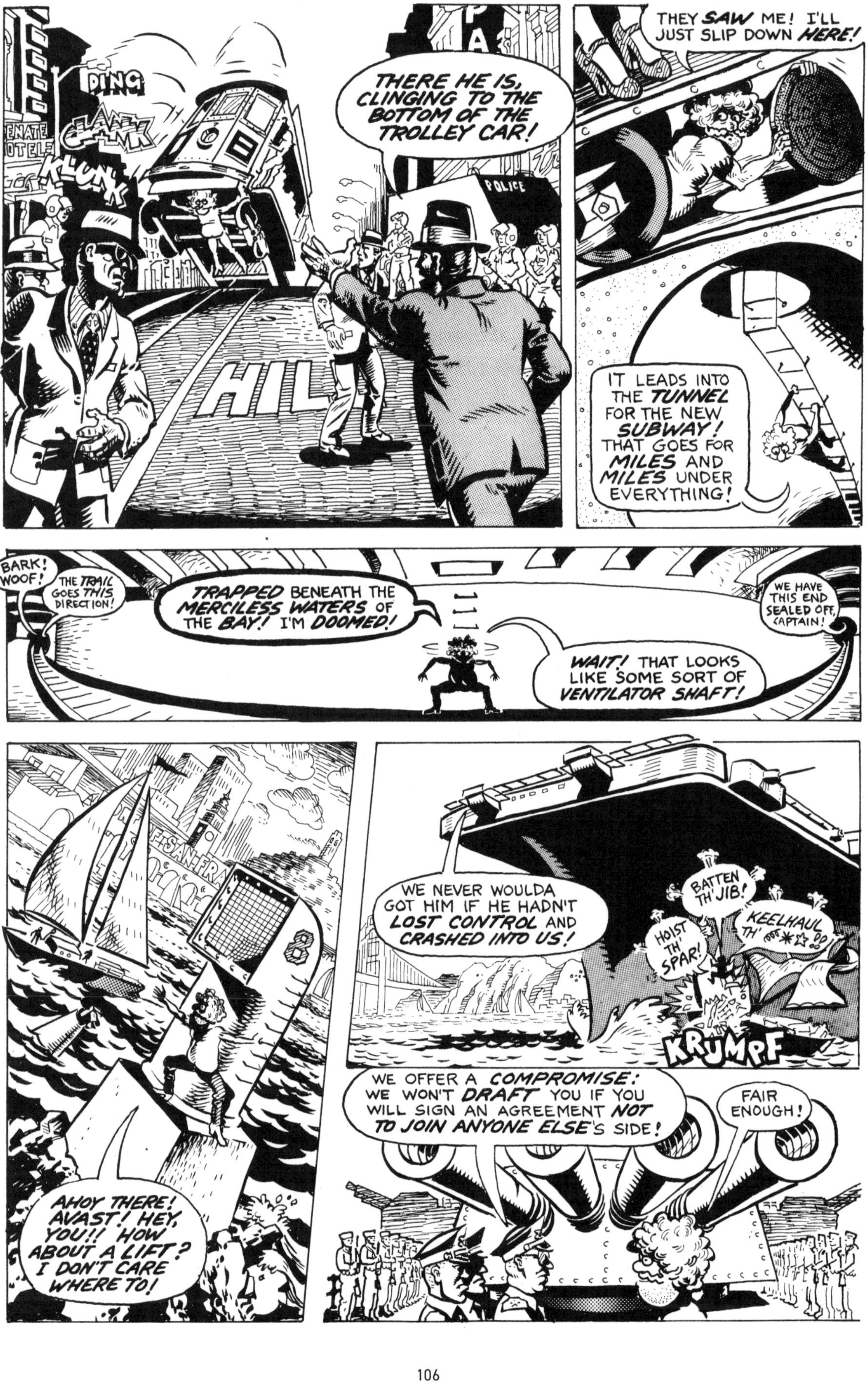
DING
CLANK
KLUNK
THERE HE IS, CLINGING TO THE BOTTOM OF THE TROLLEY CAR!
POLICE
HILL
THEY SAW ME! I'LL JUST SLIP DOWN HERE!
IT LEADS INTO THE TUNNEL FOR THE NEW SUBWAY! THAT GOES FOR MILES AND MILES UNDER EVERYTHING!
BARK! WOOF!
THE TRAIL GOES THIS DIRECTION!
TRAPPED BENEATH THE MERCILESS WATERS OF THE BAY! I'M DOOMED!
WE HAVE THIS END SEALED OFF, CAPTAIN!
WAIT! THAT LOOKS LIKE SOME SORT OF VENTILATOR SHAFT!
AHOY THERE! AVAST! HEY, YOU!! HOW ABOUT A LIFT? I DON'T CARE WHERE TO!
WE NEVER WOULDA GOT HIM IF HE HADN'T LOST CONTROL AND CRASHED INTO US!
BATTEN TH' JIB!
HOIST TH' SPAR!
KEELHAUL TH'
KRUMPF
WE OFFER A COMPROMISE: WE WON'T DRAFT YOU IF YOU WILL SIGN AN AGREEMENT NOT TO JOIN ANYONE ELSE'S SIDE!
FAIR ENOUGH!

GOODNESS! IS THAT TRULY FAIR, NOW? WELL, ALL'S FAIR IN LOVE AND WAR, AS THEY SAY. FAIR'S FAIR, THEY SAY, TOO. NOT GOOD, JUST FAIR. ALL'S NOT GOOD IN LOVE AND WAR. BUT ANYHOW... YOU'VE HEARD OF GOOD, REAL, AND TRUE LOVE, BUT HAVE YOU EVER HEARD OF A FAIR LOVE? YOU'RE ABOUT TO! HERE'S A FAIRLY GOOD, FAIRLY REAL, AND FAIRLY TRUTHFUL EPISODE FROM THE ANNALS OF

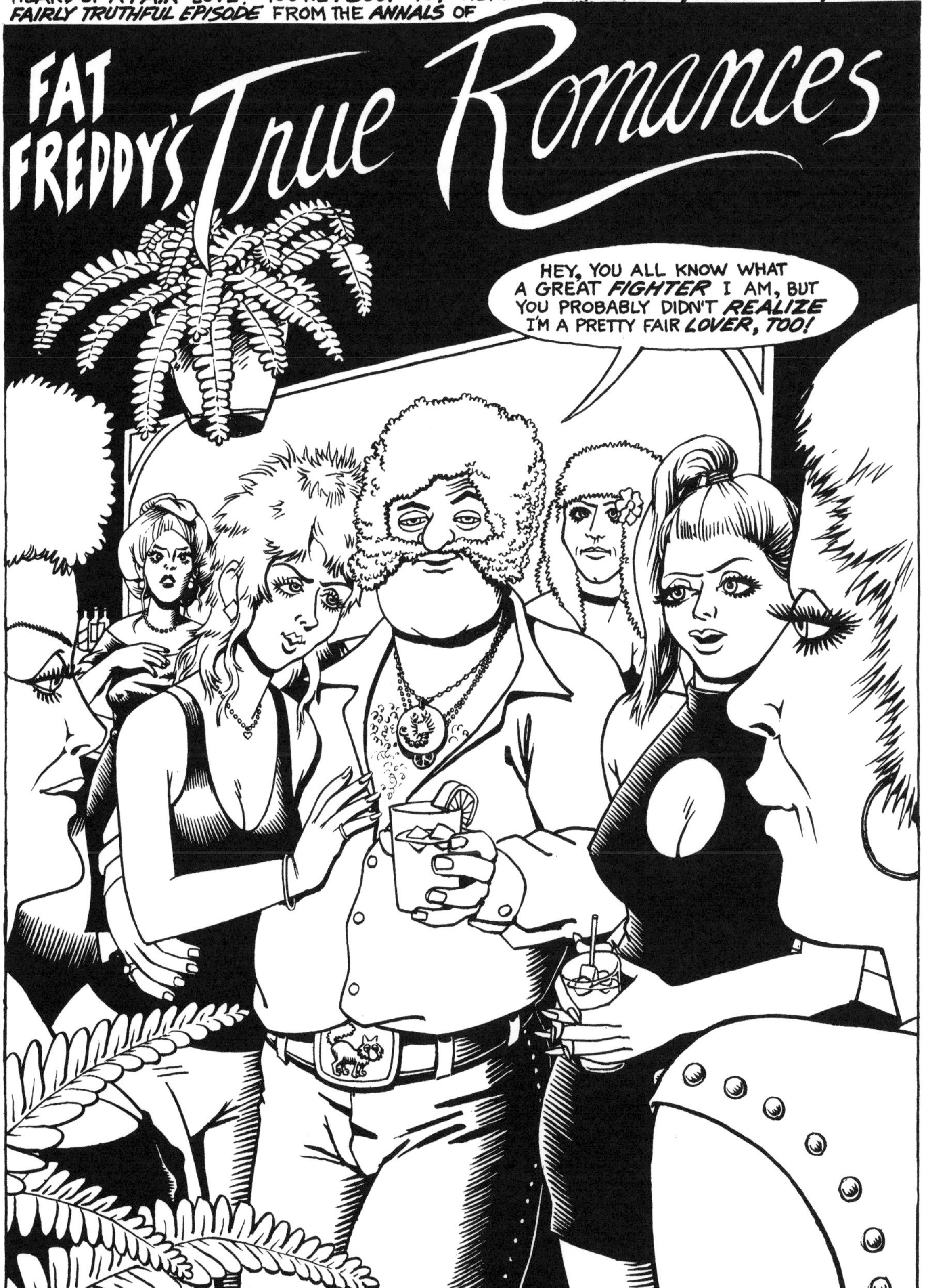
FAT FREDDY'S True Romances
HEY, YOU ALL KNOW WHAT A GREAT FIGHTER I AM, BUT YOU PROBABLY DIDN'T REALIZE I'M A PRETTY FAIR LOVER, TOO!
GUY COLWELL ©R.O.P. INC.

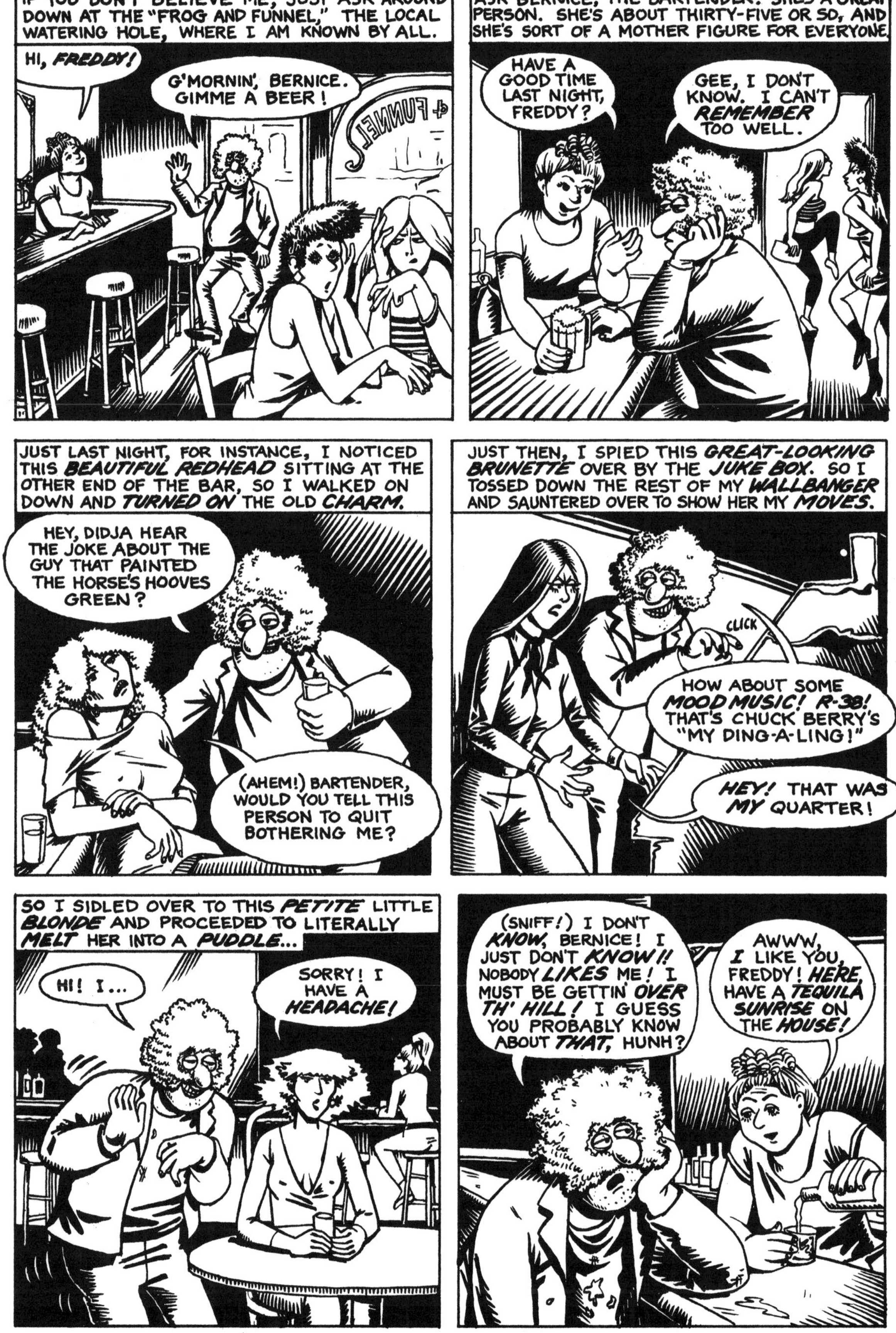
IF YOU DON'T BELIEVE ME, JUST ASK AROUND DOWN AT THE "FROG AND FUNNEL," THE LOCAL WATERING HOLE, WHERE I AM KNOWN BY ALL.
HI, FREDDY!
G'MORNIN', BERNICE. GIMME A BEER!
& FUNNEL
ASK BERNICE, THE BARTENDER. SHE'S A GREAT PERSON. SHE'S ABOUT THIRTY-FIVE OR SO, AND SHE'S SORT OF A MOTHER FIGURE FOR EVERYONE.
HAVE A GOOD TIME LAST NIGHT, FREDDY?
GEE, I DON'T KNOW. I CAN'T REMEMBER TOO WELL.
JUST LAST NIGHT, FOR INSTANCE, I NOTICED THIS BEAUTIFUL REDHEAD SITTING AT THE OTHER END OF THE BAR, SO I WALKED ON DOWN AND TURNED ON THE OLD CHARM.
HEY, DIDJA HEAR THE JOKE ABOUT THE GUY THAT PAINTED THE HORSE'S HOOVES GREEN?
(AHEM!) BARTENDER, WOULD YOU TELL THIS PERSON TO QUIT BOTHERING ME?
JUST THEN, I SPIED THIS GREAT-LOOKING BRUNETTE OVER BY THE JUKE BOX. SO I TOSSED DOWN THE REST OF MY WALLBANGER AND SAUNTERED OVER TO SHOW HER MY MOVES.
CLICK
HOW ABOUT SOME MOOD MUSIC! R-38! THAT'S CHUCK BERRY'S "MY DING-A-LING!"
HEY! THAT WAS MY QUARTER!
SO I SIDLED OVER TO THIS PETITE LITTLE BLONDE AND PROCEEDED TO LITERALLY MELT HER INTO A PUDDLE...
HI! I...
SORRY! I HAVE A HEADACHE!
(SNIFF!) I DON'T KNOW, BERNICE! I JUST DON'T KNOW!! NOBODY LIKES ME! I MUST BE GETTIN' OVER TH' HILL! I GUESS YOU PROBABLY KNOW ABOUT THAT, HUNH?
AWWW, I LIKE YOU, FREDDY! HERE, HAVE A TEQUILA SUNRISE ON THE HOUSE!

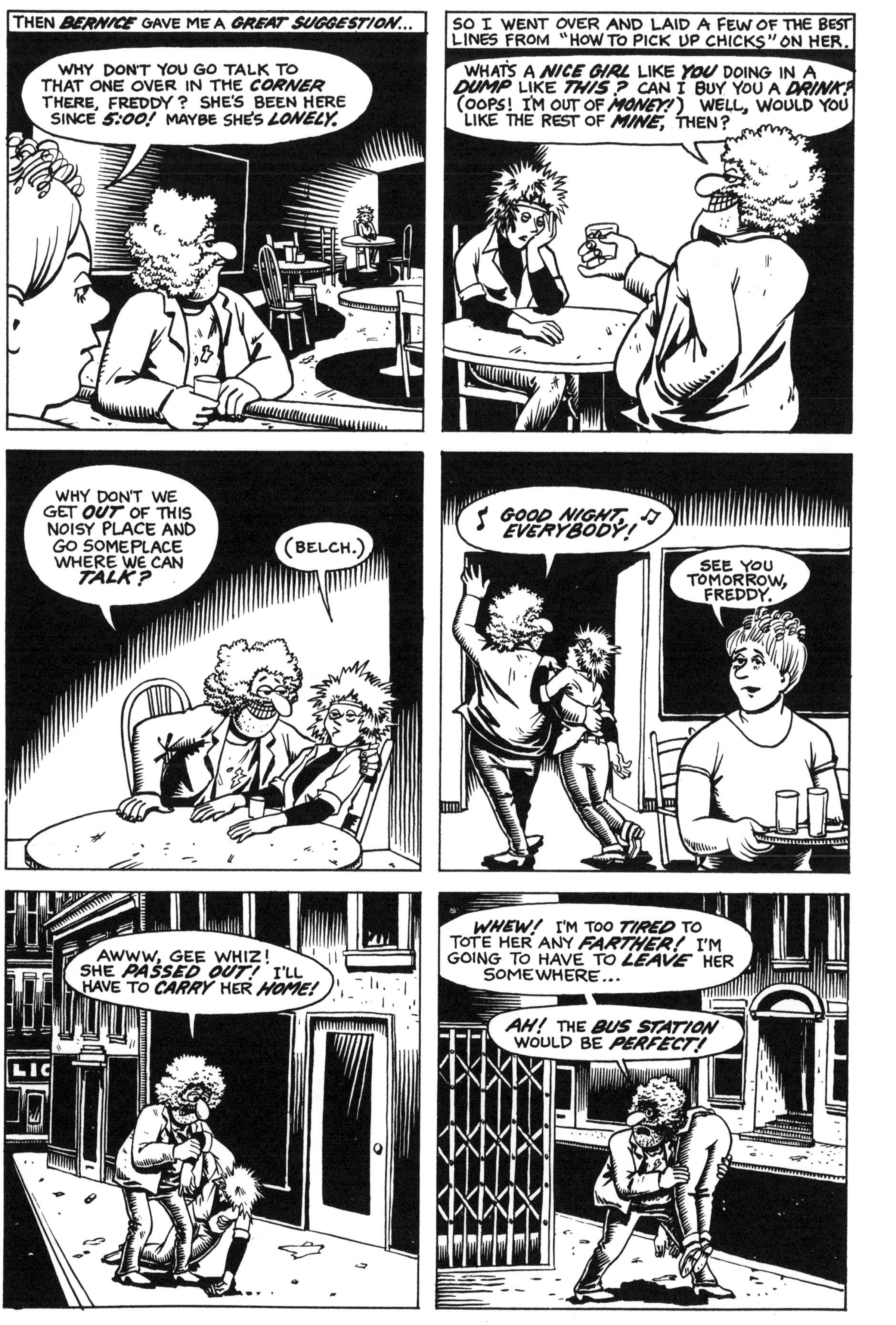
THEN BERNICE GAVE ME A GREAT SUGGESTION...
WHY DON'T YOU GO TALK TO THAT ONE OVER IN THE CORNER THERE, FREDDY? SHE'S BEEN HERE SINCE 5:00! MAYBE SHE'S LONELY.
SO I WENT OVER AND LAID A FEW OF THE BEST LINES FROM "HOW TO PICK UP CHICKS" ON HER.
WHAT'S A NICE GIRL LIKE YOU DOING IN A DUMP LIKE THIS? CAN I BUY YOU A DRINK? (OOPS! I'M OUT OF MONEY!) WELL, WOULD YOU LIKE THE REST OF MINE, THEN?
WHY DON'T WE GET OUT OF THIS NOISY PLACE AND GO SOMEPLACE WHERE WE CAN TALK?
(BELCH.)
GOOD NIGHT, EVERYBODY!
SEE YOU TOMORROW, FREDDY.
AWWW, GEE WHIZ! SHE PASSED OUT! I'LL HAVE TO CARRY HER HOME!
LIC
WHEW! I'M TOO TIRED TO TOTE HER ANY FARTHER! I'M GOING TO HAVE TO LEAVE HER SOMEWHERE...
AH! THE BUS STATION WOULD BE PERFECT!

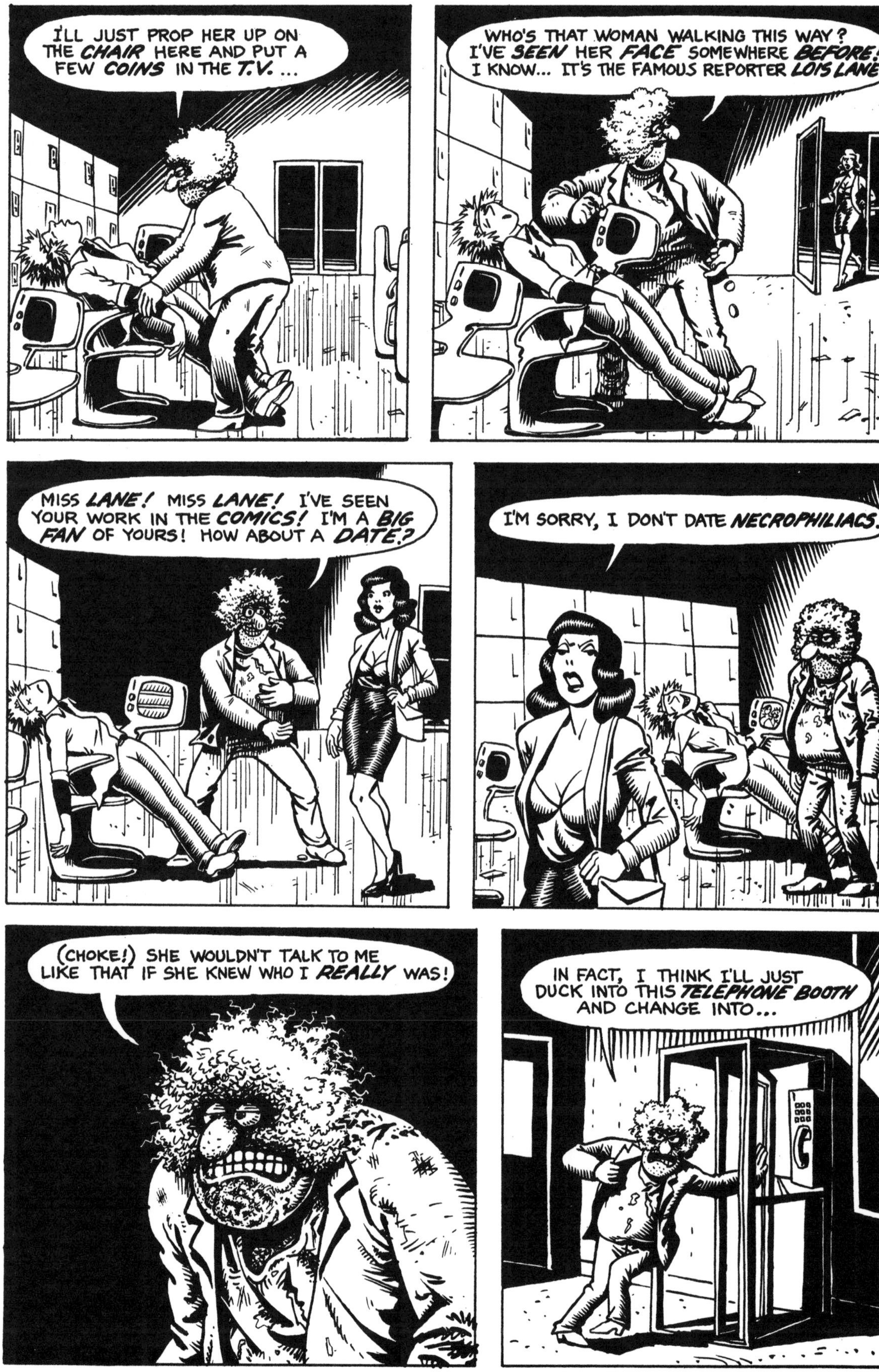
I'LL JUST PROP HER UP ON THE CHAIR HERE AND PUT A FEW COINS IN THE T.V. ...
WHO'S THAT WOMAN WALKING THIS WAY? I'VE SEEN HER FACE SOMEWHERE BEFORE! I KNOW... IT'S THE FAMOUS REPORTER LOIS LANE!
MISS LANE! MISS LANE! I'VE SEEN YOUR WORK IN THE COMICS! I'M A BIG FAN OF YOURS! HOW ABOUT A DATE?
I'M SORRY, I DON'T DATE NECROPHILIACS.
(CHOKE!) SHE WOULDN'T TALK TO ME LIKE THAT IF SHE KNEW WHO I REALLY WAS!
IN FACT, I THINK I'LL JUST DUCK INTO THIS TELEPHONE BOOTH AND CHANGE INTO...

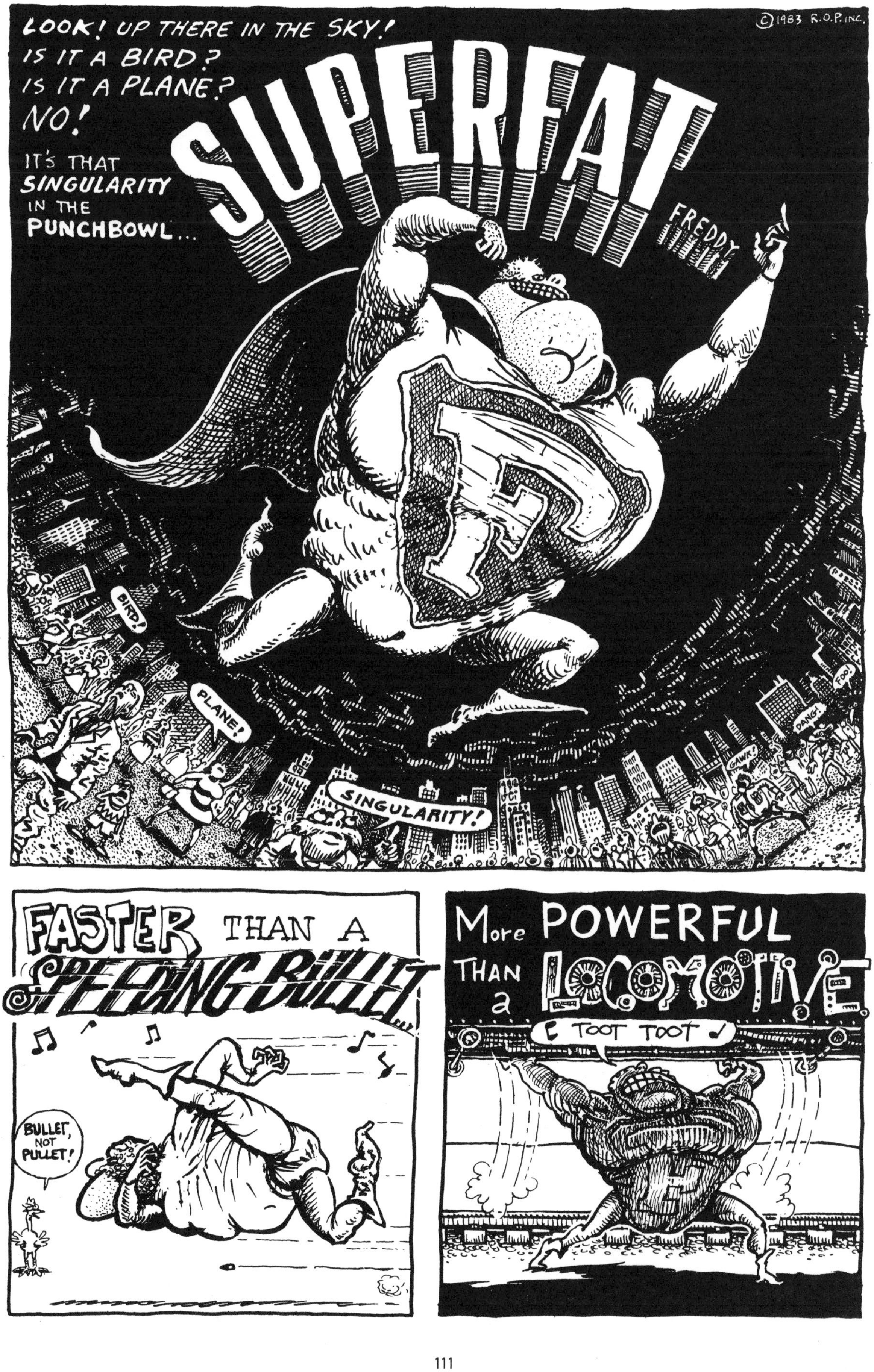
LOOK! UP THERE IN THE SKY!
IS IT A BIRD?
IS IT A PLANE?
NO!
IT'S THAT SINGULARITY IN THE PUNCHBOWL...
SUPERFAT
FREDDY
©1983 R.O.P. INC.
BIRD!
PLANE!
SINGULARITY!
FASTER THAN A SPEEDING BULLET
BULLET, NOT PULLET!
More POWERFUL THAN a LOCOMOTIVE
TOOT TOOT

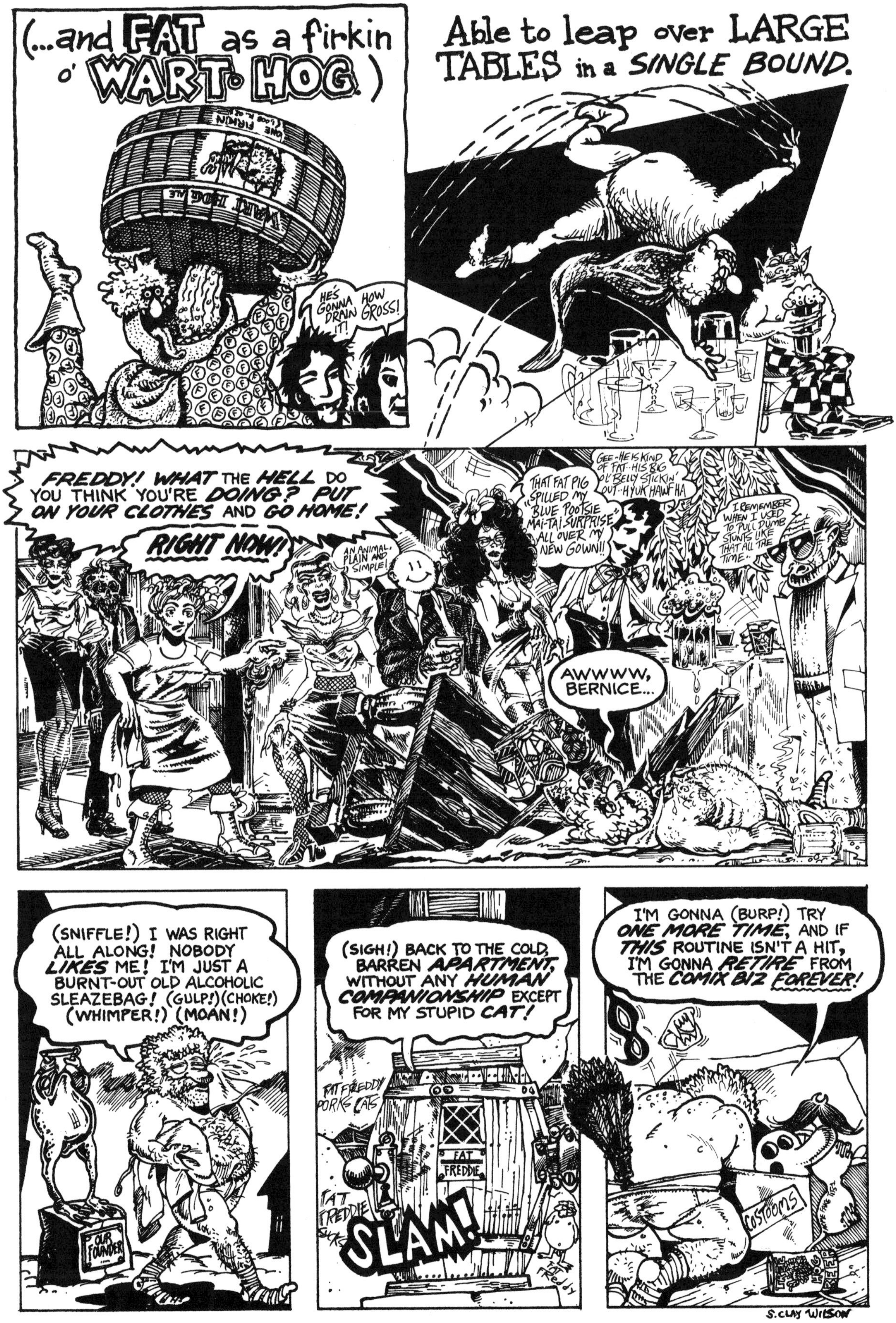
(...and FAT as a firkin o' WART-HOG)
ONE FIRKIN
WART HOG ALE
HE'S GONNA DRAIN IT!
HOW GROSS!
Able to leap over LARGE TABLES in a SINGLE BOUND.
FREDDY! WHAT THE HELL DO YOU THINK YOU'RE DOING? PUT ON YOUR CLOTHES AND GO HOME!
RIGHT NOW!
AN ANIMAL, PLAIN AND SIMPLE!
THAT FAT PIG SPILLED MY "BLUE POOTSIE MAI-TAI SURPRISE" ALL OVER MY NEW GOWN!!
GEE-HE IS KIND OF FAT.. HIS BIG OL' BELLY STICKIN' OUT.. HYUK HAWF HA
I REMEMBER WHEN I USED TO PULL DUMB STUNTS LIKE THAT ALL THE TIME..
AWWWW, BERNICE...
(SNIFFLE!) I WAS RIGHT ALL ALONG! NOBODY LIKES ME! I'M JUST A BURNT-OUT OLD ALCOHOLIC SLEAZEBAG! (GULP!)(CHOKE!) (WHIMPER!) (MOAN!)
OUR FOUNDER
(SIGH!) BACK TO THE COLD, BARREN APARTMENT, WITHOUT ANY HUMAN COMPANIONSHIP EXCEPT FOR MY STUPID CAT!
FAT FREDDY PORKS CATS
FAT FREDDIE
FAT FREDDIE SUCKS
SLAM!
I'M GONNA (BURP!) TRY ONE MORE TIME, AND IF THIS ROUTINE ISN'T A HIT, I'M GONNA RETIRE FROM THE COMIX BIZ FOREVER!
COSTOOMS
S. CLAY WILSON

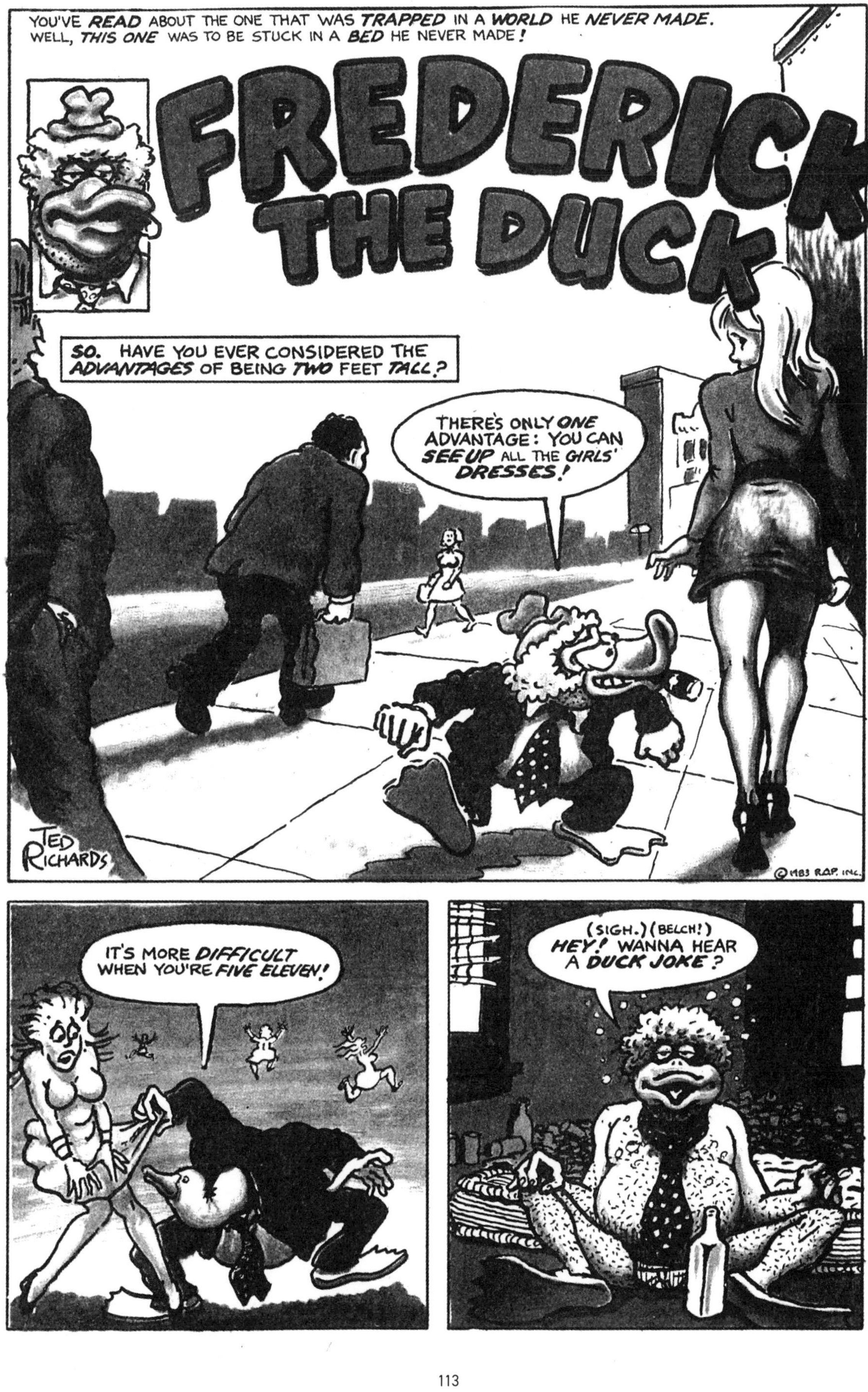
YOU'VE READ ABOUT THE ONE THAT WAS TRAPPED IN A WORLD HE NEVER MADE.
WELL, THIS ONE WAS TO BE STUCK IN A BED HE NEVER MADE!
FREDERICK THE DUCK
SO. HAVE YOU EVER CONSIDERED THE ADVANTAGES OF BEING TWO FEET TALL?
THERE'S ONLY ONE ADVANTAGE: YOU CAN SEE UP ALL THE GIRLS' DRESSES!
TED RICHARDS
© 1983 RAP, INC.
IT'S MORE DIFFICULT WHEN YOU'RE FIVE ELEVEN!
(SIGH.) (BELCH!) HEY! WANNA HEAR A DUCK JOKE?

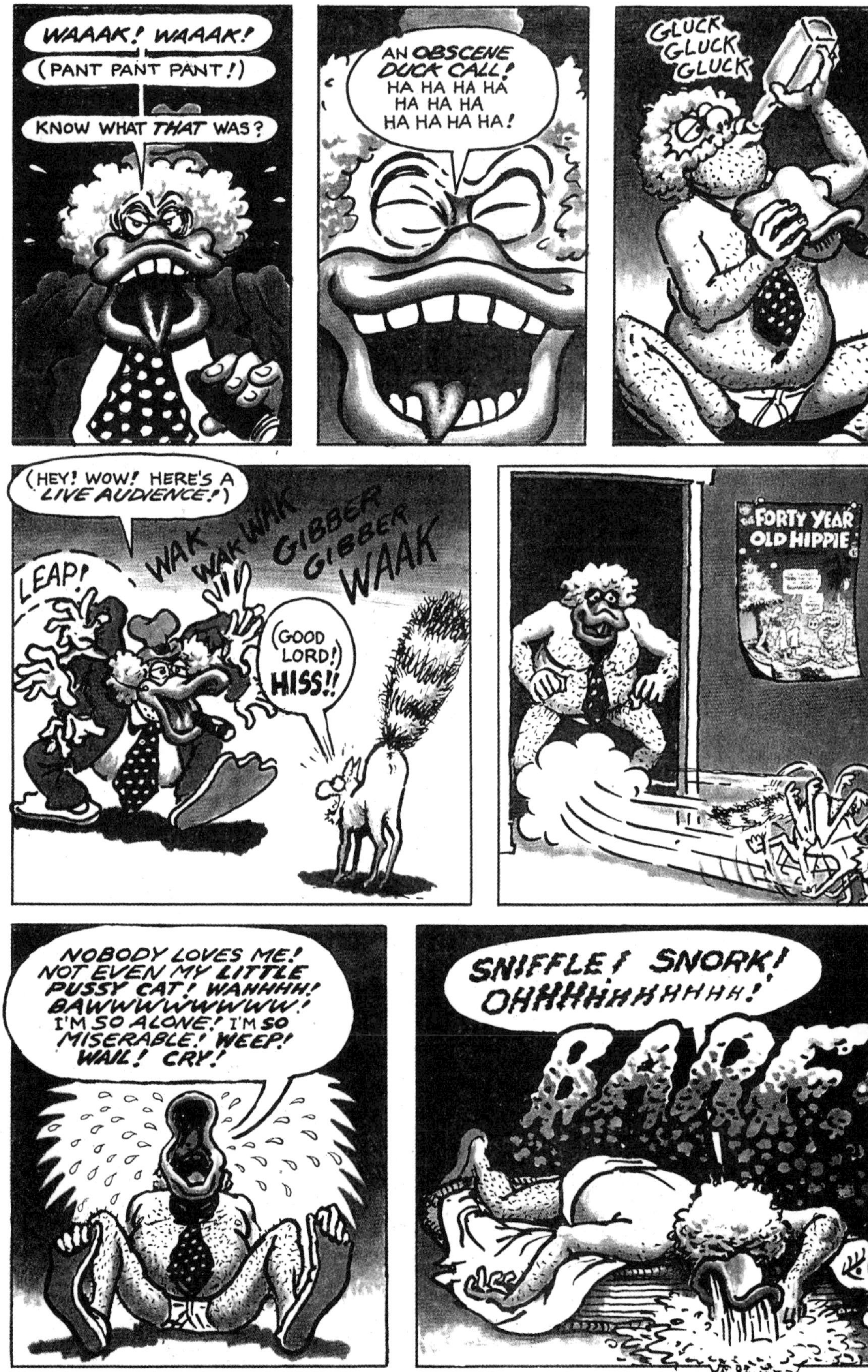
WAAAK! WAAAK!
(PANT PANT PANT!)
KNOW WHAT THAT WAS?
AN OBSCENE DUCK CALL! HA HA HA HA HA HA HA HA HA HA HA!
GLUCK GLUCK GLUCK
(HEY! WOW! HERE'S A LIVE AUDIENCE!)
LEAP!
WAK WAK WAK
GIBBER GIBBER WAAK
(GOOD LORD!) HISS!!
FORTY YEAR OLD HIPPIE
NOBODY LOVES ME! NOT EVEN MY LITTLE PUSSY CAT! WANHHH! BAWWWWWWWWW! I'M SO ALONE! I'M SO MISERABLE! WEEP! WAIL! CRY!
SNIFFLE! SNORK! OHHHHHHHHHH!
BARF!

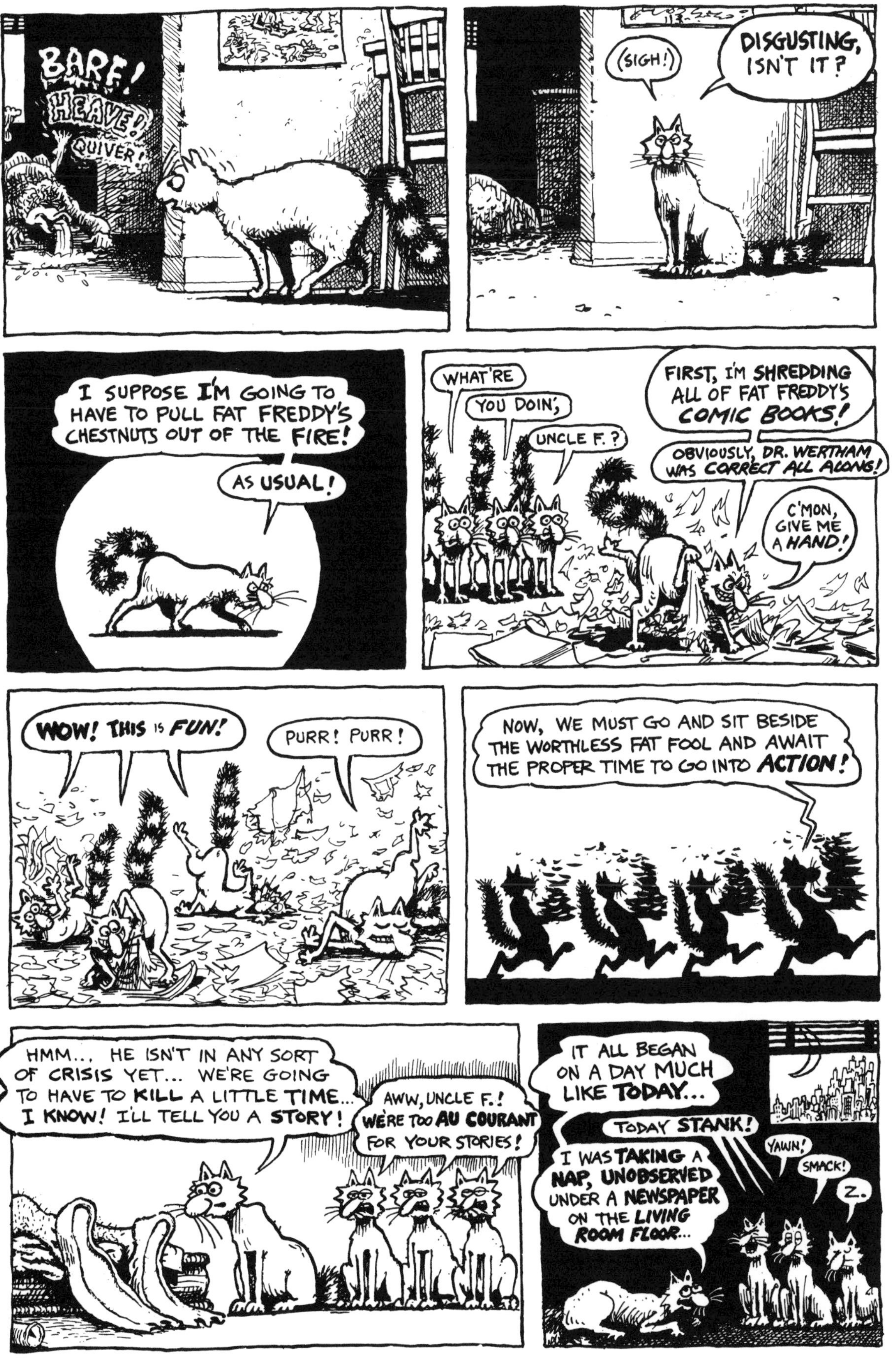
BARF!
HEAVE!
QUIVER!
(SIGH!)
DISGUSTING, ISN'T IT?
I SUPPOSE I'M GOING TO HAVE TO PULL FAT FREDDY'S CHESTNUTS OUT OF THE FIRE!
AS USUAL!
WHAT'RE
YOU DOIN',
UNCLE F.?
FIRST, I'M SHREDDING ALL OF FAT FREDDY'S COMIC BOOKS!
OBVIOUSLY, DR. WERTHAM WAS CORRECT ALL ALONG!
C'MON, GIVE ME A HAND!
WOW! THIS IS FUN!
PURR! PURR!
NOW, WE MUST GO AND SIT BESIDE THE WORTHLESS FAT FOOL AND AWAIT THE PROPER TIME TO GO INTO ACTION!
HMM... HE ISN'T IN ANY SORT OF CRISIS YET... WE'RE GOING TO HAVE TO KILL A LITTLE TIME... I KNOW! I'LL TELL YOU A STORY!
AWW, UNCLE F.! WE'RE TOO AU COURANT FOR YOUR STORIES!
IT ALL BEGAN ON A DAY MUCH LIKE TODAY...
TODAY STANK!
I WAS TAKING A NAP, UNOBSERVED UNDER A NEWSPAPER ON THE LIVING ROOM FLOOR...
YAWN!
SMACK!
Z.

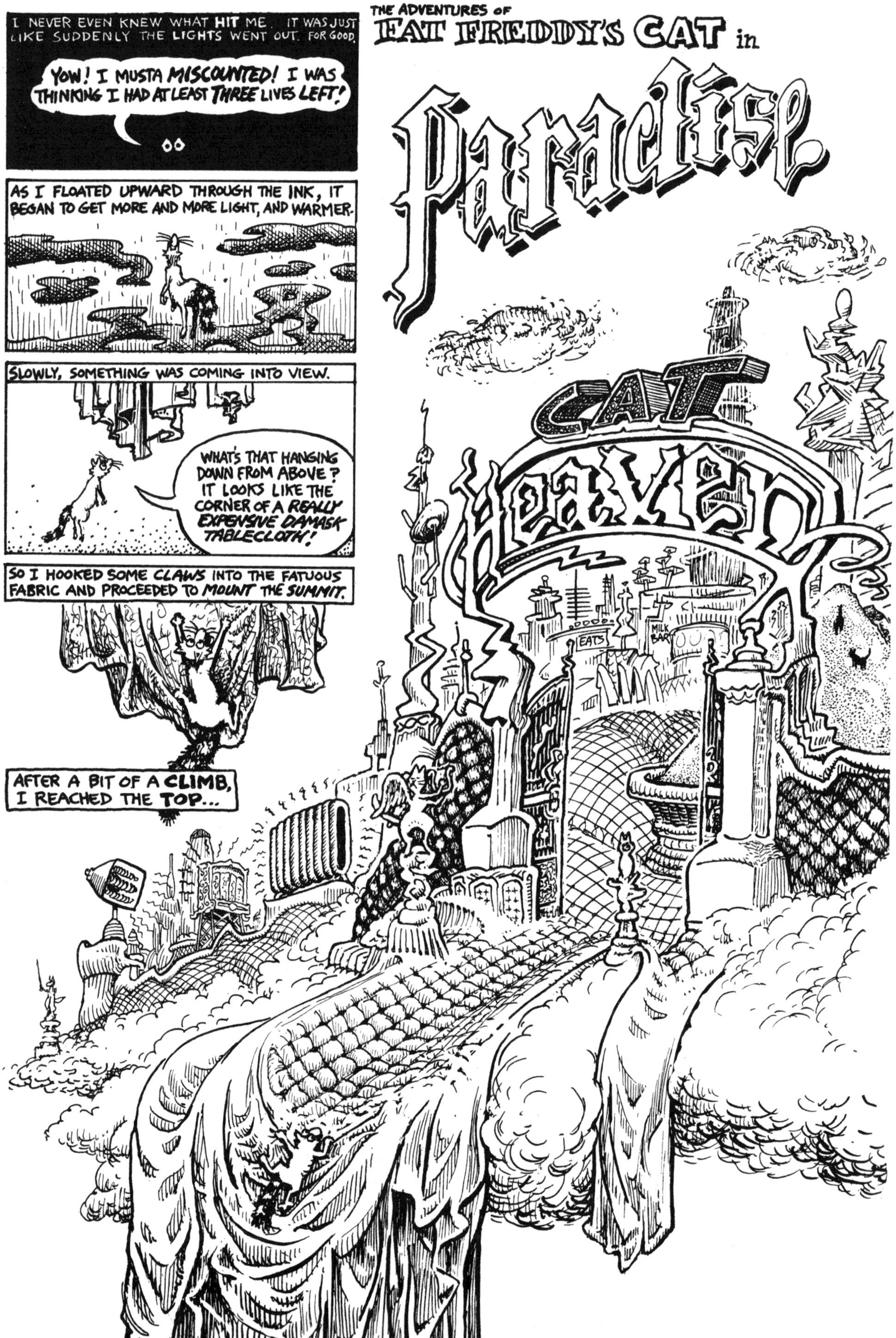
I NEVER EVEN KNEW WHAT HIT ME. IT WAS JUST LIKE SUDDENLY THE LIGHTS WENT OUT. FOR GOOD.
YOW! I MUSTA MISCOUNTED! I WAS THINKING I HAD AT LEAST THREE LIVES LEFT!
THE ADVENTURES OF FAT FREDDY'S CAT in
Paradise
AS I FLOATED UPWARD THROUGH THE INK, IT BEGAN TO GET MORE AND MORE LIGHT, AND WARMER.
SLOWLY, SOMETHING WAS COMING INTO VIEW.
WHAT'S THAT HANGING DOWN FROM ABOVE? IT LOOKS LIKE THE CORNER OF A REALLY EXPENSIVE DAMASK TABLECLOTH!
SO I HOOKED SOME CLAWS INTO THE FATUOUS FABRIC AND PROCEEDED TO MOUNT THE SUMMIT.
AFTER A BIT OF A CLIMB, I REACHED THE TOP...
CAT HEAVEN
EATS
MILK BAR

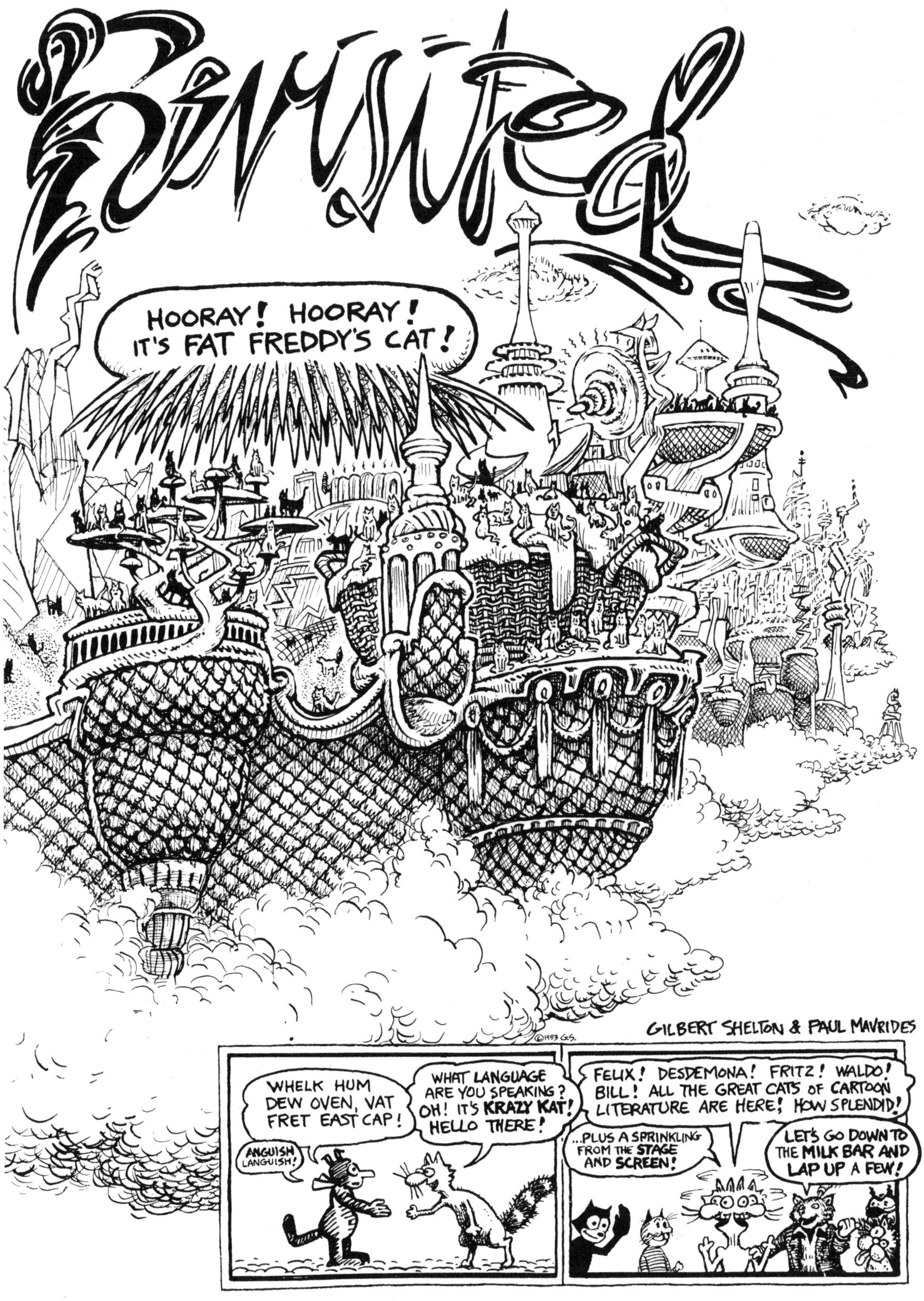
HOORAY! HOORAY! IT'S FAT FREDDY'S CAT!
GILBERT SHELTON & PAUL MAVRIDES
©1983 G.S.
WHELK HUM DEW OVEN, VAT FRET EAST CAP!
ANGUISH! LANGUISH!
WHAT LANGUAGE ARE YOU SPEAKING? OH! IT'S KRAZY KAT! HELLO THERE!
FELIX! DESDEMONA! FRITZ! WALDO! BILL! ALL THE GREAT CATS OF CARTOON LITERATURE ARE HERE! HOW SPLENDID!
...PLUS A SPRINKLING FROM THE STAGE AND SCREEN!
LET'S GO DOWN TO THE MILK BAR AND LAP UP A FEW!

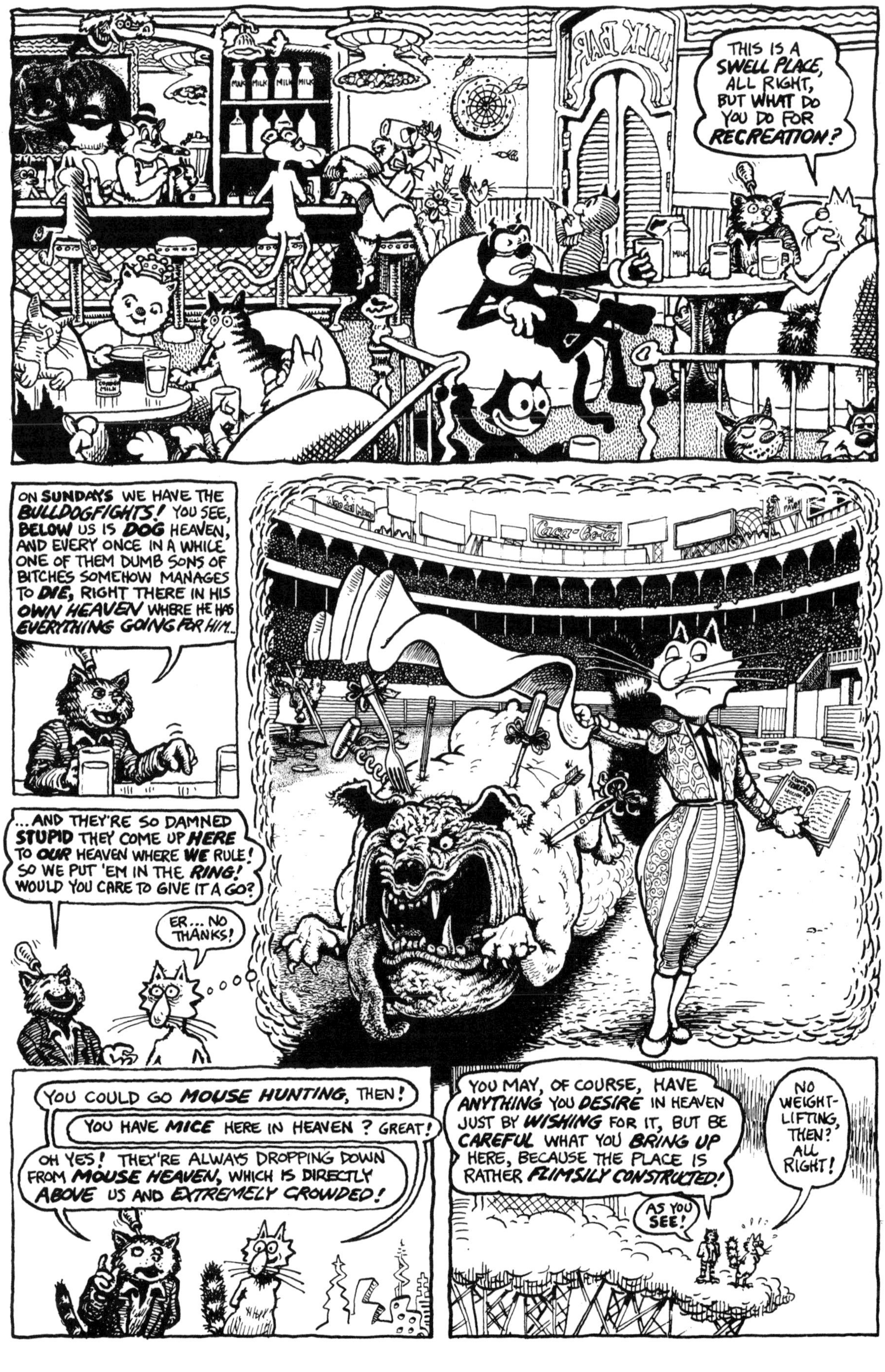

MILK BAR
MILK MILK MILK MILK
THIS IS A SWELL PLACE, ALL RIGHT, BUT WHAT DO YOU DO FOR RECREATION?
ON SUNDAYS WE HAVE THE BULLDOGFIGHTS! YOU SEE, BELOW US IS DOG HEAVEN, AND EVERY ONCE IN A WHILE ONE OF THEM DUMB SONS OF BITCHES SOMEHOW MANAGES TO DIE, RIGHT THERE IN HIS OWN HEAVEN WHERE HE HAS EVERYTHING GOING FOR HIM...
Caca-Cola
...AND THEY'RE SO DAMNED STUPID THEY COME UP HERE TO OUR HEAVEN WHERE WE RULE! SO WE PUT 'EM IN THE RING! WOULD YOU CARE TO GIVE IT A GO?
ER... NO THANKS!
YOU COULD GO MOUSE HUNTING, THEN!
YOU HAVE MICE HERE IN HEAVEN ? GREAT!
OH YES! THEY'RE ALWAYS DROPPING DOWN FROM MOUSE HEAVEN, WHICH IS DIRECTLY ABOVE US AND EXTREMELY CROWDED!
YOU MAY, OF COURSE, HAVE ANYTHING YOU DESIRE IN HEAVEN JUST BY WISHING FOR IT, BUT BE CAREFUL WHAT YOU BRING UP HERE, BECAUSE THE PLACE IS RATHER FLIMSILY CONSTRUCTED!
NO WEIGHT-LIFTING, THEN? ALL RIGHT!
AS YOU SEE!

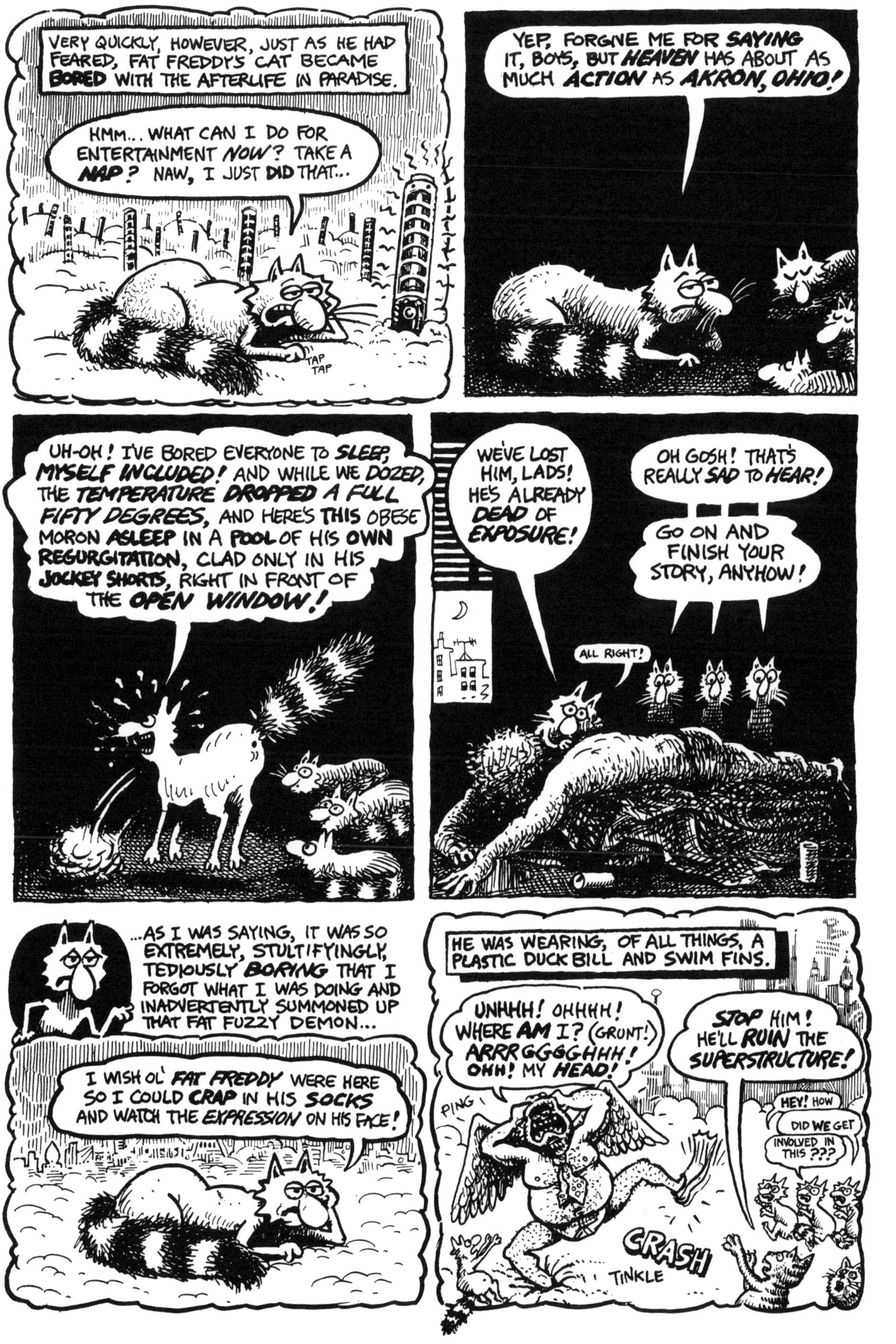
VERY QUICKLY, HOWEVER, JUST AS HE HAD FEARED, FAT FREDDY'S CAT BECAME BORED WITH THE AFTERLIFE IN PARADISE.
HMM... WHAT CAN I DO FOR ENTERTAINMENT NOW? TAKE A NAP? NAW, I JUST DID THAT...
TAP TAP
YEP, FORGIVE ME FOR SAYING IT, BOYS, BUT HEAVEN HAS ABOUT AS MUCH ACTION AS AKRON, OHIO!
UH-OH! I'VE BORED EVERYONE TO SLEEP, MYSELF INCLUDED! AND WHILE WE DOZED, THE TEMPERATURE DROPPED A FULL FIFTY DEGREES, AND HERE'S THIS OBESE MORON ASLEEP IN A POOL OF HIS OWN REGURGITATION, CLAD ONLY IN HIS JOCKEY SHORTS, RIGHT IN FRONT OF THE OPEN WINDOW!
WE'VE LOST HIM, LADS! HE'S ALREADY DEAD OF EXPOSURE!
OH GOSH! THAT'S REALLY SAD TO HEAR!
GO ON AND FINISH YOUR STORY, ANYHOW!
ALL RIGHT!
...AS I WAS SAYING, IT WAS SO EXTREMELY, STULTIFYINGLY, TEDIOUSLY BORING THAT I FORGOT WHAT I WAS DOING AND INADVERTENTLY SUMMONED UP THAT FAT FUZZY DEMON...
I WISH OL' FAT FREDDY WERE HERE SO I COULD CRAP IN HIS SOCKS AND WATCH THE EXPRESSION ON HIS FACE!
HE WAS WEARING, OF ALL THINGS, A PLASTIC DUCK BILL AND SWIM FINS.
UNHHH! OHHHH! WHERE AM I? (GRUNT!) ARRRGGGGHHH! OHH! MY HEAD!
STOP HIM! HE'LL RUIN THE SUPERSTRUCTURE!
PING
HEY! HOW DID WE GET INVOLVED IN THIS???
CRASH
TINKLE

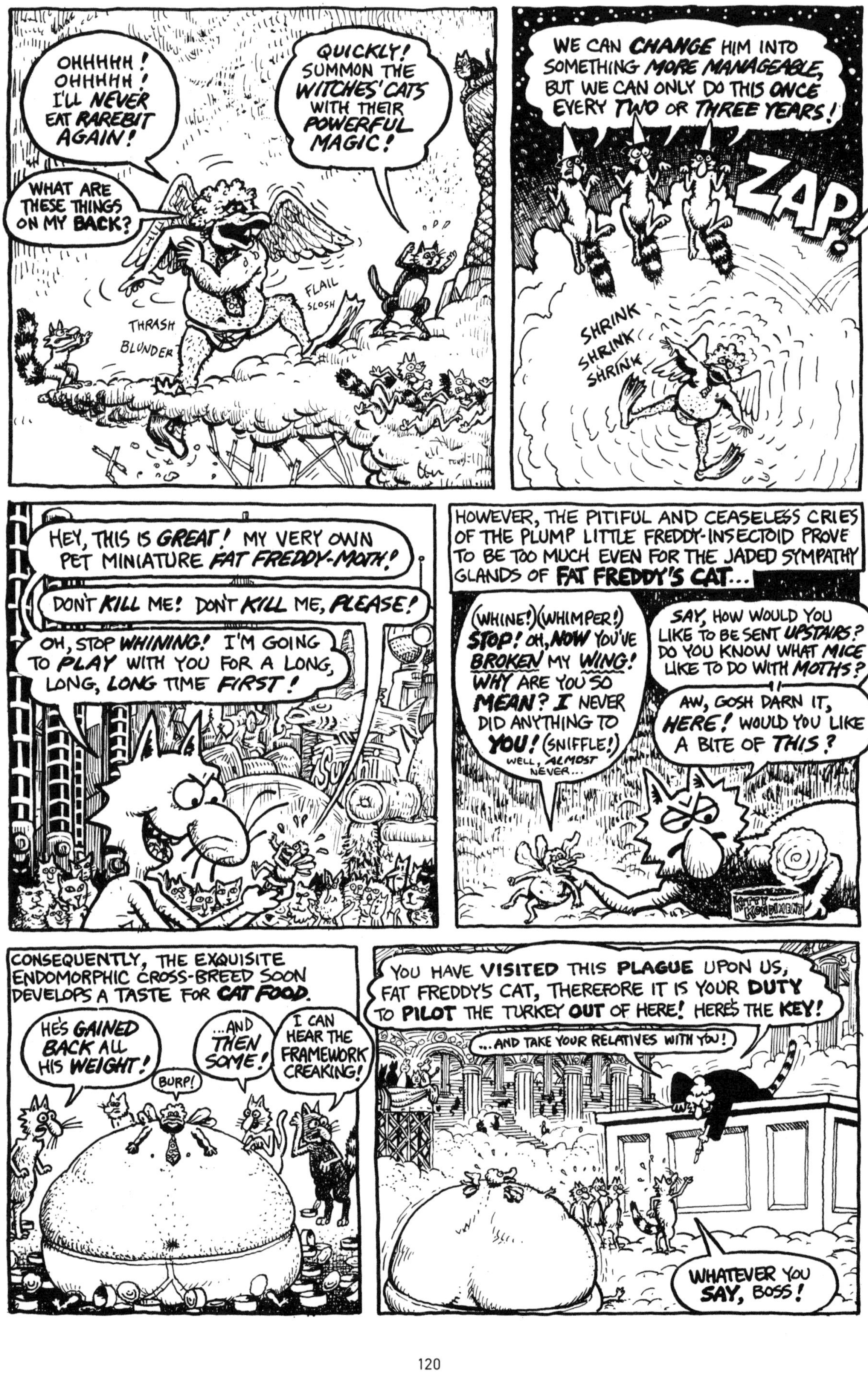

OHHHHH! OHHHHH! I'LL NEVER EAT RAREBIT AGAIN!
WHAT ARE THESE THINGS ON MY BACK?
QUICKLY! SUMMON THE WITCHES' CATS WITH THEIR POWERFUL MAGIC!
FLAIL
SLOSH
THRASH
BLUNDER
WE CAN CHANGE HIM INTO SOMETHING MORE MANAGEABLE, BUT WE CAN ONLY DO THIS ONCE EVERY TWO OR THREE YEARS!
ZAP!
SHRINK
SHRINK
SHRINK
HEY, THIS IS GREAT! MY VERY OWN PET MINIATURE FAT FREDDY-MOTH!
DON'T KILL ME! DON'T KILL ME, PLEASE!
OH, STOP WHINING! I'M GOING TO PLAY WITH YOU FOR A LONG, LONG, LONG TIME FIRST!
HOWEVER, THE PITIFUL AND CEASELESS CRIES OF THE PLUMP LITTLE FREDDY-INSECTOID PROVE TO BE TOO MUCH EVEN FOR THE JADED SYMPATHY GLANDS OF FAT FREDDY'S CAT...
(WHINE!)(WHIMPER!) STOP! OH, NOW YOU'VE BROKEN MY WING! WHY ARE YOU SO MEAN? I NEVER DID ANYTHING TO YOU! (SNIFFLE!)
WELL, ALMOST NEVER...
SAY, HOW WOULD YOU LIKE TO BE SENT UPSTAIRS? DO YOU KNOW WHAT MICE LIKE TO DO WITH MOTHS?
AW, GOSH DARN IT, HERE! WOULD YOU LIKE A BITE OF THIS?
KITTY KONDIMENT
CONSEQUENTLY, THE EXQUISITE ENDOMORPHIC CROSS-BREED SOON DEVELOPS A TASTE FOR CAT FOOD.
HE'S GAINED BACK ALL HIS WEIGHT!
BURP!
...AND THEN SOME!
I CAN HEAR THE FRAMEWORK CREAKING!
YOU HAVE VISITED THIS PLAGUE UPON US, FAT FREDDY'S CAT, THEREFORE IT IS YOUR DUTY TO PILOT THE TURKEY OUT OF HERE! HERE'S THE KEY!
...AND TAKE YOUR RELATIVES WITH YOU!
WHATEVER YOU SAY, BOSS!

OFF FLY OUR HEROES, LIKE AN ANVIL. OR, MORE PRECISELY, A BLUE-GREEN 1950 STUDEBAKER COMMANDER CONVERTIBLE.

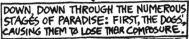

DOWN, DOWN THROUGH THE NUMEROUS STAGES OF PARADISE: FIRST, THE DOGS, CAUSING THEM TO LOSE THEIR COMPOSURE.

OOPS! NOW HE'S A 1947 HARLEY!

AND LATER, SOMEWHERE TOWARD THE BOTTOM, THE ANTHROPOMORPHIC LEVEL.

IF AH EVAH CATCH YEW SPEEDIN' THROUGH MAH BAILIWICK AGAIN, BWAH, AH'M TAKIN' AWAY YOAH LICENSE!

FORGIVE THEM, FATHER, FOR THEY KNOW NOT WHAT THEY DO!

THEY MUSTA BEEN DOIN' TWO HUNDRED!

EARTH HO!!!

PUT ON THE BRAKES NOW.

OR THE FLAPS, OR WHATEVER!

I THINK I DETECT A VERY FAINT HEARTBEAT!

DON'T STOP EMITTING THAT INFRARED MEN! WE CAN PULL HIM OUT!

I BELIEVE THERE'S A DIM GLIMMER! PILE ON MORE COMICS, GUYS!

HE'S STIRRING! HE'S COMING AWAKE!

WE'VE SAVED HIM! HOORAY!

AARRRRRRGHH!? WHICH ONE OF YOU CATS BARFED ON MY COMIC BOOKS?!

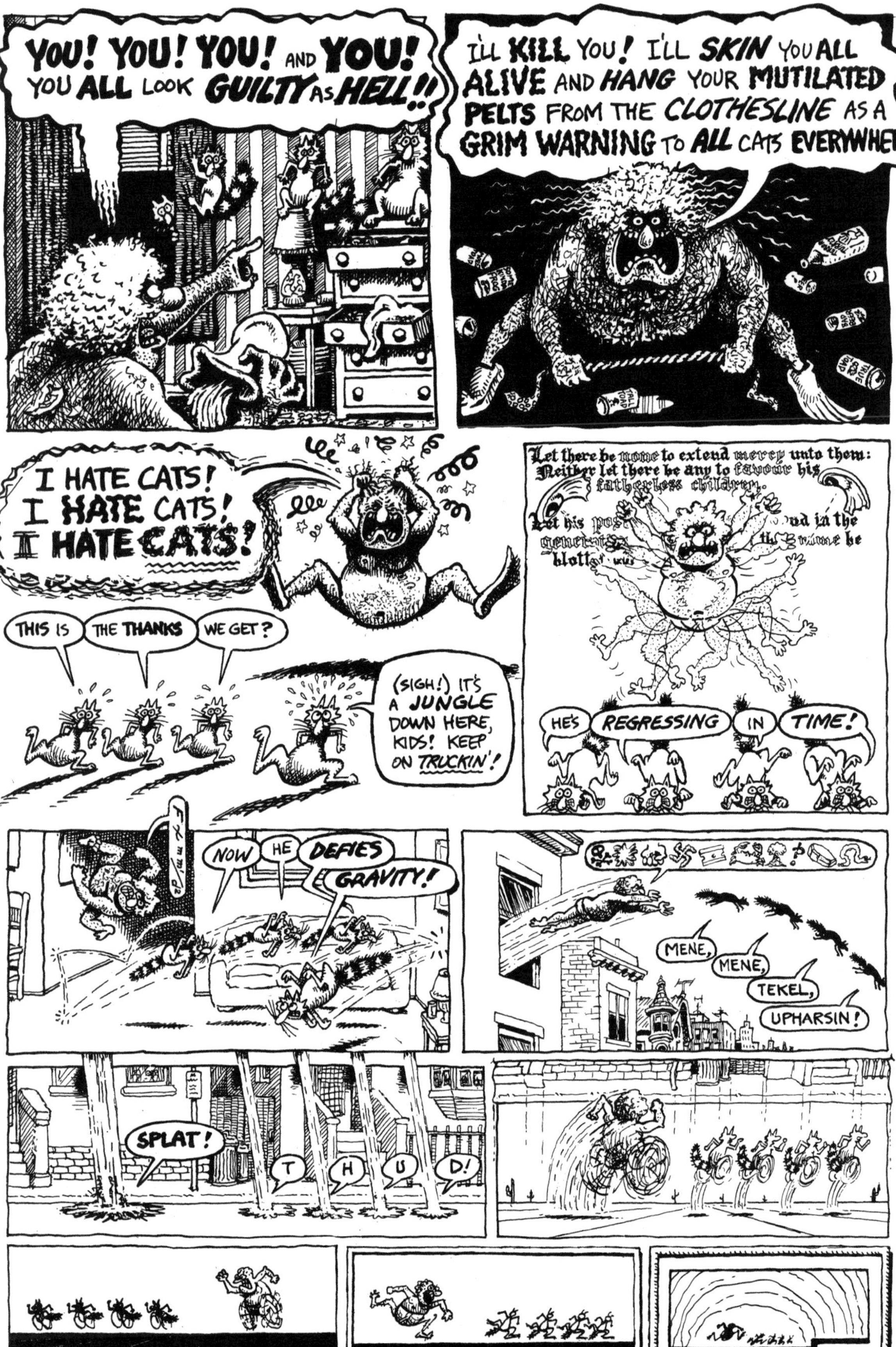
YOU! YOU! YOU! AND YOU! YOU ALL LOOK GUILTY AS HELL!!
I'LL KILL YOU! I'LL SKIN YOU ALL ALIVE AND HANG YOUR MUTILATED PELTS FROM THE CLOTHESLINE AS A GRIM WARNING TO ALL CATS EVERYWHERE!
TRUE
I HATE CATS! I HATE CATS! I HATE CATS!
Let there be none to extend mercy unto them:
Neither let there be any to favour his fatherless children.
THIS IS
THE THANKS
WE GET?
(SIGH!) IT'S A JUNGLE DOWN HERE, KIDS! KEEP ON TRUCKIN'!
HE'S
REGRESSING
IN
TIME!
NOW
HE
DEFIES
GRAVITY!
MENE,
MENE,
TEKEL,
UPHARSIN!
SPLAT!
T
H
U
D!
The END

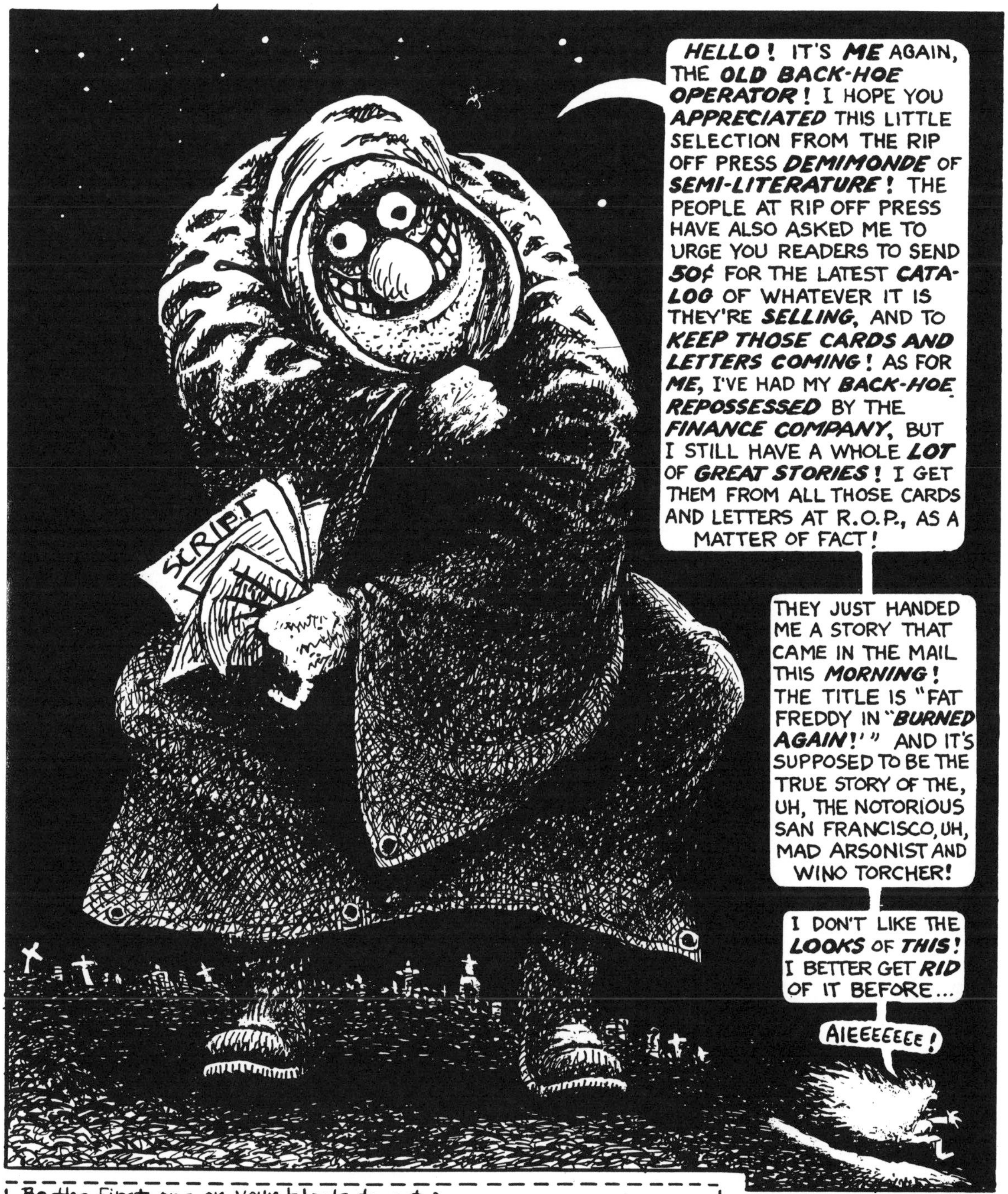
HELLO! IT'S ME AGAIN, THE OLD BACK-HOE OPERATOR! I HOPE YOU APPRECIATED THIS LITTLE SELECTION FROM THE RIP OFF PRESS DEMIMONDE OF SEMI-LITERATURE! THE PEOPLE AT RIP OFF PRESS HAVE ALSO ASKED ME TO URGE YOU READERS TO SEND 50¢ FOR THE LATEST CATALOG OF WHATEVER IT IS THEY'RE SELLING, AND TO KEEP THOSE CARDS AND LETTERS COMING! AS FOR ME, I'VE HAD MY BACK-HOE REPOSSESSED BY THE FINANCE COMPANY, BUT I STILL HAVE A WHOLE LOT OF GREAT STORIES! I GET THEM FROM ALL THOSE CARDS AND LETTERS AT R.O.P., AS A MATTER OF FACT!
THEY JUST HANDED ME A STORY THAT CAME IN THE MAIL THIS MORNING! THE TITLE IS "FAT FREDDY IN "BURNED AGAIN!'" AND IT'S SUPPOSED TO BE THE TRUE STORY OF THE, UH, THE NOTORIOUS SAN FRANCISCO, UH, MAD ARSONIST AND WINO TORCHER!
I DON'T LIKE THE LOOKS OF THIS! I BETTER GET RID OF IT BEFORE...
AIEEEEEEE!
SCRIPT

Be the first one on your block to get a

LIFETIME SUBSCRIPTION
To FAT FREDDY'S COMICS & STORIES

(CHECK HERE)

☐ I WANT A LIFETIME SUBSCRIPTION TO FAT FREDDY'S COMICS & STORIES. ENCLOSED IS A CASHIERS CHECK FOR THE AMOUNT OF $50,000.00 MADE OUT TO FREDDY FREEKOWTSKI AND SEND IT CARE OF RIP OFF PRESS INC. P.O. BOX 4686 AUBURN CA 95604
SORRY, LIFETIME SUBSCRIPTIONS ONLY, PLEASE.

NAME ____________________
ADDRESS ____________________
CITY __________ STATE __________ ZIP __________

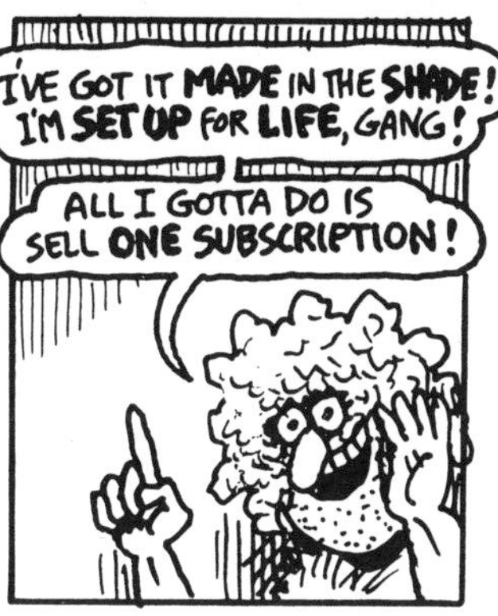
I'VE GOT IT MADE IN THE SHADE! I'M SET UP FOR LIFE, GANG!
ALL I GOTTA DO IS SELL ONE SUBSCRIPTION!

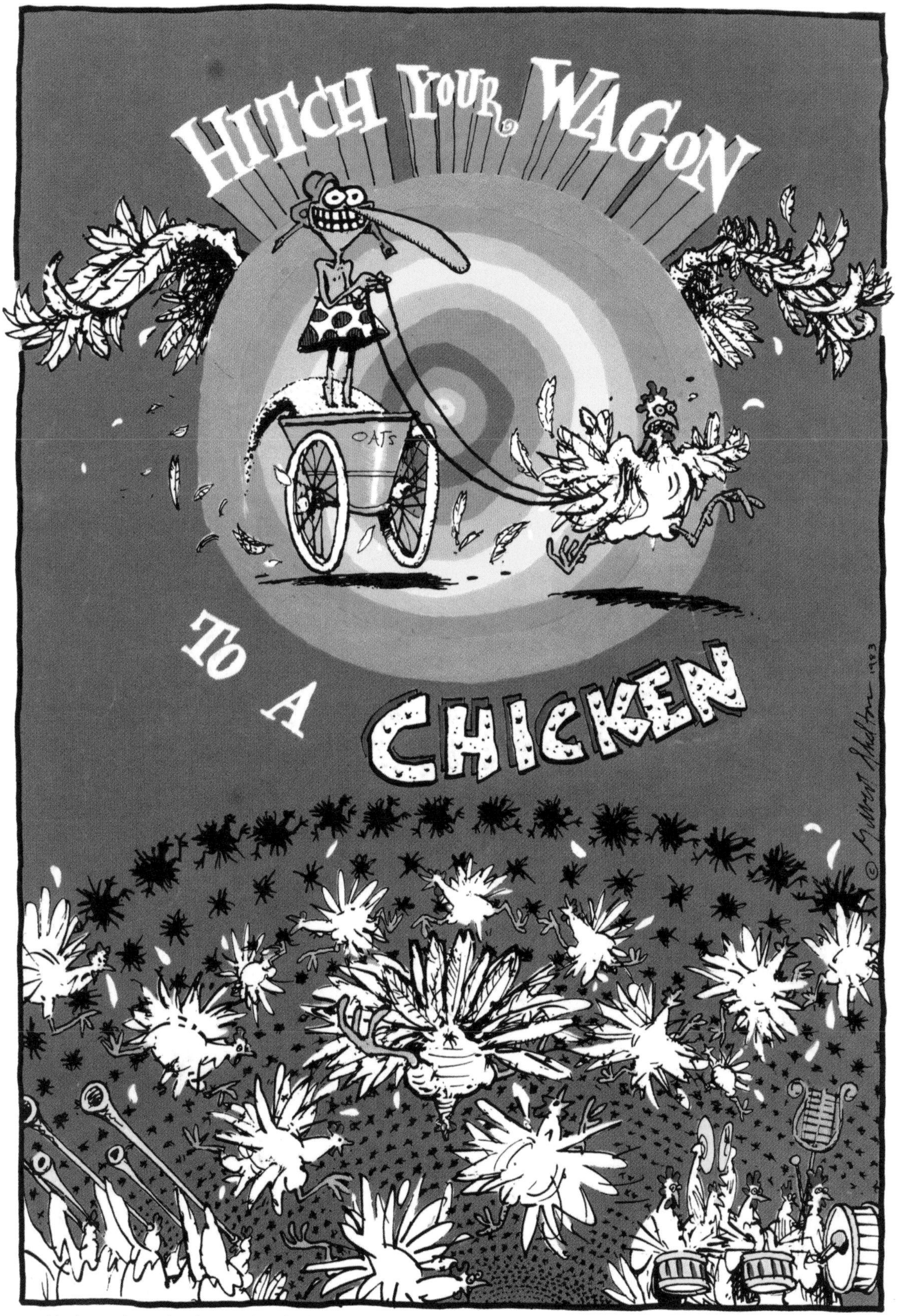
HITCH YOUR WAGON
OATS
TO A
CHICKEN

Number one in a series of great sayings for the eighties.
Brought to you by Rip Off Press, Inc., as a public service.
Illustrated by Gilbert Shelton.
Colored by Guy Colwell using the Fluorotint® color reproduction procedure.

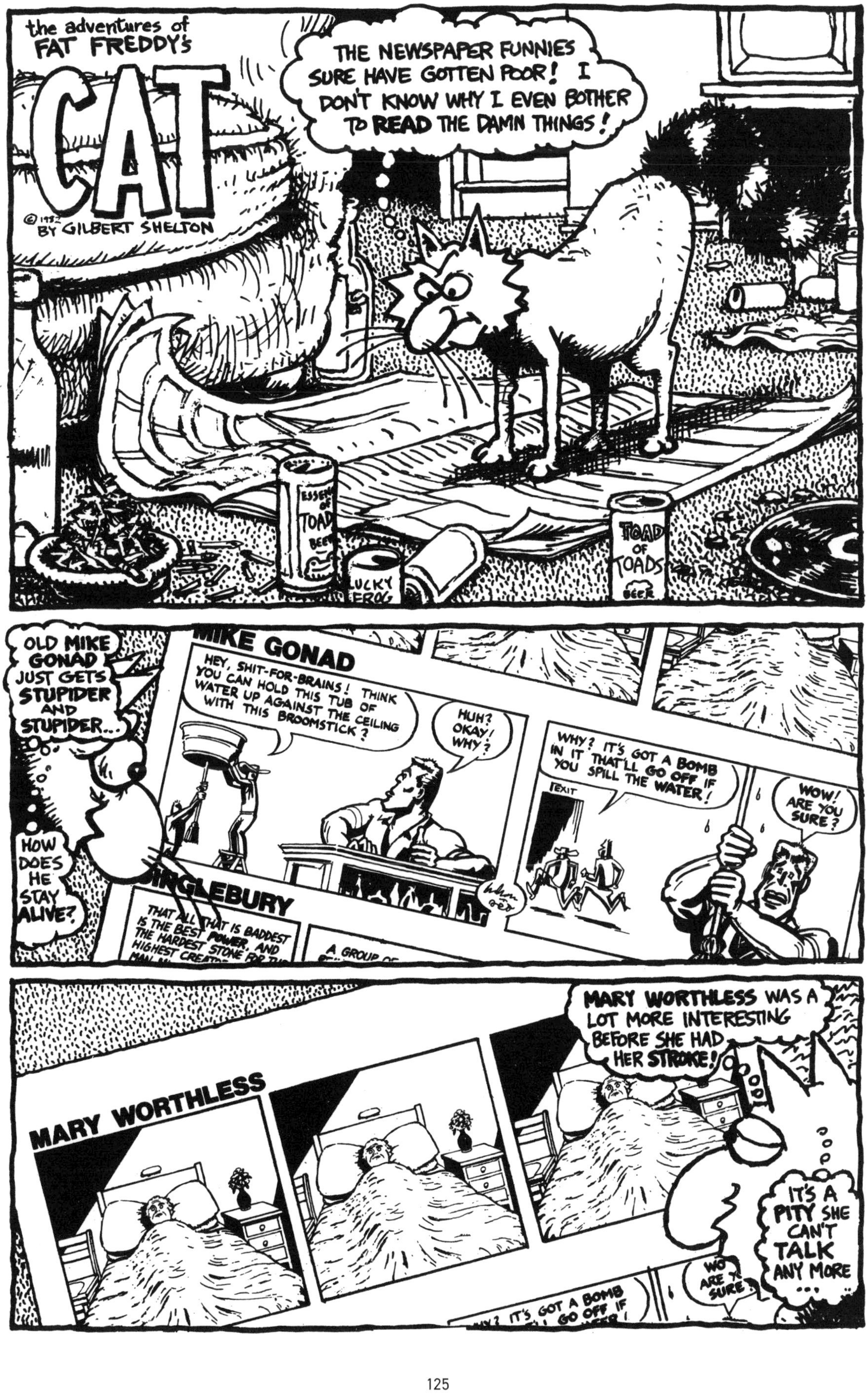
the adventures of
FAT FREDDY'S
CAT
© 1982 BY GILBERT SHELTON
THE NEWSPAPER FUNNIES SURE HAVE GOTTEN POOR! I DON'T KNOW WHY I EVEN BOTHER TO READ THE DAMN THINGS!
ESSENCE OF TOAD BEER
LUCKY FROG
TOAD OF TOADS BEER
OLD MIKE GONAD JUST GETS STUPIDER AND STUPIDER...
MIKE GONAD
HEY, SHIT-FOR-BRAINS! THINK YOU CAN HOLD THIS TUB OF WATER UP AGAINST THE CEILING WITH THIS BROOMSTICK?
HUH? OKAY! WHY?
WHY? IT'S GOT A BOMB IN IT THAT'LL GO OFF IF YOU SPILL THE WATER!
EXIT
WOW! ARE YOU SURE?
HOW DOES HE STAY ALIVE?
DINGLEBURY
THAT ALL THAT IS BADDEST IS THE BEST POWER, AND THE HARDEST STONE FOR THE
A GROUP OF
MARY WORTHLESS WAS A LOT MORE INTERESTING BEFORE SHE HAD HER STROKE!
MARY WORTHLESS
IT'S A PITY SHE CAN'T TALK ANY MORE...
IT'S GOT A BOMB
GO OFF IF

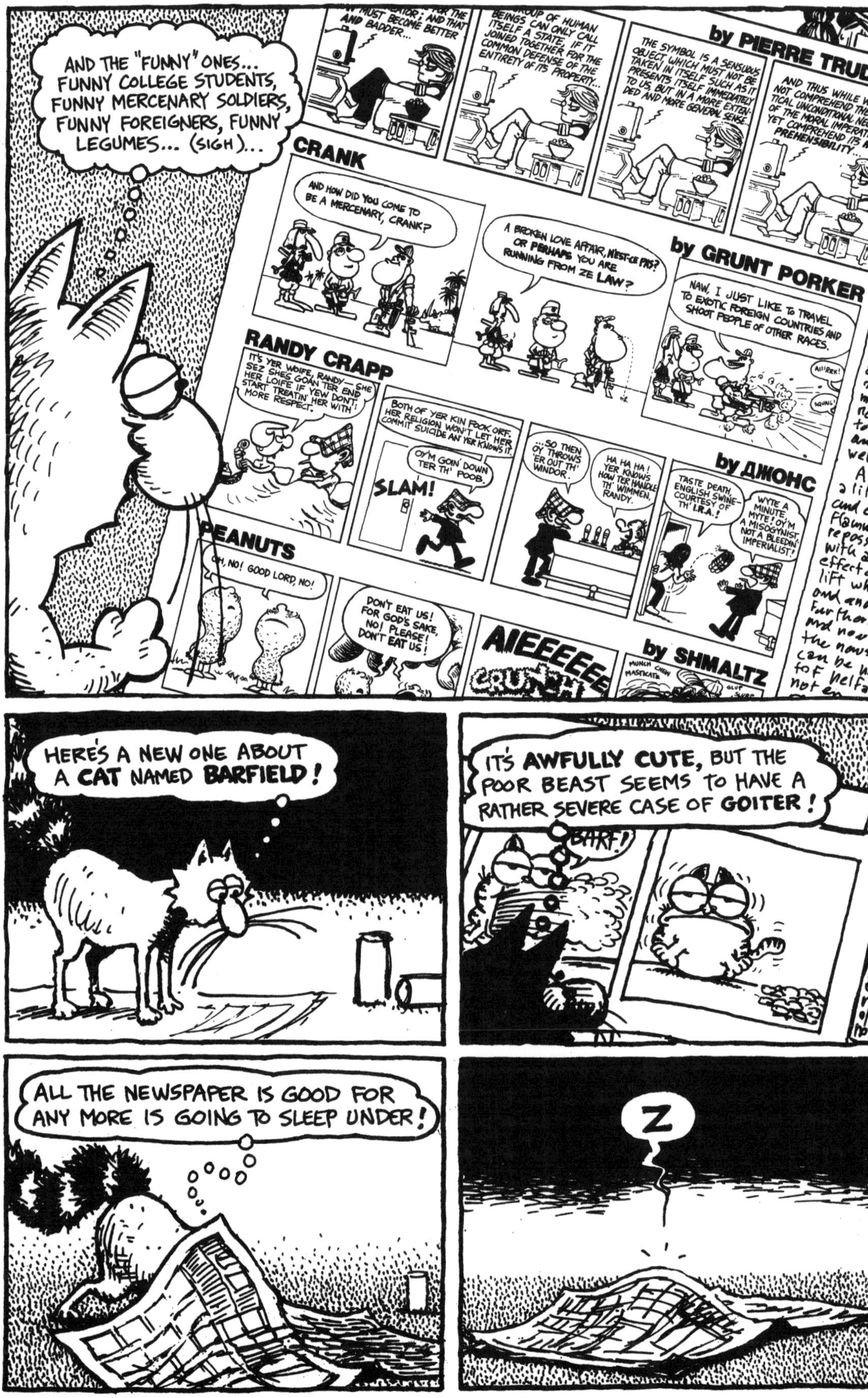
AND THE "FUNNY" ONES... FUNNY COLLEGE STUDENTS, FUNNY MERCENARY SOLDIERS, FUNNY FOREIGNERS, FUNNY LEGUMES... (SIGH)...
BEINGS CAN ONLY CALL ITSELF A STATE IF IT JOINED TOGETHER FOR THE COMMON DEFENSE OF THE ENTIRETY OF ITS PROPERTY...
by PIERRE TRUDEA
THE SYMBOL IS A SENSUOUS OBJECT, WHICH MUST NOT BE TAKEN IN ITSELF SUCH AS IT PRESENTS ITSELF IMMEDIATELY TO US, BUT IN A MORE EXTENDED AND MORE GENERAL SENSE...
AND THUS WHILE WE DO NOT COMPREHEND THE PRACTICAL UNCONDITIONAL NECESSITY OF THE MORAL IMPERATIVE, WE YET COMPREHEND ITS INCOMPREHENSIBILITY...
CRANK
AND HOW DID YOU COME TO BE A MERCENARY, CRANK?
A BROKEN LOVE AFFAIR, N'EST-CE PAS? OR PERHAPS YOU ARE RUNNING FROM ZE LAW?
by GRUNT PORKER
NAW, I JUST LIKE TO TRAVEL TO EXOTIC FOREIGN COUNTRIES AND SHOOT PEOPLE OF OTHER RACES.
RANDY CRAPP
IT'S YER WOIFE, RANDY— SHE SEZ SHE'S GOAN TER END HER LOIFE IF YEW DON'T START TREATIN' HER WITH MORE RESPECT.
BOTH OF YER KIN FOOK ORF. HER RELIGION WON'T LET HER COMMIT SUICIDE AN' YER KNOWS IT.
OY'M GOIN' DOWN TER TH' POOB.
SLAM!
...SO THEN OY THROWS 'ER OUT TH' WINDOR.
HA HA HA! YER KNOWS HOW TER HANDLE TH' WIMMEN, RANDY.
by ДЖОНС
TASTE DEATH, ENGLISH SWINE— COURTESY OF TH' I.R.A.!
WYTE A MINUTE, MYTE! OY'M A MISOGYNIST, NOT A BLEEDIN' IMPERIALIST!
PEANUTS
OH, NO! GOOD LORD, NO!
DON'T EAT US! FOR GOD'S SAKE, NO! PLEASE! DON'T EAT US!
AIEEEEEE
by SHMALTZ
MUNCH CHEW MASTICATE
HERE'S A NEW ONE ABOUT A CAT NAMED BARFIELD!
IT'S AWFULLY CUTE, BUT THE POOR BEAST SEEMS TO HAVE A RATHER SEVERE CASE OF GOITER!
BARF!
ALL THE NEWSPAPER IS GOOD FOR ANY MORE IS GOING TO SLEEP UNDER!
Z

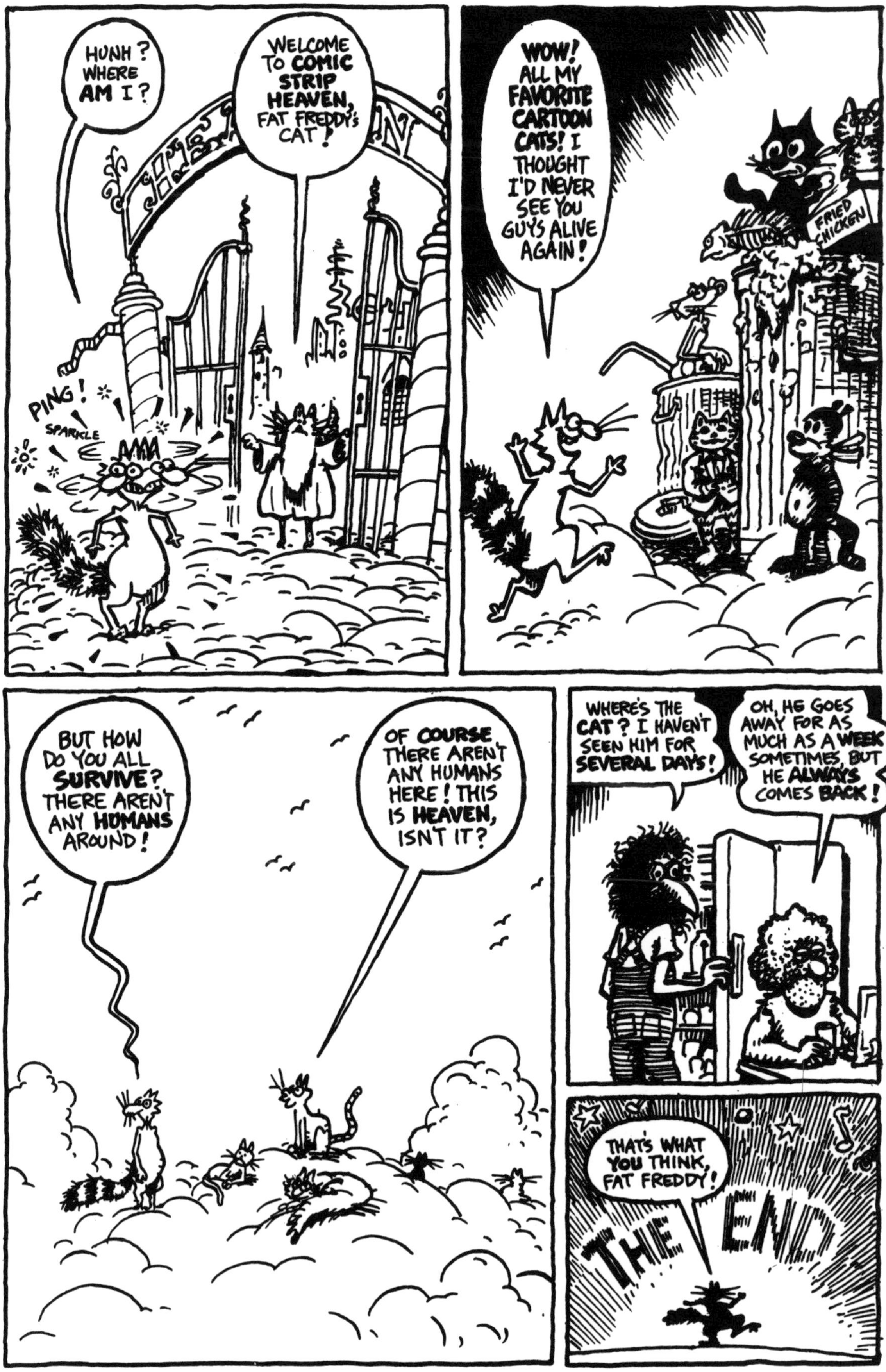
HUNH? WHERE AM I?
WELCOME TO COMIC STRIP HEAVEN, FAT FREDDY'S CAT!
PING!
SPARKLE
WOW! ALL MY FAVORITE CARTOON CATS! I THOUGHT I'D NEVER SEE YOU GUYS ALIVE AGAIN!
FRIED CHICKEN
BUT HOW DO YOU ALL SURVIVE? THERE AREN'T ANY HUMANS AROUND!
OF COURSE THERE AREN'T ANY HUMANS HERE! THIS IS HEAVEN, ISN'T IT?
WHERE'S THE CAT? I HAVEN'T SEEN HIM FOR SEVERAL DAYS!
OH, HE GOES AWAY FOR AS MUCH AS A WEEK SOMETIMES, BUT HE ALWAYS COMES BACK!
THAT'S WHAT YOU THINK, FAT FREDDY!
THE END

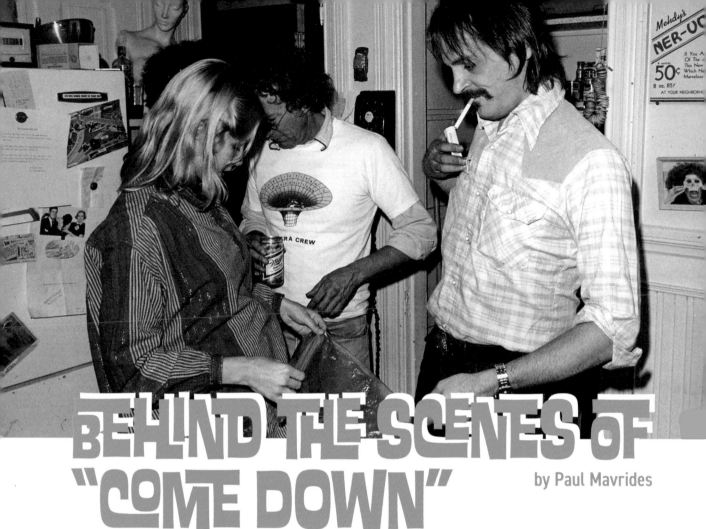

BEHIND THE SCENES OF "COME DOWN"

by Paul Mavrides

"Come Down" (p. 65) was, I think, my idea, and it wound up entailing a serious graphic effort. What would happen if the Freak Brothers stopped getting high all the time? So Gilbert and Dave and I came up with this story where the trio become real flesh-and-blood humans. The idea was that the cartoon drawings would slowly turn into photographic images of the "real" Freak Brothers in a real room facing real problems in the real passage of time, and eventually they would just go, "OK, enough of this," and get high and turn back into cartoon characters.

Of course, for such an undertaking, you need real people. So we enlisted Peter Weber, the darkroom guy at Rip Off Press, to play Phineas and Don Baumgart, the distribution guy there, to play Fat Freddy. Dave played Franklin. My roommate at that time, another cartoonist from Ohio, Becky Wilson, had a cat named Denise

that jumped onto the table in the middle of the shoot and integrated herself into it, thus becoming Fat Freddy's cat.

We did all the photography in my kitchen (which is still my kitchen). I directed the shoot, and Fred Todd, the publisher of Rip Off, was the photographer.

We blew the photos up, and I retouched them. They were black-and-white photos (called "grayscale" or "continuous tone" in the printing trade), which we washed very carefully to get silverprints, and I used grayscale retouching paints to paint over the actors and the cat and added certain touches to make it seem real. I decided to make the boys still have big noses and other familiar characteristics, so they weren't actual normal-looking people, they were just kind of

ABOVE: Dava Sheridan, Don Baumgart, and Dave Sheridan.
OPPOSITE: An unretouched Dave Sheridan. Photos by Paul Mavrides.

modeled in full grayscale versions with real bodies. We then halftoned the retouched photographs for print using a very rough, large-dot screen so that when they were reduced, it would help make the illusion better.

Gilbert and I wrote the final dialogue, and Gilbert lettered the text for the word balloons.

"Come Down," sadly, was the last thing we worked on together. Dave started a couple of panels at the beginning of the story, but then he didn't feel well and went to the doctor, and that was that. He died in relatively short order.

Finishing "Come Down" was one of the hardest things I've ever had to do. Gilbert came back from his sojourn in Europe at that point and ended up staying in San Francisco for a year or two, and we began "The Idiots Abroad" (volume 6 in this series). Gilbert then moved to Paris, and at that point, I got to go to Paris on a regular basis.

I remember Dave's funeral. We took his ashes to scatter in the waters off Angel Island State Park in San Francisco Bay on a Neptune Society boat. It was really kind of rough weather in the Bay that day, a lot of dark, a lot of waves, and it felt dramatic. I went out and hung onto the bow of the ship, which was crashing through the pounding waves.

But as soon as we got around to the far side of the island, the rain stopped, a little bit of sun came out, and the waters calmed. A priest and other people spoke, and then Dave's ashes were scattered, and everybody was crying. Poster artist (and Dave's one-time art partner) Pat Ryan and a few others had arranged to hand out joints to everyone, so while Dave's ashes were floating on the water with flowers on them, we all threw the joints into the water on top of the flowers.

This article was adapted from "The Fabulous Furry Freak Brothers" by Paul Mavrides in *Dave Sheridan: Life with Dealer McDope, the Leather Nun, and the Fabulous Furry Freak Brothers*, edited by Mark Burstein (F.U. Press, 2018).

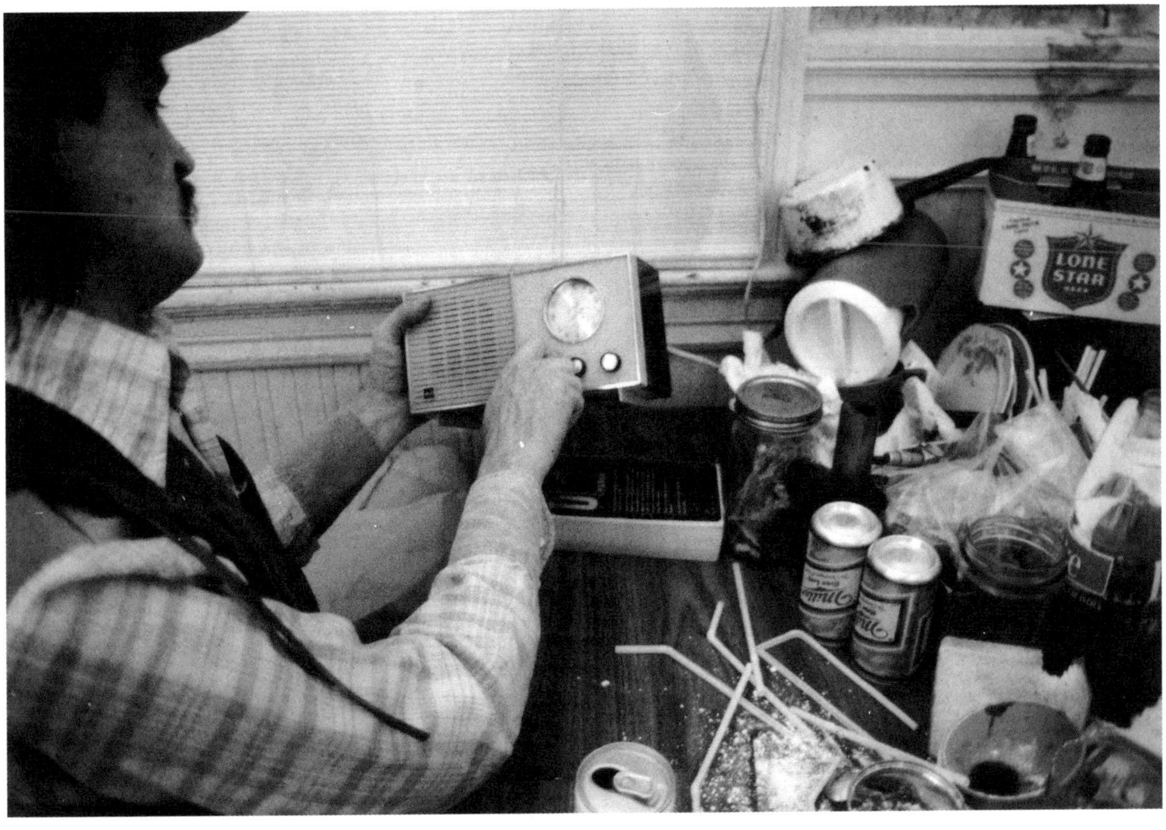
LONE STAR

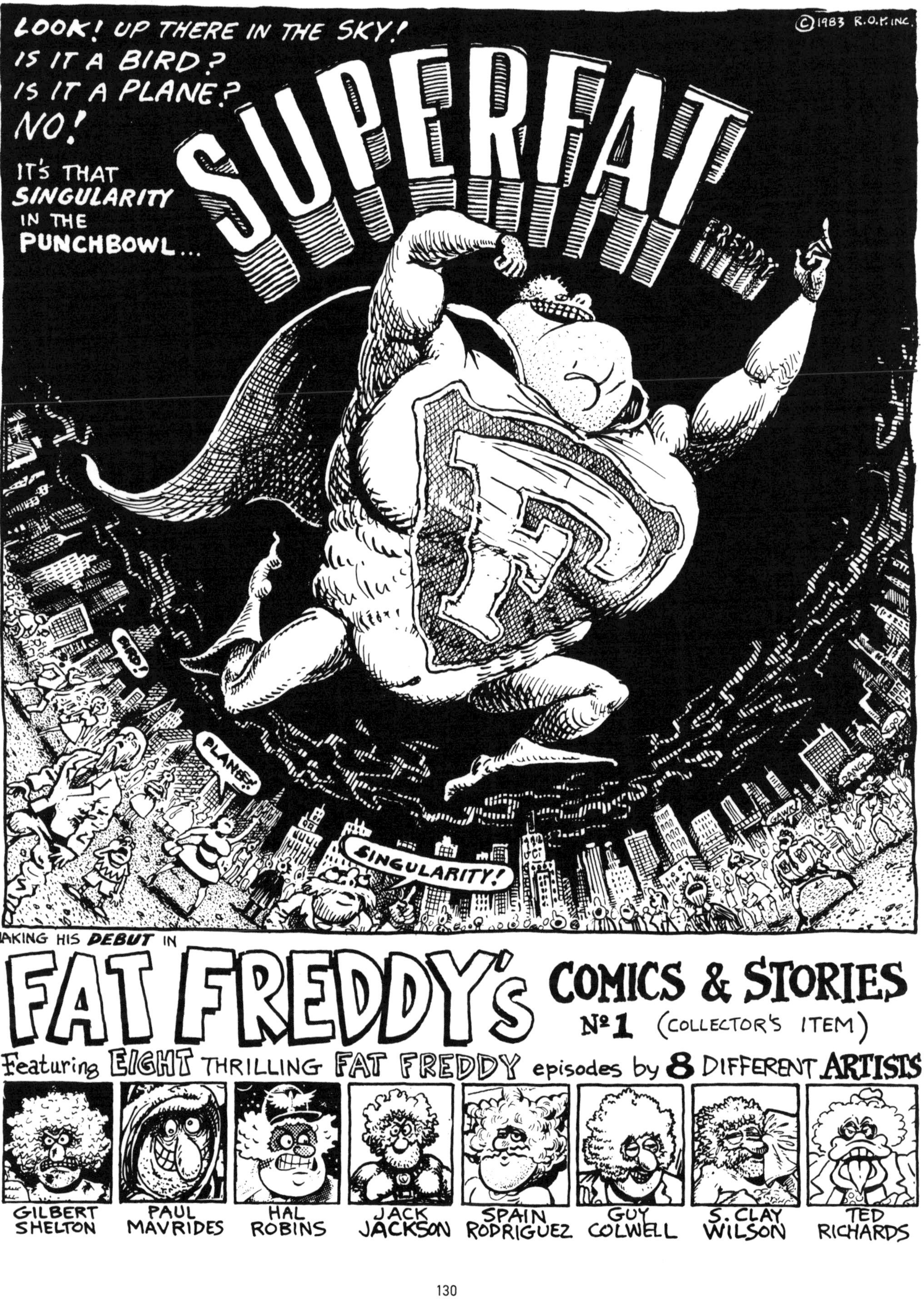
©1983 R.O.K. INC.
LOOK! UP THERE IN THE SKY!
IS IT A BIRD?
IS IT A PLANE?
NO!
IT'S THAT SINGULARITY IN THE PUNCHBOWL...
SUPERFAT
BIRD!
PLANE!
SINGULARITY!
MAKING HIS DEBUT IN
FAT FREDDY'S COMICS & STORIES
Nº1 (COLLECTOR'S ITEM)
Featuring EIGHT THRILLING FAT FREDDY episodes by 8 DIFFERENT ARTISTS
GILBERT SHELTON
PAUL MAVRIDES
HAL ROBINS
JACK JACKSON
SPAIN RODRIGUEZ
GUY COLWELL
S. CLAY WILSON
TED RICHARDS

THE ARTISTS

Gilbert Shelton, 1977. Photo by Clay Geerdes.

Gilbert Shelton (b. 1940, Houston, Texas) began his career as a cartoonist on *The Texas Ranger*, the humor magazine for the University of Texas in Austin, where he also served as editor. It was there that he debuted his superhero parody, Wonder Wart-Hog. The Hog of Steel won him fame throughout the 1960s, but his creation of the Fabulous Furry Freak Brothers in 1969 heralded a new phase in his career. After a move to San Francisco, Shelton co-founded Rip Off Press to publish his own and other underground comix work.

OPPOSITE: The artboard for a 1983 poster to promote *Fat Freddy's Comics & Stories* #1.

The rapid success of early Freak Brothers shorts led to a weekly(ish) newspaper strip and the expansion of Rip Off into a distribution syndicate, supplying a full comics page to alt-weeklies and campus newspapers. Sometimes this would be a Freak Brothers adventure with a Fat Freddy's Cat "bottom strip." Fat Freddy's Cat also eventually graduated to his own solo strip.

Through the 1970s, Shelton contributed to underground anthologies including *Zap Comix* and *Arcade*, continued to issue occasional Wonder Wart-Hog stories, periodically collected Freak Brothers stories in their own comics and books, had a years-long run of painted Freak Brothers stories in *High Times* magazine, and was the driving author behind *Give Me Liberty: A Revised History of the American Revolution*, a satirical comics history of the American Revolution, issued by Rip Off for the US Bicentennial in 1976.

Burnt out on the dual responsibilities of publishing and cartooning, Shelton took an extended visit to Europe in 1979 and ultimately relocated to France. He divested his interest in Rip Off Press but continued to publish there and through other magazines and publishers around the globe.

His work can also be found in *The Complete Zap Comix* (Fantagraphics, 2014), *Zap Comix #16* (Fantagraphics, 2016), and other volumes in *The Fabulous Furry Freak Brothers Follies*.

Dave Sheridan, 1981. Photo by Clay Geerdes.

Dave Sheridan (1943–1982, b. Cleveland, Ohio) arrived in San Francisco in 1969 and became involved in the burgeoning comix scene while also working as a commercial illustrator and album cover artist. His Dealer McDope was syndicated through Rip Off Press, and in 1974, he began collaborating with Gilbert Shelton on Freak Brothers strips and stories, a role he continued until his death in 1982.

Dave Sheridan: Life With Dealer McDope, The Leather Nun, And The Fabulous Furry Freak Brothers (Fantagraphics, 2018), edited by Mark Burstein, serves as both a biography and a greatest hits collection. His work can also be found in other volumes in *The Fabulous Furry Freak Brothers Follies*.

Paul Mavrides, 1981. Photo by Clay Geerdes.

Paul Mavrides moved to the Bay Area in 1975 and collaborated with Jay Kinney on the strip *Cover-Up Lowdown*, collected by Rip Off Press in 1977. He was soon recruited by Shelton as an art assistant on the Freak Brothers and eventually became co-writer as well. In 1979, he co-founded The Church of The Sub-Genius and continued to be a prime force in that satirical organization while collaborating trans-Atlantically with Shelton for many decades.

He was a contributing editor to *Rip Off Comix* in the 1980s, did his own short comics for various anthologies, and issued a sketchbook volume, *Skull Farmer*, in 1991. His work as the final member to join the Zap collective can also be found in *The Complete Zap Comix* (Fantagraphics, 2014), *Zap Comix #16* (Fantagraphics, 2016), and other volumes in *The Fabulous Furry Freak Brothers Follies*.

Hal Robins, 1977. Photo by Clay Geerdes.

Hal Robins (b. 1950) has divided his career between commercial illustration, underground comix (including *Young Lust* and R. Crumb's *Weirdo* magazine), and a prominent role in The Church of The Sub-Genius (as Dr. Howland Owll). He collaborated with Paul Mavrides on Dinoboy for *Rip Off Comix* and other anthologies.

A 1999 collection, *Grave Yarns*, exhibits the same flair for EC-style horror stories as his work in this volume.

Jack Jackson, 1972. Photo by Clay Geerdes.

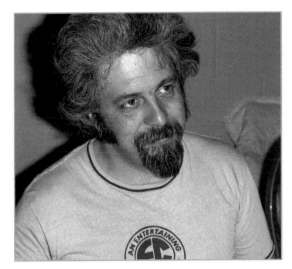

Spain Rodriguez, 1981. Photo by Clay Geerdes.

Jack Jackson (a.k.a. Jaxon) (1941–2006) was first published under Shelton's editorship of *The Texas Ranger*, and in 1964, he self-published one of the first proto-underground comics, *God Nose*. Despite being one of the co-founders of Rip Off Press, Jaxon mostly published elsewhere — his work in Last Gasp's *Slow Death* also shows an affinity for EC horror. By the late 1970s, his work began to focus on historical subjects, particularly first nations' peoples of Texas and North America. He died by suicide in Texas in 2006.

Jackson's *Los Tejanos* (1982) was one of Fantagraphics's earliest graphic albums. His other books from Fantagraphics include *Optimism Of Youth* (1991), *God's Bosom* (1995), and the collection *Jack Jackson's American History: Los Tejanos & Lost Cause* (2013), which incorporated his 1982 book.

Spain Rodriguez (1940–2012, b. Buffalo, New York) contributed his early writing and cartooning to New York's *East Village Other*, where he debuted his character Trashman. His 1968 *Zodiac Mindwarp* tabloid was one of the earliest underground comix, before the comic book format became the standard for the form. He joined *Zap Comix* with #4 in 1969 (one issue after Shelton), moved to San Francisco in 1970, and began publishing Trashman regularly. Much of his other work was divided between autobiographical/

reportage and celebratory sado-masochism. He died in San Francisco in 2012.

His work can also be found in *The Complete Zap Comix* (Fantagraphics, 2014) and *Zap Comix* #16 (Fantagraphics, 2016). Spain's other books with Fantagraphics include *Cruisin' With the Hound: The Life and Times of Fred Toote'* (2012) and three volumes of a complete collection, *Street Fighting Men* (2017), *Warrior Women* (2018), and *My Life & Times* (2021).

Guy Colwell, 1981. Photo by Clay Geerdes.

Guy Colwell (b. 1945, Oakland, California) completed two years at the California College of Arts and Crafts, then dropped out specifically to resist the draft and "bring on the consequences." He worked at Mattel Toy Co. doing sculpture through 1966 and 1967, then endured those consequences by serving two years in federal prison for refusing the draft. That experience only focused his commitment to both art and social justice, with his work in the following decades divided between comics like *Inner City Romance*, social commentary through fine art as a painter, and in-the-field activist illustration on the Great Peace March for Nuclear Disarmament. He supported his art with staff work at Rip Off Press through the 1980s and continues to paint in Berkeley, California.

Fantagraphics has published collections of Colwell's comics *Inner City Romance* (2015) and *Doll* (2019), a portfolio of drawings entitled Street Scenes (2015), and an original all-ages graphic novel, *In Fox's Forest*.

S. Clay Wilson, 1982. Photo by Clay Geerdes.

S. Clay Wilson (1941–2021, b. Lincoln, Nebraska) was first published in 1966 in *Grist*, a literary journal in Lawrence, Kansas. One of the *Grist* editors also commissioned and published a portfolio by Wilson, which he used as a calling card upon his arrival in San Francisco in 1968. His first stop was at a print shop that happened to be running off *Zap Comix* #1 at that very moment. By *Zap Comix* #2, Wilson was part of the first expansion of *Zap* contributors. His bold, scabrous, and profane comics were an influence on Crumb himself, and titles like *Pork*, *Snatch Comics*, *Bent*, and *Felch Cumics* blatantly warned buyers what they were in for. He worked for Rip Off Press on *The Rip Off Review of Western Culture* and was interviewed for the third issue. Wilson

continued drawing, illustrating, and painting until suffering a severe brain injury in 2008. He died at home in San Francisco in 2021.

The Mythology of S. Clay Wilson, a three-volume series written and edited by Patrick Rosenkranz for Fantagraphics, mixes biography with anthology: *Pirates in the Heartland* (2014), *Demons and Angels* (2015), and *Belgian Lace From Hell* (2017). His work can also be found in *The Complete Zap Comix* (Fantagraphics, 2014) and *Zap Comix* #16 (Fantagraphics, 2016).

Ted Richards, 1977. Photo by Clay Geerdes.

Ted Richards (b. 1946, Fort Bragg, North Carolina) spent the last three years of his teens in the Air Force, which gave him experience in the combination of marijuana and military life that inspired his character Dopin' Dan — who had a guest strip in *The Fabulous Furry Freak Brothers* #2. Richards moved to San Francisco in 1969, and by 1975 he was living on-site at Rip Off Press and collaborating with Shelton on *Give Me Liberty: A Revised History of the American Revolution*. He wrote and drew *The 40-Year-Old Hippie* for the Rip Off syndicate. He ultimately lost a massive lawsuit filed by Disney against the Air Pirates cartooning collective (detailed in *The Pirates and the Mouse: Disney's War Against the Counterculture* by Bob Levin, Fantagraphics, 2003).

He subsequently escaped comics and has worked as a software designer, computer graphics artist, and web designer since 1981.

FIRST APPEARANCES

While we have attempted to identify the first published appearance of every story in this volume, we were unable to pinpoint everything, particularly strips that first appeared outside of Rip Off Press's comic book catalog. We welcome corrections and additions.

The stories in this volume were first printed or reprinted in comic book form in the following comic books and comics collections. A key to abbreviations appears below.

ABBREVIATIONS

FFFB06 Six Snappy Sockeroos From the Archives of the Fabulous Furry Freak Brothers (Freak Brothers #6), 1980

FFFB07 Several Short Stories From the Fabulous Furry Freak Brothers (Freak Brothers #7), 1982

FFFBL04 The Fabulous Furry Freak Brothers Library Volume 4, 1988

FFC05 Fat Freddy's Cat #5, [November] 1980

FFC&S01 Fat Freddy's Comics & Stories #1, 1983

FFC&S02 Fat Freddy's Comics & Stories #2, 1986

PP83 Promotional poster, 1983

ROC07 Rip Off Comix #7, 1980

ROC08 Rip Off Comix #8, [April] 1981

ROC09 Rip Off Comix #9, 1981

ROC10 Rip Off Comix #10, 1982

ROC11 Rip Off #11, Fall 1982

ROC12 Rip Off #12, 1983

ROC15 Rip Off Comix #15, June 1987

ROC21 Rip Off Comix #21, Winter 1988

ROC31 Rip Off Comix #31, 1991

TRIP81 Thoroughly Ripped With The Fabulous Furry Freak Brothers and Fat Freddy's Cat, Revised Edition 1981

OVERLEAF: When Shelton left a blank layout for a Fat Freddy's Cat strip laying about the office, Mavrides, Colwell, and Bill Griffith challenged each other in a round-robin jam. 1984.

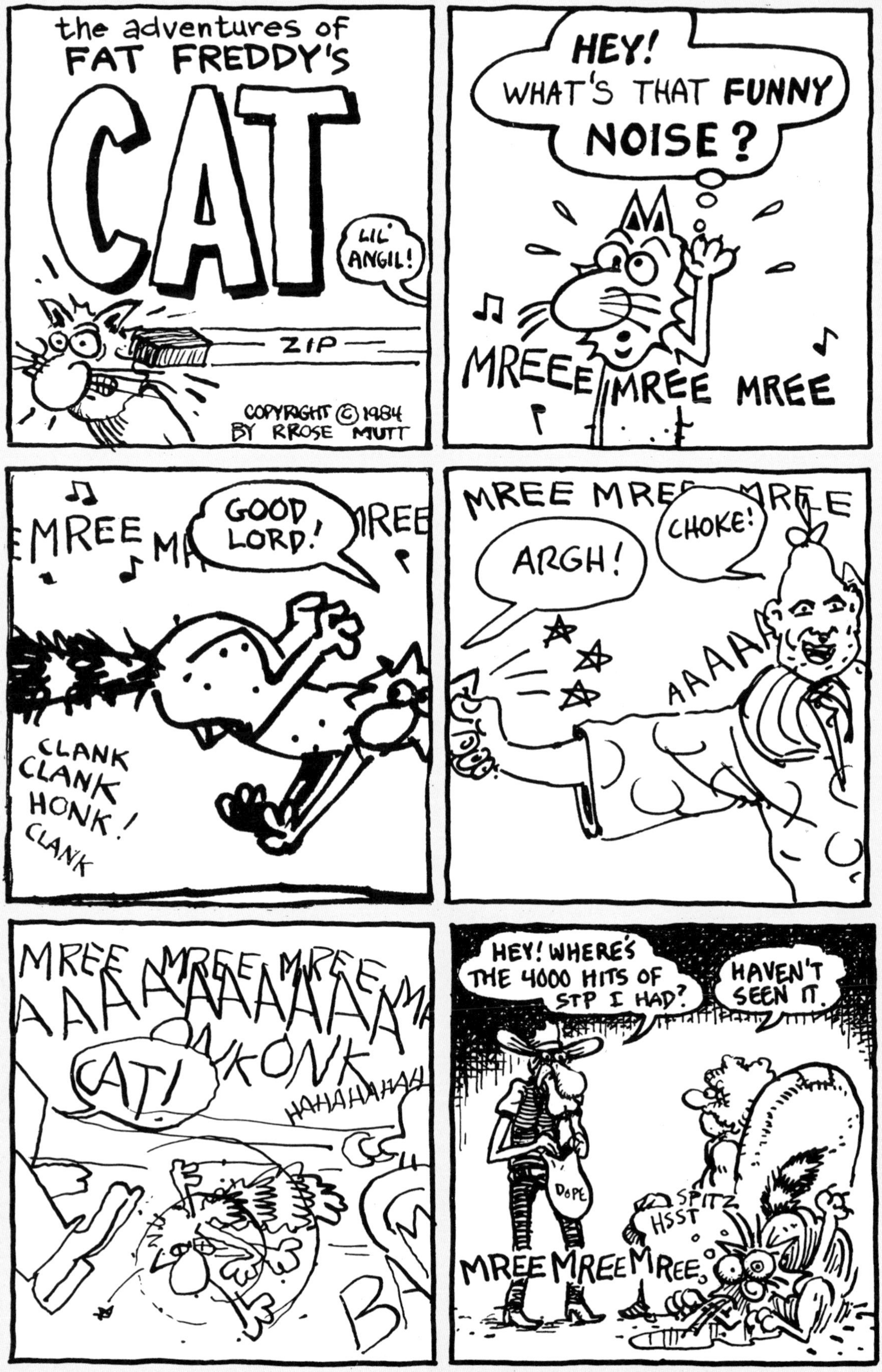
the adventures of
FAT FREDDY'S
CAT
LIL' ANGIL!
ZIP
COPYRIGHT © 1984 BY RROSE MUTT
HEY! WHAT'S THAT FUNNY NOISE?
MREEE MREE MREE
MREE
GOOD LORD!
CLANK CLANK HONK! CLANK
MREE MREE MREE
ARGH!
CHOKE!
AAAAA
MREE MREE MREE
AAAAAAAAAA
CAT!
KONK
HAHAHAHAH
HEY! WHERE'S THE 4000 HITS OF STP I HAD?
HAVEN'T SEEN IT.
DOPE
SPITZ
HSST
MREE MREE MREE

Logo and panel borders: Shelton. Panels 1, 3, 6: Mavrides. Panel 2: Robins. Panel 4: Griffith. Panel 5: Colwell.

FREEWHEELIN'
FRANKLY
FRANK
FREDD
FRANCES
& FTO FREDDY'S CAT